An Introduction to Sociology

For Eirene

An Introduction to Sociology

Third Edition

KEN BROWNE

301
BRO

polity

First published in 2005 by Polity Press

Polity Press
65 Bridge Street
Cambridge CB2 1UR, UK.

Polity Press
350 Main Street
Malden, MA 02148, USA

ISBN: 0-7456-3257-2
ISBN: 0-7456-3258-0 (pb)

A catalogue record for this book is available from the British Library.

Typeset in 10.25 on 12pt QuadraatSans.
by Servis Filmsetting Limited, Manchester.
Printed and bound by Tien Wah Press, Singapore.

The publisher has used its best endeavours to ensure that the URLs for
external websites referred to in this book are correct and active at the time
of going to press. However, the publisher has no responsibility for the
websites and can make no guarantee that a site will remain live or that the
content is or will remain appropriate.

Every effort has been made to trace all copyright holders, but if any have
been inadvertently overlooked the publishers will be pleased to include
any necessary credits in any subsequent reprint or edition.

For further information on Polity, visit our website: www.polity.co.uk

Contents

Preface by Laurie Taylor   xi
Introduction to the Third Edition   xiii
Acknowledgements   xiv
How to Use this Book   xv
Useful Websites   xvi

1 Introducing Sociology   1

What is Sociology?   1
Some Key Introductory Ideas   5
Consensus and Conflict Views of Society   8
Chapter Summary   9
Key Terms   10

2 Social Stratification   11

Systems of Stratification   13
Four Views of Social Class   16
The Class Structure of Britain   27
Chapter Summary   27
Key Terms   28
Coursework Suggestions   28

3 Social Class in Modern Britain   29

Class Inequalities   29
Changes in the Class Structure   33
Social Mobility   39
Chapter Summary   45
Key Terms   45
Coursework Suggestions   46

4 Wealth, Welfare, and Poverty   47

Wealth and Income   47
Poverty   51
The Welfare State   63
The Persistence of Poverty: Why the Poor Remain Poor   68
Chapter Summary   76
Key Terms   77
Coursework Suggestions   77

5   Gender   78

Sex and Gender   78
Gender and Biology   79
Gender and Identity   80
Gender Socialization and Stereotyping in Britain   80
Are Gender Roles and Identities Changing?   92
The Sexual Division of Labour   95
The Changing Status of Women in Britain   95
Women at Work   100
Conclusion   109
Chapter Summary   110
Key Terms   110
Coursework Suggestions   111

6   Ethnicity and Race   112

Race, Ethnicity, and Minority Ethnic Groups   112
Ethnicity and Identity   112
The Pattern of Immigration   113
Who are the Minority Ethnic Groups?   113
Some Inequalities Facing Minority Ethnic Groups   114
The Causes of Racism   125
Are Relations between Ethnic Groups Improving?   125
Chapter Summary   128
Key Terms   129
Coursework Suggestions   129

7   Power, Politics, Citizenship, and Protest   130

Types of Political System   131
Citizenship   132
Political Parties in Britain   133
Influences on Voting Behaviour   135
Why do People Abstain in Elections?   142
Opinion Polls and Elections   143
Influencing Decision-Making in a Democracy   147
Is Britain a Democracy?   156
Chapter Summary   158
Key Terms   159
Coursework Suggestions   159

8   The Mass Media   161

The Power of the Media: Key Questions   161
Formal Controls on the Media   162
Ownership of the Mass Media   164
Newspaper Readership and Social Class   165
The Mass Media, Public Opinion, and Social Control   168

Bias in the Media: What Affects Media Content? 171
Stereotyping and the Media 179
Crime, Deviance, and the Media 182
The Effects of the Mass Media 185
Violence and the Media 187
The Mass Media and Democracy 188
Into the Future 188
Chapter Summary 190
Key Terms 191
Coursework Suggestions 191

9 **Social Control, Deviance, and Crime** 192

Agencies of Social Control 192
Crime and Deviance 196
The Pattern of Crime 200
What's Wrong with the Official Crime Statistics? 208
Is the Crime Rate Increasing? 215
Explaining Crime and Deviance 216
Government Initiatives and Policy Solutions to Crime 221
Conclusion: Deviance, Crime, and Social Change 221
Chapter Summary 223
Key Terms 224
Coursework Suggestions 224

10 **The Family** 225

What is the Family? 225
Consensus and Conflict Approaches to the Family 225
Different Forms of the Family and Marriage 226
Changes in the Family in Britain 231
Family Diversity and the Myth of 'Cereal Packet' Families 251
Critical Views of the Family 257
Alternatives to the Family 261
Are Marriage and the Family Declining Social Institutions? 263
Chapter Summary 264
Key Terms 265
Coursework Suggestions 266

11 **Schooling in Britain** 267

Education in Britain before the 1970s 267
Comprehensive Schools and Selection 268
The Key Aims of Educational Change 271
Recent Developments in Education 272
The Role of Education in Society 278
Chapter Summary 283
Key Terms 284
Coursework Suggestions 284

12 Inequality in Education 285

Social Class and Underachievement 285
Compensatory Education 295
Ethnicity and Underachievement 296
Gender Differences in Education: The Underachievement of
  Boys 299
Private Education: The Independent Schools 306
Is Equality of Educational Opportunity Possible to Achieve? 309
Chapter Summary 309
Key Terms 310
Coursework Suggestions 310

13 Religion 311

Defining Religion 311
The Role of Religion in Society 312
Religion, Social Conflict, and Social Change 315
Religious Organizations 315
New Religious Movements 316
The Secularization Thesis 321
Conclusion: Belief without Belonging? 333
Chapter Summary 334
Key Terms 334
Coursework Suggestions 335

14 Work and Leisure 336

The Importance of Work 336
Attitudes to Work 337
Work and Identity 338
Unemployment 338
Craft Production, Industrial Society, and the Division of
  Labour 343
Fordism and Post-Fordism 344
The Effects of Changing Technology on Society 348
Alienation and Job Satisfaction 350
The Changing Occupational Structure and Patterns of
  Employment 353
Trade Unions 359
Leisure 362
Chapter Summary 368
Key Terms 369
Coursework Suggestions 369

15 Population 370

The Importance of Information on Population 370
Key Terms Used in the Study of Population 371

Population Size 373
Population Change in the United Kingdom 373
Urbanization 389
Rural and Urban Life 393
Chapter Summary 395
Key Terms 396
Coursework Suggestions 396

16 Health and Illness 397

What is Meant by 'Health', 'Illness', and 'Disease'? 398
The Medical and Social Models of Health 399
Becoming a Health Statistic 400
Medicine and Social Control: The Sick Role 400
How Society Influences Health 402
The Food Industry 405
Inequalities in Health 406
Chapter Summary 414
Key Terms 414
Coursework Suggestions 415

17 Doing Sociological Research 416

Key Issues in Social Research 416
Quantitative and Qualitative Data 417
Primary and Secondary Sources 418
Social Surveys 420
Observation 432
Doing Your Own Research: Coursework 436
Chapter Summary 439
Key Terms 439

Appendix: Reading Statistical Data 440

Statistical Tables 440
Describing a Trend 442
Graphs 442
Bar Charts 445
Pie Charts 446

Glossary 448
Index 462

Preface

Sociologists are not exactly renowned for the accuracy of their predictions, so I'm delighted that Ken Browne has asked me to write a new preface for this third edition of his textbook. It gives me the perfect opportunity to brag about how accurate I was in describing the first edition as a book that would go on to become a classic introductory text to sociology.

It wasn't really that tricky a forecast. There are plenty of sociology introductions on the market but very few of their authors can hold a candle to Browne when it comes to combining a comprehensive survey of the territory with a passionate commitment to gaining new enthusiasts.

So, while he covers all the topics specified by the GCSE's examining boards, he also finds plenty of space for excellent examples of how such familiar sociological concepts as gender, deviance, ethnicity, and power impact upon our daily lives.

This is not the sort of warmed-over sociology that is occasionally served in books announcing themselves as introductory. Browne is bang up-to-date, bringing sociological analysis to bear upon today's newspaper headlines. There are excellent sections here on such diverse topics as spin doctors (the former Iraqi Minister of Information – 'Comical Ali' – rates a special mention), the aftermath of the twin towers tragedy, and the impact that new forms of technology are having on the development of contemporary social movements.

Browne is not an over-opinionated sociologist. All sides are given a fair hearing and there are plenty of references to the impossibility of ever producing anything that might count as a final truth. Neither does he choose to sensationalize. There is an evenness of pace about the entire book which allows the reader the comfortable sensation of being led across unfamiliar territory by a knowledgeable and unhurried guide. But there is nothing at all patronizing about this guidance. At every opportunity the author suggests fascinating ways in which new students of sociology might carry out their own investigations. Sociology, as Browne explains in the opening section, does repeatedly challenge the self-evident notions called 'common sense', but that certainly does not mean that it should create its own mystifications.

In my preface to the first edition I praised Browne's ability to keep his readers' attention by employing textual variety. This skill is even more evident in this new, third edition. Cartoons, tables, diagrams, and photographs routinely break up the pages, but without ever distracting from the thread of the argument.

I predict that this new edition will prove even more successful than its excellent predecessors. And I do so happily. After all, there is nothing quite so pleasurable as backing certainties.

Laurie Taylor

Introduction to the Third Edition

This book is intended as an elementary introduction to sociology for both the general reader and those studying at GCSE and other courses at a similar level. No previous knowledge of sociology is assumed. All the key issues and areas included in GCSE and other introductory sociology courses are covered, with each chapter closely modelled on the syllabus content of the major GCSE examining boards.

This third edition has been completely revised and updated, including a range of new material and statistics reflecting more contemporary social changes and social trends, and new cartoons, photographs and graphics have been added.

The book is particularly suited to further education students studying for GCSE on one-year courses, who require a clear and concise account of each topic area. It is also suitable for use by students on other introductory courses which have a sociological component, such as nursing, social work, and health and social care courses. This book will enable the content of such courses to be covered easily and thoroughly, and allow time for students and teachers or lecturers to discuss, pursue the acquisition of skills and carry out the coursework assignments which are often important aspects of such courses. Students studying at home or on other distance-learning courses will find the book a valuable companion to their studies. Those who are considering taking an AS- or A-level or Access sociology course or an AVCE in health and social care will find the book very useful both as preparatory reading and as an easy-to-read foundation text to get them started in sociology.

Reading about sociology is no substitute for getting involved in the fascination and difficulties of doing an actual piece of research. Chapter 17 provides a comprehensive guide to sociological research methods and the way to tackle coursework. Suggestions on appropriate research topics are included at the end of every chapter except chapters 1 and 17.

Acknowledgements

Thanks must go once again to my students at North Warwickshire and Hinckley College who, unwittingly, have helped me to gauge the accessibility of both the text and the level. I must also thank Eirene Mitsos, Natalie Walford, and Polity's three anonymous readers who provided valuable input into the preparation of this third edition, and Ken Pyne for producing the new cartoons. Many thanks are owed to Laurie Taylor for his generosity in writing the new preface. I'd like to thank Emma Longstaff and Sarah Dancy, and all the other staff at Polity Press. Fiona Sewell has once again carried out an excellent and informed job in copy-editing the text, as has Pamela Thomas in proofreading it, and I am most grateful for their contributions.

I am grateful to all those who gave permission to reproduce copyright material, particularly Liz Kettle and the Department for Work and Pensions, the Commission for Racial Equality, and the Equal Opportunities Commission. Other thanks must go to Sinn Fein, the African National Congress, the Office of Nelson Mandela, Alison Hallam, Barrie Percival and Loughborough Grammar School, Blackwell Publishing, British Gas, Christian Research, Clara Vulliamy, the Child Poverty Action Group, David Haldane, Ford Motor Company, Fulchester Industries/IFG, Gordon Browne, Gower Publishing, HarperCollins Publishers, Keith Roberts, Leamington Courier, Macmillan, National Readership Surveys Ltd, News International, Penguin Books, Peugeot, *Punch*, Routledge, Rover Group, Sarah at <www.worldrevolution.org.uk>, Stephen Rumble, Ted Fussey, Michael Dyer, the *Guardian*, the Joseph Rowntree Foundation, and Tom at <www.lifeisajoke.com>.

The source of copyright material is acknowledged in the text. Should any copyright holder have been inadvertently overlooked, the author and publishers will be glad to make suitable arrangements at the first possible opportunity.

How to Use this Book

Most chapters in this book are fairly self-contained, and it is not necessary to read them in any particular order or to read all of them. Select chapters according to the course you are studying. Those not familiar with the interpretation of statistical data will find it useful to study the appendix fairly early on. Those doing research projects of various kinds should read chapter 17, and refer to the website list for useful reference sites. When issues are discussed in more than one chapter, cross-references are made in the text.

Throughout the book, a range of activities and discussion topics is included. These provide valuable exercises to develop your skills and understanding, and should be attempted whenever possible, though they are not essential for understanding each chapter. Important terms are printed in coloured type when they first appear. These are normally explained in the text, and listed at the end of the chapter. They are also included in a comprehensive glossary at the end of the book. Unfamiliar terms should be checked in the glossary or index for further clarification or explanation. The contents pages or the index should be used to find particular themes or references.

Chapter summaries outline the key points that should have been learnt after reading each chapter. These should be used as checklists for revision – if you cannot do what is asked, then refer back to the chapter to refresh your memory. The glossary at the end of the book also provides both a valuable reference source and a revision aid, as you can check the meaning of terms.

A last word: do not look on this book as your final and absolute source of authority – see it as your friend rather than your boss. Much of sociology is controversial and the subject of intense and heated debate, and even apparently 'factual' statistics are open to a variety of interpretations. Discuss with others what you read in this book, and adopt a questioning and critical approach to your studies. 'The truth' may be out there somewhere, but, like the executioner's face, it is often well hidden, so take nothing for granted and do not accept things at face value. Above all, enjoy sociology.

Useful Websites

The Internet is an invaluable source of information for sociologists, and for exploring the topics in this book. This might particularly be the case if you are doing coursework. You should be prepared to click on links and surf the web to explore the topics you're interested in, though always be cautious as there is a lot of rubbish on some sites, and you can't always believe what they say. Internet site addresses often change or disappear, but below are a few sites that are very well run, kept very up to date, and carry an excellent range of contemporary information, articles and statistics of relevance to the topics covered in this book. The information found on them can generally be regarded as accurate and trustworthy, and used by sociologists as evidence or to develop arguments. Other useful websites are referred to throughout this book.

Current affairs and useful general information

<www.google.com> is one of the best search engines to search for topics generally.

<www.guardian.co.uk> – this is the site of the *Guardian* newspaper, which is packed with useful stuff.

<www.bbc.co.uk> – the BBC, widely regarded as one of the best websites in the world. You're bound to find something useful.

Sociology for schools and colleges

<www.sociology.org.uk> – an excellent sociology site created for GCSE-, AS- and A-level students, and run by Chris Livesey.

<www.atss.org.uk> – the site of the ATSS (Association for the Teaching of Social Science). You will find a range of material, including worksheets, notes, and a list of websites of use to sociologists.

<www.cultsock.ndirect.co.uk/MUHome/cshtml/index.html> – a site containing just about everything you need on the mass media, for both teachers and students.

<www.chrisgardner.clara.net> – part of the National Grid for Learning, this is a Sociology Learning Support site.

<www.ngfl.gov.uk> – the National Grid for Learning, always worth checking.

<www.religioustolerance.org> – a very useful site for researching all aspects of religion.

Government and other 'official' sites

<www.statistics.gov.uk> – the site of the Office for National Statistics, which contains a huge range of contemporary data on all the topics covered in this book.

<www.statistics.gov.uk/census2001> – the Office for National Statistics 2001 census site.

<www.ukonline.gov.uk> – the British government site is an excellent starting point for locating all government ministries and departments, including the police. Some of the government ministries that may be of particular use are:

- <www.homeoffice.gov.uk> – the Home Office, for a whole host of crime and deviance issues, and a range of other issues;
- <www.dfes.gov.uk> – the Department for Education and Skills (DfES), for all information on education;
- <www.standards.dfes.gov.uk> – the standards site of the DfES;
- <www.doh.gov.uk> – the Department of Health;
- <www.dwp.gov.uk> – the Department for Work and Pensions, where the latest benefit and poverty statistics are available, as well as the 'Beat-a-Cheat' site.

<www.parliament.uk> – Parliament, for political research and contacting your MP.

<www.eoc.org.uk> – the Equal Opportunities Commission.

<www.cre.gov.uk> – the Commission for Racial Equality.

<http://europa.eu.int/> – the European Union, in case you want to see what is happening in other European countries in comparison to Britain.

<www.socialexclusionunit.gov.uk> – the Social Exclusion Unit at the Office of the deputy prime minister.

<www.ofcom.org.uk> – the Office of Communications (the media regulator).

<www.pcc.org.uk> – the Press Complaints Commission.

<www.tuc.org.uk> – the site of the Trades Union Congress, a useful site for exploring trade union and labour force issues.

<www.who.int/en> – the site of the World Health Organization.

Voluntary and campaigning groups

<www.jrf.org.uk> – the site of the Joseph Rowntree Foundation; the best site for finding out all the latest research about poverty and inequality.

<www.cpag.org.uk> – the site of the Child Poverty Action Group, the major campaigning group against poverty.

<www.newint.org.uk> – the site of the *New Internationalist* magazine, where global poverty and international inequalities between nations are discussed.

1 Introducing Sociology

KEY ISSUES

- What is sociology?
- Sociology and science.
- Key introductory ideas and important terms.
- Consensus and conflict views of society.

Newcomers to sociology often have only a vague idea as to what the subject is about, though they frequently have an interest in people. This interest is a good start, because the focus of sociology is on the influences from society which mould the behaviour of people, their experiences, and their interpretations of the world around them. To learn sociology is to learn about how human societies are constructed, and where our beliefs and daily routines come from and how our social identities are formed; it is to re-examine in a new light many of the taken-for-granted assumptions which we all hold, and which influence the way we think about ourselves and others. Sociology is above all about developing a critical understanding of society. In developing this, sociology can itself contribute to changes in society, for example by highlighting and explaining social problems like divorce, crime, and poverty. The study of sociology can provide the essential tools for a better understanding of the world we live in, and therefore the means for improving it.

WHAT IS SOCIOLOGY?

Sociology is the systematic (or planned and organized) study of human groups and social life in modern societies. It is concerned with the study of social institutions. These are the various organized social arrangements which are found in all societies. For example, the family is an institution which is concerned with arrangements for marriage, such as at what age people can marry, whom they can marry and how many partners they can have, and the upbringing of children. The education system establishes ways of passing on attitudes, knowledge, and skills from one generation to the next. Work and the economic system organize the way the production of goods will be carried out, and religious institutions are concerned with people's relations with the supernatural. These social institutions make up a society's social structure – the building blocks of society.

Sociology tries to understand how these various social institutions operate, and how they relate to one another, such as the influence the family might have on how well children perform in the education system. Sociology is also concerned with describing and explaining the patterns of inequality, deprivation, and conflict which are a feature of nearly all societies.

Sociology and common sense

Sociology is concerned with studying many things which most people already know something about. Everyone will have some knowledge and understanding of family life, the education system, work, the mass media, and religion simply by living as a member of society. This leads many people to assume that the topics studied by sociologists and the explanations sociologists produce are really just common sense: what 'everyone knows'.

This is a very mistaken assumption. Sociological research has shown many widely held 'common-sense' ideas and explanations to be false. Ideas such as that there is no real poverty left in modern Britain; that the poor and unemployed are inadequate and lazy; that everyone has equal chances in life; that the rich are rich because they work harder; that men are 'naturally' superior to women; that it is obvious that men and women will fall in love and live together – these have all been questioned by sociological research. The re-examination of such common-sense views is very much the concern of sociology.

A further problem with common-sense explanations is that they are tightly bound up with the beliefs of a particular society at particular periods of time. Different societies have differing common-sense ideas. The Hopi Indians' common-sense view of why it rains is very different from our own – they do a rain dance to encourage the rain gods. Common-sense ideas also change over time in one society. In Britain, for example, we no longer burn witches when the crops fail, but seek scientific explanations for such events.

Not all the findings of sociologists undermine common sense, and the work of sociologists has made important contributions to the common-sense understandings of members of society. For example, the knowledge which most people have about the changing family in Britain, with rising rates of divorce and growing numbers of lone parents, is largely due to the work of sociologists. However, sociology differs from common sense in two important ways:

- Sociologists use a sociological imagination. This means that, while they study the familiar routines of daily life, sociologists look at them in unfamiliar ways or from a different angle. They ask if things really are as common sense says they are. Sociologists re-examine existing assumptions, by studying how things were in the past, how they've changed, how they differ between societies, and how they might change in the future.

- Sociologists look at evidence on issues before making up their minds. The explanations and conclusions of sociologists are based on precise evidence which has been collected through painstaking research using established research procedures.

Sociology and naturalistic explanations

Naturalistic explanations are those which assume that various kinds of human behaviour are natural or based on innate (in-born) biological characteristics. If this were the case, then one would expect human behaviour to be the same in all societies, as people's biological make-up doesn't change between societies. In fact, by comparing different societies, sociologists have discovered that there are very wide differences between societies in customs, values, beliefs, and social behaviour. For example, there are wide differences between societies in the roles of men and women and what is considered appropriate 'masculine' and 'feminine' behaviour. This can only be because people learn to behave in different ways in different societies, as their biological make-up is the same. Sociological explanations recognize that most human behaviour is learnt by individuals as members of society, rather than being something with which they are born. Individuals learn how to behave from a wide range of social institutions right throughout their lives. Sociologists call this process of learning socialization.

Sociology and science

Sociology is one of a group of subjects, including economics, psychology, and politics, which are known as the social sciences. The idea that sociology might be considered a science poses a number of problems. This is because the term 'science' is usually associated with the study of the natural world, in subjects like physics, chemistry, and biology that make up the natural sciences.

However, the study of society by sociologists presents a range of problems which do not exist in the natural sciences, as the comparison on page 4 suggests.

Is sociology scientific?

The differences between the natural sciences and sociology mean that sociologists cannot follow exactly the same procedures or produce such precise findings as those in the natural sciences. Despite this, sociology

Natural science

Social science

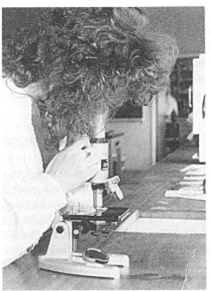

Photos: Michael Dyer LRPS

Natural science	Sociology
■ Experiments can be carried out to test and prove ideas and it is possible to isolate causes in laboratory conditions.	■ Human beings have rights, and might well object to being experimented upon. For example, the idea of removing children from their parents and raising them in isolation to test the influence of society on human behaviour would be regarded by most people as outrageous. Sociology also wants to study society in its normal state, not in the artificial conditions of an experiment.
■ As a result of experiments, natural scientists can accurately predict what will happen in the same circumstances in the future. For example, the chemist can predict with certainty, as a result of experiments in laboratory conditions, that some combinations of chemicals will cause explosions.	■ Human behaviour cannot be predicted with such certainty: in two similar situations, people may react differently, according to how they interpret what is going on around them; and people can change their minds.
■ In the natural sciences, the presence of the scientist doesn't affect the behaviour of chemicals or objects.	■ Sociologists studying people may change the behaviour of those being studied, who may become embarrassed, be more defensive and careful about what they say, or act differently because they have been selected for study. If this happens, then the results obtained will not give a true picture of how people behave normally.
■ The natural scientist does not have to persuade objects, chemicals, or, usually, animals to cooperate in research.	■ People may refuse to answer questions or otherwise cooperate, making sociological research difficult or impossible. They can lie or otherwise distort and conceal the truth when they are being researched, making the findings of research suspect.

might still be regarded as adopting a scientific approach to the study of society as long as it has the following features:

■ Value freedom – the personal beliefs and prejudices of the sociologist should not be allowed to influence the way research is carried out and evidence interpreted. Obviously the personal interests and beliefs of the sociologist will influence the choice of topic he or she studies, but the research itself should not be distorted by these beliefs. In other words, sociologists should not 'cook the books' to make their point.

■ Objectivity – the sociologist should approach topics with an open mind, and be prepared to consider all the evidence in a detached way.

■ The use of systematic research methods – sociologists collect evidence about topics using planned and organized methods. These are discussed fully in chapter 17.

■ The use of evidence – sociological descriptions of social life, and the explanations and conclusions drawn, are based on carefully collected evidence.

■ The capacity for being checked – the findings and conclusions of sociological research are open to inspection, criticism, and testing by other researchers. 'Bad' sociology, using inadequate evidence to reach unjustifiable conclusions, is likely to be torn to shreds by others interested in the topic.

SOME KEY INTRODUCTORY IDEAS

Socialization, culture and identity

Socialization is the life-long process of learning the culture of any society. The term 'culture' refers to the language, beliefs, values and norms, customs, roles, knowledge, and skills which combine to make up the 'way of life' of any society. This culture is socially transmitted (passed on through socialization) from one generation to the next.

Socialization plays a crucial part in forming our identities. Identity is about how we see and define ourselves – our personalities – and how other people see and define us. For example, we might define ourselves as gay, black, a Muslim, Welsh, English, a woman, a student, or a mother. Many aspects of our individual identities will be formed through the socialization process, with the family, friends, school, the mass media, the workplace, and other agencies of socialization helping to form our individual personalities. Figure 1.1 on page 6 illustrates the various factors which influence our identities and how others see us, and many chapters in this book refer to aspects of this socialization process, and the forming of our identities.

However, while life-long socialization plays a very important part in forming our identities, individuals also have the free will to enable them to 'carve out' their own personal identities and influence how others see them, rather than simply being influenced by them. Individuals are not simply the passive victims of the socialization process. Figure 1.1 shows a range of factors that influence our identities. Note the arrows go both ways, suggesting that while individual identities are formed by various forces of socialization, the choices individuals and groups make and how they react to these forces can also have an influence. For example, while the mass media might influence our lifestyles, attitudes, and values, as well as how we see ourselves and how others see us, individuals may also react to what they read, see, or hear in the media in different ways. A woman from a minority ethnic background may define herself as black or Asian, but she may also see herself mainly as a woman, a mother, a teacher, or a Muslim. Similarly, we have some choices in the consumption goods we buy, the clothes we wear, and the leisure activities we choose to follow. Through these choices, we can influence how others see us, and the image of ourselves we project to them.

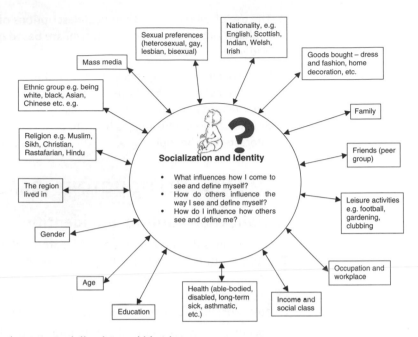

Figure 1.1 Socialization and identity

Refer to figure 1.1:

1 Suggest one example in each case of how the various factors may influence the individual's sense of identity.

2 Suggest five ways that individuals can influence how others see them.

3 Describe the five most important factors that you think have influenced how *you* define yourself and how others see you. Explain your answer with examples.

4 Suggest three ways *you* can influence how others see and define you – for example, as a particular 'type' of person, such as 'trendy', 'odd', 'sporty', 'Goth', etc.

Roles and role conflict

Roles are the patterns of behaviour which are expected from people in different positions in society – they are very much like the roles actors play in a television series. People in society play many different roles in their lifetimes, such as those of a boy or girl, a child and an adult, a student, a parent, a friend, and work roles like factory worker, police officer, or teacher. People in these roles are expected by society to behave in particular ways. The police officer who steals, or the teacher who is drunk in the classroom, show what these expectations of behaviour are.

One person plays many roles at the same time. For example, a woman may play the roles of woman, mother, worker, sister, and wife at the same time. This may lead to role conflict, where the successful performance of two or more roles at the same time may lead to conflict, such as the conflict between the roles of full-time worker and mother which some women experience.

Role conflict for working women

1 List all the roles you play, and briefly outline what others expect of you in each of these roles. For example, how are you expected to behave as a student, and what activities are you expected to carry out which you wouldn't have to if you were not a student?

2 From your list of roles, try to pick out those which conflict with each other, as suggested in the cartoon above.

Values and norms

Values are ideas and beliefs about what is 'right' and 'wrong', and the important standards which are worth maintaining and achieving in any society. They provide general guidelines for behaviour. In Britain, values include beliefs about respect for human life, privacy, and private property, about the importance of marriage and the importance of money and success. There are often strong pressures on people to conform to a society's values, which are frequently written down as laws. These are official legal rules which are formally enforced by the police, courts, and prison, and involve legal punishment if they are broken. Laws against murder, for example, enforce the value attached to human life in our society.

Norms are social rules which define correct and acceptable behaviour in a society or social group to which people are expected to conform. Norms are much more specific than values: they put values (general guidelines) into practice in particular situations. The rule that someone should not generally enter rooms without knocking reflects the value of privacy, and rules about not drinking and driving reflect the value of respect for human life. Norms exist in all areas of social life. In Britain, those who are late for work, jump queues in supermarkets, laugh during funerals, walk through the streets naked, or never say hello to friends are likely to be seen as annoying, rude, or odd because they are not following the norms of accepted behaviour. Norms are mainly informally enforced – by the disapproval of other people, embarrassment, or a 'telling off' from parents.

Customs are norms which have existed for a long time and have become a part of society's traditions – kissing under the mistletoe at Christmas, buying Easter eggs, or lighting candles at Divali are typical customs found in Britain.

Values and norms are part of the culture of a society, and are learned and passed on through socialization. They differ between societies – the values and norms of an African tribe are very different from those of people in modern Britain. They may also change over time and vary between social groups in the same society. In Britain, cohabitation (living together without being married) is much more accepted today than it was in the past, and wearing turbans – which is seen as normal dress among Sikh men – would be seen as a bit weird among white teenagers.

Social control

Social control is the term given to the various methods used to persuade or force individuals to conform to those social values and norms which have been learnt through socialization, and to prevent deviance – a failure to conform to social norms.

Sanctions are the rewards and punishments by which social control is achieved and conformity to norms and values enforced. These may be either *positive sanctions*, rewards of various kinds, or *negative sanctions*, various types of punishment. The type of sanction will depend on the seriousness of the norm: positive sanctions may range from gifts of sweets from parents to children, to merits and prizes at school, to knighthoods and medals; negative sanctions may range from a feeling of embarrassment, to being ridiculed or gossiped about or regarded as a bit eccentric or 'a bit odd', to being fined or imprisoned.

| DISCUSSION | Discuss the various positive and negative sanctions which affect the way you behave in your daily life. |

CONSENSUS AND CONFLICT VIEWS OF SOCIETY

Is society based on harmony and agreement between individuals and groups? Or is society based on conflict and antagonism between them? These two questions reflect different views among sociologists about the way society works. These two approaches are often referred to as consensus and conflict theories.

Consensus theory

Consensus theory is the approach adopted by Functionalist sociologists. Functionalism sees society as built up and working like the human body, made up of interrelated parts working together to maintain society. For example, just as the heart, lungs, and brain in the human body work together to maintain human life, social institutions like the family, education, and the law work together to maintain society.

Stability in society is based on socialization into norms and values on which most people agree. These shared norms and values are known as a value consensus. Consensus theorists, when studying society, emphasize these shared norms and shared values that exist between people, and see society as made up of individuals and social institutions working together in harmony, without much conflict between people and groups.

Conflict theory

Conflict theory has its origins in the work of Karl Marx (1818–83) and Max Weber (1864–1920).

Rather than viewing society as essentially peaceful and harmonious, conflict theorists emphasize social differences and conflicts, with inequalities in wealth, power, and status all creating conflicts between individuals and social groups. For example, there are conflicts between men and women, black and white people, employers and employees, and the rich and the poor. These groups have different interests and values, and there is no value consensus. This approach sees differences and conflicts between individuals, groups, and classes as important features of contemporary society, and conflict theorists tend to emphasize these conflicts when describing and explaining society.

CHAPTER SUMMARY

After studying this chapter, you should be able to:

- Explain why sociology is different from common-sense and naturalistic explanations.

- Explain some of the problems sociologists face compared with those working in the natural sciences.

- Explain why sociology is scientific.

- Define the meaning of socialization, culture, identity, roles, role conflict, values, laws, norms, social control, deviance, and positive and negative sanctions, and explain their importance in understanding human behaviour in human society.

- Explain briefly what is meant by consensus and conflict approaches to the study of society.

KEY TERMS

conflict theory
consensus theory
culture
customs
deviance
identity
laws
norms
objectivity
role conflict
roles
sanctions
social control
social institutions
social structure
socialization
sociology
value freedom
values

2 Social Stratification

KEY ISSUES

- Social stratification.
- Systems of stratification.
- Four views of social class.
- The class structure of Britain.

Most people would agree that few societies are really equal. The study of social stratification is of central concern to sociologists, because modern societies display such a wide range of inequalities. These include inequalities between rich and poor, between social classes, between men and women, and between black and white. Inequalities exist in a wide range of areas of social life, such as in job security, leisure opportunities, health, housing, income, and the power to influence events in society. Much of this book is concerned with describing and explaining these inequalities, so an understanding of social stratification provides a necessary starting point for the newcomer to sociology.

The word 'stratification' comes from 'strata' or layers, as in the way different types of rock are piled on top of one another to form rock strata. Social stratification refers to the division of society into a pattern of layers or strata made up of a hierarchy of unequal social groups. These stand in relations of advantage and disadvantage to one another in terms of features such as income, wealth, occupational status, race, or sex, depending on the stratification system. Those at the top of the stratification hierarchy will generally have more power in society than those at the bottom.

A stratification hierarchy

ACTIVITY

Make a list of what you consider to be the most important inequalities in society today. Explain in all cases why you think they are important in people's lives and how they affect the chances people get in life.

KEY TERMS USED IN THE STUDY OF SOCIAL STRATIFICATION

- **Economic inequality** refers to all those material things which affect the lives of individuals, such as their wealth, their income, and the hours they work. These inequalities can be measured, and continue to exist regardless of whether people recognize them as important or not.

- **Life chances** are the chances of obtaining those things defined as desirable and of avoiding those things defined as undesirable in any society. Life chances include the chances of obtaining things like good-quality housing, good health, holidays, job security, and educational success, and avoiding things like ill-health and unemployment.

- **Status** refers to the differing amounts of prestige or respect given to different positions in a group or society by other members of that group or society. Status involves people's social standing in the eyes of others. Status inequalities only exist so long as other people in a group or society continue to recognize them. For example, a vicar in a Christian society is generally given high status, but is unlikely to be given such status in a society practising witchcraft or voodoo.

- **Status groups** are groups of people sharing a similar status. For example, teachers generally share the same status.

- **Ascribed status** is status which is given to an individual at birth and usually can't be changed. Examples of such status include a person's age, race, sex, or place or family of birth. Members of the royal family in Britain have ascribed status.

- **Achieved status** refers to status that individuals have achieved through their own efforts, such as in education, skill, or promotion at work and career success.

- **Status symbols** are things that 'show off' people's status to others, such as the kind of job they have, the way they spend their money, the sort of house they live in, the car they drive, and their general lifestyle. All these things may be highly or lowly rated by other members of society.

- **Social mobility** is the term used to describe the movement up or down the social hierarchy between levels of a stratification system. For example, a person who came from a working-class family but became a middle-class doctor would have achieved upward social mobility. An **open society** is one where social mobility is possible; a **closed society** is one where no social mobility is possible.

SYSTEMS OF STRATIFICATION

Sociologists have identified three major types of stratification system, which have important differences between them: the caste system, feudal estates, and social class.

The caste system

The caste system is the most rigid system of stratification and is associated with India. The levels of the social hierarchy are called castes, and this hierarchy is fixed and clearly defined. The social position of individuals is ascribed at birth in accordance with Hindu religious beliefs and customs. Hindus believe in reincarnation – that people are born again after death. Hinduism suggests that people's behaviour in their previous life will decide the caste they are born into after rebirth. Since people believe the social position they are born into (their caste) is god-given, they generally accept their ascribed caste position.

A caste society is a closed society, with no social mobility possible from one caste to another. Each caste is completely closed off from others by religious rules and restrictions, which ensure that very little social contact occurs between members of different castes. The purity of each caste is maintained by endogamy. This means that marriage is only permitted to a person of the same caste. Besides the choice of marriage partner, caste membership also determines social status and occupation.

In the Indian system, the Hindu religion divides the population into five major castes:

1 Brahmins – the highest caste of priests and religious people.

2 Kshatriya – rulers and administrators.

3 Vaisya – merchants and farmers.

4 Sudras – manual workers.

5 The 'Untouchables' – literally, a group without a caste: social outcasts.

Despite recent attempts by the Indian government to remove the inequalities of the caste system, the system still continues, as many people still accept the Hindu religious beliefs on which it is based.

It has been suggested that the apartheid regime in South Africa, which was only abolished in the 1990s, showed some similarities with the caste system. Here people were stratified according to ascribed racial characteristics (white, coloured, and Bantu or black populations), with legal restrictions on mixing/marriage between different races, and with an almost 'religious' ideology of white supremacy.

Feudal estates

Feudalism was typically found in medieval Europe. The levels of the social hierarchy were called estates, and based on ownership of land. There was

The monarch, aristocracy, and gentry (knights, barons, and earls)

FIRST ESTATE

The church (bishops, abbots, and other clergy

SECOND ESTATE

Merchants, artisans, free peasants, and serfs

THIRD ESTATE

The feudal hierarchy

no legal equality between estates, and people in higher estates had more legal rights and privileges than those in lower ones. The lower estates had obligations and duties to those higher up the hierarchy, which were backed up by laws. For example, there was an obligation for serfs to work one day a week on the master's land. Membership of any estate was determined largely by birth, with social position, power, and status all ascribed at birth.

Feudalism was, like the caste system, a closed society, with social mobility from one estate to another extremely limited. However, some upward mobility to a higher estate was possible, for example through gifts of land as a reward for outstanding military service. In general, estates were preserved by endogamy, and intermarriage was only rarely allowed between individuals of different estates.

The feudal system of stratification looked something like the diagram above.

Social class

Social class is the form of stratification found in industrial societies, like modern Britain. Social classes can be defined as broad groups of people who share a similar economic situation, such as occupation, income, and ownership of wealth. Often, these criteria are closely related to each other and to other aspects of individuals' lives, such as their level of education, their status and lifestyle (for example, housing, car ownership, and leisure activities), and how much power and influence they have in society.

The main differences between the social class system and the caste and feudal systems are:

■ Social class is based not on religion or law, but mainly on economic criteria such as occupation, wealth, and income.

■ The levels of the social hierarchy (social classes) are not clearly separated from one another: the divisions between social classes are frequently quite vague – it is hard to say, for example, where the working class ends and the middle class begins.

■ Social class differences are not backed up by legal differences. All members of society in theory have equal legal rights, and those in higher social classes do not have legal authority over those in lower classes.

■ There are no legal or religious restrictions on intermarriage between people of different social classes. In theory people can marry whom they like; in practice people tend to marry someone in their own social class.

■ Social class societies are open societies. There are no legal or religious restrictions on the movement of individuals from one social class to another, and social mobility is possible.

■ The social class system is generally meritocratic. A meritocracy is a society where social positions are generally achieved by merit, such as educational qualifications, talent, and skill, rather than ascribed from birth. However, the social class of the family into which a child is born can have an important effect on his or her life chances. Entry into the propertied upper class is still mainly through inherited wealth, and therefore social positions here remain mainly ascribed rather than achieved.

'Look. Don't judge me by the clothes I wear, the car I drive, the books I read, the food I eat, the music I like, the friends I see, the money I earn, the place I live, the job I have, the things I say or the way I act. OK?'

Reproduced by permission of Punch

Social class and status

An individual's social class and status are often closely linked, and a member of a high social class will usually have high status as well. This is because the amount of social respect individuals get is often influenced by the same factors as their social class – their wealth, their income, and their occupation.

However, while an individual can only belong to one social class, he or she may have several statuses. For example, a person with a low-status, working-class job such as a refuse collector may achieve high status as a local councillor. Similarly, it is quite possible for two people to share the same social class but to have different statuses. For example, a white semi-skilled manual worker will find it easier to achieve status in a group of racist white workers than a black or Asian immigrant, who may be given lower status simply because of his or her race, even if he or she has the same occupation and income as the white worker.

| ACTIVITY | 1 If you were trying to decide a person's social class, what features would you take into account? Think about issues such as her or his job, speech, dress, housing, leisure activities and lifestyle, level of education, and car ownership. List all the features you can think of. |
| | 2 Now put your list into order of importance, with the most important features first. Explain why you have put them in that order. |

FOUR VIEWS OF SOCIAL CLASS

In the last activity, you listed the most important features that you would take into account in deciding a person's social class. The features you think important, though, may not be the same as those chosen by others. A similar dispute exists among sociologists. While most sociologists would agree that social classes consist of groups of people who share a similar economic situation, there are different views regarding exactly which aspect of that economic situation is the most important in defining a person's social class. The following discussion deals with four of the most common definitions and explanations of social class inequality which are used by sociologists: the consensus view of the Functionalists, the conflict views of Marx and Weber, and the definition of class by a person's occupation.

The consensus view of social class

Consensus theorists believe that social class inequalities are both necessary and inevitable. Functionalist writers suggest this is because:

- Some jobs in society are more important than others in maintaining society, requiring specialized skills that not everyone in society has the talent and ability to acquire.

- Those who do have the ability to do these jobs must be motivated and encouraged to train for these important positions with the promise of future high rewards in terms of income, wealth, status, and power. There must therefore be a system of unequal rewards to make sure the most able people get into the most important social positions. These unequal rewards are agreed and accepted by all (a consensus), as it is suggested that the most qualified and able people, who have the highest rewards, are working for everyone's benefit by doing society's most important jobs.

The difficulty with this approach is that there are many poorly rewarded occupations which can still be seen as vital in maintaining society. For example, a rich business executive can only become rich through the work of his or her employees, and a refuse collector is no less important than a doctor in maintaining society's health.

Conflict views of social class

The Marxist theory of social class

Much sociological discussion about social class has been influenced by the writings of Karl Marx. Marxist explanations suggest that the main reason for social class inequalities lies in the private ownership of the means of production – the key resources like land, property, factories, and businesses which are necessary to produce society's goods. For Marx, an individual's social class was defined by whether or not she or he owned the means of production. The concentration of ownership of the means of production in the hands of a small upper class brought to their owners an unearned income in the form of profit, and laid the basis for social class inequalities in wealth and income.

Karl Marx, 1818–83

Bourgeoisie and proletariat

Marx argued there were two basic social classes in capitalist industrial society: the class of owners of the means of production (whom he called the bourgeoisie or capitalists) and the class of non-owners (whom he called the proletariat or working class). The proletariat, since they owned no means of production, had no alternative means of livelihood but to work for the bourgeoisie. The bourgeoisie exploited the proletariat, making profits out of them by keeping wages low and paying them as little as possible instead of giving them the full payment for their work.

The ruling class

The class of owners was also a ruling class, according to Marx. For example, because they owned the means of production, the bourgeoisie could decide where factories should be located and whether they should be opened or closed down, and they could control the workforce through hiring and firing. Democratically elected governments could not afford to ignore the power of the bourgeoisie, otherwise they might face rising unemployment and other social problems if the bourgeoisie decided not to invest its money.

The ruling ideas

The ruling ideas in society – what Marx called the 'dominant ideology' – were those of the owning class, and the major institutions in society reflected these ideas. For example, the laws protected the owning class rather than the workers; religion acted as the 'opium of the people', persuading the proletariat to accept their position as just and natural (rather than rebelling against it), by promising future rewards in heaven for putting up with their present suffering; the bourgeoisie's ownership of the mass media meant only their ideas were put forward. In this way, the working class were almost brainwashed into accepting their position. They failed to recognize they were being exploited and therefore did not rebel against the bourgeoisie, because they thought their position was 'natural' and they could see no alternative to it. Marx called this lack of awareness by the proletariat of their own interests false consciousness.

A Marxist view of false consciousness and class consciousness

Exploitation, class conflict, and revolution

Marx predicted the working class would become poorer and poorer and society would become divided into two major social classes: a small, wealthy, and powerful bourgeoisie and a large, poverty-stricken proletariat. The exploitation of the proletariat by the bourgeoisie, Marx believed, would eventually lead to major class conflict between the poverty-stricken proletariat and the bourgeoisie. The proletariat would struggle against the bourgeoisie through strikes, demonstrations, and other forms of protest. The proletariat would then develop class consciousness – an awareness of their common working-class interests and their exploitation – until eventually they would make a socialist revolution and overthrow the bourgeoisie.

Communism

After the revolution, the proletariat would nationalize the means of production (which were formerly the private property of the bourgeoisie) by putting them in the hands of the state. The means of production would therefore be collectively owned and run in the interests of everyone, not just of the bourgeoisie. Capitalism would be destroyed and a new type of society would be created, which would be without exploitation, without classes, and without class conflict. This equal, classless society Marx called Communism.

A SUMMARY OF MARX'S THEORY OF CLASS

Marx's theory of social class is based on a model of two social classes, defined by whether or not they own the means of production. The bourgeoisie (the owning class) is a ruling class which exploits the proletariat (the non-owning class). This exploitation gives rise to class conflict between these two major classes. The proletariat will eventually overthrow the bourgeoisie in the socialist revolution, and create an equal, classless society called Communism.

The strengths and weaknesses of Marx's theory of class

There has been much discussion of the Marxist view of social class, particularly whether it can still be applied in modern industrial societies like Britain. One of the more obvious criticisms is that the revolution Marx predicted has not happened in Britain or any of the Western industrialized societies. While many of the class inequalities and conflicts which Marx identified remain in modern capitalist industrial societies, the communist solutions he proposed do not seem to have worked in the way he foresaw. In those countries where revolutions did occur, Communism did not succeed in creating an equal society, and there emerged a new 'ruling class' of people who were better off than the majority. From 1989 onwards, a major wave of popular revolts shook Eastern Europe and the Soviet Union, and swept away the former Communist regimes. There is now no communist country left in Europe.

STRENGTHS

■ There is still evidence of opposing class interests and class conflict, such as strikes and industrial sabotage in the workplace. The British

Social Attitudes Survey has reported that over half of the population of modern Britain still believe there are strong conflicts between rich and poor and between managers and workers.

■ The means of production remain mostly privately owned in the hands of a small minority of the population. There are still great inequalities of wealth and income in modern Britain, and widespread poverty: 10 per cent of the population own over 72 per cent of the wealth, and about 22 per cent of people are living in poverty.

■ There remains much evidence of major social class inequalities in life chances, such as in health, housing, levels of educational achievements and job security.

■ The owners of the means of production still have much more power and influence than the majority. For example, the major positions in the state, industry, and banking are held by the privileged rich who have attended public schools, and who also own the mass media.

WEAKNESSES

■ While great inequalities in wealth and income continue to exist, the working class has not got poorer as Marx predicted. Living standards have improved vastly since Marx's day, and the welfare state and compulsory state education have given the working class a better lifestyle than Marx predicted.

■ Compulsory education has given the working class more chances of upward social mobility, and the welfare state provides a safety net guaranteeing a minimum income for all. Housing, health, and educational standards are much improved compared with the nineteenth century.

■ Unemployment benefits help to reduce the more severe hardships which were associated with unemployment in Marx's day.

■ Marx suggested only the two opposing classes of bourgeoisie and proletariat would emerge, but this approach does not easily explain the wide inequalities that exist between people who do not own the means of production. The past century has seen the emergence of a new middle class of professionals, managers, and office workers between the bourgeoisie and proletariat. While these groups do not own the means of production, they benefit from exercising authority on behalf of the bourgeoisie and have higher status and better income and life chances than the working class. They generally have no interest in overthrowing the bourgeoisie.

DISCUSSION

1 Discuss the strengths and weaknesses of Marx's theory of class given above. Do you think Marx's ideas are still relevant in any way in the modern world, or do you think they are basically old-fashioned and out of date? Try to think of other evidence and examples to back up your viewpoint besides those given above.

> 2 To what extent do you think there are conflicts between groups of people in modern Britain, such as conflicts between rich and poor, managers and workers, and the unemployed and people with jobs? Why do you think these conflicts might exist? How might society be made more equal, with reduced conflicts between people?

Weber's theory of social class

Max Weber (1864–1920) agreed with Marx that people's ownership or non-ownership of the means of production was important in creating social class differences and conflicts between classes. However, Weber suggested that differences in people's market situation were also important in creating social class inequalities. 'Market situation' simply means that some people are able to get higher incomes when they sell their abilities and skills in the job market because they have rare skills, talents, or qualifications that are in demand, such as doctors and lawyers. It might also be because society values some skills and talents more highly than others and rewards them accordingly, as might be the case with football, film and music stars and other celebrities, or with some business executives and company owners. This means there are many different social classes differing in their market situations.

The difficulty with Weber's approach is that it does not easily explain the position of those who inherit their wealth and do not sell their skills in the labour market, as they live on unearned incomes rather than those earned through employment.

However, Weber thought that to understand social inequality and social conflict fully it was necessary to look at status differences between people as well as their economic position. For example, status characteristics like gender, religion, age, and ethnicity can all create conflicts between people regardless of their wealth and income. There are conflicts between status groups like men and women, Protestant and Catholic (as in Northern Ireland), young people and older people, and black and white people.

For Weber, therefore, society was divided by conflict between many competing social classes and status groups, rather than just the two social classes Marx considered.

Defining class by occupation

Occupation or socio-economic group is the most common basis for the definition of social class used by governments, by advertising agencies when doing market research, and by sociologists when doing surveys. This is because a person's occupation is an easy piece of information to obtain, and people's occupations are generally a good guide to their skills, qualifications, and experience, their income, their life chances, and other important aspects of their lives. Occupation is also a major factor influencing people's power and status in society, and most people judge the social standing of themselves and others by the jobs they do.

ACTIVITY

List all the ways you can think of that a person's occupation might affect other aspects of his or her life, such as family life, status in society, housing, health, leisure activities, beliefs and values, future planning, and so on. Make sure you explain precisely how the effects you mention are linked to a person's job.

There is a wide range of occupational scales in use, but three of the best-known and most widely used definitions of class by occupation are the National Statistics Socio-economic Classification (NS-SEC), the Standard Occupational Classification (SOC2000), and the Institute of Practitioners in Advertising (IPA) Scale. The NS-SEC is used for all official statistics and surveys, and the IPA Scale is widely used in market research and many surveys, including opinion polls. These three scales are shown on pages 24–6, with a reference to what these classes roughly refer to in the everyday language used by sociologists, and as used to describe the middle-class and working-class categories found in this book.

The middle-class occupations are generally non-manual, with people working primarily in offices, doing mainly mental rather than physical work. The term white-collar workers is sometimes used to refer to lower middle-class clerical and sales occupations.

The working-class occupations are mainly manual, with people working primarily with their hands, in jobs requiring physical work. These are sometimes referred to as blue-collar workers.

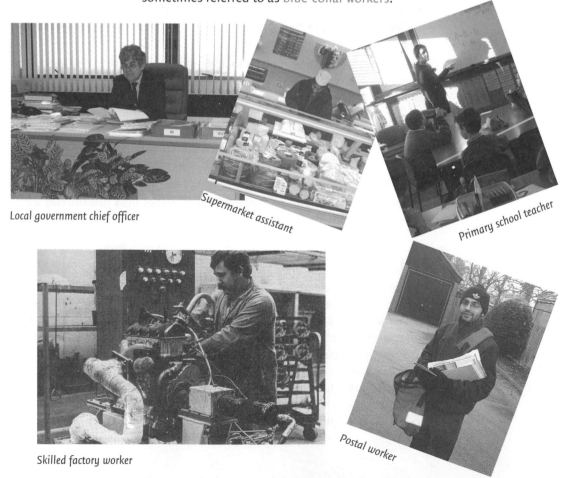

Local government chief officer

Supermarket assistant

Primary school teacher

Skilled factory worker

Postal worker

Secretary

Scaffolders

Sociology lecturer

Road maintenance workers

Recycling centre operative

Call centre workers

Cleaner

ACTIVITY

1 Classify each of the twelve occupations shown as either manual or non-manual work.

2 Put the pictures in the order of pay and status in society that you think each occupation is given, numbering them 1 to 12, beginning with 1 as the highest pay and status. Give reasons for your answer.

3 Do you think the gender or ethnicity of those doing any of these jobs might influence the status or pay that is given to the jobs? Explain your answer, with examples of particular jobs.

The National Statistics Socio-economic Classification (NS-SEC)

This occupational scale is based upon occupational source and security of income, prospects of economic advancement, and amount of authority and control at work.

Social class	Commonly called	Examples of occupations
Class 1 Higher managerial and professional occupations		
Class 1a Large employers and higher managerial occupations	Class 1 Upper middle class	Large employer, higher manager, company director, senior police/fire/prison/ military officer, newspaper editor, football manager
Class 1b Higher professional occupations		Doctor, solicitor, engineer, teacher, airline pilot
Class 2 Lower managerial and professional occupations	Class 2 Middle class	Journalist, nurse/midwife, actor, musician, junior police officer (constable), lower manager
Class 3 Intermediate occupations	Class 3 (Non-manual) Lower middle class	Secretary, air stewardess, driving instructor, footballer, telephone operator
Class 4 Small employers and own-account workers		Small employer/manager, self-employed publican, plumber
Class 5 Lower supervisory and technical occupations	Class 3 (Manual) Skilled manual workers/upper working class	Lower supervisor, electrician, mechanic, train driver, bus inspector
Class 6 Semi-routine occupations	Class 4 Semi-skilled manual/working class	Traffic warden, caretaker, gardener, supermarket shelf-stacker, assembly-line worker, shop assistant
Class 7 Routine occupations	Class 5 Unskilled manual/ lower working class	Cleaner, waiter/waitress, bar staff, road worker
Class 8 Never worked and long-term unemployed	The poor, and sometimes the underclass	Long-term unemployed, long-term sick, never worked

The Standard Occupational Classification (2000) (SOC2000)

This occupational scale ranks occupations according to their similarity of qualifications, training, skills and experience

Social class	Commonly called	Examples of occupations
Class 1 Managers and senior officials	Class 1 Upper middle class	Senior sales manager, police officer (inspector and above), senior manager or administrator in national and local government and large companies
Class 2 Professional		University or college lecturer, teacher, doctor, solicitor, architect, vicar, social worker, pharmacist, civil engineer, librarian
Class 3 Associate professional and technical	Class 2 Middle class	Surveyor, computer programmer, nurse, youth worker, journalist, airline pilot, laboratory technician, police officer (sergeant and below), fitness instructor
Class 4 Administrative and secretarial	Class 3 (Non-manual) Lower middle class	Clerical worker, secretary, receptionist, market research interviewer, school secretary
Class 5 Skilled trades	Class 3 (Manual) Skilled manual workers/upper working class	Bricklayer, electrician, plumber, motor mechanic, butcher, baker, chef/cook, computer maintenance and installation engineer
Class 6 Personal services		Hairdresser and beautician, nursery nurse, travel agent, child-minder and related
Class 7 Sales and customer service	Class 4 Semi-skilled manual/working class	Sales rep, sales assistant, supermarket check-out operator, call centre operator
Class 8 Process, plant, and machine operatives		Assembly-line worker, packer, bus/lorry/van/taxi-driver, tyre and exhaust fitter, driving instructor
Class 9 Elementary	Class 5 Unskilled manual/lower working class	Farm worker, refuse collector, postal worker, road sweeper, cleaner, hospital porter, waiter/waitress, bar staff, traffic warden, shelf-filler, school crossing patrol attendant

The Institute of Practitioners in Advertising (IPA) Scale

Advertisers are mainly interested in selling things to people, so their scale ranks occupations primarily on the basis of income. They obviously want to know how much money people have so they can target their advertising at the right people. This scale is very widely used in surveys of all kinds.

Social class	Commonly called	Examples of occupations
Class A Higher managerial, administrative, or professional occupations	Upper middle class	Opticians, judges, solicitors, senior civil servants, surgeons, senior managers (in large companies), accountants, architects
Class B Intermediate managerial, administrative, or professional occupations	Middle class	Airline pilots, MPs, teachers, social workers, middle managers, police inspectors
Class C1 Supervisory or clerical and junior managerial, administrative, or professional occupations	Lower middle class	Clerical workers, computer operators, receptionists, sales assistants, secretaries, nurses, technicians
Class C2 Skilled manual workers	Upper working class	Carpenters, bricklayers, electricians, chefs/cooks, plumbers
Class D Semi-skilled and unskilled manual workers	Semi-skilled and lower working class	Postal workers, bar workers, office cleaners, road sweepers, machine minders, farm labourers
Class E Those on the lowest levels of income	The poor	Pensioners (on state pensions), casual workers, long-term unemployed, and others on income support and the lowest levels of income

The problems of defining class by occupation

While occupation is very commonly used to define social class, the use of occupation and occupational scales presents a number of problems for the sociologist:

- The use of occupation excludes the wealthy upper class, who own property and have a great deal of power but often don't have an occupation. Occupational scales therefore do not reveal major differences in wealth and income within and between social classes.

- Groups outside paid employment are excluded, such as housewives and the never-employed unemployed. Housework is not recognized as an occupation.

- Social class is based primarily on the occupation of the highest-earning member of the household, but the use of a single head of household may ignore dual-worker families, where both partners are working. Such families have much better life chances than single-income households in the same class. Their combined incomes might even give them the lifestyle of a higher social class.

■ The classes on occupational scales tend to be very broad, and disguise major differences within each class. For example, a grouping like 'professionals' may include both poorly paid junior NHS doctors and rich Harley Street private specialists. There are major differences in income and life chances between such people, yet they are placed in the same class.

THE CLASS STRUCTURE OF BRITAIN

Often, when talking of social class, sociologists will refer to terms quite loosely. Figure 2.1 illustrates which groups of occupations are generally being referred to when particular social classes in modern Britain are mentioned. Note that the main division between working class and middle class is generally accepted as being that between manual and non-manual occupations. The controversial idea of the underclass is discussed in chapter 4.

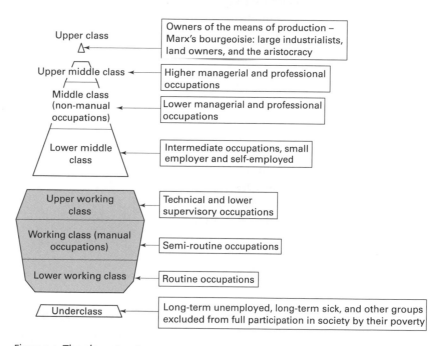

Figure 2.1 The class structure

CHAPTER SUMMARY

After studying this chapter, you should be able to:

■ Explain what is meant by social stratification.

■ Describe the main features of the caste, estate, and class systems, and the differences between them.

■ Explain what is meant by the term 'status'.

■ Define the term 'social class'.

■ Describe the main features of consensus and conflict theories of social class, and some problems with them.

■ Explain why sociologists often use occupation as an indicator of social class, and explain the problems in the use of occupation and occupational scales.

■ Outline the main social classes in Britain today.

KEY TERMS

achieved status
ascribed status
blue-collar workers
bourgeoisie
caste system
class consciousness
closed society
Communism
endogamy
false consciousness
feudalism
life chances
market situation
means of production
meritocracy
open society
proletariat
social class
social mobility
social stratification
status
status groups
white-collar workers

COURSEWORK SUGGESTIONS

1   Ask a sample of people about their attitudes to social class – what they think it is, what is the most important factor defining it, whether it is still important, whether everyone has the same chances in life. Ask them to describe themselves as middle or working class, and to say why.

2   Carry out a survey among a group of people, and ask them whether they believe there are conflicts between the rich and the poor in Britain, and, if they say yes, ask them why they think these problems exist.

3 Social Class in Modern Britain

Many people assume that social class is not really very important today, often blaming sociologists for highlighting class inequalities which don't really have much impact on people's lives. Others suggest that social class is no longer an important influence on people's lifestyles – the goods they choose to consume and the choices they make in how they live their lives – as people can choose from a range of different lifestyles presented to them through the mass media and available to them through their consumer spending.

However, pretending that social classes don't exist will not make them go away, any more than not being able to see a plate glass door will stop you from hurting yourself when you walk into it. Ask yourself why you don't buy expensive clothes, houses, and cars, or travel first class by train. Why don't you go to exotic foreign countries for long holidays several times a year? Why don't you eat out at restaurants all the time instead of cooking? Why don't you try to skip National Health Service waiting lists by paying for private medicine?

ACTIVITY

1 What social class do you think you belong to? Give reasons for your answer.

2 Think of all the differences you can between social classes in modern Britain. How would you explain the class differences you have identified?

3 Conduct a survey among people you know to see how they identify social class and what social class they would put themselves in, and why.

Social classes do not exist merely in the mind of the sociologist: there are wide, measurable differences in life chances between social classes. The higher the social class of an individual, the more access she or he will have to society's resources – such as better housing, cars, food, holidays, income, and job security – and the more influence he or she will have in society. The following section examines some examples of these class differences, and further examples are discussed in other parts of this book (see particularly chapters 12 and 16 on inequalities in education and health).

CLASS INEQUALITIES

Wealth and income

In 2001–2, 5 per cent of the population owned 57 per cent of the UK's wealth, and 10 per cent of the population owned over 72 per cent of the wealth. The poorest 50 per cent of the population owned just 1 per cent of the UK's wealth; the top 20 per cent of income earners got over five times the share of the bottom 20 per cent; and Britain had one of the widest gaps between the high-paid and the low-paid in Europe. Poverty remains widespread, with 22 per cent of the population of Britain – about 12 and a half million people – living in poverty in 2001–2. These issues are discussed in the next chapter.

Health and life expectancy

Despite the welfare state and the National Health Service, major differences in health continue to exist between social classes. A man from social class 1 on average lives seven years longer than a man from social class 5. As shown in figure 3.1, nearly twice as many babies die at birth or in the first week of life (a perinatal death) or in the first year of life (infant mortality) in social class 5 as in social class 1. Figure 3.2 shows how chronic sickness and acute sickness rise as one moves down the social class hierarchy (chronic sickness is long-standing illness or disability;

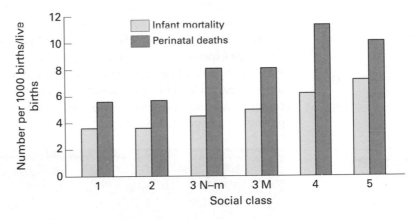

Figure 3.1 Perinatal deaths and infant mortality (for births within marriage only): by social class of father, England and Wales, 2001

Source: Office for National Statistics

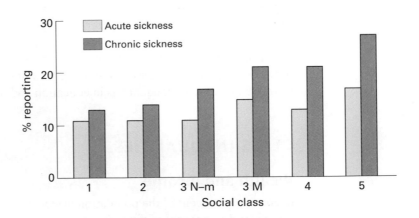

Figure 3.2 Chronic and acute sickness: by social class, Great Britain, 2001

Source: Calculated from General Household Survey, 2001

acute sickness refers to restriction of normal activity due to illness or injury in the previous two weeks before interview). A survey in the 1990s showed the death rate from heart disease was about one half higher than average for people in social class 5, compared with one half lower than average for those in social class 1. This is just part of a mass of evidence which shows that lower-working-class people suffer more from almost all diseases than those in the upper middle class.

These issues of health and illness are discussed further in chapter 16.

<table>
<tr><td>ACTIVITY</td><td>

Study figures 3.1 and 3.2 and then answer the following questions:

1 Which social class has the highest level of infant mortality?

2 Which social class has about 10 perinatal deaths per thousand births?

3 Which two social classes have the lowest level of infant mortality?

4 What is the approximate difference between the number per thousand of perinatal deaths in class 1 and in class 5?

5 What is the difference between the percentage of people reporting chronic sickness in class 1 and in class 5?

6 Which three social classes reported the highest levels of chronic sickness?

7 Figure 3.1 shows more babies dying within the first week or within the first year of life in social class 5 than in social class 1. Suggest explanations for this.

</td></tr>
</table>

Explaining class differences in health and life expectancy

These differences are often explained by the following features of working-class life, which are less likely to be experienced by those in middle-class occupations:

■ Longer working hours, with shiftwork and overtime.

■ Poorer conditions at work, with more risks to health and safety through accidents and industrial diseases.

■ Less time off work with pay to visit the doctor.

■ Lower income, leading to poorer diets and housing.

■ More likelihood of working-class areas being at risk through industrial and traffic pollution.

■ Poorer medical care in working-class areas, with long hospital waiting lists and overworked GPs, and lack of enough income to make use of private medicine.

■ Lower levels of education, which often mean less awareness of health and the services which are available, and less self-confidence in questioning the judgements of health professionals.

■ Poverty in old age, due to the lack of an occupational pension and inadequate earnings while working to save for old age.

■ Smoking, which tends to be more common in the working class.

■ Higher levels of unemployment and poverty, and therefore more stress-related illnesses.

Class differences in employment

The different status of occupations is backed up by different terms and conditions of employment under which people work. These improve with movement upward through the social class hierarchy.

Even the lowest level of non-manual workers, routine clerical workers, often have better terms and conditions of employment than manual workers, although they don't always earn more. In general, manual workers, compared with the non-manual middle class:

- Get lower pay, despite working longer hours with shiftwork and overtime (see table 3.1).

- Have shorter holidays.

- Work in more dangerous and less hygienic conditions, with greater risks of accident and disease.

- Are more supervised at work, having to clock in, getting pay 'docked' for lateness, and not being allowed time off with pay for personal reasons.

- Receive less training in their work.

- Are less likely to receive full pay during sickness, or to belong to an employer's pension scheme.

- Have much less job security: the risk of unemployment is seven times greater for an unskilled manual worker than for someone in social class 1.

Table 3.1 Levels of average pay and hours: full-time employees on adult rates, Great Britain, April 2002

	Males		Females		All employees (males and females)	
	Manual	Non-manual	Manual	Non-manual	Manual	Non-manual
Average gross[a] weekly earnings (£ before deductions)	£368	£610	£251	£405	£346	£514
Of which (%):						
Overtime payments	12%	2%	6%	2%	11%	2%
Incentive, etc., payments	3%	5%	2%	2%	5%	4%
Shift, etc., premium payments	3%	1%	3%	1%	3%	1%
Average total weekly hours	43.9	38.9	39.7	37.1	43.1	38.1
Of which overtime hours (%)	10%	3%	4%	2%	9%	2%

Note:
[a]Gross earnings are those before deductions of income tax, national insurance, pensions, etc.
Source: Data adapted from *New Earnings Survey,* 2002

DISCUSSION

How might the terms and conditions of employment of manual workers affect their attitudes to work, their leisure activities, and their plans for the future?

ACTIVITY

Refer to table 3.1:

1 Which occupational group of males and females worked the shortest hours?

2 Which occupational group of males and females worked the most overtime?

3 Which group of all employees had the largest percentage of their pay made up of incentive payments?

4 Which group of all employees had the lowest percentage of their pay made up of payments for working shifts?

5 Which occupational group of males and females had the lowest gross weekly earnings in April 2002?

6 What differences does the table show between male and female full-time employees? Suggest possible explanations for the differences you identify.

Explaining class differences in employment

Class differences in employment are often explained or justified by the higher education, training, and increased management responsibility of many non-manual workers, and the need to retain their commitment and loyalty to the firm and thus protect the firm's interests and investment. Even routine office workers often have some knowledge of the firm's 'secrets', such as profit levels, accounts, sales, and orders, and the management might want to conceal these 'secrets' from manual workers, particularly if they are submitting a pay claim. It is therefore in the firm's interest to try to retain the loyalty and commitment of non-manual staff. The tighter control and poorer conditions of work of manual workers suggest they are not trusted by management, are considered more dispensable, and can be more easily replaced. The generally poorer pay of women, whether manual or non-manual, compared with males (illustrated in table 3.1) is fully discussed in chapter 5.

CHANGES IN THE CLASS STRUCTURE

The changing occupational structure

At the beginning of the twentieth century, the majority of people in Britain were working in manual working-class occupations, with less than a quarter being considered upper or middle class. However, in the last hundred years, changes in the economy have occurred which have changed the occupational structure. These changes include:

■ A growth in the tertiary sector of the economy, which is concerned with the provision of services, such as administration, sales, finance and insurance, transport, distribution, and the running of government services (like the welfare state and education). This has created more middle-class jobs, particularly routine, low-level, non-manual jobs.

- A decline in semi-skilled and unskilled manual work, as technology takes over these tasks, and creates more skilled jobs.

- A steady increase in the percentage of the workforce engaged in non-manual occupations, especially white-collar occupations such as routine clerical work.

- An increase in lower professional occupations, like teachers and social workers.

These developments have led to a change in the shape of the social structure, with unskilled and semi-skilled manual occupations getting smaller and skilled manual and lower-middle-class occupations getting larger. There has also emerged what some people regard as an 'underclass' of long-term unemployed and other groups who are excluded by their poverty from full participation in society. The underclass is discussed more fully in the following chapter. As shown in figure 3.3, the social structure has changed from the pyramid shape that existed about a century ago to the shape of a diamond.

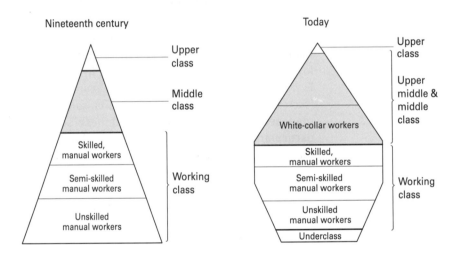

Figure 3.3 The changing shape of the class structure in Britain

The changing working class: the 'traditional' and 'new' working classes

Since the 1960s, the wages and living standards of skilled manual workers have improved greatly, often exceeding those of some of the middle class. These highly paid manual workers – sometimes called affluent workers – could afford to buy their own homes and live in middle-class areas, and to buy the consumer goods which previously only the middle class could afford. This gave rise to the idea of embourgeoisement.

DEFINITION Embourgeoisement is the idea that the differences between the middle class and working class are disappearing, with well-paid manual workers merging into the middle class.

However, despite big improvements in living standards and lifestyles, the following differences still separate affluent manual workers from the middle class, suggesting that embourgeoisement has not occurred:

Embourgeoisement

Middle class

⬆

Working class

■ Their high wages are only obtained at the cost of overtime and shiftworking – working conditions which are rarely experienced by non-manual workers.

■ They lack some 'fringe benefits' which non-manual workers receive, such as employers' pension and sick pay schemes.

■ They have more limited promotion opportunities and less job security than non-manual workers.

■ They have an instrumental attitude to work. This means their main concern is with money. The purpose of work is not to achieve status, promotion, or job satisfaction (as in the middle class), but to get money to enjoy life outside work.

■ Even though they often live on the same estates as non-manual workers, manual workers tend to prefer the company of other manual workers like themselves.

While manual workers are not merging into the middle class, there has been the emergence of a new working class, with a decline in the numbers of the traditional working class. This new working class has a much more affluent lifestyle and a more privatized family life than the traditional working class, and has an instrumental attitude to the Labour Party and trade unions, supporting them only for selfish motives of personal gain rather than out of a sense of loyalty to their workmates and the communities in which they grew up. The main features of these two sections of the working class are summarized on page 36.

Traditional working class

- Declining in size.
- Found mainly in the north of England and Scotland in traditional (long-established) basic industries, such as mining, docking, iron and steel, and shipbuilding. These industries have been in decline since the 1960s.
- People work in the same industry generation after generation and live near one another and near the place of work. There is, as a result, a close-knit community living and working together, with high levels of involvement in community life.
- There is a strong sense of working-class identity and class solidarity. Therefore there is a strong commitment to trade unions, and support for the Labour Party, seen as 'the party of the working class'.

- A large majority live in social (rented) housing (council and housing association houses).
- There is seen to be a basic conflict between the social classes, with society divided by power differences between 'us' (the workers) and 'them' (the bosses).

New working class

- Growing in size.
- More likely to be found in the south of England. They are generally well-paid, 'affluent' workers with more secure jobs in newer, more technologically advanced and other light manufacturing industries.

- People live a privatized, home-centred family lifestyle, with little involvement with neighbours or the wider community.

- They have an instrumental approach to politics and trade unions – their support depends on what they can personally get out of them. There is little sense of loyalty to others in the same class. They are less likely to belong to trade unions and prefer to vote for the political party bringing them the most personal benefits, regardless of which political party that is.
- Many are home-owners and have lifestyles more like the middle class.

- Social class is not seen as very important – the only real difference between people is that some have more money and possessions than others.

ACTIVITY

Refer to the section above and list the following statements as true or false:

1 Traditional working-class people are more likely to vote Labour.
2 Members of the new working class are more likely to own their own homes.
3 The traditional working class is likely to have a lifestyle more like the lower middle class.
4 People in the new working class are more likely to live in a tight-knit community.
5 Traditional working-class people are more likely to be trade union members.
6 The new working class is more likely to be found in the north of England.
7 Members of the new working class are likely to be better paid.
8 Members of the traditional working class are more likely to see society as divided by conflict between opposing social classes.

The changing nature of clerical work: the proletarianization of white-collar workers

DEFINITION

> **Proletarianization** is the opposite of embourgeoisement. It is the suggestion that, rather than affluent workers becoming middle class, some middle-class groups (particularly clerical and administrative workers) are descending into the working class.

Proletarianization

Middle class

⬇

Working class

Traditionally, clerical workers had higher levels of education, higher pay, shorter working hours, and better working conditions and career opportunities than manual workers, and were seen as having a middle-class status and lifetyle.

The proletarianization thesis suggests that these advantages once enjoyed by clerical workers compared to the manual working class are declining or have been lost altogether.

The declining status of clerical work

Throughout the last century, the position of the clerical worker changed in a number of important ways, and it continues to change today:

- The relative pay of clerical workers has declined dramatically, and today is generally little better (and often worse) than that of manual workers.

- Promotion opportunities have been reduced. There is little chance of a clerical worker today 'working his or her way up' into management, as managerial jobs are often filled directly by graduates of universities and colleges.

- Clerical workers have lost their close association with management and they face increased supervision of their work by line managers.

- Office technology such as calculators, computers, and copiers has reduced the skills of clerical work – this is called deskilling – and much clerical work has become more like routine and repetitious factory work.

- With compulsory education, the skills required for clerical work (which have themselves become simplified through deskilling) are far more common today, so the educational differences that once existed between clerical and manual workers have been eroded and many more people have the basic skills to do clerical work. This has contributed to the decline in pay.

Technology is changing clerical work

These changes have brought about a relative decline in status, and in terms of educational level, housing, and living standards there are few differences between clerical and manual workers. A further factor contributing to this decline in status has been the 'feminization' of clerical work – it has become more defined as 'women's work', when it was once seen as a respectable middle-class job for men. In a world dominated by men, women's jobs are often seen, quite unfairly, as less important simply because they are done by women. In the face of these changes, clerical workers have turned more to trade unions to protect their position, and this brings them more in line with working-class methods for defending pay and conditions.

DISCUSSION   Do you agree that clerical work has become more defined as 'women's work'? Why are women more likely than men to take up such work?

Are clerical workers now working class?

While there is no doubt that the position of clerical workers has declined dramatically since the early twentieth century, clerical workers still have a number of differences from manual workers:

- They have more job security (though this is rapidly disappearing).

- They work shorter hours, have better fringe benefits, such as pension schemes and sickness benefits, and have longer holidays.

- They are still less supervised at work than manual workers: many do not have to clock in, have no pay knocked off for lateness, and have more flexibility in working hours (flexitime).

- They often share canteen and other facilities with management, and they are more likely to cooperate with management, rather than display the mistrust of management shown by manual workers.

- Despite the growth of white-collar trade unions, these unions often maintain a separate identity from manual unions, and they are often concerned with 'staying ahead' of manual workers in terms of pay and conditions and maintaining status differences, rather than recognizing shared or common interests with manual workers.

These differences continue to separate clerical workers from manual workers, though these differences are diminishing. Proletarianization is an on-going process and the social position of clerical workers may continue to decline as changes in office technology and tighter management control make office work more and more like factory work.

SOCIAL MOBILITY

Social mobility refers to the movement of people up or down the social class hierarchy, either during the course of the individual's lifetime or compared to the social class into which she or he was born. Modern industrial societies are said to be open societies because social mobility is possible, and people can move up or down the social class hierarchy.

Why study social mobility?

The study of social mobility is important because it enables sociologists to find out how open society is – how much people move from the social class into which they were born, and how much they improve their social position during their adult lives. Social mobility studies can show to what extent society is meritocratic – whether people's social position is achieved solely on the basis of their talents, abilities, skills, and qualifications, or whether the social class into which they were born, and other factors like their gender or ethnic origin, influence the positions they can achieve as adults. In short, these studies can show whether or not everyone has equal opportunities of reaching the top social classes.

Measuring social mobility

Sociologists use the criterion of occupation to measure mobility, using occupational scales like the National Statistics Socio-economic Classification discussed in chapter 2.

This means that there are problems with the measuring 'tools' used in social mobility studies. For example, social mobility studies often exclude women, and sociologists differ in the occupational scales they use – some rank occupations according to their status, others by income – so the results of different mobility studies are often hard to compare. Also, the status of occupations changes over time and new occupations (like computer programmers and system analysts) may emerge, while other occupations may disappear.

As we saw earlier, clerical work has changed dramatically since the early twentieth century, so someone doing a clerical job in the 1950s may actually have had a much higher-status job than someone doing a clerical job today. Social mobility is usually measured in one of two ways:

- Inter-generational social mobility compares an adult's present occupation with that of the family she or he was born into (usually measured against the father's occupation). It therefore shows social class mobility between two generations. For example, a refuse collector's daughter who becomes a doctor has experienced upward social mobility compared with the class into which she was born.

- Intra-generational social mobility compares a person's present occupation with her or his first occupation, therefore showing how much mobility she or he has achieved in his or her lifetime. An example would be the person who began her or his working life as a small shopkeeper, but who eventually built up a massive supermarket empire.

How much social mobility is there in Britain?

Social mobility in modern Britain is relatively limited, and most people stay in the broad social class they were born into. The main findings suggest the following conclusions.

Inter-generational social mobility

- A considerable number of children from working-class backgrounds now achieve upward mobility to the middle class. This is largely because there are declining numbers of working-class jobs, and growing numbers of middle-class jobs – there is 'more room at the top', enabling middle-class children to stay middle class, while also enabling more working-class children to become middle class.

- Nearly 80 per cent of the adults in the working class, and about three-quarters of the middle class, were born to parents of the same class.

- There is a close link between the social class of origin (the class people are born into) and the social class of destination (the one they end up in as adults).

- There are fairly high levels of inter-generational mobility, but most of this is short-range mobility, such as movement from class 5 to class 3, and there is relatively little long-range mobility across several occupational classes, such as from class 5 to class 1.

- Not everyone has the same chance of achieving upward social mobility. A child from a working-class background has only about half the chance of entering classes 1 and 2 as an adult compared to one from the lower middle class. A child born into social classes 1 and 2 has about three times the chance of being in these classes as an adult compared to one from a working class background. This shows a clear lack of equal opportunity for all to have the same chance of getting the top jobs.

The 1:2:3 pattern of unequal opportunity

Whatever the chance a boy from a working-class background has of reaching social class 1 or 2, a boy from a lower-middle-class family has about twice the chance and a boy from an upper-middle-class family has about three times the chance of entering class 1 or 2 as an adult. This clearly shows an inequality of opportunity in the chances of upward mobility in Britain.

- There is a high level of self-recruitment at the two extremes of the class hierarchy. This means many children born into class 1 themselves enter class 1 as adults, and many children born into class 5 themselves enter class 5.

- Despite more social mobility today, the propertied upper class still remains largely closed, as much wealth is inherited rather than achieved through work or talent. The best way to get rich in modern Britain is still to be born to rich parents.

Intra-generational social mobility

The chances of upward mobility during a person's career, such as moving from a manual job to a higher-status professional and managerial or technical job, have declined. Higher-status positions are increasingly filled directly by graduates from the education system, and most of these graduates themselves come from higher social class backgrounds.

ACTIVITY

Go through the following list, writing down for each one 'upward mobility', 'downward mobility', or 'no change', *and* 'inter-generational mobility' or 'intra-generational mobility'. Refer to the occupational scales in the previous chapter if you find any difficulty.

1 A nurse who decides to become a labourer on a building site.

2 The daughter of a miner who becomes a bank manager.

3 A teacher who decides to retrain as a social worker.

4 A doctor's son who becomes a taxi-driver.

5 An immigrant from a poor farming background in Africa who gets a job in Britain as a farm labourer.

6 The daughter of a skilled manual worker who becomes a routine clerical worker.

7 A postal worker who becomes a traffic warden.

8 A pilot whose son becomes a police constable.

9 The owner of a small shop whose daughter becomes the manager of a large supermarket.

10 A sales assistant in a shop who becomes a priest.

Women and social mobility

Studies of social mobility have in the past tended to ignore women, because of the mistaken assumption that most women are married, work as housewives, and depend on their husbands for their income. Women have therefore been seen as having their class decided by their husband's occupation. However, this is a wildly outdated view, and ignores the large number of non-married working women and the rapid increase in recent years in the numbers of working married women. More recent studies suggest:

■ Women have traditionally had poorer chances of mobility than men, because they have been mainly concentrated in semi-skilled manual occupations, routine clerical work, and the lower professions such as teaching and nursing. However, the better performance of women in education, their growing participation in the labour force, and equal opportunities policies at work are now giving women more favourable opportunities for upward mobility than men.

■ Women face major difficulties in entering skilled manual and managerial, technical, and top professional occupations.

■ There are very few women compared with men in the top elite positions in society – those small groups of people holding a great deal of power in society, such as judges, leaders of industry, top civil servants, and MPs and government ministers.

■ Women still have less chance of promotion than men, and it is still often women who experience downward mobility when they abandon careers with bright futures to take care of children, only to return to work at a lower status, and with less pay, than when they left. The reasons for this pattern are discussed more fully in chapter 5.

Ethnicity and social mobility

There have been relatively few studies of social mobility and ethnicity. However, minority ethnic groups experience more upward and downward mobility than the white majority. While some minority ethnic groups are experiencing rapid upward mobility, they still face a range of disadvantages. For example, while 90 per cent of white British graduates are in middle-class jobs, only 56 per cent of Pakistani, 62 per cent of Indian and 68 per cent of African-Caribbean graduates are in such jobs. These issues are considered further in chapter 6.

Explanations for social mobility

More room at the top

The last century has seen a relative decline in the proportion of semi- and unskilled manual occupations and an expansion in non-manual professional, managerial, and routine clerical occupations. This has increased the opportunities for upward mobility for the working class, as there is more room at the top. There are fewer middle-class children than extra top jobs. This means that, even if all middle-class children go into middle-class jobs, there are still higher-level job vacancies to be filled by 'promoting' people from lower down the social scale.

Improved educational opportunities

Free and compulsory secondary education since 1944, and the development of comprehensive education in the 1960s, have enabled more working-class children to obtain the educational qualifications required for upward mobility. This is particularly important as intra-generational mobility is generally achieved through promotion at work, which increasingly depends on educational qualifications, and inter-generational mobility is also achieved mainly through educational qualifications. However, as chapter 12 shows, the educational qualifications that someone obtains are closely related to the social class of the family into which they were born.

Marriage

Some people may achieve upward mobility through marrying a partner from a higher social class. It is mainly women who achieve upward mobility through marriage, but such cross-class marriages are uncommon and most people marry within their own social class.

Exceptional talents and luck

Exceptional talents, such as in sport or entertainment, or luck, like winning the lottery, provide a route for upward mobility, but only for an extremely small number of people.

Obstacles to social mobility

While levels of social mobility have grown in recent years, there remain a number of obstacles to social mobility and the development of a truly 'open' society. The issues summarized below are discussed further in chapters 5, 6, and 12.

- Despite free and compulsory state education, there remains widespread inequality of educational opportunity. Many working-class children face a number of obstacles and disadvantages to success in education, which mean they do not do as well as their ability should allow them to, and this restricts their chances of upward mobility. Middle-class families are generally in a better position to secure for their children a middle-class occupation, as they are more able to afford to support their children in further and higher education in a wide number of ways.

- There remain biases in recruitment to the upper-middle-class elite jobs. For example, judges and top civil servants are recruited almost exclusively from people who have attended very expensive boys' public schools and then gone to Oxford or Cambridge universities. This is a major obstacle for children from working-class backgrounds, who can't afford these schools and are therefore often denied the chance of getting into these top jobs.

- Women face a range of obstacles in achieving upward mobility, because of a range of factors which hinder their ability to compete in the labour market on equal terms with men (see chapter 5).

- Disadvantages in education, and racism in education, training, and employment, often present obstacles to the upward social mobility of some minority ethnic groups. Consequently, a high percentage of people of African-Caribbean and Pakistani/Bangladeshi origin are represented in the working class.

DISCUSSION

Do you think everyone who has intelligence, initiative, and skill can make it to the 'top' in modern Britain if they really try? Are those at the top and the bottom of the social class hierarchy there because they deserve to be?

ACTIVITY

1 Explain how each of the factors below might encourage or limit the possibilities of upward social mobility.

2 Suggest what steps you might take to ensure that the most well-paid and responsible positions in society are filled by the most able and committed people, regardless of their social class, gender, or ethnic origins.

Factors encouraging social mobility
- Family support for children, in the form of money, support in education, values and networks of contacts.
- Raising educational standards and ensuring access to further and higher education for all.
- Equality of opportunity for all, based on merit, with fairer recruitment policies by employers.
- Drive, ambition, and a willingness to take up opportunities and take risks.

Factors limiting social mobility
- Lack of success in education.
- Lack of family support.
- Poor attitudes, low expectations, and lack of ambition.
- Barriers to some occupations, like the legal profession, for those from the 'wrong' social class background.
- Racial and sexual discrimination.
- Childhood poverty.

This chapter has shown that social class differences persist as major features of life in contemporary Britain, and most people do not achieve much upward social mobility from the family into which they are born. These class inequalities become even more apparent when the two extremes of the social class hierarchy are studied: the rich and the poor. These themes are explored in the following chapter.

CHAPTER SUMMARY

After studying this chapter, you should be able to:

- Describe and explain a range of social class differences.

- Describe and explain the main changes in the class structure over the last century.

- Explain and criticize the suggestion that embourgeoisement has occurred.

- Describe the differences between the 'traditional' and 'new' working classes.

- Describe and explain how the position of clerical workers has changed.

- Describe and explain the patterns of social mobility in Britain, and outline the obstacles to social mobility.

KEY TERMS

affluent worker
deskilling
elite
embourgeoisement
infant mortality
inter-generational social mobility
intra-generational social mobility

perinatal death
proletarianization
racism

COURSEWORK SUGGESTIONS

1   Using secondary sources, do a study of some aspect of social class inequality, such as in health, at work, or in education.

2   Interview a sample of manual and non-manual workers and try to discover what differences exist in their terms and conditions of employment and their experience of work.

4 Wealth, Welfare, and Poverty

KEY ISSUES

- Wealth and income.
- Poverty.
- The welfare state.
- The persistence of poverty.

Many believe that large differences in wealth and income and the contrasts between the very rich and the very poor have largely disappeared in modern Britain. Surely the welfare state has got rid of poverty? However, a walk through the streets of any large city will reveal stark contrasts between the mansions, the luxury cars, and the expensive lifestyle of the rich, and the poverty and hardship of many of those who are unemployed, sick, or old, who are lone parents, who are homeless or living in decaying housing, and who are faced with a future of hopelessness and despair. This chapter will show the common assumption that the welfare state has resolved the problem of poverty to be exaggerated, and demonstrate that massive inequalities in wealth and income and widespread poverty remain in modern Britain.

WEALTH AND INCOME

■ Wealth refers to property which can be sold and turned into cash for the benefit of the owner. The main forms of wealth are property such as homes and land, stocks and shares in companies, and personal possessions. Productive property is wealth which provides an unearned income for its owner, for example houses which are rented, factories and land, or stocks and shares which provide dividends. Consumption property is wealth for use by the owner, such as consumer goods like fridges, cars, and stereo systems, or owning your own home, which do not produce any income.

■ Income refers to the flow of money which people obtain from work, from their investments, or from the state. This may be earned income, received from paid employment (wages and salaries), or unearned income, which is received from investments, such as rent on property, interest on savings, and dividends on shares.

The distribution of wealth and income

Figure 4.1 shows that in 2001–2 the poorest 50 per cent of the population owned only 1 per cent of the wealth, while the richest 5 per cent owned 57 per cent. One-tenth of the population possessed nearly three-quarters of the nation's wealth. These figures are official figures from the Inland Revenue (the government's tax collectors), and they therefore underestimate the inequalities of wealth, as the wealthy have an interest in concealing their wealth to avoid taxation.

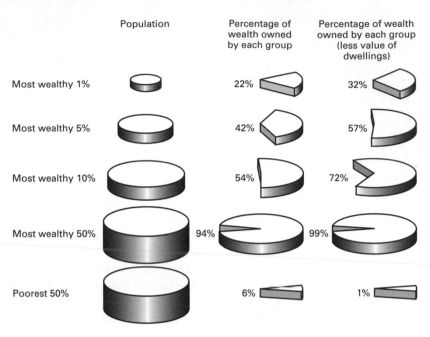

Figure 4.1 Distribution of wealth: United Kingdom. 2000

Source: Inland Revenue, 2003

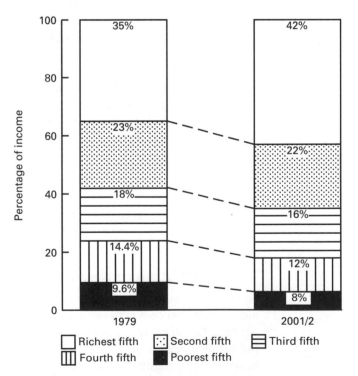

Figure 4.2 Distribution of income: by fifths of the population, United Kingdom, 1979 and 2001/2

Source: Households Below Average Income (Department for Work and Pensions, 2003)

As figure 4.2 shows, income is also unequally distributed, with the richest fifth of income earners getting about 42 per cent of all income in 2001–2 – more than twice their 'fair share' if income were equally distributed, and more than the bottom three-fifths of income earners got between them. The poorest fifth got only about 8 per cent, just two-fifths of their 'fair share'.

ACTIVITY

Study figure 4.2 and answer the following questions:

1 Which group increased its share of income between 1979 and 2001–2?

2 Which group suffered the least cut in its income share between 1979 and 2001–2?

3 By how much did the percentage share of the poorest fifth of the population fall between 1979 and 2001–2?

4 How might the evidence in figure 4.2 be used to show that the rich were getting richer between 1979 and 2001–2 while the poor, in comparison, were getting poorer?

5 Draw a pie chart to illustrate the distribution of income in 2001–2.

Who are the rich?

The rich are:

- *The aristocracy*. They are major land owners, such as the Duke of Westminster, who owns sizeable chunks of London, Cheshire, the Scottish Highlands, Vancouver, and Hawaii, and whose wealth amounts to an estimated £5.0 billion, according to the *Sunday Times* 2004 'Rich List'.

- *The owners of industry and commerce* – the 'corporate rich' of the business world. This includes Richard Branson of Virgin, Britain's sixth-richest person in 2004 with estimated assets of £2.6 billion.

- *Stars of entertainment and the media*, such as former Beatle Paul McCartney (£760 million), Mick Jagger (£180 million), Elton John (£175 million), and the relatively impoverished Sean Connery on £82 million, Robbie Williams on £78 million, and David and Victoria Beckham on £65 million.

The first two of these groups make up Marx's bourgeoisie.

Most wealth is inherited, with those inheriting doing nothing to earn their wealth. Most of the rich live on unearned income from investments rather than from employment.

High-income earners do not necessarily put in more work than those who receive low pay; it is simply that society places different values on people in different positions, and rewards them more or less highly. A senior executive in a large company or a rock star will probably not have to work as hard for his or her high income as an unskilled manual labourer working long hours in a low-paid job. Whenever one hears about 'hard-working royalty', it is worth bearing in mind that Britain's queen is one of

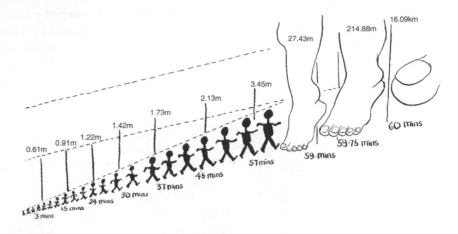

The UK income procession

Imagine that everyone's height was based on their income, so the more you earned, the taller you were. Suppose the entire population of Britain marched past you in one hour, ranked in order of their income. This is what you would see.

  For the first 30 minutes, you would be greeted by a parade of very small people, between 61 cm and 1.22 m high. The first person of average height (income) – 1.73 m – wouldn't go by until 37 minutes had passed. After 57 minutes, mini-giants of 3.45 m appear. In the last minute, super-rich giants of 27.43 m appear, but these are dwarfed by the unbelievably rich super-giants (214.88 m tall) who go by in the final few seconds. The last person is so rich that his or her over-16-km height makes all the others look tiny.

Britain's richest women, with personal assets estimated at £250 million. If the queen were to pop this into her local building society, she would receive in unearned income each year (after tax) an amount that would take a manual worker on average wages about 375 years to earn.

Attempts to redistribute wealth and income

The massive inequalities in wealth and income mentioned above, and the inequalities in life chances these have caused, have provoked various measures by governments to redistribute wealth and income more equally. Some of these measures are:

■ Inheritance tax, which is a tax payable when people give gifts of wealth either before or after death, and is intended to limit the inheritance of vast quantities of wealth from one generation to the next.

■ Capital gains tax, which is intended to reduce profits from dealing in property or shares, and is payable whenever these are sold.

■ Income tax, which is payable on unearned and earned income, and rises as earnings increase.

■ Social welfare benefits from the state, like income support, which are attempts to divert the resources obtained through taxation to the needy sections of society.

Why have these attempts failed?

Despite these measures, attempts to redistribute wealth and income have been largely unsuccessful. Little real redistribution has occurred, and what redistribution has taken place has mainly been between the very rich and the already well off. There are five main reasons for this:

- Their investments often mean the wealthy can make their wealth grow at a faster rate than the rate at which it is taxed.

- The state allows tax relief – money normally used to pay income tax – on a wide variety of things such as business expenses, school fees, and private pensions. These are expenses which only the better off are likely to have. This means that they pay a smaller proportion of their income in tax than a person who is poorer but who does not have these expenses.

- Tax avoidance schemes, which are perfectly legal, are often thought up by financial advisers and accountants to find loopholes in the tax laws and beat the tax system, thereby saving the rich from paying some tax. Such schemes involve things like living outside of Britain for most of the year, investing in pension schemes to avoid income tax, investing in tax-free or low-tax areas like the Channel Islands, giving wealth away to kin well before death to avoid inheritance tax, or putting companies in other people's names, such as those of husband/wife, children, or other kin.

- Tax evasion involves people not declaring wealth and income to the Inland Revenue. This is illegal, but is suspected to be a common practice among the rich.

- Many people fail to claim the welfare benefits to which they are entitled. Some reasons for this are discussed later in this chapter.

POVERTY

While there are great inequalities in the distribution of wealth and income in Britain, with a small section of the population possessing large amounts, there is at the other extreme the continued existence of widespread poverty. One of the key issues in discussing poverty, and certainly the most controversial, is the problem of defining what poverty is.

Absolute poverty

Absolute poverty or subsistence poverty refers to a person's biological needs for food, water, clothing, and shelter – the minimum requirements necessary to subsist and maintain life, health, and physical efficiency. A person in absolute poverty lacks the minimum necessary for healthy survival. While the minimum needed to maintain a healthy life might vary, for example, between hot and cold climates and between people in

Absolute poverty
Photo: Gordon Browne

occupations with different physical demands, absolute or subsistence poverty is roughly the same in every society. People in absolute poverty would be poor anywhere at any time – the standard does not change much over time. The solution to absolute poverty is to raise the living standards of the poor above subsistence level. Absolute poverty is most associated with the countries of the Third World, where it remains a widespread problem. It is unlikely many people live in absolute poverty in Britain today, where poverty is basically relative poverty.

Relative poverty: poverty as social exclusion

Relative poverty involves defining poverty in relation to a generally accepted standard of living in a specific society at a particular time. This takes into account social and cultural needs as well as biological needs. Townsend has provided the classic definition of relative poverty:

DEFINITION

Individuals . . . can be said to be in poverty when they lack the resources to obtain the types of diets, participate in the activities and have the living conditions and amenities which are customary, or at least widely encouraged or approved, in the societies to which they belong. Their resources are so seriously below those commanded by the average individual or family that they are, in effect, excluded from ordinary living patterns, customs or activities.

P. Townsend, *Poverty in the United Kingdom* (Penguin)

THE GLOBAL EXTENT OF ABSOLUTE POVERTY

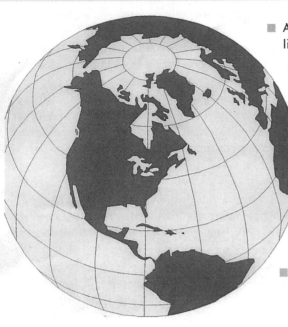

- Around 1.2 billion people in the world are living on a dollar (about 60p) a day or less.

  - Eight hundred and twenty-eight million people are moderately or severely malnourished.

    - One-fifth of the world's population are not expected to live beyond the age of 40.

    - The world's richest 1 per cent of people receive as much income as the poorest 57 per cent.

    - Nearly one billion people in the world are illiterate.

    - Easily preventable diseases, like pneumonia, diarrhoea, malaria, and measles, kill nearly eleven million children under the age of 5 each year – 30,000 every day.

- About 1.3 billion people lack safe water.

- Five hundred thousand women a year die in pregnancy or childbirth – about one every minute.

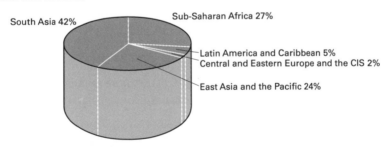

Income poverty
Regional distribution of people living on less than $1 a day
Global total 1.2 billion

South Asia 42%
Sub-Saharan Africa 27%
Latin America and Caribbean 5%
Central and Eastern Europe and the CIS 2%
East Asia and the Pacific 24%

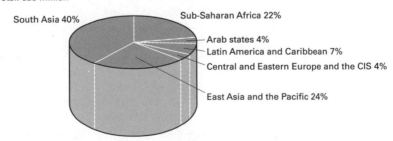

Hunger
Undernourished people as a percentage of total population
Total: 828 million

South Asia 40%
Sub-Saharan Africa 22%
Arab states 4%
Latin America and Caribbean 7%
Central and Eastern Europe and the CIS 4%
East Asia and the Pacific 24%

Source: UNICEF; *United Nations Human Development Report,* 2003

Relative poverty is a condition where individuals or families are deprived of the opportunities, comforts, and self-respect which the majority of people in their society enjoy. Minimum needs are then related to the standard of living in any society at any one time, and will therefore vary over time and between societies, as standards of living change. For example, those living in slum housing in Britain would be regarded as poor here, but their housing would appear as relative luxury to poor peasants in the Third World. Similarly, running hot water and an inside bathroom and toilet would have been seen as luxuries one hundred years ago in Britain, but today are seen as basic necessities, and those without them would be regarded as poor by most people.

Social exclusion

The relative definition of poverty is closely linked with the idea of social exclusion. This involves people being marginalized or excluded from participation in education, work, and community life, and from access to services and other aspects of life seen as part of being a full and participating member of mainstream society. (Marginalization refers to the process whereby some groups are pushed by poverty, ill-health, or ignorance to the margins of society and are unable to take part in the life enjoyed by the majority of citizens.) Those who live in relative poverty don't have the resources to live a normal life, and are excluded from the opportunity to participate fully in society, and are denied the opportunities most people take for granted.

The consensual idea of poverty

A third idea of poverty is to ask the public what they regard as being poor, and what items they think are necessary for a minimum standard of living in Britain. In this way it is hoped to establish a widespread agreement (a consensus) on what ordinary people think makes up the minimum standards required for life in Britain at the beginning of the twenty-first century. The 'Poverty and Social Exclusion' list of some popular items (opposite) and the activity below explore this idea of a consensual notion of poverty.

ACTIVITY

1 Either alone or through majority agreement in a group, go through the 'Poverty and Social Exclusion' list opposite, ticking those items which you think are necessities, which all adults should be able to afford, and no one should have to go without.

2 Compare your list with another person's or group's. How do your decisions compare with others? Were some items clear-cut and others borderline? Discuss the reasons for any differences of opinion about what counts as necessities.

3 The 'Poverty and Social Exclusion in Britain' national survey, conducted in 2000, found that items 1–35 were considered necessities by 50 per cent or more of the population. At least two out of three members of the public classed items 1–25 as necessities which no one should have to go without. How far does your list agree or disagree with these national findings?

4 Do you think if you were in a very poor country you would have the same list of necessities? Give reasons for your answer.

The Poverty and Social Exclusion Survey list

1. Beds and bedding for everyone
2. Heating to warm living areas of the home
3. Damp-free home
4. Visiting friends or family in hospital
5. Two meals a day
6. Medicines prescribed by doctor
7. Refrigerator
8. Fresh fruit and vegetables daily
9. Warm, waterproof coat
10. Replace or repair broken electrical goods
11. Visits to friends or family
12. Celebrations on special occasions such as Christmas
13. Money to keep home in a decent state of decoration
14. Visits to school e.g. sports day
15. Attending weddings, funerals
16. Meat, fish or vegetarian equivalent every other day
17. Insurance of contents of dwelling
18. Hobby or leisure activity
19. Washing machine
20. Collect children from school
21. Telephone
22. Appropriate clothes for job interviews
23. Deep freezer/fridge freezer
24. Carpets in living rooms and bedrooms
25. Regular savings (of £10 per month) for rainy days or retirement
26. Two pairs of all-weather shoes
27. Friends or family round for a meal
28. A small amount of money to spend on self weekly, not on family
29. Television
30. Roast joint/vegetarian equivalent once a week
31. Presents for friends/family once a year
32. A holiday away from home once a year not with relatives
33. Replace worn-out furniture
34. Dictionary
35. An outfit for social occasions
36. New, not second-hand, clothes
37. Attending place of worship
38. Car
39. Coach/train fares to visit friends/family quarterly
40. An evening out once a fortnight
41. Dressing gown
42. Having a daily newspaper
43. A meal in a restaurant/pub monthly
44. Microwave oven
45. Tumble dryer
46. Going to the pub once a fortnight
47. Video cassette recorder
48. Holidays abroad once a year
49. CD player
50. Home computer
51. Dishwasher
52. Mobile phone
53. Access to the Internet
54. Satellite television

Source: Adapted from David Gordon et al., *Poverty and Social Exclusion in Britain* (Joseph Rowntree Foundation, 2000). Reproduced by permission of the Joseph Rowntree Foundation.

The 'Poverty and Social Exclusion in Britain' survey (2000) found:

- 24 per cent of the population lacked three or more of these items.

- About 9½ million people could not afford adequate housing conditions.

- About 6½ million adults went without essential clothing.

- About 2 million children went without at least two things they needed.

- 25 per cent of the population cannot afford regular savings of £10 a month for rainy days or retirement.

- About 7 per cent of the population are not properly fed by today's standards, lacking enough money to afford fresh fruit and vegetables, or two meals a day, for example.

The controversy over poverty

The idea of relative poverty and its measurement have been particularly controversial. Many conservative politicians attack the idea of relative poverty and the suggestion that many people in Britain are poor. Item A below presents this view. Item B presents an alternative view put forward by the Child Poverty Action Group, with which many sociologists would agree.

ACTIVITY

Read item A and item B and then answer the questions which follow (opposite):

Item A

Some Conservatives attack the idea of relative poverty and the view that many people in Britain are poor. They argue that poverty in the old absolute sense of hunger and want has been wiped out, and it is simply that some people today are 'less equal' than others. They claim that the lifestyle of the poorest 20 per cent of families today represents affluence beyond the wildest dreams of the Victorians. Starving children and squalid slums have disappeared, and they point out that half of today's so-called 'poor' have a telephone, car, and central heating and virtually all have a refrigerator and television set. They argue that it is therefore absurd to suggest that more than a fifth of the population is today living in poverty. They claim the idea of relative poverty amounts to no more than simple inequality, and that the use of the concept of relative poverty means that however rich a society becomes, the relatively poor will never disappear as long as there is social inequality. As one former Conservative minister commented, 'The poverty lobby would, on their definition, find poverty in Paradise.'

Item B

The Child Poverty Action Group (CPAG) supports the view that poverty should be seen in relation to minimum needs established by the standard of living in a particular society, and all members of the population should have the right to an income which allows them to participate fully in society rather than merely exist. Such participation involves having the means to fulfil responsibilities to others – as parents, sons and daughters, neighbours, friends, workers, and citizens. Poverty filters into every aspect of life. It is about not having access to material goods and services such as decent housing, adequate heating, nutritious food, public transport, credit, and consumer goods.

But living on the breadline is not simply about doing without things; it is also about experiencing poor health, isolation, stress, stigma and **exclusion**:

> Poverty curtails freedom of choice. The freedom to eat as you wish, to go where and when you like, to seek the leisure pursuits or political activities which others accept; all are denied to those without the resources . . . **poverty is most comprehensively understood as a state of partial citizenship**. (P. Golding, ed., Excluding the Poor (CPAG, 1986))

The gradual raising of the poverty line simply reflects the fact that society generally has become more prosperous and therefore has a more generous definition of a minimum income. The poor should not be excluded as the general level of prosperity rises.

Source: Adapted from Carey Oppenheim, *Poverty: The Facts* (CPAG)

1 With reference to item A, explain briefly in your own words Conservative objections to the idea of relative poverty.

2 Explain in your own words what the former Conservative minister meant when he said 'The poverty lobby would, on their definition, find poverty in Paradise' (end of Item A).

3 On the basis of what you have studied so far in this chapter, what definition of poverty do you think the Conservatives in item A support? Give reasons for your answer.

4 With reference to item B, identify three factors apart from material goods and services which the CPAG thinks should be taken into account when defining poverty.

5 Explain what is meant by 'exclusion' and 'poverty is most comprehensively understood as a state of partial citizenship' in item B (highlighted).

6 What definition of poverty do you think the CPAG supports? Give reasons for your answer.

DISCUSSION

Do you think poverty really exists in modern Britain, given the starving populations in Africa?

The measurement of poverty in Britain: the poverty line

DEFINITION

The poverty line is the dividing point between those who are poor and those who are not. The official poverty line used in Britain today is 60 per cent of average income – the definition of poverty used by the European Union.

Sociologists often also take into account those who are living on the margins of this poverty line, as those whose incomes are low often slip between being on or below the poverty line and just above it.

The extent of poverty in Britain

In 2001–2 in Britain:

■ Twelve and a half million people were living in poverty (below 60 per cent of average income) – 22 per cent of the population.

■ Nearly a third (30 per cent) of all children were living in poverty.

■ There were more children living in poverty than in any other European country, according to Eurostat, the European Union statistics agency.

The numbers of the poor, and the changes between 1994/5 and 2001/2 are shown in figure 4.3 on page 58.

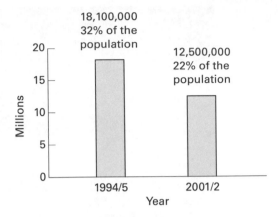

Figure 4.3 Numbers of people living in poverty (below 60 per cent of average income after housing costs): Great Britain, 1994/5 and 2001/2

Source: *Households Below Average Income* (Department for Work and Pensions, 2003)

ACTIVITY

Study figure 4.3 and answer the following questions:

1 By how much did the percentage of the population living below 60 per cent of average income decrease between 1994/5 and 2001/2?

2 What percentage of the population had below 60 per cent of average income in 1994/5?

3 How many fewer people had below 60 per cent of average income in 2001/2 than in 1994/5?

4 What percentage of the population were living below 60 per cent of average income in 2001/2?

5 Suggest possible reasons for the decrease in the numbers of those living in poverty between 1994/5 and 2001/2.

THE FEMINIZATION OF POVERTY

Women are far more likely than men to experience poverty. In 2002, about two-thirds of adults receiving income support were women. Women face a higher risk of poverty than men because:

■ Women are more likely to be in low-paid and part-time work. In 2003, around three-quarters of low-paid workers were women.

■ They are more likely than men to be lone parents with sole responsibility for children, leading to reduced possibilities for employment, and dependence on inadequate state benefits.

■ Women live longer than men and retire earlier, and therefore spend a greater proportion of their lives beyond retirement age. However, because of low pay throughout their lives they are less likely than men to have savings, and are less likely than men to be entitled to employers' pensions.

■ In many low-income households, it is often mothers rather than fathers who bear the burden of trying to make ends meet, and in the face of poverty sacrifice their own standard of living to provide food, clothing, and extras for the children.

Who are the poor?

Poverty and social exclusion are essentially problems of the working class, because other classes have savings, occupational pensions, and sick pay schemes to protect them when adversity strikes or old age arrives. The identity of the major groups in poverty suggests that poverty is caused not by idleness, but by social circumstances beyond the control of the poor themselves. The unemployed, the low-paid, and pensioners account for most of the poor. Of those living in poverty (60 per cent of average income) in 2001/2:

- 62 per cent were workless.

- 38 per cent were in full-time or part-time work. Many of the poor work long hours in low-paid jobs.

- 21 per cent were pensioners. Many elderly retired people depend on state pensions for support, and these are inadequate for maintaining other than a very basic standard of living.

- 21 per cent were lone parents. Lone parents are often prevented from getting a full-time job by the lack of childcare facilities, or only work part-time, which generally gets lower rates of pay. The costs of childcare often mean lone parents cannot afford to work. The majority of lone parents are women, who in any case get less pay than men.

- The sick and disabled are likely to be highly represented among the poor, particularly in the unemployed and low-paid sectors. Disability brings with it poorer employment opportunities, lower pay, and dependence on state benefits.

- There were nearly 4 million children living in poverty – around 1 in 3 of all children. 74 per cent of Bangladeshi and Pakistani children live in poverty.

Figure 4.4 illustrates which groups make up most of those living in poverty in 2001/2, by family type and by economic status, and figure 4.5 shows the risk of being in poverty by various groupings (see page 60).

Criticisms of the poverty line

Many people are critical of the definition of poverty simply in terms of income, because it takes no account of all the extras most of the population take for granted, such as coping with household emergencies, going on holiday, going out for a drink with friends, and taking part in other leisure activities. Poverty is not simply a matter of how much income someone has, but can also involve other aspects of life such as the quality of housing and the quality and availability of public services like transport, hospitals, schools, and play areas for children.

Let us briefly outline some aspects and consequences of poverty apart from shortage of income. While not all of those in poverty will experience

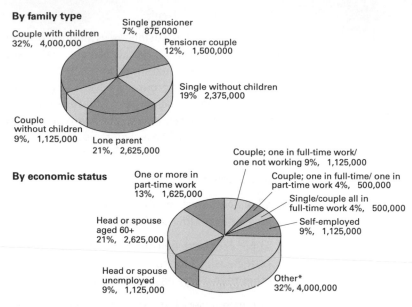

By family type

Single pensioner
7%, 875,000

Pensioner couple
12%, 1,500,000

Couple with children
32%, 4,000,000

Single without children
19% 2,375,000

Couple without children
9%, 1,125,000

Lone parent
21%, 2,625,000

By economic status

One or more in part-time work
13%, 1,625,000

Couple; one in full-time work/ one not working 9%, 1,125,000

Couple; one in full-time/ one in part-time work 4%, 500,000

Single/couple all in full-time work 4%, 500,000

Self-employed
9%, 1,125,000

Head or spouse aged 60+
21%, 2,625,000

Head or spouse unemployed
9%, 1,125,000

Other*
32%, 4,000,000

* Other = all those not included in previous groups

Figure 4.4 Who are the poor? Number of individuals living below 60 per cent of average income after housing costs: 2001/2

Source: Households Below Average Income (Department for Work and Pensions, 2003)

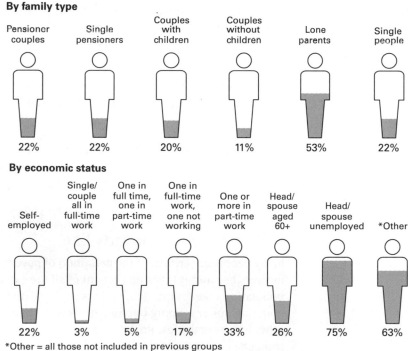

By family type

Pensioner couples	Single pensioners	Couples with children	Couples without children	Lone parents	Single people
22%	22%	20%	11%	53%	22%

By economic status

Self-employed	Single/ couple all in full-time work	One in full time, one in part-time work	One in full-time work, one not working	One or more in part-time work	Head/ spouse aged 60+	Head/ spouse unemployed	*Other
22%	3%	5%	17%	33%	26%	75%	63%

*Other = all those not included in previous groups

Figure 4.5 The risk of poverty: proportion of individuals in particular groups living in poverty (below 60 per cent of average income after housing costs): United Kingdom, 2001/2

Source: Households Below Average Income (Department for Work and Pensions, 2003)

ACTIVITY

Refer to figure 4.5 and answer the following questions:

1 What percentage of self-employed people were living in poverty in 2001/2?

2 What percentage of couples with children were living in poverty?

3 What evidence is there in figure 4.5 that might be used to show that low pay is a cause of poverty?

4 What difference is there between the proportion of couples with children and couples without children living in poverty?

5 Which two groups overall have the highest risk of poverty?

6 Which group overall has the least risk of being in poverty?

7 Suggest how the evidence in figure 4.5 might be used to show that the poor are victims of unfortunate circumstances rather than being themselves to blame for their poverty. Could any of the evidence in the figure be used to support the opposite view?

all of these multiple deprivations, the list below shows how poverty can be like a spider's web, trapping the poor in a deprived lifestyle in many aspects of their lives.

■ *Homelessness.* In 2003, around 129,000 households were officially accepted as intentionally or unintentionally homeless and in priority need by local authorities in England, and around 91,000 households were living in temporary accommodation.

■ *Poverty in healthcare.*
  – There are fewer doctors practising in inner-city areas (where many of the poor live), and those who do are often overworked, because the poor have more health problems.
  – The poor are less likely to get time off work with pay to visit the doctor.
  – They face long hospital waiting lists.
  – Many are not fully aware of what health services are available to them, and the poor tend to be less vocal in demanding proper standards of care from doctors.

■ *Poverty at school.*
  – Inner-city schools often have older buildings and poorer facilities.
  – There is often a concentration of social problems in these schools, such as drugs and vandalism, and consequently a higher turnover of teachers.
  – Parents are less able to help their children with their education, and have less money than non-poor parents to enable the school to buy extra resources.

■ *Poverty at work.*
  – *Poor working conditions.* These include a neglect of health and safety standards and a high accident rate; working at night and long periods of overtime because the pay is so low; lack of trade union organization to protect the workers' interests; lack of entitlement to paid holidays; and no employers' sick pay or pension schemes.
  – *Insecure employment,* often with very short notice of dismissal.

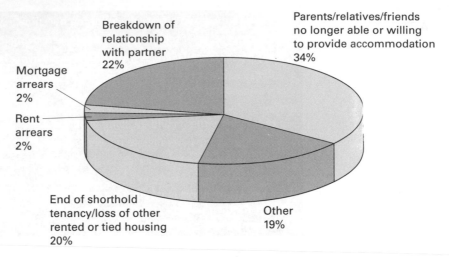

Figure 4.6 Reasons for homelessness: households officially accepted as homeless in priority need, England, 2003

Source: Office of the Deputy Prime Minister

DEFINITION	Poverty means going short materially, socially and emotionally. It means spending less on food, on heating, and clothing than someone on an average income. But it is not what is spent that matters, but what isn't. Poverty means staying at home, often being bored, not seeing friends, not going out for a drink and not being able to take the children out for a trip or treat or a holiday. It means coping with the stresses of managing on very little money, often for months or even years. It means having to withstand the onslaught of society's pressure to consume. It impinges on relationships with others and with yourself. Above all, poverty takes away the tools to build the blocks for the future – your 'life chances'. It steals away the opportunity to have a life unmarked by sickness, a decent education, a secure home and a long retirement. It stops people being able to take control of their lives. *Source*: Carey Oppenheim, *Poverty: The Facts* (CPAG)

- ■ *Poor health*, such as respiratory problems like asthma and infectious diseases, as a result of poor diet and damp, overcrowded housing.

- ■ *Going short of food, clothing, and heating*, and not being able to replace household goods or carry out household repairs and decoration. A survey in 2002 suggested that 1 in 20 mothers go without enough food so they can try to satisfy the needs of their children. Lone parents on income support are 14 times more likely to go without enough food than mothers not receiving benefits. Many poor families have an unhealthy diet, not because they don't know or care about a nutritionally healthy diet, but because they can't afford it.

■ *Isolation and boredom*. Making friends may be hard because there is no money to get involved in social activities.

■ *Stress*, in the face of mounting bills and debts, perhaps leading to domestic violence, family breakdown, and mental illness.

■ *Low self-esteem*, brought on by dependence on others, the lack of access to the activities and facilities others have, and difficulties in coping with day-to-day life.

THE WELFARE STATE

The main measures taken to help the poor have largely developed with the welfare state, which began with the Beveridge Report of 1942. This recommended the development of welfare services aimed at the destruction of the 'five giants' of want, disease, squalor, ignorance, and idleness, and the creation of a society where each individual would have the right to be cared for by the state from womb to tomb. The welfare state as we know it today came into effect on 5 July 1948 – the date of the foundation of the National Health Service.

The welfare state provides a wide range of benefits and services including:

■ A range of welfare benefits through the social security system for many groups such as the unemployed, those injured at work, the sick and disabled, widows, the retired, expectant mothers, lone parents, and children. Examples are state pensions, Job Seekers' Allowance, Incapacity Benefit, and Income Support.

■ A comprehensive and largely free National Health Service, including ante- and post-natal care, hospitals, GPs, dentists, and opticians (although some charges are payable – for example to dentists and opticians).

■ A free and compulsory state education for all to the age of 16.

■ Social services provided by local councils, such as social workers, and special facilities for the disabled, the elderly, and children. Local councils are also responsible for housing the homeless, and for the adoption and fostering of children.

The structure and key services of the welfare state (as they were in early 2004) are shown on the next page in figure 4.7.

Other providers of welfare

The welfare state, run by national and local government, is not the only provider of welfare. The informal, voluntary, and private sectors also play important roles, often working alongside the state provision.

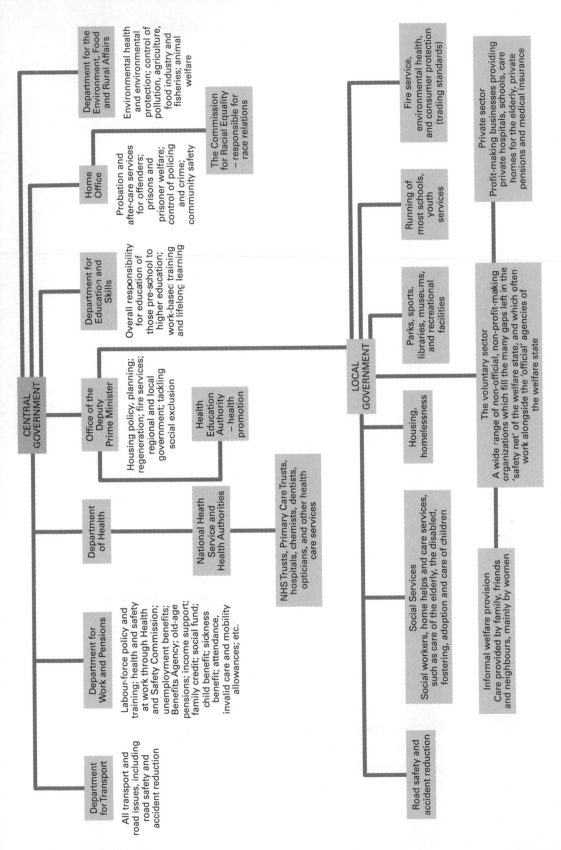

Figure 4.7 'Womb-to-tomb' care: the structure and key services of the welfare state

CENTRAL GOVERNMENT

Department for Transport
All transport and road issues, including road safety and accident reduction

Department for Work and Pensions
Labour-force policy and training; health and safety at work through Health and Safety Commission; unemployment benefits; Benefits Agency: old-age pensions; income support; family credit; social fund; child benefit; sickness benefit; attendance, invalid care and mobility allowances; etc.

Department of Health

National Heath Service and Health Authorities
NHS Trusts, Primary Care Trusts, hospitals, chemists, dentists, opticians, and other health care services

Office of the Deputy Prime Minister
Housing policy, planning; regeneration; fire services; regional and local government; tackling social exclusion

Health Education Authority – health promotion

Department for Education and Skills
Overall responsibility for education of those pre-school to higher education; work-basec training and lifelong learning

Home Office
Probation and after-care services for offenders; prisons and prisoner welfare; control of policing and crime; community safety

The Commission for Racial Equality – responsible for race relations

Department for the Environment, Food and Rural Affairs
Environmental health and environmental protection; control of pollution, agriculture, food industry and fisheries; animal welfare

LOCAL GOVERNMENT

Road safety and accident reduction

Social Services
Social workers, home helps and care services, such as care of the elderly, the disabled, fostering, adoption and care of children

Housing, homelessness

Parks, sports, libraries, museums, and recreational facilities

Running of most schools, youth services

Fire service, environmental health, and consumer protection (trading standards)

The voluntary sector
A wide range of non-official, non-profit-making organizations which fill the many gaps left in the 'safety net' of the welfare state, and which often work alongside the 'official' agencies of the welfare state

Informal welfare provision
Care provided by family, friends and neighbours, mainly by women

Private sector
Profit-making businesses providing private hospitals, schools, care homes for the elderly, private pensions and medical insurance

Informal welfare provision

Much welfare provision is provided informally by family, friends, and neighbours, and this often means care by women, as it is women who tend to take on the main caring responsibilities in the family for the dependent elderly, the disabled, and the sick.

The voluntary sector: voluntary organizations

Voluntary organizations are non-official, non-profit-making organizations, often charities, which are 'voluntary' in the sense that they are neither created by, nor controlled by, the government. They employ both salaried staff and voluntary helpers, and are funded by donations from the public and grants from, or sale of services to, central and local government. Voluntary organizations try to fill some of the gaps left by the 'safety net' provided by the state, by providing help and information in areas where state assistance is too little or non-existent.

Voluntary organizations include groups such as the Salvation Army, which provides hostel accommodation and soup kitchens; Shelter, which campaigns for the homeless and helps with finding accommodation; Help the Aged and Age Concern; the NSPCC (the National Society for the Prevention of Cruelty to Children) and the Child Poverty Action Group, which promotes action for the relief of poverty among children and families with children. The churches also provide a range of welfare support, particularly to the elderly.

Voluntary organizations have high levels of expert knowledge, and work in specialized areas, like domestic violence, homelessness, debt, or AIDS, where state provision may be under pressure, inadequate, or non-existent. However, voluntary organizations often lack adequate funds to be as effective as they might otherwise be, and they do not exist in all areas where they are needed.

Voluntary organizations also play important roles as pressure groups. These seek to put pressure, through public campaigns, on those in positions of power in society to improve welfare benefits and services for the poor and socially excluded. Voluntary organizations play a major role in highlighting the weaknesses of the welfare state, and keeping problems such as poverty, homelessness, and the care of the mentally ill in the public eye. They frequently provide expert knowledge and make recommendations to governments for changes to improve social welfare.

The private sector

The private sector consists of profit-making private businesses, from which individuals or local and central government purchase services or benefits. This sector provides welfare services such as private hospitals, schools, care homes for the elderly, private pensions, and medical insurance.

Access to the private sector is generally only available to those who can afford it, and poor people may therefore not get services at all, if the state doesn't provide or pay for them.

Table 4.1 Three voluntary organizations in Britain

Organization	Aim	Activities
Citizens Advice Bureau	To provide free, confidential, impartial, and independent advice	Advice and practical support with the problems people face in their daily lives, including debt and consumer issues, benefits, housing, legal issues, employment and immigration.
NACRO National Association for the Care and Resettlement of Offenders)	To work towards a more effective approach to preventing crime and more humane treatment of offenders	Provides a housing association and employment training for ex-offenders. Runs youth training, education, and advice projects. Works with local communities to develop crime prevention schemes.
National Debtline	To provide free, confidential and independent advice on debt problems	Provides a national telephone helpline for people with debt problems, backed up with written self-help materials.

ACTIVITY

1 Do you think the state should be the main provider of welfare for all? What are the advantages and disadvantages of welfare provision by the state compared to the voluntary and private sectors?

2 Suggest reasons why informal welfare provision is mainly carried out by women. What consequences do you think this might have for women's lives and careers?

The future of the welfare state

The development of the welfare state rested on the assumption that the government should be mainly responsible for social welfare, and for action to eliminate problems such as unemployment, ill-health, and poverty, and to provide care for the disabled, children in need, the elderly, and other vulnerable and socially excluded or marginalized groups.

This traditional view of the role of the state in providing welfare seems to be changing. The period of Conservative government between 1979 and 1997 involved the state reducing its welfare support, and there were savage cuts in welfare spending. More people were left to help themselves through the use of informal, voluntary, and private services. Poverty and social exclusion rose dramatically.

The Labour government first elected in 1997 began to reverse the cuts of the Conservative years, and announced that tackling social exclusion and poverty were to be its priorities. A number of policies were implemented to tackle poverty and social exclusion:

- Benefit and pension levels were increased, with pensioners given a huge increase in help with their winter fuel bills.

- More money was spent on health and education to improve standards.

- The National Minimum Wage was introduced, helping the poorest paid.

- A system of Tax Credits was established to help the most disadvantaged.

- 'New Deals' were established to help the young, lone parents, the long-term unemployed, and the disabled to move from welfare into work.

- More childcare was made available, and pre-schooling was extended to all 3-year-olds.

- Health and Education Action Zones were established to help improve the health and education of the most disadvantaged.

Despite these big improvements, the soaring costs of the welfare state suggest the following will be the major concerns of all governments in the future:

- Tackling dependency on welfare benefits by moving people into employment through 'welfare to work' schemes – getting people off welfare benefits and into paid employment.

- Cutting the soaring levels of state spending on welfare provision.

- Making more people pay for the services they receive, through more means-testing.

- Putting greater emphasis on provision by the voluntary and private sectors.

- Getting people to help themselves through the family and community, and encouraging people to save to pay for their own welfare services.

- Making welfare state institutions like hospitals, surgeries, social services, and schools more efficient, and introducing competition between them so they give clients better-quality services at lower costs, with more choice for clients. Welfare state institutions are increasingly being run more like private businesses.

Is the welfare state succeeding?

Huge sums of taxpayers' money are spent on the welfare state, and there are constant disputes about whether or not it is successful in tackling the problems of poverty and ill-health, and therefore whether more, or less, money should be spent on it. A few of these competing arguments are outlined below, some of which are discussed in other chapters.

IS THE WELFARE STATE SUCCEEDING?

Yes

- State support has eliminated absolute poverty in childhood and old age, and in periods of ill-health, unemployment, and disability throughout our lives. The standard of social (council and housing association) housing has massively improved, and slums have disappeared.
- All have access to free medical care, and the health of the nation has improved immeasurably.

- All have free education from the age of 3 to the age of 18.

- Many vulnerable groups have a range of state agencies and other organizations to assist them, such as social services, GPs' clinics, and Help the Aged.

- Everyone is guaranteed 'cradle-to-grave' security

No

- Many people still live a deprived lifestyle compared to most people, because welfare benefits are inadequate. There remain huge inequalities in wealth, income, education, housing, health, and employment. Relative poverty and social exclusion remain serious social problems.
- The welfare state is failing to cope with the demands placed on it. For example, there are often long delays for hospital treatment, and there remain huge inequalities in health and access to health care (see chapter 16).
- The middle class still benefit the most in education, and those from poorer families still suffer huge disadvantages (see chapter 12).
- There are many vulnerable groups who slip through the safety net, or for whom there is inadequate or no state provision. They have to turn to a poorly funded voluntary sector, or just cope, or not cope, alone.
- Generous welfare benefits create a nation of scrounging social misfits who are prepared just to live off benefits without ever working. The welfare state has undermined personal responsibility and self-help.

THE PERSISTENCE OF POVERTY: WHY THE POOR REMAIN POOR

The welfare state in Britain was originally seen as a way of providing 'womb-to-tomb' care, and of eradicating poverty. However, while it may have removed the worst excesses of absolute poverty, widespread deprivation remains in modern Britain. The welfare state, as this chapter suggests, has yet to solve the real problems of relative poverty. Why is this?

A good way to remember the various explanations of poverty is to think of them as 'blaming theories' – where is the blame placed for poverty?

The explanations below variously:

- Blame the *generosity* of the welfare state (the 'nanny state').
- Blame the *inadequacy* of the welfare state.
- Blame the culture of the poor.
- Blame the cycle of deprivation.
- Blame the unequal structure of power and wealth in society.

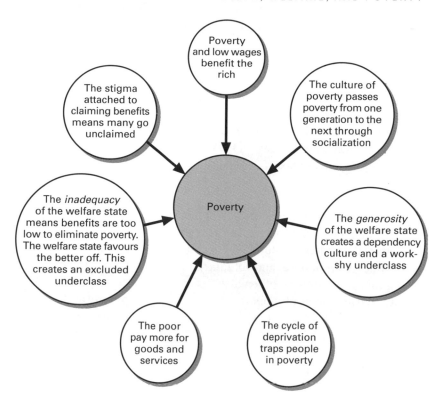

Figure 4.8 Why the poor remain poor

The circles around the central "Poverty" circle contain:

- Poverty and low wages benefit the rich
- The culture of poverty passes poverty from one generation to the next through socialization
- The stigma attached to claiming benefits means many go unclaimed
- The *inadequacy* of the welfare state means benefits are too low to eliminate poverty. The welfare state favours the better off. This creates an excluded underclass
- The *generosity* of the welfare state creates a dependency culture and a work-shy underclass
- The poor pay more for goods and services
- The cycle of deprivation traps people in poverty

Blaming the generosity of the welfare state: the dependency culture and the underclass (version 1)

Some Conservatives argue that poverty arises because the welfare state is too generous in the benefits it hands out. The generosity of 'handouts' from the 'nanny' welfare state has, they say, created incentives for staying unemployed, leading to a situation where people learn to become dependent on others. This discourages the poor from taking action to help themselves, and undermines self-help and self-reliance. This is what has been called a dependency culture – a set of values and beliefs, and a way of life, centred on dependence on others.

Universal versus selective, means-tested benefits

Such writers believe that universal welfare benefits (which are available to everyone regardless of income, such as the basic state pension, and free health care and education) should be withdrawn from all those who are capable of supporting themselves. These benefits should instead be targeted only on those who genuinely need them, such as the disabled and the long-term sick. Universal benefits should therefore be replaced by selective benefits, targeted by means-testing. Means-testing involves people having to pass a test of their income and savings (their 'means') before receiving any benefits, and only if these were low enough would they receive any benefits. The arguments over means-testing are presented below.

ARE MEANS-TESTED BENEFITS A GOOD IDEA?

Yes

- Benefits are targeted only on those who really need them. People who are able to work should support themselves. Money is saved on universal benefits which most people don't need and shouldn't have. More money is available to invest in the economy, create jobs and cut taxes.

- Means-testing stops unemployment being an option for some people, and fights the welfare dependency culture.

- Families, communities and voluntary organizations are strengthened as alternative sources of support.

- Selective means-tested benefits will enable more benefits for the most disadvantaged, by no longer wasting money on those who can afford to support themselves.

No

- Means-tested benefits, which are received only by the very poor, may lead to some people being worse off if they take a low-paid job. They may lose means-tested benefits like housing or council tax benefits, and the extra they earn by working is not enough to compensate for the lost benefits. This 'poverty trap' discourages people from taking work. Universal benefits avoid this.

- Because of the poverty trap, means-testing might drive people into a dependency culture and a reluctance to get a job.

- Families and communities caught in the poverty trap are likely to be weakened by poverty and stress. Some will be encouraged to become 'benefit cheats' through concealing income and savings to get around means-testing. Universal benefits keep everyone's standards up to an acceptable minimum level.

- Often the most deprived do not take up or make full use of even universal benefits, as they're unsure of how to do so. Means-tested benefits attach a stigma to those who claim them, and make it even more unlikely they will claim benefits to which they are entitled.

UNCLAIMED BENEFITS

Many poor people do not claim the welfare benefits to which they are entitled, particularly those which are means-tested. Each year, around 800,000 families fail to claim state benefits to which they are entitled. According to the Department for Work and Pensions' own statistics, released in 2003, as much as £4.5 billion of income-related benefits go unclaimed each year, with pensioners being the group least likely to claim. Overall, about 1 in 5 people are not claiming benefits to which they are entitled. This is often because of:

- The complexity of the benefits and tax system.
- Inadequate publicity.
- The obscure language of leaflets and complex means-testing forms, which means people often do not know what their rights are or the procedures for claiming benefits.

These bureaucratic hurdles are so great that many people are deterred from claiming what they are entitled to. This is particularly important as the poor are among the least educated sections of the population. The mass media periodically run campaigns about welfare 'scroungers' – like 'Stuff the spongers' – which help to attach a stigma to claiming benefits which may deter some people from doing so. The establishment of the Department of Work and Pensions 'Targeting Benefit Fraud' website and phone line gives such a stigma official support.

The Department for Work and Pensions' 'Targeting Fraud' campaign declares its aims to be 'to positively reinforce honest behaviour, create a climate of intolerance to fraud and to undermine its social acceptability'. By far the majority of benefit claimants are honest, but fraud (dishonest claims) is a serious problem which costs the government around £2 billion each year.

Reproduced by permission of the Department for Work and Pensions

The underclass – version 1: the poor as welfare scroungers and social misfits

Some have argued that the generosity of the welfare state, and the dependency culture, have created an underclass of people – right at the bottom of the social hierarchy – who have developed a lifestyle and set of attitudes which make them reluctant to take jobs. They are willing simply to live off the welfare state. Supporters of this view of the underclass also regard some of the poor as social misfits, pointing to their lack of morality, high crime levels, cohabitation, and large numbers of lone parents. However, many sociologists reject this view, arguing that the attitudes and values of the poor are no different from those of the non-poor: they want the same things as the rest of society, but just lack the means to achieve them. This alternative view of the underclass is explored below in version 2.

These ideas of the dependency culture and the underclass are also implied in the later 'culture of poverty' explanation (see page 74).

(see page 74)

DISCUSSION

Refer to the 'Unclaimed benefits' box on p. 70:

1 Do you agree the media give the impression that people receiving benefits are 'scroungers'?

2 Do you think most people receiving welfare benefits are deserving?

3 Do you think benefits discourage people from taking more responsibility for their own lives?

4 Do you think people should be expected to take a job even if they will be worse off than if they received benefits?

Blaming the inadequacy of the welfare state: the underclass (version 2)

An alternative explanation for the persistence of poverty is offered by those who argue that benefit levels are too low to lift people out of poverty. From this viewpoint, the welfare state is not generous enough, and middle-class people gain more from the welfare state than the poor. For example, the middle class gain more from state spending on education, because they keep their children in education longer (in further and higher education). The middle class also gain more from the health service, partly because they are more demanding and assertive in their dealings with doctors, and partly because the middle class are generally healthier. This means that doctors in middle-class areas are less overworked, and so are able to spend more time dealing with patients and their problems. Poor people, by contrast, get less time with their doctors and face longer hospital waiting lists. Tax relief on private pensions also benefits the middle class more, as they are more likely to have private pension schemes. In general, then, the middle class gain more from the welfare state than the poor. This bias towards the middle class has been called the inverse care law – that those whose need is greatest get the least resources, and those whose need is least get the greatest resources. This is discussed more in chapter 16 on health.

The underclass – version 2: poverty and social exclusion

This failure of the welfare state to provide sufficient help to the poor has led to an alternative view of the underclass to that discussed above. This alternative view suggests the underclass consists of disadvantaged groups whose poverty means they are excluded from taking part in society to the same extent as the non-poor. This excluded underclass consists of groups such as the disadvantaged elderly retired, lone-parent families, and the long-term unemployed. These groups are forced to rely upon inadequate state benefits which are too low to give them an acceptable standard of living. This prevents them from participating fully in society, and gives them little opportunity to escape the poverty trap.

This view of the underclass suggests it is not the attitudes of poor people which are to blame for their poverty, but the difficulties and misfortune they face which are beyond their control, like unemployment, disability, or sickness. The poor live depressingly deprived lifestyles, and want many of the things most of society already has, like secure and decently paid jobs and opportunities. In this view, it is government policies which have neglected to tackle unemployment, failed to improve the living standards of those on some benefits, and failed to give the poor the opportunities and incentives needed to get off benefits. It is this, not the attitudes of the poor, which leaves them excluded from full participation in society. This view suggests government policies should tackle unemployment, improve the living standards of those on benefits (for example through higher pensions and benefit levels), and give incentives to the poor to get off benefits by ensuring there are enough decently paid jobs available. Only in this way will the excluded underclass disappear in our society.

ACTIVITY

Two views of the underclass

Version 1

A group who have developed a lifestyle and set of attitudes which means they are no longer willing to take jobs. They have evolved a dependency culture, which means they are not prepared to help themselves but are prepared to live off the welfare state. They lack morality and have high levels of crime, cohabitation, and lone parenthood. Their work-shy 'sponging' attitudes and lack of social responsibility are responsible for their poverty. Most of the poor have only themselves to blame.

Version 2

A group whose poverty means they are excluded from taking part in society to the same extent as the non-poor do, even though they want to. They consist of groups like the disadvantaged elderly retired, one-parent families, and the long-term unemployed. Their attitudes are the same as those of the rest of society, but they are forced to rely upon inadequate state benefits which are too low to give them an acceptable standard of living. This prevents them from participating fully in society, and gives them little opportunity to fulfil their ambitions and escape the poverty trap.

Compare the two models of the underclass above:

1 Which view do you think provides the most accurate picture of poor people?

2 What solutions to the problem of the underclass would you adopt for each version?

Blaming the culture of the poor: the culture of poverty

Another explanation for the persistence of poverty is the theory of the culture of poverty. This suggests it is the characteristics of the poor themselves, their values and culture, that cause poverty and social exclusion. It is suggested the poor form an underclass who are resigned to their situation. They seldom take opportunities when they arise, are reluctant to work, and don't plan for the future. They seem, in this view, to make little effort to change their situation, or to help themselves overcome their social exclusion. They won't use their initiative and involve themselves in mainstream society and try to break free of their poverty, even when opportunities to do so arise. Children grow up in this culture, and learn these values from their parents, and so this culturally poor underclass, poverty, and social exclusion continue from one generation to the next.

The weakness of this type of explanation is that it tends to blame the poor for their own poverty, and implies that if only the poor would change their values, then poverty would disappear. However, if the poor do develop a culture of poverty – and this is hotly disputed – it may well be a result of poverty rather than a cause of it. For example, the poor cannot afford to save for a 'rainy day'; planning for the future is difficult when the future is so uncertain; and it is hard not to give up and become resigned to being unemployed after endless searching for non-existent jobs.

TRAPPED IN POVERTY: THE POOR PAY MORE

One of the great ironies of poverty is that the cost of living is higher for the poor than the non-poor, and this hinders the poor in their attempts to escape poverty. The poor pay more because:

- They often live in poor-quality housing, which is expensive to heat and maintain.
- They live mainly in inner-city areas, where rents are high.
- The price of goods and services is higher in poorer areas, owing to factors like shoplifting and vandalism.
- They have to buy cheap clothing, which wears out quickly and is therefore more expensive in the long run.
- They have to pay more for food as they can only afford to buy it in small quantities (which is more expensive), and from small, expensive corner shops as they haven't cars to travel to supermarkets. They also lack storage facilities like freezers for buying in bulk.
- The poor pay more for house and car insurance, owing to higher levels of theft and vandalism in poor areas.
- They pay more for credit; banks and building societies won't lend them money as they consider them a poor risk. Loans are therefore often obtained from 'loan sharks' at exorbitant rates of interest.
- They suffer more ill-health, and so have to spend more on non-prescription medicines.

The culture-of-poverty explanation, and the earlier 'dependency culture' one, are convenient ones for those in positions of power, as they put the blame for poverty on the poor themselves. If these explanations are adopted, then the problem of poverty will be solved by policies such as cutting welfare benefits to the poor, to make them 'stand on their own two feet', and job training programmes to move them from welfare to work.

Blaming the cycle of deprivation

A further explanation for poverty is what has been called the cycle of deprivation. This suggests that poverty is cumulative, in the sense that one aspect of poverty can lead to further poverty. This builds up into a vicious circle which the poor find hard to escape from, and it then carries on with their children. Figure 4.9 illustrates examples of possible cycles of deprivation. The problem with this explanation is that, while it explains why poverty continues, it does not explain how poverty begins in the first place. The final type of explanation does try to do this.

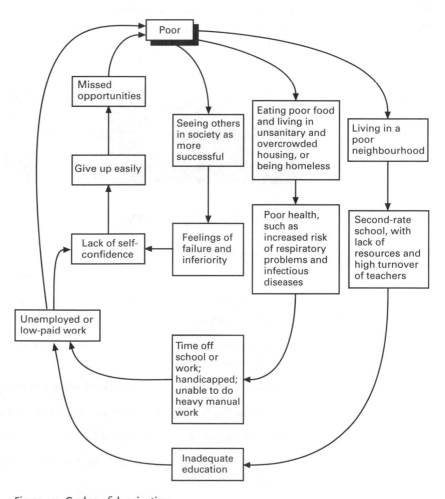

Figure 4.9 Cycles of deprivation

Blaming the unequal structure of power and wealth in society

These are structural explanations, which explain poverty in terms of the structure of society, with its unequal distribution of wealth and income and the inadequate assistance given to the poor. These are mainly Marxist arguments, which suggest that the reason the poor remain poor is because they are exploited by the rich. The owners of society's key resources make profits by paying low wages – and their wealthy position depends on poverty. Poverty ensures the dangerous, menial jobs are done, and the poor help to limit the wage demands of those who are non-poor by providing a threat to their jobs. The poor lack power to change their position, because they do not have the financial resources to change public opinion. In this view, it is not being unemployed, a lone parent, long-term sick, disabled, or old that causes poverty. Rather, it is government policy and the structure of society which mean people facing misfortune, through no fault of their own, are penalized for it by inadequate benefits.

Structural explanations suggest that any serious attempt to abolish poverty would involve a widespread redistribution of wealth and income. This would mean the creation of improved social services, higher welfare benefits, and more and better-paid jobs, with the introduction of higher taxes on the rich to pay for these reforms.

ACTIVITY

Imagine you have become the prime minister, with a huge majority in Parliament enabling you to carry through a successful campaign against poverty. Think carefully about all the explanations for poverty you have read of in this chapter, and the groups in poverty. Devise a series of policies which would help to reduce poverty. Explain in each case why you think your proposed policy would help to reduce poverty.

CHAPTER SUMMARY

After studying this chapter, you should be able to:

- Explain the difference between wealth and income.

- Describe the attempts made to redistribute wealth and income, and explain why these measures have failed.

- Explain the difference between absolute, relative, and consensual definitions of poverty.

- Explain what is meant by social exclusion and marginalization.

- Describe the poverty line in Britain, and make criticisms of it.

- Describe aspects of poverty apart from lack of income.

- Identify the main groups in poverty in modern Britain, and explain why each of them is poor.

- Explain why women are more likely to be in poverty than men.

■ Outline the main features of the welfare state.

■ Explain, with examples, the role of informal care, voluntary organizations, and the private sector in providing welfare.

■ Identify some arguments for and against the success of the welfare state.

■ Explain why the cost of living is higher for the poor than for those who are not poor.

■ Explain the advantages and disadvantages of means-testing.

■ Give a number of explanations why the poor remain poor, despite the welfare state.

■ Discuss the different versions of the view that the poor are an underclass.

KEY TERMS

absolute poverty
consumption property
culture of poverty
dependency culture
income
inverse care law
marginalization
poverty line
pressure groups
productive property
relative poverty
social exclusion
underclass
wealth

COURSEWORK SUGGESTIONS

1   Carry out a survey asking people about poverty in Britain today. Do they think it still exists? What do they mean by 'poor'? Draw up a list of items and ask people whether they think they are essential for a basic standard of living. You could use the list of items in the 'Poverty and Social Exclusion' survey earlier in this chapter to help you. Try to draw some conclusions about the ideas of relative poverty, and the consensus view of poverty.

2   Interview a sample of people generally thought to be living in poverty, such as the unemployed or lone parents, and try to discover what difficulties they experience compared with those who aren't poor. You will need to approach this topic with great sensitivity so as not to offend those concerned, and you should not make it obvious you regard them as poor.

3   Do a case study of the activities of a local voluntary organization.

5 Gender

Stratification by sex is a feature found in most societies, with men generally being in a more dominant position in society than women. Our sex has major influences on how we think about ourselves, how others think about us, and the opportunities and life chances open to us. Men have traditionally been seen in a wide range of active and creative roles – as warriors, hunters, and workers, as political leaders or successful business executives, as scientists, engineers, inventors, or great artists.

And what roles have women been traditionally seen in? As housewives and mothers confined to the home and caring for their husbands and children. Even when working outside the home, women's jobs often seem to be an extension of their caring role in the home, looking after others as receptionists, secretaries, nurses, teachers, social workers, shop and kitchen assistants, or cleaners. We might almost be forgiven for thinking that men and women exist in two different worlds, united only by belonging to the same species. Are these differences simply an extension of the biological make-up of males and females, or are they a product of the ways that males and females are brought up in society? This chapter will examine this question, and discuss how the social differences between men and women are constructed by socialization in modern Britain. The continuing inequalities between women and men, which are, in part, a product of this socialization, are also considered.

SEX AND GENDER

■ The term sex (whether someone is male or female) refers to the natural or biological differences between men and women, such as differences in genitals, internal reproductive organs, and body hair.

■ Gender (whether someone is masculine or feminine) refers to the cultural, socially constructed differences between the two sexes. It refers to the way a society encourages and teaches the two sexes to behave in different ways through socialization.

■ A gender role is the pattern of behaviour and activity which society expects from individuals of either sex – how a boy/man or girl/woman should behave in society. Gender roles may sometimes be referred to as sex roles.

■ Gender identity refers to how much people see themselves, and others see them, in terms of their gender roles and biological sex.

The difference between the terms 'sex' and 'gender' is best illustrated by the case of transsexuals – people who biologically belong to one sex, but are convinced they belong to the opposite sex, for example a woman 'trapped' in a man's body. When these people try to change their biological

KEY ISSUES

- Sex and gender.
- Gender and biology.
- Gender and identity.
- Gender socialization and stereotyping in Britain.
- Are gender roles and identities changing?
- The sexual division of labour.
- The changing status of women in Britain.
- Women and domestic labour (housework).
- Women in paid employment and the inequalities facing women at work.

sex, through surgery and hormone treatment, they also have to learn to act in a different way and adopt new masculine or feminine gender roles. The *Independent on Sunday* reported the case of a man who changed sex twice: from male to female and back again. On taking on the female role, he had to adopt a new feminine gender identity, like changing his name from Colin to Cathy, wearing a dress and high-heeled shoes, putting on a black wig as his hair was too masculine in texture, and shaving off his beard. However, the importance of gender identity meant that, while he was losing his male friends, barriers remained in forming close relations with female friends. He felt he was simply changing from acting as a man to acting as a woman, and that the only group with which he could find full acceptance was that of other transsexuals. After three years of living as a woman, the pressures of being accepted as neither male nor female meant he stopped hormone treatment, reverted to his former male identity, and started dressing as a man again. It is experiences such as these that show the fundamental importance of gender identities, and how influential they are, not only in how we see ourselves, but in how others see us too.

GENDER AND BIOLOGY

It is sometimes suggested that the different gender roles played by women and men are 'obvious' extensions of the biological differences between the sexes. Therefore women are thought to be 'natural' mothers, with a maternal and caring 'instinct' and a biological inclination towards child rearing and domestic tasks. It is suggested that men, on the other hand, are 'naturally' assertive and dominant members of society, inclined towards the 'breadwinner' role of supporting the family.

If this argument were correct, then one would expect the typical roles played by men and women in Britain to be the same in every society: after all, the biological differences between men and women are the same everywhere. However, the comparative study of other societies suggests this is not the case.

Three tribes in New Guinea

Margaret Mead described three tribes in New Guinea (*Sex and Temperament*, 1935) where the roles of men and women were quite different from those found in modern Britain.

■ Among the *Mundugumar*, both sexes showed what we in Britain would regard as masculine characteristics – both sexes were aggressive, both hated childbirth and child rearing, and both treated children in an offhand way.

■ Among the *Arapesh*, there were few 'natural' differences between the behaviour of the sexes. Both sexes were gentle and passive; women did the heavy carrying; the men tried to share the pains of childbirth with their wives by lying with them during it. Both sexes shared equally the tasks of bringing up children (women's traditional role in Britain).

■ In the *Tchambuli* tribe, the traditional gender roles found in modern Britain were reversed – it was the men who displayed what we would regard as 'feminine' characteristics, such as doing the shopping and putting on make-up and jewellery to make themselves attractive. Women were the more aggressive, practical ones, who made the sexual advances to men and did all the trading.

These three examples suggest that gender roles are not natural, since they differ between societies even though biological differences remain the same. It is evidence like this which has led sociologists to conclude that masculine and feminine gender identities are primarily constructed through socialization, rather than simply a result of the biological differences between men and women.

GENDER AND IDENTITY

Throughout our lives, our gender – whether we see ourselves as masculine or feminine – influences how we think about ourselves, how we behave towards others, how others see us, the expectations they have of us, and the way they treat us.

Having a 'feminine' or 'masculine' identity enables us to share things with others (a night out with the girls or the lads?) and gives us guidelines for socially approved behaviour, for example the way we dress, the language we use, the way we sit, and our hair styles. While we may be able to some extent to influence the exact details of our own gender identities – after all, men and women do not display the same masculine and feminine characteristics in a uniform, unchanging way – the options available to us are not unlimited. We are influenced by agencies of socialization such as the family, the school, the peer group, and the mass media, which frequently promote socially approved forms of masculine and feminine behaviour.

ACTIVITY

1 List some of the socially approved ways that men and women are expected to behave, and expected *not* to behave, in contemporary Britain.

2 Suggest ways in which these expectations might be beginning to change.

GENDER SOCIALIZATION AND STEREOTYPING IN BRITAIN

A gender stereotype is a generalized view of the 'typical' or 'ideal' characteristics of men and women. In modern Britain, for example, girls and women are often expected to show the 'feminine' characteristics of

DEFINITION

A stereotype is a generalized, oversimplified view of the features of a social group, allowing for few individual differences among members of the group. The assumption is made that all members of the group share the same features. Examples of stereotypes include views such as 'all women are lousy drivers', 'all young people are vandals and layabouts', or 'the unemployed are all on the fiddle'.

Gender stereotyping of the worst kind

This was how Mr Justice Harman responded when someone explained to him the difference between Miss, Mrs, and Ms.

being pretty, slim, gentle, caring, sensitive, submissive, non-competitive, dependent, and focused on people (people-oriented, for example in concern for their family, maintaining friendships, and keeping customers happy).

The masculine stereotype, on the other hand, emphasizes characteristics like physical strength, aggression and assertiveness, independence, competitiveness, ambition, and focusing on 'doing things' (task-oriented, for example work success, making things, DIY in the home, or activities to escape from work).

Girls and women who fail to conform to the feminine stereotype are liable to be seen as 'tomboys', while men and boys who fail to conform to the masculine stereotype are likely to be seen as 'wimps'. It is still the case that one of the worst taunts a male child can face is to be called a 'girl' by his peer group.

Some jobs and activities are also stereotyped as more suitable for men or women; housework and childcare, for example, are still seen as predominantly 'women's work', while 'men's work' is predominantly seen as something that takes place outside the home in paid employment.

There is a wide range of social institutions which influence the socialization of males and females into their gender roles in modern Britain, but here the family, the education system, the peer group, and the mass media will be focused on.

The role of the family

Children begin to learn their gender roles at a very early age, and by the time children start school they have already learnt much about masculine and feminine roles. For example, a survey conducted in 1991 for the National Association of Schoolmasters/Union of Women Teachers (NAS/UWT) and the Engineering Council among 5-year-olds found that car-repairing, woodwork, fire-fighting, mountain-climbing, and seeing war films were seen by most children to be mainly for men, and 73 per cent of the boys and 66 per cent of the girls thought that only men could be scientists. The family plays a very important part in this primary socialization.

Parents' stereotypes

Gender socialization begins with the simple question from new parents: 'Is it a boy or a girl?' Parents and relatives tend to hold stereotyped views of the 'typical' or 'ideal' characteristics of boys and girls, and they often try to bring up their children in accordance with this view of 'normal' masculine or feminine behaviour. For example, research shows that baby boys are treated differently from baby girls, with boys more likely to be 'bounced' in physical play, whereas girls are treated more gently and are

ACTIVITY

1 What other groups of people tend to get stereotyped in the world today apart from men and women?

2 What are the main features of these stereotypes?

3 Do you consider these stereotypes to be flattering or insulting to the groups concerned? Give reasons for your answer.

4 Look at the following list of words, and divide them into three groups: those you might use to describe women, those you might use to describe men, and those you might use to describe both men and women.

clever	passive	sulky	thoughtful	bastard
powerful	assertive	gentle	caring	attractive
bimbo	emotional	spinster	elegant	soft
aggressive	pretty	tart	kind	tender
cold	sweet	logical	quiet	competitive
sly	ruthless	delicate	brave	active
muscular	bitchy	weak	clinging	slag
domineering	slim	submissive	frigid	gracious
hideous	hunk	handsome	raving	plain
hysterical	blonde	beautiful	bachelor	stud
cute	babe	fit	mover	dickhead
loose	dog	trophy bird	easy	slut

5 Now compare the two lists of words used to describe men and women. Do they present gender stereotypes? You will probably have found there are some words in both lists that have a similar meaning. Why are some words generally restricted to one gender? Discuss why these words are not used to describe both sexes, and how they show stereotyped assumptions about women and men.

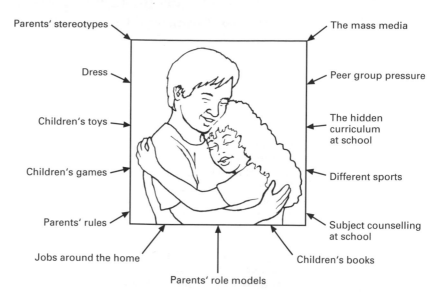

Parents' stereotypes

Dress

Children's toys

Children's games

Parents' rules

Jobs around the home

Parents' role models

The mass media

Peer group pressure

The hidden curriculum at school

Different sports

Subject counselling at school

Children's books

Figure 5.1 The social construction of gender differences through socialization

more likely to be cuddled. Parental praise like 'you're a good boy or good girl' are likely to reward behaviour which is seen as appropriate for their gender, and young children soon learn that approval from parents and relatives often depends on conforming to gender stereotypes. From birth, girls and boys are frequently dressed in different clothes and colours – 'blue for a boy, pink for a girl' – and parents generally buy girls clothes which are more 'colourful' and 'pretty', and boys more practical clothing. Such different forms of dress generally continue, of course, right throughout life.

Children's toys

Children are generally given different sorts of toys to play with according to their sex. This increases the pressure on them to follow at an early age the different roles to which they will be expected to conform in adult life. Table 5.1 on page 84 illustrates the way toys tend to be stereotyped according to their suitability for either boys or girls.

Boys tend to be given (and choose to play with), for example, construction kits, cricket bats, footballs, chemistry sets, electronic toys, guns, cars and trucks, aeroplanes, and computers: more active and technical toys, which take them outside the home, both physically and in their imagination. On the other hand, girls are generally given toys like sewing machines, dolls, prams, toy hoovers, cookers, tea sets, and drawing books – toys which are often played with inside the home, and serve to restrict girls to the domestic situation.

Table 5.1 Sex-stereotyping of toys

Masculine toys		Either sex		Feminine toys	
Toy	Rating	Toy	Rating	Toy	Rating
Football	1.5	Banjo	4.5	Skipping rope	7.0
Plane	1.7	Rocking horse	4.6	Sewing machine	8.2
Toolset	2.0	Alphabet ball	4.9	Dish cabinet	8.3
Racing car	2.2	Paddling pool	5.0	Cleaning set	8.4
Dumper truck	2.5	Blackboard	5.3	Dolls' pram	8.5
Construction set	2.7	Roller skates	5.3	Dolls' wardrobe	8.7
Tractor	3.0	Telephone	5.6	Cosmetics	8.8
Wheelbarrow	3.2	Teddy bear	5.8		
Sports car	3.6				

The ratings were made by 20-year-old psychology students, and were found to correspond strongly with the choices made by children of either sex. 1 = strongly masculine, 5 = appropriate for both sexes, 9 = strongly feminine.
Source: Data adapted from A. Oakley, *Sex, Gender and Society* (Gower)

ACTIVITY

1 Look at the two lists of strongly masculine and strongly feminine toys in table 5.1, and add any other toys to the lists you can think of.

2 Explain all the main differences you can between the masculine and feminine toys, and suggest how these differences might encourage boys and girls to learn different skills and behave differently as adults. Make sure you refer to examples of particular toys and particular adult roles in your answer.

Little girls' dreams?

More than one billion Barbies (and members of her family) have been sold worldwide since 1959. If all the Barbies sold were placed head to toe, they would circle the world more than eleven times. But do such toys make girls overconcerned with their own bodies and image?

Photo: Ted Fussey

Children's games

Children's games frequently involve practising adult gender roles, such as girls playing the role of nurse to their brothers' doctor, or girls playing at being mothers or housewives by playing with dolls, trying on make-up, cooking, or serving tea to brothers with toy tea sets. A short time in a nursery shows that by the age of 3 most little girls are already acting out the stereotyped female gender role. Boys play more aggressive and dominant games, such as war games or cowboys and Indians.

Parents' rules

Research has suggested that girls face different rules to boys of the same age, and are more strictly supervised by parents. Girls are more likely to be collected by parents from school than boys, and are less likely to be allowed to play outside or in the street. Girls are also more likely to be told to be in at a certain time, and to have to tell their parents where they are going.

Jobs around the home

As table 5.2 shows, participation by children in household duties shows a marked difference between the sexes, with girls more likely to do indoor housework, generally helping their mothers with domestic jobs, while boys are more likely to do outdoor jobs with their fathers, like cleaning the car, sweeping the paths, and being shown how to do repairs and make things.

Table 5.2 Eleven-year-olds' participation in household duties

Duty	Boys %	Girls %	Both %
Washing up	40	63	51
Indoor housework (tidying, vacuum cleaning, dusting, bedmaking, etc.)	19	44	32
Miscellaneous dirty/outside jobs (gardening, sweeping, cleaning car or windows, making or mending fires, peeling potatoes, shoe cleaning, emptying bin, etc.)	36	8	22
Going on errands	39	21	30

Source: Adapted from J. Newson, E. Newson, D. Richardson, and J. Scaife, 'Perspectives in sex role stereotyping', in J. Chetwynd and O. Hartnett (eds), *The Sex Role System: Psychological and Sociological Perspectives* (Routledge and Kegan Paul)

ACTIVITY

Study table 5.2 and answer the following questions:

1 What household duty is most likely to be performed by both sexes?

2 What household duty is least likely to be performed by (a) boys and (b) girls?

3 How do you think the divisions in household duties among 11-year-olds could be seen as preparation for adult gender roles? Give examples of particular adult roles.

Watching and imitating parents

Small children mainly learn by watching and imitating the role models provided by others. A role model is simply a pattern of behaviour which others model their behaviour on. Children often observe their parents carrying out their respective gender roles every day. If children see their mothers spending more time in the home while their fathers go out to work, their mothers spending more time doing cooking, cleaning, and other housework than their fathers, and their mothers, rather than their fathers, taking time off work to look after them when they are sick, or taking them to the doctor, then children may well begin to view these roles as the 'normal' ways for men and women to behave. In general, small children are brought up by women, surrounded by women, and it is women who nearly always care for them, whether mothers, child-minders, or teachers. It is perhaps not surprising, then, that many girls still grow up today seeing childcare as being a major part of their role in life.

The role of the school

The process of gender socialization begun in the home often carries on through schooling. Much of this socialization goes on through the school's hidden curriculum. This consists of the hidden teaching of attitudes and behaviour, which are taught at school through the school's organization and teachers' attitudes but which are not part of the formal timetable. This is discussed in more detail in chapter 11. Despite equal opportunities policies, the hidden curriculum still often emphasizes the differences between males and females, and encourages different forms of behaviour. Three examples help to illustrate this.

Teachers' attitudes

Teachers have also been socialized into gender roles, and there is evidence suggesting that teachers have traditionally had higher expectations of boys than girls, encouraging them more (especially in sciences and computing), and placing more emphasis on their progress than that of girls, because they expect boys to be the main future 'breadwinners'. Teachers may also give different career advice to boys and girls, such as steering girls towards nursing and office work, and boys towards a much wider range of occupations.

Boys demand more of the teacher's time, and disruptive, unruly behaviour from boys is more likely to be tolerated than the same behaviour from girls. Girl 'trouble-makers', who fight in the playground or are disruptive in class, for example, are likely to be punished more severely than boys displaying similar behaviour, since girls are not expected to show such 'unfeminine' behaviour.

Schoolbooks

Reading books in infant schools have often shown women and little girls in the housewife/mother role, such as helping mother in the home, or watching their brothers climbing trees, mending the car, and 'getting into mischief'. Boys are more likely to be portrayed as playing with cars or trains, playing football, exploring, building things, climbing trees, and so on. Schools and textbook publishers are now tackling such stereotypes, but the effects of these changes will take time, and of course schools alone cannot reverse the stereotyping that goes on in a wide range of areas.

In secondary school, gender differences are reinforced by the illustrations in textbooks for different subjects – science books rarely show girls doing science, and boys rarely appear in home economics books. These suggest that some subjects are more suited to one sex rather than the other. Evidence suggests that the examples used in science books are still more in keeping with the experiences of boys than with girls.

Subject choice

Girls and boys have traditionally been counselled by parents and teachers into taking different subjects. Girls have been more likely to take arts subjects (like English literature, history, and foreign languages) and study home economics and commerce, while boys have been more likely to take sciences, technical drawing, and design and technology – subjects which are more likely to lead to more skilled and technical occupations after school. This gender division is also found in sport, with rugby and cricket for the boys and hockey and netball for the girls. Under the National Curriculum introduced in 1988 (see chapter 11), *all* 11–14-year-olds have to take technology, which includes home economics, business studies, and design and technology. This means that these gender divisions between subjects were broken down to some extent during the 1990s. However, even within the National Curriculum, there are gender differences within option choices. For example, girls are more likely to take home economics, textiles, and food technology, while boys are more likely to opt for electronics, woodwork, or graphics, and after age 16 other subject divisions still remain, as chapter 12 on education shows.

DISCUSSION

On the basis of your own experiences at both primary and secondary school, discuss any difficulties or pressures you might have experienced at school because of your sex in choosing subjects and options that you wanted to do. Take into account factors such as the views of your parents, friends, and teachers, and the advice of careers and subject teachers.

The importance of the peer group

A peer group is a group of people of similar age and status with whom a person mixes socially. Generally, people try to gain acceptance among their peers by conforming to the norms of their peer group. These norms frequently involve stereotyped masculine and feminine roles. For example, among male peer groups, interests and norms often centre on activities like football, music, cars, motor-bikes, stereo equipment, and computers. Female interests often centre on things such as fashion, make-up, and dancing. The peer group can exert strong pressure to conform to these interests: a boy, for example, who collected soft toys would be quite likely to find himself ridiculed by his peer group; a girl who played rugby or was into boxing might be seen as a bit of a 'tomboy'. Young people who fail to conform to gender stereotypes may find themselves ridiculed by their peer group, or excluded from group activities. Such pressures can help to discourage participation in activities which don't conform to gender stereotypes.

Double standards

Among teenage boys (and often adult men too) sexual promiscuity and sexual 'conquest' are often encouraged and admired as approved masculine behaviour, and are seen as a means of achieving status in the male peer group. However, males will condemn this same promiscuity among women – promiscuous girls and women are likely to be seen as 'up for it', and called 'loose' or 'slags' or some other insulting term. This attitude is often reinforced even by the female peer group, where sexual relations for girls are only approved in the context of a steady, close relationship. Girls and women who have sex outside some 'steady relationship' are therefore likely to find themselves condemned by men and women alike. In short, promiscuous men are seen as 'stags' or 'studs'; promiscuous women are seen as 'slags' or 'sluts'. This double standard helps to encourage conformity to separate gender identities for men and women, with the stereotyped man as 'sexual athlete' and woman as the passive and faithful lover, wife, or 'girlfriend'.

ACTIVITY/ DISCUSSION

1 Explain the influences your peer group has had in forming your gender identity, and, drawing on your own experiences, suggest ways it does this.
2 Do you believe that there is a 'double standard' applied to the behaviour of males and females when it comes to sexual activity?

The role of the mass media

The mass media include films, videos and DVDs, television, newspapers, CDs and tapes, radio, advertising, books, comics, magazines, and the Internet. The mass media create and reinforce gender stereotypes in a number of ways.

Comics, for example, present different images of men and women: girls are usually presented as pretty, romantic, helpless, easily upset and emotional, and dependent on boys – who are strong, independent, unemotional, and assertive – for support and guidance, and boys and girls are often presented in traditional stereotyped gender roles such as soldiers (boys) or nurses (girls). A similar pattern is shown on children's television, and much TV advertising shows gender stereotypes. Around 80 per cent of TV advertising voice-overs are male voices, suggesting authority. The media, particularly advertising, often promotes the 'beauty myth' – the idea that women should be assessed primarily in terms of their appearance.

ACTIVITY

Examine some children's reading books, comics, or male or female adult magazines, or study TV adverts, and see if you can identify any pattern in the different roles and interests allocated to boys and girls or men and women. Provide evidence for your conclusions.

You may have found from the previous activity that there are often very different types of story and magazine aimed at males and females. Romantic fiction is almost exclusively aimed at a female readership. A glance at the magazine shelves of any large newsagents will reveal a 'women's interests' section, consisting almost exclusively of magazines on cooking, home care and housekeeping, health and slimming, lifestyle, fashion and hair care, knitting, mother and baby, and weddings.

This shows very clearly the way the media both encourage and cater for a particular view of a woman's role. Similar 'men's interests' sections are much less common. However, men (and not women) can often be seen queuing up to read magazines (classified as of 'general interest') concerned with photography, stereos, computers, DIY, and all manner of transport: cars, motor-bikes, aircraft, trains, and boats. The 'top shelf' soft-porn magazines are aimed exclusively at men.

Images of men and women

When women appear in the mass media, it has traditionally been in a limited number of stereotyped roles. These include:

■ As a 'sex object' – the image of the slim, sexually seductive, scantily clad figure typically found on page 3 of the *Sun* newspaper is used by the advertising industry to sell everything from peanuts to motor-bikes and newspapers. 'Supermodels' are the beauty queens of today, at a time when Miss World beauty contests are seen by many as unacceptable.

■ In their relationships with men, such as bosses, husbands, and lovers.

■ As emotional and unpredictable.

■ In the housewife/mother role – as the content, capable, and caring housewife and mother, whose constant concern is with the whiteness of clothes, the cleanliness of floors, and the evening meal, and as the person who keeps the family together and manages its emotions.

When men appear in the media, it is in a very wide range of roles which have no particular reference to their gender. Women's roles often involve being women first – that is, women play limited roles restricted to their gender. The masculine stereotype of the physically well-built, muscular, handsome, brave, unemotional, non-domestic male still often appears. These differing roles of men and women are most evident in advertising, even when young children are used. For example, television advertisements for washing-up liquid or washing powder nearly always show mothers and small daughters working together, and boys are usually the ones who come in covered in dirt. While men and small boys hardly ever appear in such advertisements, when they do appear in a domestic role it is nearly always made clear it is an exception, or that they are not very good at domestic tasks.

ACTIVITY

A psychological study of the 'lonely heart' personal columns found that gender stereotyping was still the norm. Putting together the main features of the advertising, the study drew up the 'typical' male and female lonely hearts advertisements.

Male advert

Male, high wage earner, own home, with caring genuine nature, attractive, with sense of humour and interested in home building, seeks attractive, loving young woman for genuine partnership.

Female advert

Female, attractive, slim, tall shapely blonde, loving and sensitive, seeks financially secure caring man with good sense of humour and own home for genuine relationship.

1 What are the differences between the two advertisements in the qualities expected of a male and female?

2 Look at the personal columns of a local or national newspaper, and see if you can spot any common themes in the qualities men look for in women, and that women look for in men. Link your findings, if you can, to gender stereotyping.

In recent years, media images of gender have been changing. 'Girl power' was a phenomenon in the 1990s, challenging more traditional stereotypes of women as housewives or low-status workers, with more emphasis on women being themselves, and doing things by themselves. Films, for example, now show more self-confident, tough, intelligent, and independent female lead characters, though ones who can also maintain perfect make-up and hair. Such new role models might include Lara Croft and Sarah Michelle Gellar (Buffy the Vampire Slayer).

The masculine ideals of toughness, self-reliance and emotional coldness now exist alongside an emphasis on men's emotions, and the problems of masculinity. Such changing gender identities are shown by the feminized David Beckham – one of the world's most famous role models for both sexes.

ACTIVITY

1 What do the two cartoons below suggest are the main forces which contribute to the gender socialization process?

2 Study the result of the socialization of men shown in the cartoons, and describe the stereotype of a 'typical male'.

3 Do you think the cartoons give an accurate impression of present masculine behaviour? Back up your view with evidence of both child and adult male behaviour.

4 To what extent do you think media stereotyping of females and males is changing? Give examples to illustrate your answer.

Some consequences of media stereotyping

The images of men and women presented in the mass media in most cases do not conform to the reality of people's everyday lives. However, they may succeed in inducing feelings of guilt, inadequacy, and lack of self-confidence among the majority of women who don't 'measure up' to the 'sex object' or the 'happy housewife' images still often appearing in the media. Research in 2001 from Glasgow University found women were up to ten times more likely to be worried about their weight than men, even when they were not overweight. A 1995 report on the mental health of teenagers found girls were very sensitive about their appearance. They continually sought reassurance about their hair, weight, and skin, and felt put down when this was not forthcoming. This may partly explain why so many women are concerned with slimming and dieting, why anorexia and other eating disorders are illnesses affecting mainly teenage girls, and why many housewives in this country are on tranquillizers. Men who fail to 'measure up' to media stereotypes may face very similar feelings of inadequacy, and cases of eating disorders are growing among male teenagers. However, with men, the consequences of media stereotyping may take a more sinister turn. It is possible that violent crime, including violence against women, and the 'yobbish' behaviour of some men might in part be traced back to media stereotypes of macho men resolving problems through violence and aggression.

ARE GENDER ROLES AND IDENTITIES CHANGING?

In recent years, there has been evidence of some change in traditional ideas about masculine and feminine gender identities, and related sexuality. Soap operas give us insights into lesbian and gay relationships, and other images of sexual identities with which we may not be very familiar. Younger people are becoming more tolerant of gays and lesbians, and more accepting of cohabitation.

More males and females are adopting gender identities which combine elements of both genders, and these are constantly changing. We see more unisex hairstyles and clothing, more men wearing what were once seen as 'women's jewellery' or 'women's clothes', and using a range of cosmetics. A number of changes have led some writers to suggest that the old conceptions of 'masculinity' and 'femininity' are outdated, and that gender identities are changing, with more people choosing to ignore the traditional gender stereotypes.

Changing female identities?

Females are now doing better than males in education, and more positive role models are replacing traditional stereotypes in daily life and in the media. Women are becoming more successful than men in many areas of the labour market, such as in the music industry and in business and the professions, like law and medicine. Females often have better 'people' and communication skills than males, and these are the skills which are required for success in the new service economy – dealing with customers, orders, clients, and complaints. The traditional stereotype of women as mothers and carers, with prime responsibility for running the home and family, is being replaced by role models of strong, independent, and successful women in all spheres of life. With women's growing labour market success, the traditional idea of a single, main, male family breadwinner is being undermined, and as women's independent income increases, their financial need for marriage reduces. A woman no longer needs a man, through marriage and the family, to achieve status in society. Women can now do everything men can do, and they are often doing it more successfully. There is now a new and wider range of roles for women, and as traditional stereotypes are eroded, so women can choose from a range of feminine identities: 'being feminine' can increasingly mean a lot of different things.

Changing male identities?

Men used to establish their identities through the public world of work and as family breadwinners, and women through the private realm of family and home. However, at the same time as women are becoming increasingly assertive and successful in a wide range of areas, the prospects for young men are diminishing. Males are underachieving in education (see chapter 12), and men's traditional employment in 'macho' manual work is disappearing, with the closure of traditional heavy industries, such as mining, shipbuilding, and steel. The traditional power of men in the family, as main breadwinner and decision-maker, in the labour market and society generally is, some suggest, increasingly under threat from women's growing equality, success and financial independence. Seventy per cent of divorces are initiated by women, and more women are choosing to remain single and childless. Marriage and parenthood are in decline. Advances in technology are reducing men's role in reproduction, and women can now have children without the necessity of a male partner. Equal opportunities laws and policies, and independent taxation and equality in pensions, have all undermined male power.

A 'New Man'?

Since the 1980s there has been a debate about the emergence of a so-called 'New Man'. This 'New Man' is allegedly more caring, sharing, gentle, emotional, sensitive in his attitudes to women, children, and his own emotional needs, and willing to do his fair share of housework (see below and chapter 10). Love, family, personal relations, and getting in touch with his own emotions are meant to be more important than achieving career success and power in the family and society. This 'New Man' is becoming more concerned with his appearance (a traditional feminine concern), with the growing use by men of cosmetic surgery, like face lifts, 'nose jobs', and 'tummy tucking', and 'beauty treatments', such as facials and waxing to remove body hair. A Mintel survey in August 2004 found men had overtaken women in buying high-fashion 'designer labels' and jewellery, and that there was a general move away from the traditional stereotype of men not caring about the way they looked and smelled. The rise of the gay movement and the growth of anti-sexist ideas have further contributed to the undermining of men's traditional role. Though the 'New Man' has turned out to be a very rare specimen, men are said to be facing anxiety, uncertainty, and confusion about what their role and identity are in today's society.

Is there a crisis of masculinity?

The factors discussed above, summarized in figure 5.2, have led to the suggestion that men are now insecure and losing their sense of purpose, with low self-esteem among many young men. Evidence for this may include the fact that young men are the group most at risk of committing suicide, and that men are more likely to get into trouble with the police, and to cause violence. Some suggest this is because of the decreasing importance and growing insecurity attached to the father and breadwinner roles. Some argue these changes are creating a 'crisis of masculinity', with men feeling 'lost' and searching for a gender identity that 'fits' in the modern world.

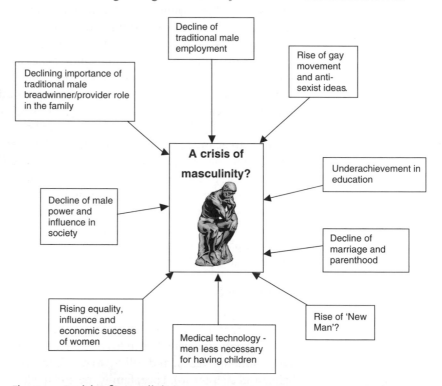

Figure 5.2 A crisis of masculinity?

DISCUSSION

1 To what extent do you think there is a 'crisis of masculinity'?
2 Do you think there is a new femininity that is more assertive and less dependent on men?
3 Do you think there is a 'New Man'?
4 To what extent do you think traditional gender identities are changing?

THE SEXUAL DIVISION OF LABOUR

Despite the discussion above of changing gender identities, the processes of gender role socialization outlined in this chapter often mean that women and men still have different experiences and expectations of life. Socialization still has the general effect of emphasizing the domestic responsibilities of girls for housework and childcare, limiting their self-confidence, and pushing them, eventually, towards marriage and the roles of housewife and mother (often alongside paid employment) as their primary roles in life. Boys, on the other hand, are still more likely to grow up conforming to the stereotype of the non-domestic, practical, unemotional, independent, and assertive male, whose role in life is that of 'the provider, the protector, and the impregnator'.

These patterns of socialization may be changing, for example through less gender stereotyping in schoolbooks and by teachers, and more role models of female success in education, the media, and the labour market. Nevertheless, the narrow, stereotyped gender roles of thirty years ago are still held by many of today's children.

Whether there is a change or not, the different socialization of males and females continues to show itself in the sexual division of labour in the job market, with jobs being divided into 'men's jobs' and 'women's jobs', and with young men and women choosing different types of work. Girls today have a strong awareness that they may one day have to balance work and a family, and many cope with this idea by aspiring only to undemanding careers. These divisions in the labour market, and the inequalities which women continue to face in a number of areas of social life, are considered below.

THE CHANGING STATUS OF WOMEN IN BRITAIN

During the twentieth century, there was a gradual improvement in the status of women in Britain, the outlines of which it is useful to list here. However, as will be seen later, women still face major inequalities with men, particularly the conflicting demands of family life and career success.

- Women have achieved more political equality with men, beginning with the powerful and often violent campaign waged by the Suffragette Movement at the beginning of the last century. By 1928, women had for the first time the same voting rights as men.

- Women today have equal rights with men in education. It is now illegal to discriminate against women or men by denying them access to certain subjects and courses at school or in further and higher education because of their sex.

- More types of job are seen as suitable for women today, and many more women are going out to work in paid employment. Women now make up about half of the workforce in Britain, which gives them more financial independence.

■ Equal opportunity laws have helped women to get a better deal and overcome prejudice and discrimination. For example, laws like the Equal Pay Act and the Sex Discrimination Act made it illegal for employers to offer different rates of pay to men and women doing the same or similar work, and to distinguish between men and women in work, leisure, and educational opportunities. The Equal Opportunities Commission helps to enforce these laws and to promote equality of opportunity between men and women.

■ Women now have equal rights with men in property ownership, and in the event of a divorce, all property now has to be divided equally between husband and wife.

■ Women have had equal rights with men in divorce since 1923.

■ The welfare state has provided more support for lone-parent families, the majority of which are headed by women, and for women caring for dependent husbands and the elderly in the home.

■ Girls have exceeded boys in educational success, and women are increasingly well qualified, and better qualified than men in the younger age groups.

Reproduced with permission of the Equal Opportunities Commission

ACTIVITY

Go to <www.eoc.org.uk>, and investigate the kinds of things done by the Equal Opportunities Commission. In the light of your findings, suggest six ways the Commission is fighting to improve the position of women, and to prevent discrimination against anyone because of their sex.

Why has the status of women changed?

The changing status of women in Britain over the last century can be explained by a number of factors.

The Suffragette Movement

The Suffragette Movement, which started at the turn of the twentieth century and lasted until 1918, aimed to achieve equal voting rights for women with men in parliamentary elections. This involved a long and often violent struggle against men's ideas about a woman's role. It was the first major struggle by women for equality with men, and began to change the ideas held by both men and women about a woman's role. The success

Figure 5.3 Why has the status of women changed over the last century?

of this campaign gave women political power for the first time in elections, and MPs had to begin to take women's interests into account if they were to be elected.

Two world wars

During the First (1914–18) and Second (1939–45) World Wars, women took over many jobs in factories and farms which were formerly done by men, as the men went off to be soldiers. Women showed during these war years that they were quite capable of doing what had previously been seen as 'men's jobs', and this began to change people's ideas about a woman's role.

Compulsory education of children

Compulsory schooling since 1880, and particularly since 1944, has reduced the time necessary for the care and supervision of children in the family. Recent improved childcare provision, and access to school for all 3- and 4-year-olds, have reduced this time further. This has given women with children a greater opportunity to go out to work than in the earlier parts of last century.

The women's movement

The women's movement (a new social movement, discussed in chapter 7) first emerged in the 1960s and is concerned with the fight to achieve equality with men in a wide range of areas. This movement was not a single group, but consisted of a large number of different women's groups with various aims, both in Britain and abroad. These groups were united by the need to improve the status and rights of women, and with ending patriarchy, which is the dominance of men in society. The women's movement challenged many ideas about the traditional role of women, particularly the stereotype that 'a woman's place is in the home'. It has campaigned for:

- Better nursery facilities.

- Free contraception and free abortion on demand, and 'a woman's right to choose' whether to have an abortion or not.

- Equal pay and job opportunities.

- The removal of tax and financial discrimination against women.

- Freedom from violence against women.

- The right of women to define their own sexuality.

The women's movement challenged many people's ideas about women, and has created a 'climate of expectation' where women now expect to be treated equally and not simply as lovers, housewives, and mothers. It is mainly because of pressures from the women's movement that equal opportunity laws have been passed, and that sexism, or prejudice and discrimination against people because of their sex, is increasingly seen as unacceptable behaviour.

ACTIVITY

1 *Either:* use the Internet and find out what you can about the kinds of actions carried out by women in their campaigns to achieve equality with men. You will find <www.fawcettsociety.org.uk> a useful website to investigate these issues, or you can find early campaigns for 'Votes for Women' explored at <www.historylearningsite.co.uk/suffragettes.htm>.

   Or: interview some older female relatives about women's fight for equality in the women's liberation movement of the 1960s. You can also find out about this by visiting <www.geocities.com/Libertyross/smvmnts.html>.

2 How do you think these activities might have changed both men's and women's views on women's traditional roles?

Reliable contraception

Modern contraception has become a much more reliable means of preventing unwanted children. Since the 1960s, the contraceptive pill has proven very effective, despite some health risks to women, and has enabled women to take control of their fertility, giving them more control over their lives.

Smaller family size

The declining size of families is both a cause and a consequence of the improving status of women. This has reduced the time spent in child rearing and given women greater opportunities to enter paid employment. A typical mother today spends about four years bearing and nursing children, and she can expect to live much longer than her nineteenth-century counterpart. This means once a woman has had children today, she still has a long life stretching ahead to pursue a career. Increasingly, women are having fewer children, or none at all, and they are having them at an older age.

More jobs for women

There are more types of job seen as suitable for women today, and legal obstacles to the employment of women have been removed in most cases. Although there still remains a lot of prejudice and discrimination by employers about the suitability of some jobs for women, the way women took over men's jobs during the world wars, the pressures of the Suffragette Movement and, more recently, the women's movement have helped to erode hostility to female workers among male bosses and workers.

This increase in employment opportunities for women has come about with the expansion of light industry, manufacturing, and the tertiary sector of the economy. The tertiary sector is concerned with services, finance, administration, distribution, transport, and government agencies, such as the NHS, the social services, and education. The expansion of this sector has increased the number of routine clerical and secretarial jobs which are overwhelmingly done by women. There has also been an increase in the number of jobs in the lower professions, such as teaching, social work, and nursing, which employ many women.

Maternity benefits and maternity leave now provide additional encouragement and opportunity for women to return to work after childbirth, as their jobs are kept open for them while they are absent having children. The fact that more women are working gives them greater financial independence and therefore more authority in both the family and society.

Technology in the home

Advances in technology have brought many improvements to the home environment, including better housing standards like central heating, labour-saving devices like freezers, washing machines, microwave cookers, food processors, and vacuum cleaners, manufactured foodstuffs such as canned and frozen foods, 'instant meals' and fast food. It has been suggested that these improvements have reduced the time spent on housework. However, others argue that these developments have simply meant higher standards are expected, and therefore more housework has to be performed. For example, automatic washing machines mean that washing is done several times a week instead of just once on 'washing day', and people change their clothes more often. This also creates, of course, more ironing. Similarly, vacuum cleaners mean that houses are expected to be kept cleaner than they used to be.

| DISCUSSION | Do you think that women are treated more equally today? What obstacles and problems do women still face that men don't? |

WOMEN AT WORK

Unpaid work: domestic labour

When talking about women at work, many people assume this refers to paid employment. However, it is important to remember there is one job which is performed full-time almost exclusively by women – unpaid housework or domestic labour. This domestic labour of women is hardly recognized as 'real work' at all, and carries little status compared with paid employment. This is partly because housework involves women in cleaning up their own and their families' self-generated dirt, doing their own and their families' washing, etc. It is also because no qualifications are needed, and housework is 'private', with no recognition by others and no praise, only complaints if the work is not done. Many women who are housewives themselves often undervalue the status of their job, as is summed up in the phrase 'I'm only a housewife'.

Women with a child under 5 spend about 65 hours a week on housework, childcare, and related tasks – far more than most people spend in paid employment. Data published by the Office for National Statistics (ONS) has shown that women spend on average nearly five hours a day cooking, cleaning, shopping, washing, and looking after the children. However, domestic labour has none of the advantages of paid employment, like regular working hours, 'clocking off' after work, chances of promotion, holiday pay, or sick pay. As table 5.3 shows, housewives experience far more monotony, fragmentation, and speed in their work than workers on even the most gruelling assembly line, but without the compensation of being paid for it.

The ONS has calculated that if the time spent on unpaid work in the home was valued at the same average pay rates as equivalent jobs in paid employment (for example, if cooking were paid as it is for chefs, or childcare as for nannies and child-minders), it would be worth £739 billion a year.

Housework and childcare are still seen as primarily the responsibility of women. As shown over the page in table 5.4, even when both partners are working full-time outside the home in paid employment, it is still women who are in most cases expected to take the major responsibility for housework and childcare. In the early 2000s, 70 per cent of women in marriages or cohabiting couples where both partners were working full-time had responsibility for general domestic duties. This means, of course, that many full-time working women have two jobs to their male partners' one.

Table 5.3 The experience of monotony, fragmentation, and speed in work: housewives and factory workers compared

| Workers | Percentage experiencing: | | |
	Monotony[a]	Fragmentation[b]	Speed[c]
Housewives	75	90	50
Factory workers	41	70	31
Assembly line workers	67	86	36

[a] Monotony refers to the feeling that the work is boring and repetitive.
[b] Fragmentation refers to the feeling that the work is divided into a series of unconnected tasks not requiring the worker's full attention.
[c] Speed refers to the feeling that the worker has too much to do, with too little time to complete the task, and so has to work at too fast a pace.
Source: A. Oakley, *The Sociology of Housework* (Martin Robertson)

ACTIVITY

Table 5.3 compares housewives' experience of their work with that of factory and assembly line workers:

1 Which group experiences the most monotony in their work?

2 Which group experiences the least speed in their work?

3 In which group did 31 per cent complain of too much speed in their work?

4 Suggest ways the evidence shown in table 5.3 might explain the finding that women who are exclusively housewives suffer more mental health problems than many of the population.

5 What differences are there between working exclusively as a housewife in the home and working in a factory which might make factory workers better able to cope with the monotony, fragmentation, and speed of their work?

6 Suggest reasons why housework is often seen by many people as not 'real work'.

Table 5.4 Who performed jobs in the home? Married or cohabiting couples with both partners working full-time: Great Britian, 1990s

Domestic job	Mainly man %	Mainly woman %	Shared equally %
Household shopping	8	45	47
Making evening meal	9	70	20
Washing evening dishes	28	33	37
Household cleaning	4	68	27
Washing and ironing	2	79	18
Small repairs around house	78	5	17
Organizing household bills/money	31	40	28
Looking after sick family members	7	48	45
Teaching children discipline	10	6	81
Summary: is responsible for general domestic duties	8	70	22

Source: Adapted from British Social Attitudes Surveys; *Social Trends*; *British and European Social Attitudes Report*, 1998

ACTIVITY

Table 5.4 looks at the way work is divided in the home where both husbands and wives, or cohabiting partners, have full-time jobs:

1 Which household task is most likely to be performed mainly by women?

2 Which household task is least likely to be shared equally?

3 Which household task is shared equally by 81 per cent of couples?

4 In the light of table 5.4, list each of the following statements as true or false:
  ■ Mostly men alone wash up the evening dishes.
  ■ Looking after sick family members is most likely to be shared by men and women today.
  ■ When their partners work full-time as well, men are most likely to make the evening meal.
  ■ Even when they work full-time, women are still mainly responsible for general domestic duties.
  ■ The only thing that men still seem to take the main responsibility for is small repairs around the house.

5 How does the evidence in table 5.4 support the view that women do two jobs compared with men's one job? Refer to particular examples to back up your case.

6 How might sociologists explain the division of household tasks shown in table 5.4?

Women in paid employment

Many of the factors discussed above explaining the changing status of women have brought about a large increase in the employment of women since the 1950s. In 2004, women made up nearly half of the workforce, compared with less than 30 per cent at the beginning of the twentieth century. Nearly 73 per cent of women of working age were in employment in 2004. Much of this increase has been among married women: less than 10 per cent of married women were working in the early twentieth century, but this has now increased to about 75 per cent (including cohabiting women), with around 1 in 10 of these women being the sole breadwinners in their families.

The inequality of women in paid employment

Although the role and status of women have gradually improved, and women have obtained job opportunities and rights previously denied to them, women still have an unequal position with men at work. Much of this inequality arises because the central role of women is still often seen by a male-dominated society as primarily that of housewife and mother. The following section summarizes the key features of women's employment situation, and describes and explains the main inequalities women face in the labour market.

The sexual division of labour

'The sexual division of labour' simply means that jobs are divided into 'men's jobs' and 'women's jobs', with women's jobs often having lower pay, poorer promotion prospects, and lower status than men's.

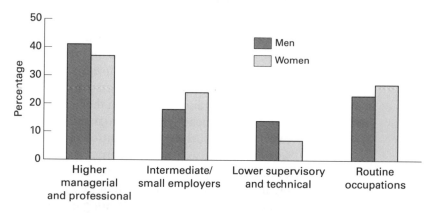

Figure 5.4 The occupations of men and women: Great Britain, 2003
Source: Data from Labour Force Survey

As shown in figure 5.4, fewer women than men are employed in the top professional and intermediate groups, and table 5.5 on page 105 shows that few women in this group are in the top professional jobs. Women are mainly employed in jobs which are concentrated at the lower end of the occupational scale: in unskilled and semi-skilled manual jobs and in routine, low-level clerical jobs like filing and keyboarding, which require little or no training. The fact that women are concentrated at the lower end of the salary and occupational status scale is known as *vertical segregation* in the labour market.

Women are also spread over a far narrower range and different types of jobs than men. This is known as *horizontal segregation*. Figure 5.5 shows that over 70 per cent of women are concentrated in four main occupational groups: professional and associate professional (mainly in education, welfare, and health); administrative and secretarial; sales and customer

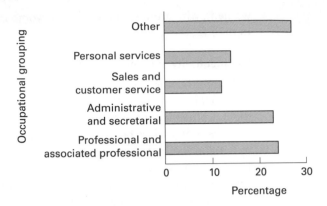

Figure 5.5 Occupational distribution of working women: Great Britain, 2003
Source: Data from Labour Force Survey

service; and personal services (like catering, cleaning, hairdressing, and other personal services).

Women are mainly employed in low-grade and low-paid jobs which are seen as 'female occupations'. These are often extensions of the traditional domestic roles of housewives and mothers into which many women continue to be socialized. These involve serving and waiting on people, caring for them, cleaning, and clearing up after others – all jobs that women have traditionally done in the home. Such jobs include nursing, primary school teaching, secretarial and routine clerical work, low-grade catering work, such as that of waitresses and canteen assistants, and working as shop assistants, supermarket 'shelf-fillers', and check-out operators. For example, secretaries serve their (still usually male) bosses, organizing the office to make things easier for them, making them coffee, and providing papers for and clearing up after their meetings; primary school teaching involves childcare; nursing is caring for the sick; catering involves cooking, serving, and clearing up meals.

Part-time work

In 2003, around four out of five part-time workers were women, and about 40 per cent of women in paid employment worked only part-time compared with 9 per cent of men. Surveys suggest this is closely related to women's responsibilities for children and other domestic tasks. Many working women are limited in the jobs they can do and the hours they can work because they are still expected to take responsibility for housework and childcare, and to be at home for the children leaving for and returning from school. There are still few workplaces today with childcare facilities which would allow working mothers to take full-time jobs. The presence of dependent children (under the age of 16), and the age of the youngest child, are the most important factors related to whether or not women are in paid employment, and whether they work full or part-time. Figure 5.6 illustrates the importance of this link between dependent children and part-time status.

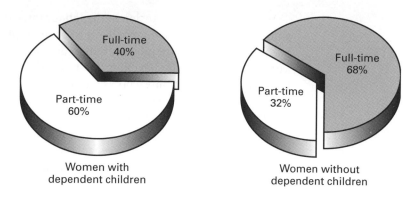

Figure 5.6 Women in employment: by dependent children and full- or part-time employment status, Great Britain, 2003

Source: Data from Labour Force Survey

Table 5.5 Women and men in top professional jobs: 2000s

Job	Women (%)	Men (%)
Senior civil servant (2002)	22	78
Senior police officer (chief/assistant chief constable) (2003)	8	92
MP (2003)	18	82
Cabinet minister (2003)	24	76
Member of the European Parliament (2002)	24	76
Local government chief executive (2002)	14	86
Army officer (lieutenant and above) (2003)	9	91
Lord Justice of Appeal (2003)	8	92
High court judge (2003)	6	94
Circuit judge (2003)	10	90
QC (silk) (2003)	7	93
Barrister (2003)	26	74
Trade union leader (2003)	13	87
Nursery and primary school headteacher (2003)	58	42
Secondary school headteacher (2003)	28	72
Head of higher education institution (universities and colleges) (2003)	13	87
General medical practitioner (GP) (2002)	36	64
Director and senior manager in top 100 UK companies (2003)	2	98
Senior manager or official (all)	30	70

Sources: Department of Health; Lord Chancellor's Department; Equal Opportunities Commission; Bar Council; Department for Education and Skills

ACTIVITY

Refer to table 5.5, which shows that there are few women in top professional jobs:

1 Why do you think this might be the case? What obstacles prevent women from getting into these jobs?

2 What steps might be taken to overcome these obstacles?

While a lot of the expansion in the labour force in recent years has been among women, with men more likely to be unemployed, much of this has been because many new jobs are temporary or part-time, which fits more with women's needs for flexibility due to the demands placed on them in the home. Much part-time work is particularly vulnerable to economic recession, and therefore involves higher risks of unemployment. Some employment protection laws may not apply to temporary or part-time workers, and often part-time workers do not belong to trade unions and so lack trade union protection. These factors mean many women often face high risks of redundancy and unemployment.

Limited career opportunities

Women have more limited career opportunities than men for a number of reasons. Because of gender stereotyping at school and the wider gender-role socialization process, women, even when they have the necessary educational qualifications for the 'top jobs', often lack the self-confidence and assertiveness to apply for them.

There is widespread male prejudice about women in career jobs and senior positions. There is evidence that some men are reluctant to be supervised by female managers, and there is a common male belief that men make better bosses. It is often assumed single women will eventually leave paid employment to marry and have children, and married women, particularly, are often seen as 'unreliable' because of the assumption they will be absent to look after sick children – although research has shown there is little difference in absence from work between men and women who share the same circumstances. Around three-quarters of all complaints of sex discrimination to the Equal Opportunities Commission come from women. A 1996 report by the Commission found that more than 1 in 4 women had experienced discrimination when applying for a job. Almost 1 in 5 had been a victim of sexism in their current employment. Even successful women in career jobs often find they come up against what has been called the glass ceiling – an invisible barrier of discrimination which makes it difficult for women to reach the same top levels in their chosen careers as similarly qualified men. These factors mean women are often overlooked for training and promotion to senior positions by male employers.

In addition, women with promising careers may have to leave jobs temporarily to have children, and therefore miss out on promotion opportunities. Research in 2003 showed that stay-at-home mothers rapidly lose their social status after leaving work. Top jobs require a continuous career pattern in the 20–30 age period – yet these are the usual childbearing years for women, so while men continue to work and get promoted, women miss their opportunities.

Finally, married or cohabiting women are still more likely to move house and area for their male partner's job promotion rather than their own. This means women interrupt their careers and have to start again, often at a lower level, in a new job, which means the men are getting promotion at the expense of lost opportunities for their partners.

Limited access to training

Women are less likely than men to enter training for better-paid and more secure skilled work. Often women are denied training, and therefore promotion opportunities, because employers, parents, teachers, and sometimes the women themselves see training as 'wasted' on women. Employers, as a result of gender socialization, may assume women will leave work to produce and raise children. They may therefore be unwilling to invest in expensive training programmes for women. Rather, they prefer to employ women in low-skilled jobs where they can be easily and quickly trained and replaced. Of the small number of women who do obtain training, the vast majority are employed in 'feminine occupations' such as hairdressing, beauty, and clerical work, which are generally low paid with limited career prospects.

Many employers still ask women discriminatory questions

THE TEN WORST-PAID JOBS IN BRITAIN . . .

Bar staff

Laundry and dry cleaning worker

Waitress

Petrol pump attendant

Kitchen porter

Catering assistant

Retail check-out operator

Hairdresser

Cleaner/Domestic

Supermarket shelf-filler

. . . and they're nearly all done by women!

Source: Low Pay Unit (2003)

Lower pay

While the Equal Pay Act gives equal pay to women if they do the same or similar work as men, it has been shown above that women often do not do the same work as men, and consequently have no one to claim equal pay with. For example, many more women work in the low-paid 'caring' occupations than men, and there may often be no males to compare their wages with. The average pay of full-time working women is only about 81 per cent of the average male wage, and in 2003 women made

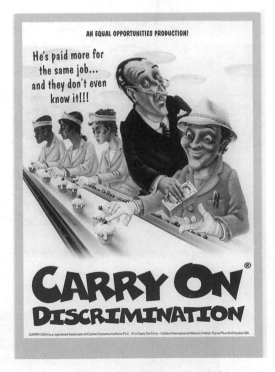

Reproduced with permission of the Equal Opportunities Commission

up around 80 per cent of all low-paid workers. Women have fewer opportunities to increase their pay through overtime, shift payments, or bonuses. Female part-time workers earn 16 per cent less each hour than male part-time workers, and full-time women workers 19 per cent less per hour than full-time men. The ten worst-paid jobs in Britain are all performed mainly by women. In a nutshell, this is because many women are concentrated in low-skilled and part-time work, which lacks promotion prospects and trade union protection, and often sick pay, holiday pay, and redundancy payments – a situation which does not apply to the majority of men.

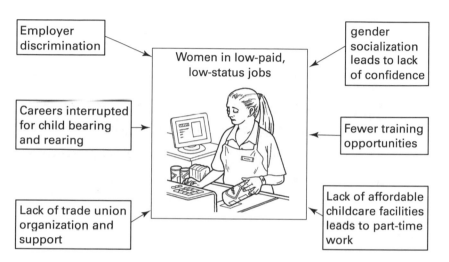

Figure 5.7 Why are women concentrated in lower-paid and lower-status jobs than men?

CONCLUSION

There have been great improvements in the position of women in the last century, particularly from the 1970s onwards under the impact of the women's movement. Attitudes have changed, and sexism has become less acceptable. Women have become more self-confident and assertive. They are now outstripping males at every level in education, and beginning to break through the glass ceiling to career success. Women are beginning to achieve more success and influence in society generally.

However, it is still women who are most likely to face poverty, and women alone head 1 in 5 families with dependent children. Women still earn less than men and have poorer career opportunities, and there are still few women in any of the top positions of power and influence in society. Housework and childcare remain the primary responsibility of women, undermining their ability to compete with men on equal terms in paid employment, reducing their financial independence, and restricting their power in society. While women have gained much over the last century, there still remains some considerable distance to travel before women achieve equality with men in many areas of life in modern Britain.

| DISCUSSION/ ACTIVITY | This chapter has mainly focused on the inequalities facing women at work. What other inequalities do women face in their daily lives compared with men? Think about things like going into pubs or clubs alone, fear of attack and sexual assault, politics, and so on.

In the light of the issues raised in this chapter and your responses to the activity above, consider what steps might be taken to break down these inequalities. To help you do this, draw three columns. In the first column, list all the inequalities you can think of that women still face today compared with men; in the second column, list the causes of these inequalities; in the third column, list the changes that would need to be made in society to remove these inequalities. |
| --- | --- |

CHAPTER SUMMARY

After studying this chapter, you should be able to:

- Explain the difference between sex and gender.

- Argue against the view that gender roles are biologically based.

- Describe the main features of gender stereotypes in modern Britain.

- Explain how gender socialization is carried out through the family, the school, the peer group, and the mass media.

- Explain some of the effects of the gender socialization process on both men and women.

- Discuss whether and how gender identities might be changing.

- Describe how and explain why the position of women has changed in Britain over the last century.

- Describe the main features of domestic labour.

- Explain why more married women are entering paid employment.

- Describe and explain a range of inequalities facing women in paid employment.

- Explain why women get only 80 per cent of the average male wage and are poorly represented in top jobs.

KEY TERMS

domestic labour
gender
gender identity
gender role
glass ceiling
hidden curriculum
patriarchy
peer group
role model

sex
sexism
sexual division of labour
stereotype

COURSEWORK SUGGESTIONS

1   Observe children in a playgroup and see if boys and girls play different types of game or play with different toys. Interview their mothers or fathers about the types of toy they had for birthday or Christmas presents. Try to reach some conclusions about gender-role socialization.

2   Study children's comics for a week (or reading books in an infant school, daily newspapers, children's books, television programmes and films, etc.), and see if boys/men and girls/women are presented in stereotyped ways. Give some detail on what the various stereotypes are and explain how they might contribute to gender-role stereotyping.

3   Examine subject or option choices, or exam entries, at your school or college and see if there are differences between males and females. Interview male and female students about why they chose their options, and interview teachers about your findings.

4   Interview a sample of married or cohabiting women in paid employment who have small children, and try to discover any problems or role conflict they experience at work and in the home.

5   Interview a sample of full-time housewives and try to discover what they enjoy most and dislike most about being full-time housewives, how much time they spend each week on housework, and how much help, if any, they get from their male partners.

6   Do a survey among men and women of different age groups asking about their attitudes to the growing equality of women.

6 Ethnicity and Race

RACE, ETHNICITY, AND MINORITY ETHNIC GROUPS

KEY ISSUES

• The meaning of race and ethnicity.

• Ethnicity and identity.

• The pattern of immigration.

• Who are the ethnic minorities?

• Some inequalities facing minority ethnic groups.

• The causes of racism.

• Are relations between ethnic groups improving?

The idea of race refers to the attempt to divide humans according to physical characteristics (like skin colour) into different racial groups, such as Caucasian (white), Negroid (black African), or Mongoloid (Chinese). Sociologists generally regard this as a rather pointless exercise, as it has no value in explaining human culture. This is because human behaviour is largely a result of socialization, and cannot be explained by purely biological characteristics.

Ethnicity is a more valuable idea. This refers to the common culture of a social group, such as language, religion, styles of dress, food, shared history and experiences, and so on. An ethnic group is any group which shares a common culture, and a minority ethnic group is a group which shares a cultural identity which is different from that of the majority population of a society. This means that groups such as gypsies, New Age travellers, and the Irish are all minority ethnic groups in Britain, as well as Asian and black communities.

DEFINITION

■ Race refers to the divisions of humans according to physical characteristics (like skin colour) into different racial groups, such as Caucasian (white) or Negroid (black African).

■ Ethnicity refers to a common culture, such as a group's language, religion, and beliefs.

■ An ethnic group is a group of people who share a common culture. A minority ethnic group is a group which shares a cultural identity that is different from that of the majority population of a society.

There is a wide range of ethnic groups who have emigrated to Britain over the years, such as the Irish, the Chinese, the Jews, the Poles, and more recently the Asians and African-Caribbeans (West Indians). However, when most people think of 'minority ethnic groups' they think of people of a different racial origin – of a different skin colour – and white people in Britain tend to think mainly of those of African-Caribbean or Asian origin. It is important to recognize that all minority ethnic groups do not share the same cultural features. For example, Asians and African-Caribbeans show especially strong cultural differences, and Indian Asians may be Sikhs (the largest group in Britain) or Hindus, while Pakistanis and Bangladeshis are more likely to be Muslims.

ETHNICITY AND IDENTITY

Ethnicity may be an important aspect of an individual's or group's identity – how they see and define themselves, and how others see them. For example, socialization may encourage people to adopt the lifestyles, dress, language, religion, food, music, values, attitudes, and beliefs of the ethnic community to which they belong. Socialization also influences the extent to which they see themselves as being 'different' from other ethnic groups, and, for example, whether they see and define themselves as being 'British', 'English', 'black', 'Muslim', 'Irish', 'Welsh', or 'Sikh'. Fortunately for race relations, a MORI poll in 2002 found that almost 9 out of 10 people said that being British is not about being white, and many seem to have embraced the idea of living in a multi-racial and multi-cultural society.

ACTIVITY

1 Think about the culture and lifestyles of ethnic groups in Britain. Identify all the features you associate with minority ethnic groups which make them in some ways different from the majority culture of society, such as the music, religion, food, attitudes, and lifestyles of African-Caribbeans, Indians, Pakistanis, or Bangladeshis.

2 To what extent do you think ethnicity is an important part of your identity?

3 What do you think is involved in 'being British'?

THE PATTERN OF IMMIGRATION

It is only since the Second World War (1939–45) that there has been a sizeable non-white population in Britain. Black people entering Britain from the British Commonwealth in the twenty years after 1945 were actively encouraged ('pulled') to come here by the British government. This was due to the serious labour shortage in the period of economic expansion following the Second World War. This 'invitation' to come to Britain was often to fill unskilled and poorly paid jobs white people refused to do. These included jobs in the NHS, London Transport, and the textile industry. Families reuniting with other relatives became an important factor in later migration. 'Push' reasons for migration included unemployment and poverty at home. Most of the early Commonwealth immigrants came from the West Indies, but later the numbers of Indians, Pakistanis, and Bangladeshis grew. The scale of this immigration has been exaggerated, and in recent years a series of racist Immigration Acts have all but ended immigration by non-white people.

WHO ARE THE MINORITY ETHNIC GROUPS?

Only about 8 per cent of the population of Britain are non-white (see table 6.1 and figure 6.1 on the next page), and these make up a small minority of all immigrants. Asians and African-Caribbeans together form about 6 per cent of the population of Britain. Well over half the minority ethnic population were actually born here, so it is misleading to regard them as immigrants, while over half of those who really are immigrants have lived here for more than thirty years.

Table 6.1 Ethnic origins of the population: United Kingdom, 2001

Ethnic group	Total (thousands)	% of the population
White	54 154	92.1
Mixed	677	1.2
Black Caribbean	566	1.0
Black African	485	0.8
Black other	98	0.2
Indian	1 053	1.8
Pakistani	747	1.3
Bangladeshi	283	0.5
Chinese	247	0.4
Other Asian	248	0.4
Other ethnic minorities	231	0.4
All ethnic groups[a]	58 789	100.00

[a] Includes those who did not state their ethnic group.
Source: Census 2001, Office for National Statistics

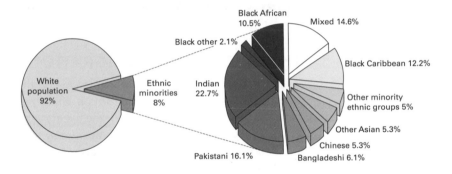

Figure 6.1 Minority ethnic population: United Kingdom, 2001

Source: Data from Census 2001, Office for National Statistics

SOME INEQUALITIES FACING MINORITY ETHNIC GROUPS

ACTIVITY

Go to <www.cre.gov.uk>, the website of the Commission for Racial Equality, and investigate five inequalities facing people from minority ethnic groups. Identify five actions that the Commission for Racial Equality is taking to try to stamp out racism and discrimination.

<www.bbc.co.uk/history/society_culture/multicultural> charts the history and experience of non-white Britons and of racism in the twentieth century. This may be useful if you want to study these issues in greater depth.

While some minority ethnic groups are doing very well in Britain, black and Asian people often face a series of disadvantages and poorer life chances than their white counterparts. Pakistanis, Bangladeshis, and African-Caribbeans in particular face a series of disadvantages in Britain compared with the white majority, although there are differences within each group. Some of these disadvantages are discussed in the chapters on education, health, and the mass media, but they also exist in a range of other areas.

Employment and unemployment

■ African-Caribbeans, Pakistanis, and Bangladeshis are less likely than white people to secure the best jobs. These groups are under-represented (that is, there are fewer of them than there should be given their proportion in the population) in non-manual occupations, particularly in managerial and professional work. They are hugely under-represented in Parliament and the top elite occupations. For example, only 52 of the 3,000 senior civil servants were from minority ethnic groups in 2001.

WHO SAYS ETHNIC MINORITIES CAN'T GET JOBS? THERE ARE OPENINGS EVERYWHERE.

Reproduced with permission of the Commission for Racial Equality

■ They are over-represented in semi-skilled and unskilled manual occupations, and often work longer and more unsociable hours (shiftwork and night work) than white people. Black and Asian people are less likely to get employed when competing with whites with the same qualifications for the same job, and have lower average earnings, even when they have the same job level as white people. On average, Pakistani and Bangladeshi men earn just over half the salary of white men, while African-Caribbean men earn about two-thirds. As figure 6.2 shows, minority ethnic groups are far more likely to be in the poorest fifth of the population.

■ People from minority ethnic groups are more likely to face unemployment, especially those of African-Caribbean, Pakistani, and Bangladeshi origin (as figure 6.3 on page 116 shows).

■ Skilled and experienced women from minority ethnic groups are twice as likely as white women to be unemployed. Black and Asian women frequently work longer hours in poorer conditions than white women or men, and receive roughly three-quarters of white women's pay, even though they are on average better educated.

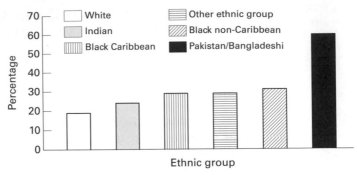

Figure 6.2 Percentage of each ethnic group in the poorest fifth of the population: United Kingdom, 2003

Source: Department for Work and Pensions, 2003

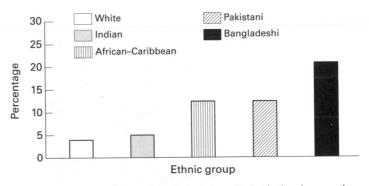

Figure 6.3 Unemployment rates: by ethnic group, United Kingdom, spring 2003

Source: Data from *Labour Market Trends*

ACTIVITY

Minority ethnic working-class women are frequently the most disadvantaged social group of all. Drawing on your knowledge of gender, ethnic, and class divisions, suggest possible explanations for this.

Housing

■ Black and Asian people tend to live in inferior housing to white people and in the 'less desirable' areas of towns and cities.

■ They tend to live in older properties than whites, and are more likely to live in a terraced house or flat.

■ They face much higher levels of overcrowding than white households (see figure 6.4).

■ As table 6.2 shows, black people are more likely to live in rented accommodation, particularly in social housing (council or housing association properties), where they are often allocated the least desirable homes. Indian Asians, however, are more likely to be owner occupiers than whites are, although the quality of the Indian Asians' housing is often poor, and tends to be in the least desirable and cheaper areas.

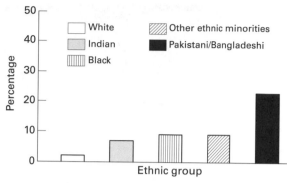

Figure 6.4 Percentage of households living in overcrowded accommodation: by ethnic group, England, 2000

Source: Data from Survey of English Housing, Office of the Deputy Prime Minister

■ It is often the case that the ethnic minorities live in areas that are different from, and poorer than, those where the white population live.

■ Black and Asian households, and single black and Asian people in particular, are more likely than whites to be homeless.

ACTIVITY

Refer to figure 6.4 and table 6.2:

1 Which ethnic group is most likely to own their home outright?
2 Which ethnic group is most likely to rent their home privately?
3 Which ethnic group is most likely to own their home with a mortgage?
4 Which ethnic group has the highest percentage in overcrowded homes?
5 Suggest explanations for the patterns of housing ownership/renting and overcrowding shown in figure 6.4 and table 6.2.

Table 6.2 Tenure: by ethnic group of household reference person, England, 2002/3

	Owned outright %	Owned with mortgage %	Rented from social sector %	Rented privately %	All tenures (=100%) thousands
Minority ethnic group					
Black Caribbean	14	41	39	6	236
Black African	2	24	47	27	139
Indian	27	51	9	13	328
Pakistani	19	51	13	17	178
Bangladeshi	4	28	60	7	67
All minority ethnic groups	17	39	28	15	1 541
White	30	42	19	9	18 697
All ethnic groups	29	42	20	10	20 238

Source: Survey of English Housing, Office of the Deputy Prime Minister

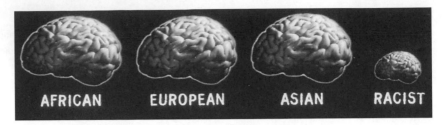

AFRICAN   EUROPEAN   ASIAN   RACIST

Reproduced with permission of the Commission for Racial Equality

Explaining racial disadvantage in employment and housing

The following explanations for racial disadvantage should be considered together, as they are cumulative, in that one aspect of discrimination or disadvantage can lead to further disadvantage in other areas.

Social class

Many of the black and Asian population are working class, and therefore face the problems encountered by all working-class people, regardless of their ethnic origin. This would explain their disadvantage compared with the population as a whole. However, there is also evidence of additional racial prejudice and racial discrimination.

> **RACIAL PREJUDICE AND DISCRIMINATION**
>
> ■ Racial prejudice is a set of assumptions about a racial group which people are reluctant to change even when they receive information which undermines those assumptions.
>
> ■ Racial discrimination is when people's racial prejudices cause them to act unfairly against a racial group. For example, a racially prejudiced police officer might use his or her power to pick on black or Asian people more than white people, perhaps by stopping them in the street and asking what they're up to.
>
> ■ Racism is believing or acting as though an individual or group is superior or inferior on the grounds of racial or ethnic origins, usually skin colour or other physical characteristics, and suggesting that groups defined as inferior have lower intelligence and abilities. Racism involves both racial prejudice and racial discrimination, and encourages hostile feelings towards groups defined as inferior.
>
> ■ Institutional racism is 'the collective failure of an organization to provide an appropriate and professional service to people because of their culture, colour or ethnic origin. It can be seen or detected in processes, attitudes and behaviour which amount to discrimination through unwitting prejudice, ignorance, thoughtless and racist stereotyping which disadvantages minority ethnic people' (Macpherson Report, 1999). (See the box on 'The Stephen Lawrence Inquiry and the Macpherson Report' on p. 124.)

ACTIVITY

With reference to the definition of institutional racism given above, suggest ways that an organization might be unwittingly (that is, not consciously) disadvantaging people from minority ethnic groups. An example might be not providing information in minority languages.

The 1976 Race Relations Act, amended in 2000, made it illegal to discriminate on the grounds of race in employment and housing, and to 'incite racial hatred', and this was strengthened by the establishment of the Commission for Racial Equality in 1976.

However, there is widespread evidence that racial discrimination in employment, housing, and other areas continues. For example, complaints of racial discrimination coming to the Commission for Racial Equality have more than doubled since the early 1990s. Part of the problem is that it is difficult to prove racial discrimination. A black or Asian person who is turned down for promotion at work in favour of a white person may be told the white person was simply more suited to the job in some way.

The most straightforward explanation for disadvantages in employment is that they result from racism and prejudice by employers, who either refuse to employ some minority ethnic groups, or employ them only in low-status and low-paid jobs, or refuse to promote them. This view has been confirmed by a number of surveys in which it was found that white workers received more positive responses in job applications than similarly qualified applicants from minority ethnic groups. For example, a 1990s survey by the Commission for Racial Equality found that white people were five times more likely to get interviews for jobs than black and Asian people with the same qualifications.

Education

Underachievement in education, with some minority ethnic groups performing below their ability in GCSEs, AS- and A- levels, AVCEs, and university entry (ethnicity and education are discussed in chapter 12), may partly explain why some minority ethnic groups are under-represented in

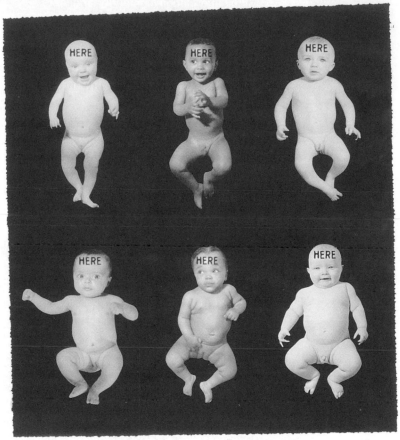

Reproduced with permission of the Commission for Racial Equality

DISCUSSION

Refer to the 'Babies' poster from the Commission for Racial Equality. What point is the poster making? What do you think the causes of racism might be?

ACTIVITY

1 Complete the questionnaire on page 121 by interviewing a group of people in your school or college. Try to get answers from people from a variety of ethnic backgrounds.

2 Analyse the results.

3 Discuss the answers in your class, considering how much racial prejudice you think might exist.

4 Suggest reasons why people might feel the way they do as shown by your interviews, taking into account any differences you found between ethnic groups.

SURVEY ON RACIAL PREJUDICE

1. To which of these groups do you consider you belong? . . .

White
Black – Caribbean
Black – African
Black – other
Indian
Pakistani
Bangladeshi
Chinese
Other

2. Do you think Britain as a society is? . . .

Very racist
Fairly racist
Fairly non-racist
Completely non-racist

3. How much prejudice is there against black and Asian people in Britain today? . . .

A lot
A little
Hardly any
Don't know

4. How prejudiced are you yourself against people of other races? . . .

Very prejudiced
A little prejudiced
Not prejudiced at all

5. How prejudiced do you think people are in your street or community? . . .

Very prejudiced
A little prejudiced
Not prejudiced at all
Don't know

6. Do you think non-whites are treated better, worse or the same as whites by? . . .

Employers:	better/worse/same
The police:	better/worse/same
Schools:	better/worse/same
The courts:	better/worse/same

7. Do you agree or disagree with the following statements?

■ People should only marry within their own ethnic group . . .   Agree/disagree

■ People of different races should keep to themselves . . .   Agree/disagree

■ I would happily have people of a different race living next door to me . . .   Agree/disagree

■ Immigration has made the variety of life better in Britain . . .   Agree/disagree

■ White people are more intelligent than black people . . .   Agree/disagree

Source: Adapted from surveys in the *Independent on Sunday* and the *Guardian*

managerial and professional work, and are more likely to be found in unskilled and semi-skilled occupations. These occupations tend to be those most at risk in times of recession, which helps to explain the higher levels of unemployment among black and Asian people. However, discrimination might well mean that they are more likely to be singled out for redundancy when the axe falls.

The generally lower pay of Asian and African-Caribbean minorities which follows from these explanations might explain their inferior housing. However, there is evidence of discrimination among landlords and council officials in allocating housing to black and Asian people.

Policing and the law

How the police go about their work – what they look out for – is guided by their ideas about who 'troublemakers' or criminals are. Black and Asian people (especially black and Asian youths) fit the police stereotype of 'troublemakers' and Black and Asian areas are therefore subject to heavier policing. People from minority ethnic groups are more likely than white people to be charged with offences such as obstruction or breach of the peace – offences which the police themselves can decide have been committed or not.

Reproduced with permission of the Commission for Racial Equality

Evidence suggests that young African-Caribbean and Asian men are more likely to be stopped and searched or questioned by the police than their white peers, and black and Asian people are more likely to be arrested than whites for the same offence. That they are more heavily policed and stopped and searched means that the police are likely to discover more crime among black and Asian people than among white people. In some cases, resentment at this treatment may actually provoke trouble and cause offences to be committed.

A 1990s survey in the *Weekly Journal* showed 92 per cent of black and Asian people felt that the police treated white people better. This confirmed the findings of a 1990s study by the National Association for the Care and Resettlement of Offenders (NACRO), which suggested there was evidence of police misconduct towards black and Asian people, who faced more unnecessarily rough treatment and abusive language than white offenders. Black and Asian people are more likely than white people to be detained after being charged by the police with an offence, and less likely to be allowed to make contact with friends, relatives, or a lawyer. The Macpherson Report of 1999 (see page 124) made clear the existence of widespread institutional racism in London's Metropolitan Police, disadvantaging minority ethnic groups. In 2003, the persistence of this racism in the Metropolitan Police led the Metropolitan Black Police Association to warn people from minority ethnic groups not to join the force.

Black and Asian people are therefore more likely to get caught, arrested, and charged, and the original police stereotype is confirmed by the activities of the police themselves. Many judges and magistrates hold similar stereotypes, and the evidence suggests that they crack down harder on black and Asian people than on white people, giving them heavier fines and sentences than white offenders committing similar offences.

- Black and Asian offenders are more likely to be charged where white offenders are cautioned for similar offences.

- Black and Asian people are more likely to be remanded than released on bail.

- Black and Asian people are more likely than whites to be given prison sentences rather than probation or community punishment.

- Black and Asian people make up only about 8 per cent of the population, but account for 21 per cent of men in prison, with black women making up 26 per cent of the female prison population.

Black and Asian people are the victims of more crimes of violence than white people, usually motivated by racism and organized by racist and fascist groups like the British National Party and Combat 18. The British Crime Survey found that both African-Caribbeans and Asians were up to 14 times more likely to be victims of racially motivated

AND YOU GET ANNOYED ABOUT JUNK MAIL.

Reproduced with permission of the Commission for Racial Equality

incidents than white people, and estimated there were around 280,000 racially motivated incidents in 2000 in Britain, including harassment, abuse, threats, intimidation, and violence – an average of over 750 incidents every day of the year. Only around 17 per cent of these were officially recorded by the police. A number of murders each year are believed to be racially motivated, such as that of black 18-year-old Stephen Lawrence, who was stabbed to death in 1993 by white youths while waiting at a bus stop in London. No one has been convicted of this murder.

The Times newspaper has reported on one estate in the West Midlands where people from minority ethnic groups had been shot at, beaten with metal bars, and had their cars set on fire in a campaign of 'ethnic cleansing' by white racists. Asian victims were particularly vulnerable to random attacks and harassment by passing groups of strangers.

This means black and Asian people often live in fear of being attacked in the streets or in their homes.

THE STEPHEN LAWRENCE INQUIRY AND THE MACPHERSON REPORT (1999)

The investigation into the police handling of the murder of black 18-year-old Stephen Lawrence by five white youths in 1993 led to the Macpherson Report in 1999. This was highly critical of the Metropolitan Police, pointing to a series of mistakes, a 'lack of urgency', and mishandling in the police investigation, including their assumption that Stephen Lawrence was involved in a street brawl rather than being the victim of an unprovoked racist attack. The Report pointed to the existence of institutional racism in the police force, and recommended a series of improvements there. These included race awareness training, more minority ethnic police officers, and stronger disciplinary action to get rid of racist police officers. The Macpherson Report established an official view of the widespread existence of institutional racism in many areas, including policing, the health services, and education, and led to a campaign to stamp out racism in a wide range of public and private organizations.

Table 6.3 Ethnic minorities and the law: United Kingdom, 2000s

Position	White %	Ethnic minority %
Law Lord	100.0	0.0
Court of Appeal judge	100.0	0.0
High Court judge	100.0	0.0
Circuit judge	98.9	1.1
Recorder	96.9	3.1
Practising barrister	91.5	8.5
Practising solicitor	98.5	1.5
Police officers	97.4	2.6

Source: Lord Chancellor's Department (2003); Home Office; Bar Council

ACTIVITY

Refer to table 6.3 and then answer the following questions:

1 Suggest reasons why the minority ethnic groups are so poorly represented, or not represented at all, in the law and the police force.

2 What difficulties do you think people from minority ethnic groups might face in joining or staying in the police force?

3 Explain carefully, with examples, how the evidence given might be used to explain the unequal treatment of black and Asian people by the law, and the high proportion of black and Asian people among those in prison.

THE CAUSES OF RACISM

There is no simple explanation of racism, but there are four factors which help to explain it:

1 *History*. Our society has a long history of white domination of African and Asian countries. Slavery and colonization were often justified on the basis of ideas about the supposed superiority of white people to those of other ethnic origins. These ideas still tend to linger on. For example, the European Youth Survey, published by MTV in the late 1990s, found almost 30 per cent of 16–24-year-olds in Britain disagreed that all races were equal, and 26 per cent said they would never consider dating someone of a different colour.

2 *Stereotyping*. A stereotype is a generalized, oversimplified view of the features of a social group, allowing for few individual differences between members of the group. Often the media portray degrading and insulting stereotypes of minority ethnic groups which fuel racism (see for example the newspaper article on page 126).

3 *Scapegoating*. Scapegoats are individuals or groups blamed for something which is not their fault. When unemployment, poverty, and crime rates rise, it becomes easy to find simple explanations by scapegoating easily identifiable minorities, such as young people, minority ethnic groups, or asylum seekers.

4 *Cultural differences*. Some argue that in any society where there are cultural differences between groups, such as in religious beliefs, values, customs, food, dress, and so on, there are bound to be conflicts from time to time between the minority cultures and the majority culture.

ARE RELATIONS BETWEEN ETHNIC GROUPS IMPROVING?

Grounds for optimism

Being black or Asian in Britain is often portrayed as a story of racial inequality, prejudice, and discrimination. Yet the news is not all bad. The existence of institutional racism has now been officially recognized, and action taken to tackle racism in a wide range of public services and private organizations. In 2003 there were, for the first time, two non-white members of the Cabinet in Downing Street.

Misdemeanour of the week. . .

Chasing the Lottery winner

VINDA LOOT!

Indian dad winner of
£18 million takeaway

IF THE lottery winner had not been "Asian" and/or "Muslim" would the tabloid press reports have been as bold and as ugly in their reaction? We are not here discussing the ethics of gambling, an activity that Islamic law does not permit, but whether the tabloids should have treated the religion of the winner in this odious manner.

"We're Hindi money", "Vinda Loot", "The Happy Chap-ati" . . . These are just some of the pernicious headlines that appeared.

As a British Muslim, I felt that my religion was being held up to ridicule and wondered where this Islamophobic tendency would lead, particularly now that certain countries in Europe are heading towards ethnic and racial intolerance.

The tabloids, willingly or unwillingly, are playing into the hands of those few racist elements in society who question "why a Paki should get all this money". What if it was a good "white" family man from Durham? If the lottery itself is based on greed then its net result brings out the worst in people, such as envy, jealousy and further greed.

The tabloid reports urging individuals and "groups" to bounty-hunt for the family do not speak of a tolerant and pluralist 20th century society. The tabloid newspapers were, in effect, encouraging the establishment of "witchfinder generals" and urging posses of fascists to search out this individual and his family, like a turkey-shoot.

Surely what was ultimately relevant here was the prize? One would have hoped that the tabloids would be in the vanguard of promoting racial harmony rather than giving fuel to a minority of bigots.

Sayyed Nadeem A Kazmi
The author is editor of the Islamic monthly, *Dialogue*

Source: Guardian

ACTIVITY

In 1994, an Asian man in Bradford won £18 million on the National Lottery. The article above is a response to the way the popular press, in particular the *Sun* newspaper, reacted. Read it, then answer the questions that follow.

1 What are the main objections of the writer to the way the story of the lottery winner was reported in the press?
2 How do you think the story might have been different if the winner had been 'a good "white" family man from Durham'?
3 Do you agree or disagree with the objections raised by the writer? Give reasons for your answer, and discuss it with your fellow students.

National and local government and some large private companies in Britain are trying to improve the representation of black people in important areas of social life. Methods adopted include the provision of training for all staff, and measures designed to increase the numbers of minority ethnic group members who apply for jobs, and to remove recruitment, selection, and promotion procedures which might discriminate against black and Asian people. These measures include advertising jobs in minority ethnic newspapers, and race awareness courses for recruiting staff. Monitoring of job applications for ethnic bias is becoming increasingly common, and equal opportunities policies to combat discrimination are being adopted by schools, colleges, and private and public sector employers. Many schools now include multi-cultural education as an important part of the curriculum, and have anti-racist policies in an attempt to promote understanding between different ethnic groups and help to overcome prejudice and discrimination based on ethnic differences. The Race Relations (Amendment) Act 2000 made school governors responsible for preventing racism, dealing firmly with it when it occurs, and actively promoting race equality.

Key parts of British society have begun to respond well to the fact that Britain is a multi-racial society. According to the largest survey of ethnic minorities ever carried out in Britain, by the Policy Studies Institute in 1997, around half of British-born Caribbean men, a third of Caribbean women, and a fifth of Indian and African Asian men now have a white partner, and about 80 per cent of 'Caribbean' children now have one white parent. A 1990s report by the Institute of Public Policy Research found about 70 per cent of white people said they wouldn't mind if a close relative married a black or Asian person. In October 2003, Britain saw the appointment of a black chief constable for the first time in history.

Racism is less acceptable than it once was, with initiatives such as the European Union's European Year Against Racism in 1997, and the development of equal opportunities policies, bringing home the message that racial prejudice has no place in a Europe of the second millennium. In some areas, such as education, some minority ethnic groups are doing better than their white counterparts. Some minority ethnic groups are much more likely to continue their education beyond the age of 16 than white people, and around 13 per cent of British university students come from minority ethnic groups – nearly double their proportion in the population as a whole. This might eventually lead to improved career prospects and bigger breakthroughs into high-status jobs. In a survey in the late 1990s for the *New Nation*, a newspaper targeted at Britain's black and Asian population, the outlook for race relations was described as positive, and over 60 per cent said things had improved in the previous five years.

Grounds for pessimism

Despite these reasons for optimism, this chapter has shown that major problems of inequality still confront the minority ethnic groups of Britain.

Racist attitudes are still widespread. A quarter of Britons admitted to being 'very' or 'a little' prejudiced against people of other races in the 2000 British Social Attitudes Survey. The 1999 Macpherson Report did show the continued widespread existence of institutional racism in some key sectors of British society.

There are no black or Asian chiefs of the armed forces, few in the police force; and there are few black or Asian people in high-status positions of power in society. There are more black and Asian university students, but black and Asian graduates face a higher unemployment rate than both graduate and non-graduate white people. A Pakistani with a university degree is as likely to be living below the poverty line as a white person with no educational qualifications. Many black and Asian people are worse off than white people with similar qualifications. More than four out of five Pakistani and Bangladeshi households are living below the poverty line.

In the 2000s, people seeking asylum in Britain from persecution abroad were viciously attacked by the media and many of the public on racist grounds, and there was a major moral panic (an exaggerated wave of public concern stirred up by the mass media) around asylum seekers. Opportunities for Britain's minority ethnic groups, whether they be in education, jobs, or housing, are still far fewer than for white people. Black and Asian people are still worse off than white people as victims of crime and in their dealings with the law. To paraphrase one writer, there still 'ain't enough black in the Union Jack'.

ACTIVITY

1   Discuss the explanations given in this chapter, and any others you can think of, for why people from minority ethnic groups, particularly African-Caribbean and Asian minorities, often face racial prejudice and discrimination. Give examples to illustrate each explanation.

2   For each explanation, suggest ways in which the causes of the prejudice and discrimination might be removed.

3   Go to <www.cre.gov.uk>, the website of the Commission for Racial Equality, and compare your suggestions in your answer to question 2 with the actions being taken by the Commission for Racial Equality.

CHAPTER SUMMARY

After studying this chapter, you should be able to:

■ Explain what is meant by the terms 'race', 'ethnicity', 'ethnic group', and 'minority ethnic group'.

■ Identify the link between ethnicity and identity.

■ Identify the main minority ethnic groups in Britain.

■ Explain how and why ethnic minorities face inequalities in employment, housing, and the law.

■ Explain what is meant by 'racial prejudice', 'racial discrimination', 'racism', and 'institutional racism'.

■ Suggest some explanations for racism.

■ Identify steps being taken to improve the position of the ethnic minorities, with examples.

KEY TERMS

ethnic group
ethnicity
institutional racism
minority ethnic group
race
racial discrimination
racial prejudice

COURSEWORK SUGGESTIONS

1   Devise a survey to question people about their attitudes to people of other ethnic groups. You might find the questionnaire included in this chapter a useful starting point.

2   Using secondary sources (see chapter 17), try to do a small-scale survey of local employment patterns to see if there is any evidence of discrimination against people from the ethnic minorities.

3   Investigate in your school, college, or workplace any efforts that are being made to create more equal opportunities for minority ethnic groups. For example, see if there are any equal opportunity policies in place or ethnic monitoring of job or student applications. Find out what steps are taken to analyse the effects of such policies, and how these findings change the actions of the institution.

7 Power, Politics, Citizenship, and Protest

KEY ISSUES

- Types of political system.
- Citizenship.
- Political parties in Britain.
- Influences on voting behaviour.
- Why people abstain in elections.
- Opinion polls.
- Influencing decision-making in a democracy.
- Pressure groups and new social movements.
- Is Britain a democracy?

When most people in Britain think about politics, they usually think about voting and elections, councillors and MPs, and often boring party political broadcasts on television. This is quite a narrow view of politics, and of course in many parts of the world people are unable to vote in elections, and don't even have the right to be bored by the television broadcasts of competing political parties. However, politics is not simply about councils and governments, but more widely about the exercise of power.

Power is the ability of people or groups to exert their will over others and get their own way, even if sometimes others resist this. Politics is concerned with the struggle to gain power and control, by getting into a position to make decisions and implement policies. This means that when partners in a personal relationship argue about decisions affecting them, we can talk about the 'politics of the personal'. In family life, disputes between husbands and wives, and parents and children, can be considered part of the 'politics of family life'. The power differences between men and women can be considered 'sexual politics'.

A distinction is often made between two types of power:

- Authority is power which is accepted as legitimate (fair and right) by those without power. We obey those with authority because we accept they have the right to tell us what to do.

- Coercion is that type of power which is not accepted as legitimate by those without power, as the power-holders rule without the consent of those they govern. People only obey because they are forced to by violence or the threat of violence.

In this chapter, the focus will be on the political system in society as a whole – the extent to which individuals can influence the decisions of governments, the policies of the political parties, and the factors which affect the way people vote. A key question will be to what extent Britain can be regarded as a democratic society.

ACTIVITY

1 Look at the following situations (below and at top of opposite page) where people are using their power in modern Britain. In each case, briefly explain whether they are using authority or coercion and give reasons for your answer. Be warned – some may involve bits of both authority and coercion, and so it may be worth discussing your answers with someone else.
- A white police officer who stops and searches people simply because they're black, and then arrests them for objecting.
- A traffic warden who gives someone a parking ticket for illegal parking.
- A school pupil who beats other pupils up if they won't give him or her money.

- ■ A teacher in a school who puts a student in detention for not doing his or her homework.
- ■ A couple who beat their children because they won't do as they're told.
- ■ A prime minister who orders his or her detectives to clear a restaurant of other customers so he or she can eat in peace.
- ■ A manager who tells workers to stop chatting and get on with their work.
- ■ A man who beats his wife because she displays too much independence.
- ■ A prison officer who puts a prisoner in solitary confinement for refusing to follow orders.

2 Depending on your answers to the activity above, explain in relation to each example how the use of coercion might be changed into authority, or how authority might become coercion. You may not find this is possible in every case.

3 What are the circumstances which influence whether the use of power is seen as fair or not?

TYPES OF POLITICAL SYSTEM

There are differences between societies in the amounts of power ordinary people have to influence government decisions, and these differences are shown in two opposing political systems: totalitarianism and democracy. While these two are presented as opposing systems, most political systems will fall somewhere between the two. It will be seen later, for example, that even in Britain, often seen as the 'home' of democracy, aspects of totalitarianism remain.

Totalitarianism

Totalitarianism is a system of government where society is controlled by a small powerful group – an elite – and ordinary people lack any control over government decision-making. There are no free elections and no civil liberties, and most of the features found in a democracy do not exist. The government rules by coercion rather than consent. People are forced to obey the government because of its control of the police, the courts, and the army. All the major social institutions, like the economy, the education system, religion, the legal system, the police, and the mass media, are strictly controlled by the government. Ideas opposed to those of the government are censored, and any opposition organizations crushed by force. Examples of totalitarian societies include Hitler's Germany and the People's Republic of China ('Communist' China).

A dictatorship is a form of totalitarianism where power tends to be concentrated in the hands of one person, such as Hitler.

Democracy

Democracy is a system of government which basically involves 'government of the people, by the people, for the people', where ordinary people have some control over government decision-making. It is impractical for everyone in society to be permanently and directly involved in political decision-making, so often representatives are elected to represent people's opinions – such as MPs (members of parliament) and local councillors in Britain. This is known as representative or parliamentary democracy, and is found in Britain, France, Germany, the other countries of the European Union, and the USA. Electing representatives is an important part of a democracy. However, a democratic society usually includes many other features to ensure that representatives can be replaced if they follow unpopular policies and that people can freely express their opinions. Figure 7.1 illustrates the main features of a democracy.

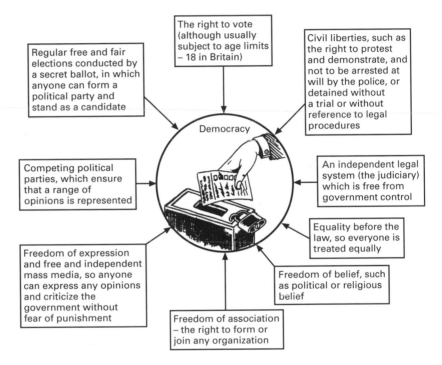

Figure 7.1 The features of a democracy

CITIZENSHIP

Citizenship is about the legal, social, civil, and political rights and responsibilities of individual citizens in a democratic society. Figure 7.1 and table 7.1 show what these citizenship rights and responsibilities mean.

In Britain in recent years there has been more emphasis placed on citizenship, as fewer and fewer people are turning out in elections, many people are not engaged in the lives of their communities, and many fail to exercise the democratic rights and responsibilities they have as citizens. The European Convention on Human Rights was incorporated into English law in 1998 as the Human Rights Act. This spelt out and protected citizens' rights, and citizenship is now a compulsory part of the National Curriculum for secondary age students.

Table 7.1 Citizenship

Area	Examples of rights	Examples of responsibilities
Legal	The right to a fair trial, a lawyer, and freedom from police harassment and arbitrary arrest; a wide range of laws protecting consumers	Legal responsibilities, like paying taxes, doing jury service, and obeying the law
Social	State-funded healthcare, education, and other welfare state services	Participating in the life of the community, getting involved in local issues and protests, looking out for the interests of the most vulnerable, and taking responsibility for one's actions
Civil and political	These include all the political and civil rights shown in figure 7.1	Going out to vote in elections, making sure politicians do what they said they'd do when elected (or trying to stop them), and protesting if they fail to do so

ACTIVITY

1 With reference to figure 7.1 and table 7.1, identify three political rights that people have as citizens in contemporary Britain.

2 Identify three social responsibilities that people might have as citizens.

3 On the basis of figure 7.1 and table 7.1, write a brief description of the 'perfect' citizen.

4 Go to <www.dfes.gov.uk/citizenship> and identify five things that students are expected to be able to understand and do as a result of following citizenship courses at school.

5 Identity the ways that Britain might be regarded as a democratic society according to figure 7.1. To what extent do you think it is true that everyone has equal rights as citizens and the same amounts of power and influence in society?

POLITICAL PARTIES IN BRITAIN

A political party is a group of people organized with the aim of forming the government in a society. In a democracy, the existence of a range of political parties is essential if voters are to have a choice of candidates and policies to choose from. The discussion below covers the major parties in Britain which put up candidates for election to local councils, the British Parliament at Westminster, or the European Parliament in Strasbourg.

The Labour Party

The Labour Party was founded in 1906, and is today one of the two main political parties in Britain. Traditionally the Labour Party placed great emphasis on state ownership and workers' control of key sectors of the economy, such as the banks, insurance companies, and all the major industrial companies, and on a very strong commitment to the welfare state, the ending of poverty, and support for trade unions. These policies traditionally meant the party was seen as the defender of working-class interests.

In the early 1990s, many of the Labour Party's traditional policies were reviewed and changed, with the party adopting policies which it was thought would have more appeal to voters. These new policies coincided with the Labour Party relaunching itself as 'New Labour', and appealing to all social classes rather than mainly the working class.

These new policies clearly succeeded with the voters. The Labour Party took power for the first time in eighteen years after winning the 1997 general election with a landslide victory, with the largest number of MPs of any party since 1945 and the largest number in the party's history. This success was repeated in 2001.

The 'centre' parties

The 'centre' parties have policies which traditionally fell between those of Labour and the Conservatives, but all the main parties seem to be increasingly sharing similar policies, differing only in detail rather than their general approach.

- The *Liberal Democrats* were founded in 1988, and they are today the main 'third party' in British politics. As well as having 53 MPs in 2003, they also have considerable influence in local government.

- The *Green Party* mainly campaigns around environmental issues, and draws support from a wide range of people who are more concerned about this than any other political issue. There is also some evidence it attracts support from those who wish to register a 'protest vote' against the other parties.

The Conservative (Tory) Party

The Conservative Party is a very long-established political party, and is today one of the two main parties in British politics. The Conservative Party gets the bulk of its funds from big business, and draws much of its traditional support from the upper and middle classes and private business. After its crushing defeats in the 1997 and 2001 general elections, the Conservative Party began to review its policies, to try to present a more caring and compassionate image, with policies likely to have more appeal to voters.

The policies of the main political parties are constantly changing, and the best way to explore the differences between the parties, and to see what their latest policies are, is to find out for yourself by doing the following activity.

ACTIVITY

1   To find out about the policies of the different political parties, go to their websites below. Take one area of interest to you, such as the environment, the welfare state, education, poverty, or the family, and see what the parties have to say. You will probably find their policies on these issues in their election manifestos. Note any differences between them, and explain which groups of people the different policies might appeal to.

2   Explore briefly some other issues, and see if you can find things that might explain why many working-class people have traditionally voted Labour, while many middle-class people have traditionally voted Conservative.

Labour Party: <www.labour.org.uk>
Conservative Party   <www.conservatives.com>
Liberal Democrats   <www.libdems.org.uk>
Green Party   <www.greenparty.org.uk>

INFLUENCES ON VOTING BEHAVIOUR

You would expect people to vote in elections purely on the issues, and on the policies held by the different parties. Some argue that 'issue-voting' has become more important in recent years, but research suggests that the political party for which people decide to vote is the result of a range of factors. Party policies are, surprisingly, a relatively minor factor among them.

The family

As a major agency of socialization, the family plays an important role in political socialization or the formation of an individual's political beliefs. Political socialization in the family, along with the other factors considered below, often means an individual will have an attachment to a particular political party, making them more 'receptive' to some views rather than others. Many people tend to share the general political beliefs and attitudes of their parents, and continue to support the political party their parents did.

Geographical area

Voting patterns seem to be associated with the geographical area in which people live. Those in the north of England, Scotland, Wales, and inner-city areas are more likely to support the Labour Party. Those in the southern parts of England and rural areas have traditionally been more likely to support the Conservative Party. This could be because of social class differences between these areas, with higher numbers of traditional working-class people, more unemployment, and social deprivation in areas supporting Labour.

Ethnic origin

The ethnic group to which people belong appears to have an influence on their voting habits. Black and Asian people have traditionally been more inclined to support the Labour Party than other parties. This is because

Labour has traditionally had more sympathetic policies on immigration and race relations, and is more concerned with reducing the racial discrimination, social deprivation, and unemployment which minority ethnic groups are more likely to encounter.

Religion

Religion is not a particularly important influence on voting in most of the United Kingdom, although members of the Church of England have traditionally been more likely to support the Conservative Party. Non-Christians (mainly members of minority ethnic groups), Roman Catholics, and those without a religion are more likely to vote Labour.

In Northern Ireland voting coincides almost exactly with the divisions between Protestants and Catholics, with Protestants supporting parties which support union with Britain, and Catholics supporting parties sympathetic to a united Ireland.

Party images and party leaders

Most people have general impressions or images of what the political parties stand for, and evidence suggests the way most people vote is influenced by this 'party image' and by whether a party appears to be the best one to handle issues like health, education, and the economy, rather than by knowledge of what the actual policies of the political parties are. For example, working-class people might vote Labour because it presents a more 'caring' image, supporting the NHS and education, and appears more sympathetic to the needs of the poor and disadvantaged than the 'uncaring' Conservatives, who seem to support big business and the well-off, and promote self-interest over the needs of the wider community.

Party images (this page and opposite)
Photos: Ted Fussey

The personalities of party leaders often have an important role in forming these images of parties and whether people vote for them – for example, whether they come across as 'likeable', honest, caring, intelligent, decisive, and 'attractive'. This is perhaps why political parties, during election campaigns, often concentrate more in their advertising and television broadcasts on presenting particular images or impressions of themselves and their leaders (such as 'caring', 'efficient', and 'friendly') rather than on explaining what their actual policies are.

The mass media

The mass media are major agencies of socialization, and have important influences on people's general beliefs and opinions. Chapter 8 shows how many of the mass media tend to present a very conservative view of society – generally supporting the 'establishment' and the way things are currently organized in society. This helps to create a long-term climate of opinion that favours the mainstream political parties at the expense of smaller parties that might want to make radical changes. In the 1997 and 2001 general elections, most newspapers – some for the first time ever – rallied behind the Labour Party, rather than the Conservative Party they had traditionally supported.

Because newspapers tend to put forward a particular political opinion, many people see them as unreliable sources of evidence, and turn to the television instead. There is little evidence to suggest that party political broadcasts on television have much influence in changing people's voting habits, except in cases when people find it difficult to make up their minds which way to vote. Floating voters are those with no fixed political opinions, who therefore regularly switch votes between parties from one election to the next. It is these voters who are most likely to be influenced by the media, and it is at these floating voters that many TV party election broadcasts are aimed.

The mass media and voting: key findings

◼ Where people already have established political views, the mass media are more likely to reinforce those views than to change them.

◼ People tend to be selective in their choice of programmes and newspapers and they only see and hear what they want to. They will either choose those that present information which confirms their existing opinions and avoid those that conflict with them, or reject those aspects which do not conform with their existing ideas. For example, there are committed Labour voters who might read a Conservative-supporting newspaper like the *Daily Mail*, but ridicule Conservative election broadcasts and ignore the paper's Tory politics.

◼ While in general the media are unlikely to change people's voting behaviour in the short term (such as in the run-up to a general election), they might be effective in changing attitudes over a longer period of time. For example, they might gradually change people's perception of a particular party or political leader. The *Sun* claimed in 1997 that 'It was the Sun wot swung it' (for Labour) by rallying behind Labour leader Tony Blair. However, an NOP/BBC poll in 1997 showed that over half of voters had decided how they would vote even before the election campaign had begun. This suggests that claims like those of the *Sun* – that newspapers can influence voters – are overstated, and newspapers are only likely to be of marginal importance in changing voters' minds, though this could be significant if election results are very close.

◼ The mass media are most likely to be influential on issues and parties which are new to people and about which people have little knowledge or experience.

◼ Floating voters are those most likely to be influenced by the media, particularly by party political broadcasts on television.

◼ Most of the media have, in the long run, supported the Conservative Party. This can create a long-term climate of opinion where more people are favourable to the Conservatives, and where opposition parties stand at a disadvantage. However, this support for the Conservatives from the media was much less in the 1997 and 2001 general elections, when there was much more support for Labour.

THE 'SPIN DOCTORS'

'Spin doctors' really came into prominence in the 1990s in Britain, particularly in the 1997 general election. Spin doctors are people who, in general, work for political parties. Their job is to manipulate the media by providing a favourable slant to a potentially unpopular or controversial news item. The term comes from the idea of 'spinning' a ball in sport to make it go in the direction you want it to. The aim of spin doctors is to grab favourable headlines (or ones damaging to other parties) in newspapers, or sound bites on TV and radio. By getting across their version of policy, controversy, and events, in stories fed to ever more demanding journalists, they hope to make the media put across a good party image to voters.

Former Iraqi information minister Mohammed Saeed al Sahhaf was nicknamed 'Comical Ali' for his 'spin-doctored' insistence in 2003 that the American and British invasion of Iraq was being crushed, at the same time as American troops were fighting their way to a military victory just one mile away from where he was speaking in Iraq's capital city Baghdad

Social class

Social class has traditionally been the single most important factor influencing the way people vote, though this has been of declining importance since the 1970s. In Britain, the Labour Party has traditionally been seen as the party with policies representing the interests of the working class, and many working-class people have tended to vote Labour. In contrast, the Conservatives have been associated with the interests of the middle and upper classes.

However, not all working-class people vote Labour, and not all middle-class people vote Conservative. Traditionally about one-third of the working class have voted Conservative, and about one-quarter of the middle class have voted Labour. In the elections between 1979 and 1992, even more manual workers than this voted Conservative, with more skilled manual workers voting Conservative than Labour in the 1987 and 1992 elections. The link between class and voting is illustrated in table 7.2 over the page. Working-class people who vote Conservative, and middle-class Labour voters, have traditionally been called deviant voters, because they are not conforming with the traditional voting habits of other people in their class, and seem to be voting against the party representing the interests of their class. Why do they do this?

Table 7.2 How the social classes voted for the three main parties: British general elections, 1987–2001

| | 1987 | | | 1992 | | | 1997 | | | 2001 | | |
| | Con. | Lab. | Lib. Dem. | Con. | Lab. | Lib. Dem. | Con. | Lab. | Lib. Dem. | Con. | Lab. | Lib. Dem. |
Class[a]	%	%	%	%	%	%	%	%	%	%	%	%
AB	56	13	31	55	23	22	40	33	22	43	34	22
C1	48	25	27	50	29	21	25	49	20	31	47	21
C2	43	36	21	41	40	19	24	56	14	32	56	11
DE	32	47	21	31	55	14	19	62	14	28	54	15

[a]See chapter 2 on 'Defining class by occupation' for details.
Source: Calculated from Ivor Crewe, 'Why did Labour lose (yet again)?', *Politics Review*, September 1992; 1997 data from BBC/NOP exit polls, *Sunday Times*, 4 May 1997; British Election Study, 2001

Working-class Conservative voters

Deference voters

Working-class deference voters are those who see members of the upper and middle class as superior in 'breeding', coming from 'better families', and making better 'natural leaders' than those from their own class. The Conservative Party contains these sorts of people, and therefore it is supported. Such voters tend to be older, be female, and have lower incomes. They are found in manual occupations where individuals are isolated from other workers, work close to their bosses, and 'know their place'. Such groups might include farmworkers, domestic servants, and those working in very small businesses.

ACTIVITY

Refer to table 7.2 and answer the questions that follow:

1 Which two social classes were least likely to support the Labour Party in 1987 and in 2001?

2 Which social classes in the table make up the working class? (Refer to chapter 2 if you're not sure.)

3 In which social class did support for the Labour Party increase the most between 1987 and 2001?

4 Which party increased its support in all social classes between 1987 and 2001?

5 In which social class did support for the Conservative Party decline the most between 1987 and 2001?

6 What evidence does the table show that the Conservative Party has traditionally been more likely to be supported by the middle class, and the Labour Party by the working class?

7 What evidence is there in the table that in the 1997 election the Labour Party succeeded in attracting more middle-class voters than at any other time between 1987 and 2001? Give evidence from the table to back up your answer.

Pragmatic voters

Pragmatic (or practical) working-class Conservative voters are those working-class people who have an instrumental attitude to voting, and will support whichever party offers them the greatest personal gain, such as more money, lower taxes and mortgage rates, and a higher standard of living. They are therefore motivated by pragmatic or practical reasons. Such voters will support the Conservative Party only so long as they feel it has more practical benefits to offer them than those of other parties.

This pragmatic, instrumental attitude means such voters have no particular party loyalty. They are more volatile, which means they are more likely to switch votes if another party offers them better personal benefits. Such workers tend to be those found in the 'new' working class, which was discussed in chapter 3.

Since the 1970s, the numbers of the traditional working class which provided the secure base of Labour support have declined, and the new 'pragmatic', instrumental part has expanded to become the largest section of the working class. This has meant that while the bulk of support for the Labour Party still comes from the working class, fewer working-class people are committed to supporting Labour. Even in the 'landslide' Labour victories of 1997 and 2001, working-class support for the Labour Party was just 56 per cent among skilled manual and 62 and 54 per cent among semi- and unskilled workers.

No longer can the Labour Party automatically rely on support from the majority of the working class, because most of them are now part of the volatile and pragmatic 'new' working class. From 1979 until Labour's victory in 1997, the Conservatives proved successful in persuading this expanding group that they had more benefits to offer than the Labour Party, and the new working class provided much of the working-class support for the Conservative Party in the general elections between 1979 and 1992. However, the Conservatives lost this support in the 1997 and 2001 elections.

The new 'pragmatism' among working-class voters suggests that social class is becoming of much less importance in affecting the way people vote than it has traditionally been, particularly where the Labour Party is concerned.

Middle-class Labour voters

About one-quarter of the middle class have traditionally voted Labour against what would appear to be their middle-class interests. These voters are most likely to be found in three main occupational groups:

- Those in the 'caring' welfare professions, like teachers and social workers, tend to vote Labour because their daily work brings them into contact with the disadvantaged and their problems, and they feel the Labour Party is more likely to tackle such issues.

- Those who have experienced upward social mobility from working-class backgrounds may vote Labour out of a sense of loyalty to their origins.

■ Routine clerical workers who are facing proletarianization may support Labour because they see their living and working conditions getting worse, and their social status declining.

Volatility, dealignment, and the expansion of the middle class

The pattern of voting in Britain since the 1970s suggests three major related changes have occurred:

■ The electorate has become more volatile – voters of all social classes are less committed to any one political party, and are more willing to change the party they vote for if another party offers them better personal benefits. People are voting more for their own self-interest rather than out of party loyalty, and on the basis of a party's policies and how well they perform, or might perform, in government. Voters have less loyalty to any one party, and the support of voters swings to and fro between different political parties.

■ There is no longer a clear alignment (a matching up) of particular social classes with one of the two main parties – in particular, the working class is no longer clearly aligned with the Labour Party, but neither is the middle class with the Conservatives. Most voters no longer show loyalty to a party according to their social class. Dealignment (a mismatch) between class and voting has occurred.

■ The middle classes have grown in size, now making up around half of the population. This means any party that wishes to win power and form a government has to get support from both the working class and the middle class. This need to appeal to middle-class voters was one of the reasons for the Labour Party dropping many of its traditional policies in the early 1990s, and remodelling itself as 'New Labour'.

ACTIVITY

1 If there were a general election tomorrow, which political party would you vote for? Give reasons for your answer, explaining carefully what influenced you in making your decision.

2 Figure 7.2 summarizes the key influences on voting behaviour that sociologists have identified. In the light of the exercise above, how far do you think the findings of sociologists confirm or deny your view? Which influences do you think are the most important?

WHY DO PEOPLE ABSTAIN IN ELECTIONS?

About 40 per cent or more of the electorate in general elections, and as many as 70 per cent or more in local elections, abstain – they fail to vote. Disadvantaged groups, such as the least educated and the poor, and younger and old people are the most likely groups to abstain from voting. In marginal seats, where the difference between the votes of the parties is very small – sometimes as little as one or two votes – abstention can actually swing the election result.

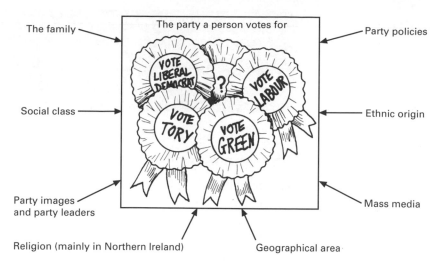

Figure 7.2 Factors influencing the way people vote

Aside from factors such as apathy, forgetfulness, bad weather, being away on holiday, or being kept in by illness (without a postal vote), people may make a positive decision to abstain for several reasons:

- In safe seats, where there has traditionally been a large majority for one party, voters may not feel it is worth voting since the outcome of the election is so predictable.

- It may be there is no candidate standing from the party people would normally vote for, or they may not support or understand the policies of any of the different parties. In 1997, an estimated two million former Conservative voters abstained, withdrawing their support from the Conservative Party, but unable to bring themselves to vote for any other party.

- Some voters might simply think elections are a waste of time, since the policies of all the parties are too similar and 'elections don't change anything anyway'. In such circumstances they may not bother to vote at all as a protest.

OPINION POLLS AND ELECTIONS

Opinion polls are social surveys which try to find out people's attitudes on many issues, and they are widely used to discover how people intend to vote in elections. They most commonly involve face-to-face interviews in the street, but telephone polls are becoming more popular in Britain.

The results of opinion polls provide the basis for reports about the 'state of the parties' which are regularly published in the newspapers, and in election periods polls are conducted daily.

ACTIVITY

1 Go to <www.mori.com/polls>, identify four recent opinion polls, and describe what these surveys found. You can search and find topics that interest you. Also make a note of the number of people who were questioned.

2 To what extent do you think public opinion polls give a true picture of what the public is thinking? Give reasons for your answer.

Why opinion polls are sometimes inaccurate

Opinion polls use sophisticated sampling techniques to obtain representative samples of the voting population. Often they can predict the outcome of elections accurately from asking no more than about 1000–1500 people. This is because the group they have questioned is a good representative cross-section of the entire population in terms of factors such as age, sex, social class, and geographical spread around the country. However, sometimes the opinion polls fail to predict the results of elections accurately (see the box on the polling disaster of 1992).

The reasons for this are quite varied, and many possible explanations are discussed in chapter 17 on the general problems of sampling and survey methods. Some possible problems with opinion polls are outlined below.

■ They may not contain a representative sample of voters, which may lead to inaccurate results. This happened in 1992 (see box).

■ Interviewer bias may mean people give inaccurate answers. People in face-to-face interviews may give the answer that they think is socially acceptable rather than what they really believe. For example, they may say they are prepared to pay higher taxes for better education and health care, but privately prefer (and vote for) tax cuts. There may be a sharp contrast between what people say to pollsters and what they actually do when it comes to voting. If a party is unpopular at the time, its supporters may be reluctant to admit to interviewers they support it – as happened with the 'silent and shy' Conservatives in 1992.

■ The format and wording of questions may affect the results of the poll. For example, respondents prefer to agree rather than disagree with statements which are put to them.

■ People may change their minds during the course of the election campaign, after the poll is conducted, when they have heard more arguments and have had more time to make up their minds. Because of this, opinion polls are likely to become more accurate the closer they are to the day of the election.

■ Some of those interviewed may decide not to vote, or are not registered to vote because they are not on the electoral register, so when it comes to the actual election, this will distort the opinion poll's predictions.

THE OPINION POLLS DISASTER OF 1992

The polls got their predictions of the election results badly wrong in 1992 . . .

Political party	Predicted result %	Actual result %
Labour	39	35
Conservative	38	43
Liberal Democrat	19	18
Others	13	14

The 1992 general election has gone down in history as the one that the opinion polls got wrong – never before had the polls been so far adrift from the actual election result. The polls predicted a small Labour victory of about 1 per cent, but the final result was a Conservative victory of about 8 per cent. An inquiry by the Market Research Society found three main reasons for this disastrous failure by the opinion polls:

1 There was a last-minute swing to the Conservatives which the opinion polls didn't pick up.

2 Those who refused to state their voting intention or said 'don't know' were more likely to be Conservative voters – the so-called 'silent and shy' Conservatives.

3 There were errors in the way the samples were selected (see chapter 17 for a discussion of sampling techniques). Samples were biased towards the lower social classes, who are more likely to be Labour voters.

The pollsters did a variety of things to overcome these errors, including:

■ Moving away from face-to-face interviews to telephone interviews. These help to overcome interviewer bias, and there is some evidence people are more honest over the telephone.

■ Changing their sampling techniques (from quota to random sampling – see chapter 17).

■ Marking 'don't knows' on the basis of the party they voted for in the previous election, who they said would make the best prime minister, which party they thought would run the economy best, and so on.

. . . but the pollsters got it right in 2001.

Political party	Predicted result %	Actual result %
Labour	45	41
Conservative	30	32
Liberal Democrat	18	18
Others	16	19

■ Opinion polls might themselves change the way people decide to vote and therefore the results of the election. This was thought to have happened in 1992, when the polls were predicting either a small Labour victory or possibly a 'hung' Parliament (where no party has overall control). This prediction may have persuaded some people to vote Conservative at the last moment to stop a predicted Labour victory.

How opinion polls might influence the results of elections

There is some evidence that opinion polls might not simply reflect voters' opinions, but actually help to form and change them, and therefore affect the eventual election results. For example, if the polls predict a large win for one party, its supporters may not bother to vote, making them complacent and thinking that it is a safe seat and the result a foregone conclusion. This could possibly result in that party actually losing the election if too many of its supporters did this. This complacency, created by the opinion polls, might cost a party an election victory.

If the polls predict that a certain party is going to win by a large margin, then supporters of another party which has no chance of winning might decide to vote for a third party in the hope of defeating the predicted winning party. This is known as tactical voting. An example might be committed Labour voters in a safe Tory seat, where Labour stands no chance of winning. If the opinion polls show that a Liberal Democrat is in second place, then Labour voters may decide to vote for the Liberal Democrat in the hope of defeating the Tory.

A final influence of opinion polls might be the *bandwagon effect*. If the polls show one party to be in the lead, people may want to 'jump on the bandwagon' and be on the side of what they think will be the winning party.

Because opinion polls can affect the results of elections, some people have actually suggested that they are banned immediately before elections, as in France and Germany, where polls are not allowed in the last seven days of election campaigns.

INFLUENCING DECISION-MAKING IN A DEMOCRACY

There are a number of ways individuals can influence the decision-making process in a democracy, or protest against policies adopted or proposed to be implemented. Joining a political party is an obvious way, which enables them to take part in formulating the policies of that party, which may eventually become government policy if the party wins a general election.

The existence of competing political parties, combined with free elections and freedom of speech, means that parties must represent a range of interests if they are to be elected or to stay in power: the need to attract voters means parties have to respond to the wishes of the electorate. Voting is the most obvious way ordinary people can influence political decisions, and is an important part of their responsibilities, as well as their rights, as citizens. A further method is by writing to their local MP or councillor to try to have their concerns taken up, or by writing to the press and using public opinion to put pressure on elected politicians. However, individuals on their own have limited power, and the most effective way of influencing decision-making is to join together with others concerned about the same issue, by forming or joining a pressure group, or identifying themselves with a new social movement (see below).

Protest movements

Every form of government needs some level of popular support if it is to stay in power, and government policies may not succeed when people show widespread resistance to them. When governments seek to implement unpopular policies, they are likely to encounter protest movements of various kinds, as people exercise their rights as citizens to influence political decision-making. Pressure groups and new social movements are the most common means of expressing protests against particular policies, or urging governments to adopt policies they favour.

Pressure groups

Pressure groups are organizations which try to put pressure on governments, councillors, and others with power to implement policies which they favour, or to prevent unpopular policies from being implemented. Pressure groups, which are sometimes called interest groups, are important in a democracy as channels for the representation of interests and opinions which might otherwise be forgotten or ignored by those with power. They therefore help to keep political parties and governments in touch with the opinions of the citizens who elected them, and are an important means for people to exercise their citizenship rights and participate in the political process.

There are two main types of pressure group.

■ *Protective or defensive groups* are concerned with defending the shared interests of their membership. Examples of these groups include the AA (the Automobile Association), Help the Aged, the NSPCC, trade unions and professional associations, and employers' organizations like the CBI (the Confederation of British Industry).

■ *Promotional groups* are concerned with promoting a particular cause rather than protecting the interests of a particular group. Examples include ASH (Action on Smoking and Health), the Child Poverty Action Group (concerned with raising welfare benefits), environmental action groups like Greenpeace and Friends of the Earth, and animal rights groups like the Animal Liberation Front. Some of these pressure groups, like Friends of the Earth or Greenpeace, are also likely to take part in the wider activities and actions of new social movements as well.

PRESSURE GROUPS AND POLITICAL PARTIES

Pressure groups differ from political parties in three main ways:

■ They do not try to take power themselves by having their members elected to Parliament and forming a government.

■ They do not claim to represent the interests of everyone, but only the particular concerns of some sections of the population.

■ They are generally concerned with only one issue or a group of related issues rather than the wide range of issues on which political parties have to form policies.

Table 7.3 gives examples of some pressure groups in Britain and indicates what the aims of each group are.

Table 7.3 Examples of pressure groups in Britain

Organization	Aim
Protective or defensive groups	
Automobile Association (AA)	To protect the interest of motorists
Age Concern	To campaign on matters of concern to the elderly and to promote dignity and quality of life for the retired
National Society for the Prevention of Cruelty to Children (NSPCC)	To protect children who are deprived, neglected, or at risk of abuse
Confederation of British Industry (CBI)	To protect and promote the interests of British business and the private enterprise system
British Medical Association (BMA)	To protect and promote the interests of doctors
Law Society	To protect and promote the interests of lawyers
Trades Union Congress (TUC)	To protect and promote the interests of affiliated trade unions and the economic and social conditions and rights of workers

Table 7.3 (continued)

Organization	Aim
National Union of Teachers (NUT)	To protect and promote the interests of teachers and children in schools

Promotional groups

Action on Smoking and Health (ASH)	To promote opposition to tobacco smoking
Child Poverty Action Group (CPAG)	To promote action for the relief of poverty among children and families with children and to campaign for higher welfare benefits
Electoral Reform Society	To secure the use of the single transferable voting system in all elections and to establish proportional representation
Greenpeace	To protect the environment and the ecological balance of the earth
Shelter	To provide assistance to the homeless and promote changes in housing policy to eliminate homelessness and poor housing

New social movements

Another way of influencing decision-making in a democracy, exercising citizenship rights to protest, and the citizenship responsibility of social and political participation, is through individuals identifying and involving themselves with a new social movement (NSM).

DEFINITION	A new social movement (NSM) is a broad movement of people who are united around the desire to promote, or block, a broad set of social changes in society. Unlike political parties or pressure groups, they are often only informally organized through a network of small, independent, locally based groups.

There are two main types of NSM:

- *Defensive NSMs* are concerned with defending a natural or social environment seen to be under threat, such as animal rights, the environment, or world peace.

- *Offensive NSMs* are concerned with establishing, defending, or extending citizenship rights to those who, to some degree, are denied them through institutional discrimination and marginalization. Examples of these include the anti-racist, women's, and gay movements.

New social movements often gain support from men and women of all social classes and ethnic groups, with a wide range of different beliefs and values. It has been suggested that NSMs represent political activity by the non-powerful, the non-wealthy, and the non-famous.

New social movements have emerged over issues like opposition to war, damage to the environment, human rights and civil liberties, and globalization.

DEFINITION	Globalization refers to the growing interdependence of societies across the world, with the spread of the same culture and economic interests across the globe. For instance, media and consumer products are often produced for a world market, by the same firms running businesses all over the world. Examples of globalization might include the way British Telecom call-centres for the UK are located in low-waged India, and Nike trainers produced at low cost in the Far East are sold for huge profits in western countries.

New social movements often become the focus for an individual's definition of himself or herself, their self-expression and identity, such as an 'environmentalist', an 'eco-warrior', an animal rights activist, an anti-racist, or gay. This identity may influence people's lifestyles, such as what they eat, the clothes they wear, the social activities they enjoy, and the general values they hold. The gay movement, for example, includes a whole gay lifestyle, of clothes, clubs, consumer products, and music. The 'pink pound' (the spending money of gay people) is now seen as a major market for advertisers and producers of all kinds of products.

Table 7.4 shows some of the typical concerns of new social movements, and examples of them.

Table 7.4 New social movements

Main focus	Some typical issues	Examples
Environment	Global warming; sustainable energy; genetically modified (GM) crops and foods; incineration of household waste	The movement against GM crops and foods, including the destruction of fields where such crops are being grown
Human and civil rights	Discrimination against minority ethnic groups, women, gays, etc.	Gay movement; women's movement; anti-racist movement
Globalization	Concern over the way the interests of a small number of American and European multinational firms seem to be dominating the world's economy and culture, and destroying local businesses and local culture, and exploiting cheap labour. Examples of such firms include Nike, Coca Cola, and McDonalds	Large and often violent demonstrations against gatherings of the world's richest nations, like those in Seattle (USA) in 1999, Genoa (Italy) in 2001, and Evian (Switzerland) in 2003
World peace	Keeping world peace, stopping international conflicts and Western countries using their military power to bully other less developed countries	Stop the War movement (2003) – against the invasion of Iraq by the USA and Britain

STOP THE WAR

The 'Stop the War' coalition in 2003, against the invasion of Iraq by Britain and the USA, was the largest coordinated political protest ever seen, with over two million people protesting on the streets of London, and many millions more across the world. These people were drawn from all sections of society, and the Internet allowed tiny groups with virtually no resources to mobilize millions of people, through websites and e-mails to press and supporters, enabling protest to spread across the globe like a Mexican wave. The Internet has enabled such new social movements to engage with people in a way the conventional political parties have failed to do, and has proven to be a key means of mobilizing support for a social protest movement.

NEW SOCIAL MOVEMENTS, POLITICAL PARTIES, AND PRESSURE GROUPS

New social movements differ from political parties and pressure groups in several ways:

- They have support from a much wider social background, with greater proportions of young people. Supporters are more likely to be involved in a range of new social movements and alternative lifestyles. NSMs are often found at peace and music festivals, like Glastonbury.

- They more commonly have international connections with other movements through the Internet.

- They are more likely to operate outside the existing political framework, and use more unconventional and sometimes illegal tactics, such as civil disobedience, demonstrations (sometimes violent), and direct action, like protesters blocking roads, breaking up meetings, and destroying animal testing laboratories.

- They cover a range of issues, rather than just the single issues of many pressure groups.

- They often focus on world issues, not just national ones.

- They are often an important part of an individual's identity and lifestyle, like the gay movement.

- They are less likely to have full-time staff and a formal national organization, and are more likely to work through the active involvement, commitment, and participation of supporters through a network of local groups, linked through the Internet.

- They are generally involved in more frequent and on-going protests.

- They are more likely to use the Internet as a means of communication and for rallying support and coordinating action (see 'Stop the War' box).

1 Go on the Internet, and try to find out about any *one* new social movement. Study the website, and see if you can guess what kind of people the site seems to be aimed at.

2 With reference to the box 'New social movements, political parties, and pressure groups', describe how far the NSM you have studied fits with the features of a NSM described there.

You may find the following websites a useful *starting* point, but be prepared to explore the sites and follow any links – remember, there is not one but a network of many groups involved in new social movements.

Environment:	<www.greenpeace.org.uk>
	<www.foe.co.uk>
Human and civil rights:	<www.liberty-human-rights.org.uk>
	<www.equalitynow.org>
	<www.stonewall.org.uk>
	<www.uk.gay.com>
Globalization/world poverty:	<www.globalpolicy.org>
	<www.oxfam.org.uk>
	<www.newint.org>
	<www.adbusters.org/home>
Animal rights:	<www.animalliberation.net>
The countryside:	<www.countryside-alliance.org>
Peace:	<www.stopwar.org.uk>
	<www.peacenews.info>

Methods used by pressure groups and new social movements

There is a range of methods used by pressure groups and new social movements to influence public opinion, political parties, and governments.

■ Contributions to the funds of political parties; for example, trade union support to the Labour Party or contributions to the Conservative Party by industry. The large contribution of the big brewers to Conservative Party funds encouraged the Conservative government in 1989 to abandon proposals aimed at eliminating the monopoly of the large breweries on pubs. Donations by the Formula One motor racing industry to the Labour Party in 1997 encouraged the Labour government to weaken proposals to ban tobacco advertising and sponsorship in motor racing. These are clear examples of powerful and wealthy pressure groups in action.

■ Lobbying MPs, government ministers, and local councillors. This means going to the entrance hall or lobby of the House of Commons or local MPs' or councillors' 'surgeries' to put the group's case.

■ Sponsorship of MPs: paying their election and other expenses in exchange for their support in the House of Commons. Trade unions and the Police Federation do this.

■ Advertising in the mass media.

- Setting up an Internet website

- Leafleting and poster campaigns.

- Organizing petitions or opinion polls to show how much support they have.

- Holding public meetings.

- Letter-writing or e-mail campaigns to newspapers, local councillors, and MPs.

- Demonstrations.

- Organizing mass campaigns, such as those against new road building, or the campaign against genetically modified crops in the 2000s.

- Civil disobedience – breaking the law to bring attention to their cause. This kind of tactic is used by the Animal Liberation Front when it breaks into laboratories and releases animals used for experiments in scientific research. In the late 1990s, tunnelling under new airport and road sites to stop development became a popular tactic for a time.

- The use of shock tactics. These might include the use of shocking and distributing images, like teddies covering their eyes so they cannot witness child abuse (used by NSPCC), or images of dead animals (used by the RSPCA), to attract the public's attention.

- Strikes, to bring economic pressure on the government to change its policies.

- The provision of expertise. Pressure groups, particularly, often have specialized knowledge gathered through research which they can put at the disposal of the government, giving them a direct influence on government policy. For example, the Child Poverty Action Group, Shelter, and the CBI are all providers of expert knowledge to governments.

- The use of the legal system to challenge or review decisions made by those with power. Examples might include the use of the Human Rights Act and the European Court of Human Rights and other legal routes to challenge and change government decisions.

ACTIVITY

Imagine that you wanted to campaign against something, such as the proposed closure of a local school, plans to build a new airport or road, or plans to build a waste incinerator in your area. Choose any issue you like, and plan out how you might organize a campaign to achieve your aims. Think carefully of how you might get people together and all the activities you might engage in to influence those with power. What obstacles, including money, might you find in carrying out a successful campaign?

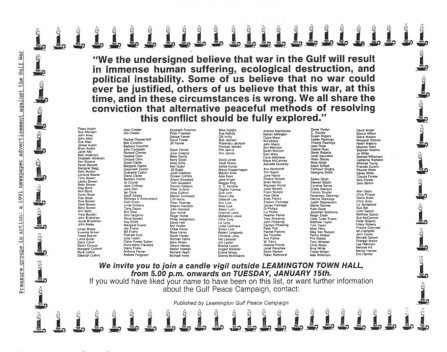

Pressure groups in action: a 1991 newspaper advertisement against the Gulf War

Protest groups in action

Clockwise from top: proposed school closure in Warwickshire; the poll tax; building Rugby airport; the second war on Iraq; the first war on Iraq

Source: Leamington Spa Courier; <worldrevolution.org.uk>

Are all protest groups equally effective?

Pressure groups and new social movements are important in a democracy as a means of representing a wide range of interests and influencing those with power. However, there are a number of criticisms of the effectiveness of such groups in influencing power-holders.

- Not all interests are represented through pressure groups and new social movements, and not all groups in the population are equally capable of forming them. Disadvantaged groups like the poor, the unemployed, minority ethnic groups, the disabled, the mentally ill, and the old often lack the resources or education to make their voices heard. Substantial wealth and education mean some groups can run more effective campaigns to make their demands heard, such as employers' organizations like the CBI.

- Not everyone has the same chance of meeting top decision-makers. Getting to see decision-makers is far easier if you are from the same social class background. 'Friends in high places' and the 'old boys' network', which is considered in the discussion of public schools in chapter 11, mean that the interests of the upper and middle classes are generally more effectively represented than those of the working class or marginalized groups.

- Some groups holding key positions in the economy are able to bring pressure to bear on the government through strike action. For example, railway workers or petrol tanker drivers can cause widespread disruption by strike action, and so are more likely to get action on their grievances than, say, old age pensioners or students.

These factors are of some concern in a democracy, as not all protest groups have the same amount of influence. Some interests get represented more effectively than others and some interests may not be represented at all.

IS BRITAIN A DEMOCRACY?

Earlier in this chapter you may have discussed whether Britain is a democracy or not. Much of this chapter has emphasized the democratic features of modern Britain, and if you look back to figure 7.1, then you may agree that many of the features listed there are indeed to be found in modern Britain. However, there are a number of weaknesses in British democracy.

Non-elected rulers

Democracy is meant to involve governments reflecting the interests of the people through elected representatives. However, the House of Lords and the monarchy are not elected, but both have considerable power in controlling which laws are passed. Unelected and unaccountable quangos (quasi-autonomous non-government organizations) have taken over many public services, in areas such as health, training, and further education.

The voting system

Voting in the UK is by the first-past-the-post system, under which the party that gets most votes in any constituency (voting area) wins that constituency. In general elections, the representative of the winning party becomes the constituency's MP, and the party getting the most MPs forms the government. This means governments are often elected which represent only a minority of voters in the country as a whole. In fact, every government in Britain since 1945 has been elected with the support of less than half of the voting population. Figure 7.3 shows that in the 2001 general election, the number of MPs elected for each party in no way represented the parties' share of the votes in the country as a whole. Such circumstances mean that, while minority parties might collect a lot of votes in the country as a whole, they get few MPs, or none at all, in Parliament and therefore no representation. Proportional representation – which means the number of MPs elected for each party reflects the share of the vote received – would ensure that minority parties and interests were more adequately represented. Figure 7.3 also shows the number of MPs that might have been elected for each party in 2001 if perfect proportional representation had been adopted.

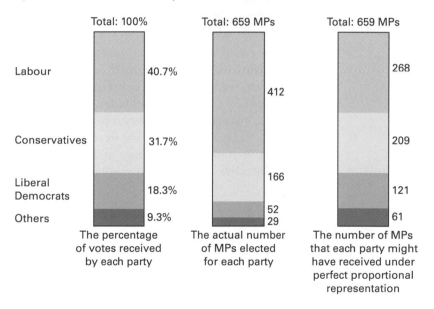

Figure 7.3 General election results: United Kingdom, 2001

Elite rule

As seen in chapter 4, wealth remains highly concentrated in the hands of a small upper class, which therefore has a major influence in economic decision-making. For example, this class can decide where factories should be located and whether they should be opened or closed down, and it can control the workforce through hiring and firing. Democratically elected governments cannot afford to ignore this power, as they might face rising unemployment and other social problems if the upper class decided not to invest its money.

Most of those in the top elite jobs which wield power and influence in this country come from public school and upper- and upper-middle-class backgrounds (see chapter 12 on this). Even among Labour MPs, less than a quarter come from working-class backgrounds. This raises questions about the extent to which working-class interests are adequately represented.

Unequal protest groups

As seen earlier in this chapter, not all interests are represented through protest groups, and some groups have a lot more wealth and power than others. It is the voices of the disadvantaged and the poor which are least likely to be heard, and it is they who are most likely to try to make their voices heard through new social movements.

Deciding the issues

The political parties – not the population as a whole – often decide what the important issues are and which ones they are going to fight elections around. The mass media are mainly privately owned, controlled by a rich and powerful minority, and have a conservative bias. They have an important role in forming 'public opinion' and, like political leaders, can decide the issues around which elections are fought.

The points raised above suggest that perhaps Britain is not quite as democratic as many people might believe, and that not everyone gets an equal chance to express her or his opinions and influence decision-making. This is likely to be true particularly of those holding radical opinions who want to change the way society is presently organized. While democracy in Britain has many strengths and freedoms which must be defended, it also has its limitations. The interests of democracy are perhaps best served by removing the limitations and reinforcing the strengths.

CHAPTER SUMMARY

After studying this chapter, you should be able to:

- Explain briefly what is meant by the terms 'power', 'authority', 'coercion', and 'politics'.

- Describe and explain the main features of a democracy, and how democracy differs from totalitarianism and dictatorship.

- Explain what is meant by 'citizenship' and identify some rights and responsibilities associated with it.

- Identify the main political parties in Britain which put up candidates in elections, and briefly describe some of their main policies.

- Discuss the range of factors influencing voting behaviour.

- Discuss how the mass media might influence political attitudes.

- Explain what is meant by 'deviant voting' and explain both working-class and middle-class deviant voting.

- Explain why social class is becoming of less importance in influencing voting.

- Suggest reasons why people abstain in elections.

- Explain why opinion polls might sometimes fail to predict accurately the outcome of elections.

- Explain how opinion polls might themselves affect election results.

- Identify ways that people can influence power-holders in a democracy.

- Explain what pressure groups are and how they differ from political parties.

- Describe, with examples, two types of pressure group.

- Explain what is meant by a new social movement, with examples, and explain how they differ from political parties and pressure groups.

- Describe the methods protest groups use to influence those with power.

- Explain why some interests are better represented by protest groups than others.

- Discuss the extent to which Britain might be regarded as a democracy.

KEY TERMS

authority
citizenship
coercion
dealignment
democracy
deviant voter
dictatorship
floating voter
globalization
new social movement
political party
politics
power
proportional representation
quango
tactical voting
totalitarianism

COURSEWORK SUGGESTIONS

1   Study the aims and activities of a local or national pressure group, or new social movement, interviewing members of the group and studying its literature and reports in newspapers. What methods does the group use to influence public opinion and how effective or successful is the group?

2   Carry out an opinion poll on the attitudes of students, workmates, or members of the public to the different political parties, their policies, and their leaders.

3   Carry out a survey among a sample of people of different ages and/or sexes and/or social classes, asking about their attitudes to some current political issue of major importance. Are there any differences between different groups?

4   Ask a sample of people what factors they think have the most influence on the way they vote, or the way they would vote if they are under voting age.

5   Carry out an opinion poll in your school, college, or workplace including the question, 'If there were a general election tomorrow, for which party would you vote?' Compare your findings with those of a current national opinion poll.

8 The Mass Media

THE POWER OF THE MEDIA: KEY QUESTIONS

The term 'mass media' refers to forms of communication which are directed at large mass audiences without any personal contact. The main media of mass communication include television, radio, newspapers and magazines, books, cinema, videos and DVDs, advertising, CDs, video games, and the Internet.

In Britain, 97 per cent of the population watch television, with those over 16 spending nearly half of all free time watching it. Around thirteen million newspapers are sold every day. The media have become important sources of information, entertainment, and leisure activity for large numbers of people, and they have become key agencies of secondary socialization and informal education. Most people will base their opinions and attitudes, not on personal experience, but on evidence and knowledge provided by newspapers and television. What we see, hear, or read in the media often has important influences on our identity – how we see ourselves and how others see us. For example, people often use the media to confirm or explore their identities, values, and interests, such as finding out and keeping up with the latest social attitudes, or trends in fashion, music, cooking, or gardening.

KEY ISSUES

- The power of the media: key questions.
- Formal controls on the media.
- Ownership of the mass media.
- Newspaper readership and social class.
- The mass media, public opinion, and social control.
- Bias in the media: what affects the content of the media?
- Stereotyping and the media.
- Crime, deviance, and the media.
- The effects of the media.
- Violence and the media
- The mass media and democracy.
- Into the future.

ACTIVITY

1. Work out approximately how many hours in a typical week you spend watching television or videos, listening to the radio or music, reading books, newspapers and magazines, or at the cinema.

2. Work out approximately how many hours a week you spend sleeping.

3. There are 168 hours in a week. Take away the number of hours you spend sleeping from this total. Now work out what percentage of your waking life you spend under the direct influence of the mass media (you can do this by dividing the number of hours spent watching TV, etc., by the number of waking hours and multiplying by 100).

4. List all the ways you think the mass media influence you in your life, such as your lifestyle and identity, knowledge about current affairs, attitudes and opinions, tastes in music and fashion, roles of men and women, etc.

You may have found from the previous activity that you spend a great deal of time under the direct influence of the mass media. You may also have found that the mass media provide the source of many of your ideas and opinions about the world.

If most of our opinions are based on knowledge obtained second-hand through the mass media, then this raises the important issue of the power of the mass media to influence our lives. Most people think and act in particular ways because of the opinions they hold and the knowledge they have, and many would agree that an 'informed' opinion – based on evidence – is the best opinion. However, do the mass media inform us about everything, and do they stress certain things in more favourable ways than others? Do they give false impressions of what is happening in society? The main mass media are privately owned and controlled, and run to make a profit. What effect does this pattern of ownership and control have on the content of the media? Does it create bias in them? What are the implications of this in a democracy? These are the sorts of questions which have interested sociologists and which will be explored in this chapter.

FORMAL CONTROLS ON THE MEDIA

Although the mass media in Britain are formally free to report whatever they like, and the state and government have no power in normal times to stop the spreading of any opinions through censorship, there are some formal limits to this freedom. The government and the state have a number of direct and indirect controls over the mass media, particularly television and radio, and there are also other 'regulators' of the mass media.

The law

The law restricts the media's freedom to report anything they choose in any way they like. The principal legal limits to the media's freedom are shown in the box below.

LEGAL LIMITS TO THE MEDIA'S FREEDOM

■ *The laws of libel* forbid the publication of an untrue statement about a person which might bring him or her into contempt, ridicule, dislike, or hostility in society.

■ *The Official Secrets Acts* make it a criminal offence to report without authorization any official government activity which the government defines as an official secret. These are extremely wide-ranging Acts, which are meant to protect the 'public interest'. However, many people argue they are often used to protect the political interests of governments.

■ *Defence or 'D' notices* are issued by the government as requests to journalists not to report certain news items which the government believes to be 'against the national interest'. These usually concern military secrets and other information which might be useful to an 'enemy'.

■ *The Race Relations Acts* forbid the expression of opinions which will encourage hatred or discrimination against people because of their race.

■ *The Obscene Publications Act* forbids the printing of anything that the high court considers to be obscene and indecent, and likely to 'deprave and corrupt' the public.

■ *Contempt of Court* provision forbids the reporting and expression of opinions about cases which are in the process of being dealt with in a court of law. This is to prevent the jury forming opinions about a case from what they see or hear in the mass media, before they have heard the evidence for themselves.

Ofcom

Ofcom (Office of Communications) is the main regulator of the mass media in the UK, with responsibilities across television, radio, telecommunications, and wireless communications services. This has responsibility for:

- Furthering the interests of consumers.

- Securing the best use of the radio spectrum.

- Ensuring that a wide range of television, radio, electronic media, and communications networks are available in the UK, with high-quality services having a broad appeal.

- Protecting the public from any offensive or potentially harmful effects of broadcast media, and safeguarding people from being unfairly treated in television and radio programmes.

ACTIVITY

Go to <www.ofcom.org.uk>, and identify and briefly describe four issues that Ofcom is currently dealing with.

The BBC

The BBC is largely a state-owned body, which is controlled by a board of governors whose members are appointed by the Home Secretary, and regulated by Ofcom. The BBC is financed by the state through the television licence fee, plus income from a series of private spin-off companies, which top up the licence fee income with substantial profits. The state can therefore have some control over the BBC by refusing to raise the licence fee. Although the BBC is not a private business run solely to make a profit like the independent commercial broadcasting services (independent TV and radio), and is not dependent on advertising for its income, it still has to compete with commercial broadcasting by attracting audiences large enough to justify the licence fee.

Independent broadcasting

Independent broadcasting includes all the non-BBC television and radio stations. These are regulated by Ofcom, which licenses the companies which can operate in the private sector, and is responsible for the amount, quality, and standard of advertising and programmes on independent television and radio, and for dealing with any complaints.

The Press Complaints Commission

The Press Complaints Commission is a voluntary body appointed by the newspaper industry itself to maintain certain standards of newspaper journalism. It deals with public complaints against newspapers, but it has no real power to enforce effective sanctions as a result of these complaints.

Table 8.1 Who owns what: national newspaper group ownership and some of their interests in publishing and television, United Kingdom, 2003

Company	Share of national daily newspaper circulation % (September 2003)	National newspapers	Also owns
News International	32.5	Sun, The Times, News of the World, Sunday Times	40% of BSkyB; HarperCollins book publishers
Trinity Mirror	19.8	Daily Mirror; Sunday Mirror; Daily Record; People; Sunday Mail	Over 250 regional newspapers
Daily Mail and General Trust	18.5	Daily Mail, Mail on Sunday	Second-largest regional newspaper owners, with over 100 papers, including London's Evening Standard; 90% of Teletext; 20% of ITN; Performance TV
Northern and Shell/Portland Investments	14.8	Daily Express, Express on Sunday, Daily Star	OK! magazine, Fantasy channel; various porn magazines and websites
Telegraph Group (part of Hollinger International)	7.1	Daily Telegraph Sunday Telegraph	Spectator
Pearson	3.0	Financial Times	Longman and Penguin book publishers
Guardian Media Group	2.9	Guardian, Observer	Over 40 local newspapers
Seven companies	98.6		

Source: Data from Audit Bureau of Circulation; corporate websites

OWNERSHIP OF THE MASS MEDIA

The mass media are very big business. The ownership of the main mass media in modern Britain is concentrated in the hands of a few large companies, which are interested in making profits. This concentration of ownership is shown in table 8.1.

Of the total circulation of national daily and Sunday newspapers, 86 per cent is controlled by just four companies, and over half by two companies (News International and Trinity Mirror). One individual, Rupert Murdoch of News International, owns the Sun and The Times, newspapers which make up about 33 per cent of all national daily newspaper sales in Britain. Rupert Murdoch alone accounted for about 33 per cent of the total daily and Sunday newspaper sales in 2003. As table 8.1 shows, this concentration extends also to other areas of the media, such as TV, and book and magazine publishing. The details of who owns what are continually changing, but in 2003 Rupert Murdoch, for example, also owned 40 per cent of BSkyB and all of HarperCollins, the world's largest English-language book publisher. The same few companies therefore control a wide range of different media, and therefore a large proportion of what we see and hear in the media. This concentration of ownership gives a lot of power to business people who are neither elected nor accountable to the public.

ACTIVITY

Explain why the concentration of ownership of the mass media might be of some concern in a democracy (refer to the previous chapter if you're not really sure what a democracy is).

Rupert Murdoch of News Corporation is now the world's most powerful media owner, with substantial interests in TV satellite broadcasting, film and newspaper, magazine, and book publishing across the world

NEWSPAPER READERSHIP AND SOCIAL CLASS

There are noticeable social class differences in newspaper readership, as shown in table 8.2 on page 167.

Newspapers can be separated into three main groups: the 'quality' newspapers, the 'middle-brow' newspapers, and the mass-circulation 'popular' newspapers, also called the tabloid press. The middle class are far more likely to read the 'quality' newspapers, and the manual working class make up the main readership of the 'popular' newspapers, particularly the *Sun*, *Daily Mirror*, and *Daily Star*. The *Daily Express* and *Daily Mail* are aimed primarily at the 'middle-brow' middle class, but have readers drawn from the whole social spectrum.

'QUALITY' NEWSPAPERS

The 'quality' newspapers are large in size (though the Independent and The Times launched tabloid versions at the end of 2003) and serious in tone and content. They are concerned with news and features about politics, economic and financial problems, sport, literature, and the arts, and give in-depth, analytical coverage in longer articles and news stories. The main 'quality' national daily newspapers in Britain are The Times, the Guardian, the Daily Telegraph, the Independent, and the Financial Times.

The **Guardian**

THE INDEPENDENT

FINANCIAL TIMES

The Daily Telegraph

THE TIMES

'MIDDLE-BROW' NEWSPAPERS

These fall between the 'quality' and the 'popular' newspapers, and include features of each. While they tend to have a more serious tone and content than the 'popular' press, they also cover a range of the more colourful issues found in the 'popular' papers and are of the tabloid type (small in page size). The Daily Mail and the Daily Express are the main 'middle-brow' papers.

Daily Express

Daily Mail

'POPULAR' NEWSPAPERS

In contrast to the 'quality' newspapers, 'popular' newspapers are of the small-size tabloid type, and are generally referred to as the tabloid press. Although they carry 'news', they are much more likely to concentrate on the sensational aspects of the news, 'human interest' stories, such as scandals and celebrities, entertainment, sport, and other 'light' topics, written in very simple language combined with large headlines and many colour photographs. The 'popular' national daily newspapers in Britain are the Daily Mirror, the Sun, and the Daily Star.

Study table 8.2 and answer the following questions:

1 What percentage of readers of the *Sun* were from social class C2 in 2003?

2 Which two daily newspapers had the largest percentage of their readers in class A?

3 Which two daily newspapers had the largest percentages of working-class readers?

4 What was the difference in the percentages of those in social classes A and E who read the *Guardian*?

5 Which Sunday newspaper had the largest percentage of its readers from social class E?

6 Compare one 'quality' and one 'popular' newspaper for the same day. Study the kinds of stories, advertisements, photographs, and cartoons, and the language they use. List all the differences between them. In the light of your findings, suggest explanations for the different social classes of their readerships.

Table 8.2 Reading of national daily and Sunday newspapers: by social class, April 2002 to March 2003

Newspaper	Social class of readership (percentages)					
	A	B	C1	C2	D	E
Daily newspapers:						
Sun	1	9	25	30	24	10
Daily Mirror	0.7	11	26	29	23	11
Daily Star	1	9	24	32	26	8
Daily Express	3	24	33	23	12	5
Daily Mail	4	27	34	19	11	4
Daily Telegraph	13	45	28	8	4	2
The Times	14	48	25	7	4	2
Guardian	9	53	25	8	4	2
Independent	12	52	23	6	6	1
Financial Times	14	53	25	6	2	0.5
Sunday newspapers:						
News of the World	1	10	25	28	25	11
Sunday Mirror	1	12	28	26	24	9
Mail on Sunday	5	28	34	19	11	3
People	1	9	24	30	26	10
Sunday Times	13	50	25	8	3	2
Sunday Express	3	24	36	21	11	5
Sunday Telegraph	14	44	27	10	4	2
Observer	8	50	27	8	5	2
Independent on Sunday	9	49	25	8	6	2

Source: National Readership Surveys Ltd

Table 8.3 How believable are the media? Newspaper readers' sources of news, and how far they believe them

Readers' attitudes	%
Main source of news	
Television	59
Newspapers	30
Radio	15
Most believable source of news	
Television	57
Newspapers	15
Radio	15
'The reporting is exactly or approximately in line with what really happened'	
Television	85
Newspapers	48
Radio	79
'The reporting is undoubtedly different from what happened or bears no relation to the event'	
Television	13
Newspapers	44
Radio	12

Sources: Adapted from *British Social Attitudes Survey* and *Sofres* for Télérama/La Croix

ACTIVITY

Study table 8.3 and answer the following questions:

1 Which of the mass media did newspaper readers use as their main source of news?

2 What percentage of newspaper readers used newspapers as their main source of news?

3 What percentage of newspaper readers saw television as the most believable source of news?

4 What percentage of newspaper readers saw newspapers as a more believable source of news than television?

5 Which medium did newspaper readers see as providing (a) the most truthful account of events and (b) the least truthful account of events?

6 Suggest reasons why most newspaper readers don't use newspapers as their main source of news and see them as less believable than television.

7 Do a small survey in your group based on the areas covered in table 8.3, and discuss the reasons why people see some of the media as more truthful than others.

THE MASS MEDIA, PUBLIC OPINION, AND SOCIAL CONTROL

The mass media play a key role in providing the ideas and images which people use to interpret and understand much of their everyday experience, and they actively shape people's ideas, attitudes, and actions. The mass media therefore have an important role in forming public opinion. The pressure of public opinion can be a significant source of social control, in so far as most people prefer to have their behaviour approved of by others rather than feel isolated and condemned by them.

The survey results in table 8.3 show that most people do use and believe the mass media, particularly television, as their main source of news. However, their reliance on such sources may be misguided. This is because the mass media don't simply show 'the facts' on which people can then form opinions. They select facts and put an interpretation on them, frequently stressing the more conservative values of society. The mass media can then be said to act as an agency of social control. They carry this out in two main ways: agenda-setting and gate-keeping, and norm-setting.

Agenda-setting and gate-keeping

Agenda-setting is the idea that the media have an important influence over the issues that people think about because the agenda, or list of subjects, for public discussion is laid down by the mass media.

Obviously, people can only discuss and form opinions about things they have been informed about, and it is the mass media which provide this information in most cases. This gives those who own, control, and work in the mass media a great deal of power in society, for what they choose to include in or leave out of their newspapers and programmes will influence the main topics of public discussion and public concern. This may mean that some subjects are never discussed by the public because they are not informed about them.

The media's refusal to cover some issues is called gate-keeping. Such issues are frequently those potentially most damaging to the values and interests of the upper class. For example, strikes are widely reported (nearly always unfavourably), while industrial injuries and diseases, which lead to a much greater loss of working hours (and life), hardly ever get reported. This means that there is more public concern with tightening up trade union laws to stop strikes than there is with improving health and safety laws. Similarly, crime committed by black people gets widely covered in the media, but little attention is paid to attacks on black people by white racists. This tends to reinforce people's racial prejudices. A final example is the way welfare benefit 'fiddles' are widely reported, but not tax evasion, with the result that there are calls for tightening up benefit claim procedures, rather than strengthening agencies concerned with chasing tax evaders.

Norm-setting

Norm-setting means the mass media emphasize and reinforce conformity to social norms, and seek to isolate those who do not conform by making them the victims of unfavourable public opinion. This is achieved in two main ways:

- *Encouraging conformist behaviour*, such as not going on strike, obeying the law, being brave, helping people, and so on. Advertising, for example, often reinforces the gender-role stereotypes of men and women.

1 Study the main newspaper headlines or major television or radio news stories for a week. Draw up a list of the key stories, perhaps under the headings of 'popular newspapers', 'quality newspapers', 'BBC TV news', 'ITN news', and 'radio news' (this is easiest to do if a group of people divide up the work). You might also research these on the web, using the following sites:

<www.bbc.co.uk>
<www.itn.co.uk>
<www.guardian.co.uk>
<www.timesonline.co.uk>
<www.thesun.co.uk>
<www.mirror.co.uk>

2 Compare your lists, and see if there is any evidence of agreement on the 'agenda' of news items for that week. If there are differences between the lists (check particularly the newspapers), suggest explanations for them.

■ *Discouraging non-conformist behaviour*. The mass media often give extensive and sensational treatment to stories about murder and other crimes of violence, riots, welfare benefit 'fiddles', football 'hooliganism', homosexuality, and so on. Such stories, by emphasizing the serious consequences which follow for those who break social norms, are giving 'lessons' in how people are expected *not* to behave. For example, the early treatment of AIDS in the mass media nearly always suggested it was a disease that only gay men could catch. This was presented as a warning to those who strayed from the paths of monogamy and hetero-sexuality – both core values of British society.

Stan Cohen illustrates this idea of norm-setting very well in the following passage:

A large amount of space in newspapers, magazines and television and a large amount of time in daily conversation are devoted to reporting and discussing behaviour which sociologists call deviant: behaviour which somehow departs from what a group expects to be done or what it considers the desirable way of doing things. We read of murders and drug-taking, vicars eloping with members of their congregation and film stars announcing the birth of their illegitimate children, football trains being wrecked and children being stolen from their prams, drunken drivers being breathalysed and accountants fiddling the books. Sometimes the stories are tragic and arouse anger, disgust or horror; sometimes they are merely absurd. Whatever the emotions, the stories are always to be found, and, indeed, so much space in the mass media is given to deviance that some sociologists have argued that this interest functions to reassure society that the boundary lines between conformist and deviant, good and bad, healthy and sick, are still valid ones. The value of the boundary line must continually be reasserted: we can only know what it is to be saintly by being told just what the shape of the devil is. The rogues, feckless fools and villains are presented to us as if they were playing parts in some gigantic morality play. (Stanley Cohen, ed., introduction to *Images of Deviance*, Penguin 1982)

ACTIVITY

1 How is deviance defined in the quoted passage by Stanley Cohen?

2 What does the passage suggest is one of the functions of the mass media's interest in deviance?

3 Give examples from the passage of (a) two types of deviant behaviour which are not regarded as criminal in modern Britain, and (b) two types of deviant behaviour which are regarded as criminal in modern Britain.

4 Think of one example of deviance which is currently receiving a lot of attention in the mass media and is of major public concern. Explain how this might be reasserting the value of the 'boundary line' between conformist and deviant behaviour.

5 Look at a range of newspapers and try to find examples of norm-setting headlines and stories. Explain in each case what types of behaviour are being encouraged or discouraged.

BIAS IN THE MEDIA: WHAT AFFECTS MEDIA CONTENT?

Bias in the media is concerned with whether the media favour one point of view at the expense of others. The mass media obviously cannot report all events and issues happening in the world. Of all the events that occur in the world every day, how is 'news' selected? Who decides which of these events is 'newsworthy'? The 'news', like any other product for sale, is a manufactured product. What factors affect the production and 'packaging' of this product? What decides the content of the mass media? The processes of agenda-setting, gate-keeping, and norm-setting discussed above influence media content. The sections below discuss some of the other factors that influence the content of the media, and may cause bias in them. Figure 8.2 on page 176 summarizes these factors.

The owners

Sometimes the private owners of the mass media will impose their own views on their editors. However, even when the owners don't directly impose their own views, it is unlikely that those who work for them will produce stories which actively oppose their owners' prejudices and interests, if they want to keep their jobs. The political leanings of the owners and editors are overwhelmingly conservative.

Making a profit

The mass media are predominantly run by large business corporations with the aim of making money, and the source of much of this profit is advertising, particularly in newspapers and commercial television. It is this dependence on advertising which explains why so much concern is expressed about 'ratings' for television programmes, the circulation figures of newspapers, and the social class of their readers. Advertisers will usually advertise only if they know that there is a large audience for their advertisements, or, if the audience is small, that it is well off and likely to buy their products or services.

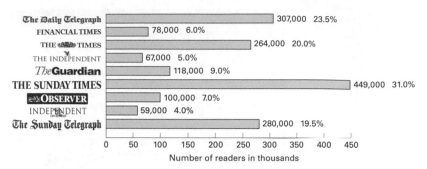

Figure 8.1 Quality newspapers read by business and professional people: United Kingdom, 2003

The percentages in the bars are the percentage share of all newspapers (national daily, or Sunday, as appropriate) read by social class A.

Source: Data from National Readership Surveys Ltd

That newspapers are very concerned about selling advertising is shown by their commissioning of readership surveys. Such statistics as those shown in figure 8.1 are important to newspapers because they help them to sell highly profitable advertising aimed at well-off business and professional people.

Advertising and media content

The importance of advertising affects the content of the media in the following ways:

■ Audiences or readers must be attracted. If they are not, then circulation figures or TV ratings will fall, advertisers will not advertise, and the particular channel or newspaper may go out of business. This means that what becomes 'news' is partly a result of commercial pressures to attract audiences by selecting and presenting the more colourful and 'interesting' events in society.

■ In order to attract the widest possible audience or readership, it becomes important to appeal to everyone and offend no one. This leads to a conservatism in the media, which tries to avoid too much criticism of the way society is organized in case it offends the readers or advertisers. This may mean that minority or unpopular points of view go unrepresented in the mass media.

■ It may lead to a distortion of the 'news' by concentrating on sensational stories, conflict, gossip, and scandal, which are more likely to attract a mass audience than more serious issues are. Alternatively, for those media which aim at a 'select' readership or audience from the upper- and upper-middle classes, it is important that the news stories chosen should generally be treated in a conservative way, so as not to offend an audience which has little to gain (and everything to lose) from changes in the existing arrangements in society.

News values and 'newsworthiness'

Journalists obviously play an important role in deciding the content of the mass media, as it is journalists who basically select what 'the news' is and decide on its style of presentation. News doesn't just happen, but is made by journalists. Research has shown that journalists operate with values and assumptions about which events are 'newsworthy' – these assumptions are called news values. These guide journalists in deciding what to report and what to leave out, and how what they choose to report should be presented.

Issues or events that are newsworthy include:

■ Issues that are easily understood.

■ Events that occur quickly or unexpectedly, such as disasters.

■ Events that involve drama, conflict, excitement, and action.

■ Events that are in some way out of the ordinary.

■ Events that have some human drama or interest to them, such as the activities of famous personalities, scandal, or armed sieges.

■ Events that are considered important – events in Britain are generally considered more important than those happening in the rest of the world, and national events are generally considered more important than local ones.

■ Stories which it is assumed will be of interest to the newspaper's readership or TV audience – giving the readers and viewers what they want. This is of great importance if the audience or readership is to continue to be attracted and viewing figures kept up or papers sold.

The idea of news values means that journalists tend to play up those elements of a story which make it more newsworthy, and the stories that are most likely to be reported are those which include many newsworthy aspects. These features affecting the content of the media suggest that the mass media present, at best, only a partial and therefore biased view of the world.

ACTIVITY

1 With reference to the list of factors making issues 'newsworthy' considered above, explain why the story in the cartoon on page 175 might be 'newsworthy'?

2 Take any current major news story which is receiving wide coverage in the mass media. List the features of this story which make it 'newsworthy'.

3 Study one 'quality' and one 'popular' newspaper of the same day and compare their coverage of this story. For example, do they sensationalize it and present new 'angles'? What evidence is there, if any, that the news values of the 'popular' press differ from those of the 'quality' press? Give examples to back up your answer.

4 Imagine you wanted to run a campaign to prevent a new road being built in your neighbourhood (or choose any issue that interests you). In the light of your expert knowledge about news values, suggest activities you might undertake to achieve media coverage of your campaign, and explain why they might be considered newsworthy.

The sudden death in a car accident of Diana, Princess of Wales, on 31 August 1997 was one of the most newsworthy stories ever. Her death dominated world newspaper and TV headlines for many days, and newspaper sales increased by up to 50 per cent. More than 31 million watched the funeral on television in Britain – three-quarters of the adult population – and an estimated one billion around the world, making it the biggest single televised event in history.

The terrorist attack on the 'twin towers' of the World Trade Center in New York on September 11, 2001, was another massive international news story. Two passenger aircraft were hijacked and deliberately crashed into the twin towers, causing both towers to collapse, and killing around 3000 people. This dominated world news for weeks and months afterwards.

Photos: Ted Fussey

News values

Selection

The processes of agenda-setting, gate-keeping, and norm-setting discussed earlier mean some events are simply not reported and brought to public attention. Some of those that are reported may be singled out for particularly unfavourable treatment. In these ways, the mass media can decide what the important issues are, what 'news' is, what the public should and should not be concerned about, and what should or should not be regarded as 'normal' behaviour in society.

The presentation of news

The way news items are presented may be important in influencing the way people are encouraged to view stories. For example, the physical position of a news story in a newspaper (front page or small inside column), the order of importance given to stories in TV news bulletins, the choice of headlines, and whether there is accompanying film or photographs will all influence the attention given to particular items. A story may be treated sensationally, and it may even be considered of such importance as to justify a TV or radio 'newsflash'. Where film is used, the pictures shown are always selected from the total footage shot, and may not accurately reflect the event. The actual images used in news films may themselves have a hidden bias. For example, in the reporting of industrial disputes, employers are often filmed in the peace and quiet of their

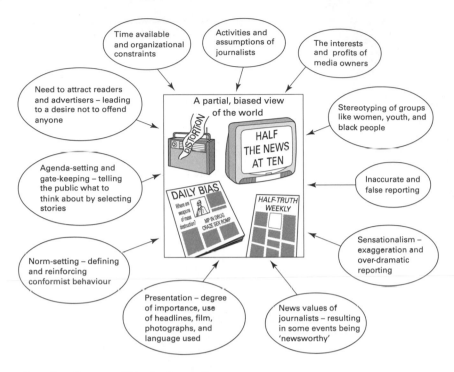

Figure 8.2 Sources of bias in the media

offices, while workers are seen shouting on the picket lines or trying to be interviewed against a background of traffic noise. This gives the impression that employers are more calm and reasonable people and have a better case than the workers.

The media can also create false or biased impressions by the sort of language used in news reporting. This bias in the use of language in newspaper reporting is shown in figure 8.3. This shows a number of expressions that were used by the British press during the first week of the 1991 (first) war against Iraq.

ACTIVITY

In figure 8.3, 'we' refers to the American, British, and other allied forces; 'they' refers to the Iraqis with whom 'we' were at war.

1 Explain with particular examples how the language used to describe Iraq differs from the language used to describe the allied forces. What general impression is given of the Iraqis?
2 Try to think of examples of other sorts of language used in newspaper stories and headlines which might give a distorted or biased impression – for example, animal rights activists being described as 'nutters'.

Inaccurate and false reporting

Other influences on media content, and possible sources of bias, lie in inaccurate reporting, because important details of a story may be incorrect. Politicians are always complaining that they have been inaccurately quoted in the press. False reporting, through either

Mad Dogs and Englishmen

We have . . .	**They have . . .**
Army, navy and air force	A war machine
Reporting guidelines	Censorship
Press briefings	Propaganda
We . . .	**They . . .**
Take out	Destroy
Suppress	Destroy
Eliminate	Kill
Neutralize	Kill
Decapitate	Kill
Dig in	Cower in their foxholes
We launch . . .	**They launch . . .**
First strikes	Sneak missile attacks
Pre-emptively	Without provocation
Our men are . . .	**Their men are . . .**
Boys	Troops
Lads	Hordes
Our boys are . . .	**Theirs are . . .**
Professional	Brainwashed
Lion-hearts	Paper tigers
Cautious	Cowardly
Confident	Desperate
Heroes	Cornered
Dare-devils	Cannon fodder
Young knights of the skies	Bastards of Baghdad
Loyal	Blindly obedient
Desert rats	Mad dogs
Resolute	Ruthless
Brave	Fanatical
Our boys are motivated by . . .	**Their boys are motivated by . . .**
An old-fashioned sense of duty	Fear of Saddam
Our boys . . .	**Their boys . . .**
Fly into the jaws of hell	Cower in concrete bunkers
Our ships are . . .	**Iraqi ships are . . .**
An armada	A navy
Israeli non-retaliation is . . .	**Iraqi non-retaliation is . . .**
An act of great statesmanship	Blundering/Cowardly
The Belgians are . . .	**The Belgians are also . . .**
Yellow	Two-faced
Our missiles are . . .	**Their missiles are . . .**
Like Luke Skywalker zapping Darth Vader	Ageing duds (*rhymes with Scuds*)
Our missiles cause . . .	**Their missiles cause . . .**
Collateral damage	Civilian casualties
We . . .	**They . . .**
Precision bomb	Fire wildly at anything in the sky
Our PoWs are . . .	**Their PoWs are . . .**
Gallant boys	Overgrown schoolchildren
George Bush is . . .	**Saddam Hussein is . . .**
At peace with himself	Demented
Resolute	Defiant
Statesmanlike	An evil tyrant
Assured	A crackpot monster
Our planes . . .	**Their planes . . .**
Suffer a high rate of attrition	Are shot out of the sky
Fail to return from missions	Are zapped

Figure 8.3 Mad dogs and Englishmen

Source: Guardian

completely making up stories or inventing a few details, and the media's tendency to dramatize events out of all proportion to their actual significance in society, typical of much reporting of the royal family, are devices used to make a story 'more interesting' and sell newspapers. This is particularly common in the mass circulation tabloid press. Such methods mean the media can be accused of manipulating their audiences.

Organizational constraints

Newspapers and TV programmes tend to work within quite tight time schedules – this is often a maximum 24-hour cycle in newspapers and even less in TV news programmes. This means that short cuts to news gathering may need to be taken, that inadequate evidence is collected to justify any conclusions drawn, and that stories aren't checked as carefully as they should be.

The assumptions and activities of journalists

The views and assumptions of journalists can have an important influence on media content – after all, they are the ones who actually write and report the news stories. Journalists tend to be mainly white, male, and middle class, and this influences whose opinions they seek for comment, what issues they see as important, and how they decide issues should be presented and explained to audiences. Journalists are likely to give greater importance to the views of powerful people, as their views appear more 'reasonable' to journalists, and they tend to ignore or treat less favourably what they regard as 'extremist' or 'radical' views.

Journalists are doing a job of work, and they like to keep their work as simple as possible. This means they often obtain information from news agencies, government press releases, 'spin doctors', public relations consultants, and so on. This means powerful and influential groups like businesses, the government, political parties, and those with power and wealth are more likely to be able to influence journalists.

All these features discussed above suggest that the mass media generally present, at best, only a partial and biased view of the world. The media stereotyping discussed below also contributes to giving biased impressions of some social groups.

STEREOTYPING AND THE MEDIA

Stereotyping of different social groups is a common feature of media coverage of events. Chapter 5 on gender-role socialization considered the way that gender stereotypes are formed and reinforced throughout the whole range of the mass media. Two other groups which are frequently victims of media stereotyping are young people and minority ethnic groups. These two groups are also often used as scapegoats for many of society's problems. Scapegoats are simply groups or individuals blamed for something which is not their fault.

Stereotyping of the young

The mass media often create a stereotype of young people as a 'problem group' in society – as trouble-makers, layabouts, and vandals. Exaggerating the occasional deviant behaviour of a few young people out of proportion to its real significance in society can generate exciting stories and sensational headlines that help to sell newspapers and attract TV viewers. The mass media provide for many people the only source of information about events, and therefore distort people's attitudes and give a misleading impression of young people as a whole. Old people, who tend to be more home-based, are particularly vulnerable to such stereotypes, as their impressions are formed very strongly by the media.

Folk devils and moral panics

In his book on the mods and rockers of the 1960s, *Folk Devils and Moral Panics*, Stan Cohen suggests that mass media stereotypes of young people, particularly where unusual or exceptional behaviour is involved, provide exciting stories and sensational headlines, and help to sell newspapers. He argues that young people have been used as a scapegoat to create a sense of unity in society, by uniting the public against a common 'enemy'. Young people are relatively powerless, and an easily identifiable group to blame for all of society's ills. Some young people who get involved in relatively trivial deviant or delinquent actions or groups, such as hooliganism, vandalism, or soft drug abuse, are labelled in the media as folk devils or groups posing a threat to society. (Labelling is defining a person or group in a certain way – as a particular 'type' of person or group.) This causes a moral panic in society – an overreaction suggesting that society itself is under threat. Editors, politicians, church people, police, magistrates, and social workers then 'pull together' to overcome this imagined threat to society. The folk devils become visible reminders of what we should not be. In this view, young people play much the same role as witches in the past – an easy scapegoat to blame for all of society's problems. As a result of these moral panics, all young people may then get labelled and stereotyped as potentially troublesome or as a 'problem group'.

ACTIVITY

Go to <http://groups.msn.com/TheSixtiesPleasureZone/yourwebpage6.msnw> and find out what you can about the mods and rockers in the 1960s. Suggest reasons, with evidence, why they might have been seen as folk devils causing a 'moral panic' in society.

'A paedophile? No, they've cornered a social worker!'

Stereotyping of minority ethnic groups

Black and Asian people are another social group which the mass media tend both to stereotype and to use as scapegoats. Minority ethnic groups make up only about 8 per cent of the population of Britain, yet frequently this small minority are presented in quite negative ways in the media, as if they were major causes of conflict and 'social problems' that otherwise wouldn't exist. Minority ethnic groups often only appear in the media in the context of 'trouble' of various kinds, and as scapegoats on which to blame social problems.

They are presented in a limited range of degrading, negative, and unsympathetic stereotypes, such as:

■ Law breakers, such as drug dealers, welfare fraudsters, and 'muggers' (committing street robbery with violence).

■ Low-paid workers.

■ People with a culture that is seen as 'alien' and a threat to British culture – a kind of 'enemy within', with immigration seen as a threat to the British way of life and the jobs of white workers.

■ People causing conflict and trouble, as in stories portraying racial problems.

■ People causing social problems, such as asylum seekers, immigrants (whether legal or illegal), rioters, welfare scroungers, lone parents, and so on, rather than as people with social problems like persecution, poverty, racial discrimination, poor housing, and being victims of racist attacks by white people.

■ People who often do well in sport and music, but are rarely portrayed as academic or professional successes.

■ People who have problems internationally – for example, who run their own countries chaotically, who live in famine conditions (images of starving babies), who are always having tribal conflicts, military coups, and so on, who need the white Western countries to help solve their problems for them.

Degrading stereotypes of black people are still frequently found in books, films, and comics. Little is heard about black people's successes and achievements, their history and culture, or about the discrimination and deprivation they often face in housing, employment, and education (see chapters 6 and 12). Attacks on black people by white racists rarely receive media coverage, and media attacks still stir up public hostility to minority ethnic asylum seekers. Such stereotyping may create, confirm, and reinforce racial prejudices about black people among whites, thereby reinforcing the racism which is deeply entrenched in British society, and leaving non-white minority ethnic groups to take the blame for problems that are not created by them at all.

However, it seems that the way minority ethnic groups are presented in the media is improving, with more positive media coverage and less stereotyping. There are more minority ethnic actors moving into more popular dramas and soaps, there are more black newscasters, and there are more programmes, TV channels, videos, and magazines being targeted at black audiences. In addition, black and Asian people are moving to satellite and cable TV faster than any other ethnic groups. This is particularly true among younger people, who are the fastest growing section of the ethnic minorities. This change is one TV networks need to take account of, if they are to retain viewers and therefore to justify the licence fee (in the case of the BBC) or to retain advertisers (in the case of commercial channels).

Do you think that the media still stereotype minority ethnic groups, young people, and women? While you are watching television (or reading newspapers or magazines, etc.) try to identify any stereotypes that you come across. Make notes on these examples, and discuss them with others in your group. What evidence, if any, can you point to that stereotyping is still occurring in the media?

CRIME, DEVIANCE, AND THE MEDIA

The mass media provide knowledge about crime and deviance for most people in society, including politicians, the police, social workers, and the public at large. The mass media tend to be very selective in their coverage of crime, exploiting the possibilities for a 'good story' by dramatizing, exaggerating, and sensationalizing some crimes out of all proportion to their actual extent in society. For example, attacks on old people and other crimes of violence – which are quite rare – are massively overreported, giving a false and misleading impression of the real pattern and extent of such crimes. This process can create many unnecessary fears among people by suggesting that violence is a normal and common feature of everyday life. This is particularly likely in the case of the housebound elderly. A Home Office report confirmed this view, arguing that TV programmes which stage reconstructions of unsolved crimes, such as the BBC's *Crimewatch*, exaggerate the level of dangerous crime and unnecessarily frighten viewers.

The media, labelling, and deviancy amplification

As seen earlier in this chapter, the media's pursuit of 'good stories' means they often distort, exaggerate, and sensationalize the activities of some groups. The media have the power to label and stereotype certain groups and activities as deviant, and present them as folk devils causing some imagined threat to society. Even if much of what is reported is untrue, this may be enough to whip up a moral panic – growing public anxiety and concern about the alleged deviance.

This can raise demands for action by the agencies of social control to stop it. Often these agencies, such as schools, social services, the police, and magistrates, will respond to the exaggerated threat presented in the media by taking harsher measures against the apparent 'trouble-makers'. Such action, particularly by the police, can often make what was a minor issue much worse, for example by causing more arrests, and amplify (or make worse) the original deviance. This is known as deviancy amplification. Groups which have fitted this pattern include mods and rockers in the 1960s and other youth sub-cultures, glue-sniffers, football 'hooligans', travellers on their way to Glastonbury or Stonehenge, and organizers of raves. Figure 8.4 illustrates the way the media can amplify deviance and generate a moral panic. Figure 8.5 on page 184 shows a range of moral panics which have arisen in Britain since the 1950s.

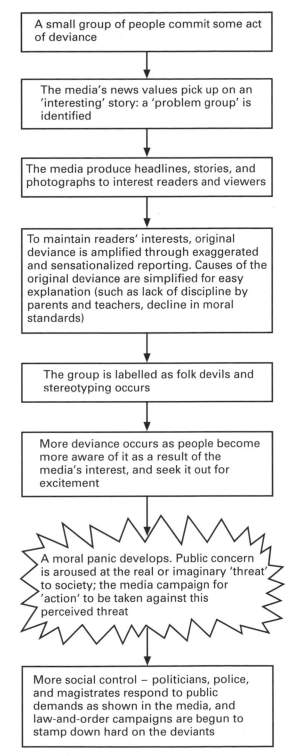

Figure 8.4 Deviancy amplification, moral panics, and the media

Study figure 8.4 and try to fill in each of the stages of any current moral panic in society

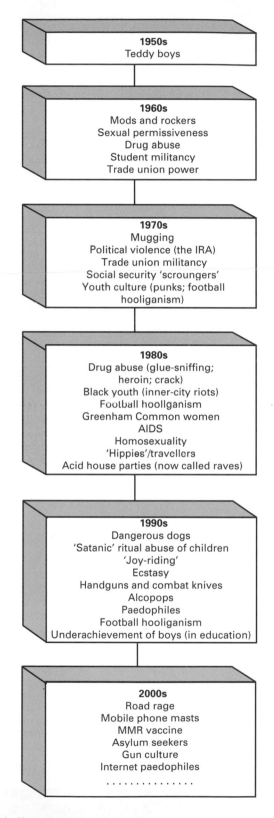

Figure 8.5 Folk devils and moral panics: United Kingdom, 1950s–2000s

THE EFFECTS OF THE MASS MEDIA

Much of this chapter suggests that the content of the media does have some effect on the audience. However, this cannot be taken for granted. People are conscious, thinking human beings, not mindless robots. They might not swallow everything they come across in the media, and they might respond in a variety of ways to what they read, hear, or see. For example, they might dismiss, reject, ignore, criticize, forget, or give a different meaning to a media message, and this is likely to be influenced by factors such as their own social experiences, ethnic origin, social class, gender, and so on. For example, a black person is likely to reject a racist message in a TV broadcast or newspaper report. It therefore becomes very difficult to generalize about the effects of the media.

We also need to be aware that the media is only one influence on the way people might think and behave, and there is a wide range of other agencies involved in people's socialization. People can form their own judgements on media content, and it would be somewhat foolhardy to suggest all behaviour can be explained by exposure to the media. Families, friends, schools, workplaces and workmates, churches, social class, ethnicity, gender, disability, age, and so on may all influence individual and group behaviour and attitudes. The question may then be not what the media do to people, but what people do with the media.

There are a number of different approaches that sociologists have adopted to the question of whether media content does actually have an influence or effect on audiences, mainly centred on the issue of whether audiences are passive dopes mindlessly consuming media content, or active interpreters of that content, giving it their own meanings and interpretations. These different approaches are summarized in table 8.4 on the next page.

Not everyone views the same media content in the same way

Table 8.4 The effects of the mass media on audiences

Approach	Features	View of media audience	Criticisms
The hypodermic syringe approach	The media act like a hypodermic syringe, injecting messages and content into the 'veins' of media audiences with immediate effects – e.g. seeing violence on television, and then going out and attacking someone.	Unthinking, passive, gullible and easily manipulated robots, who are unable to resist the 'drug' injected by the media.	Audiences don't all react the same way to the media – this will depend on their socialization and their own ideas. Little research evidence supports this view of the effects of the media.
The two-step flow approach	The media influences 'opinion leaders' (first step) – those whom others listen to and take notice of, like teachers, friends, or influential members of any social group. These 'opinion leaders' then influence audiences, passing on information and views they have picked up through the media (second step).	Relatively passive. The media don't have a direct effect on them, but they are influenced by the media's effect on opinion leaders.	It suggests that people are easily influenced by opinion leaders. It does not recognize that people may have views, opinions and experiences of their own on which to base their views of media content.
The uses and gratifications approach	This suggests the effects of the media will depend on what the audiences use the media for, and their own various pleasures and interests (gratifications). People use the media in different ways (e.g. for pleasure, information, relaxation, company, etc.) and the effects of the media are likely to vary accordingly.	Thinking, active, and critical human beings, not passive, easily manipulated robots. Many will only watch or read media that fit in with their existing views and interests (selective exposure), they will see or hear only that which fits in with their own views and interests (selective perception), and they will ignore or 'forget' material that is not in line with their views and interests (selective retention).	It underestimates the power and influence of the media and media companies to shape and influence the choices people make and the 'pleasures' they derive from the media.

ACTIVITY

1 Suppose you wanted to study the effects of a TV programme on an audience. Suggest how you might go about researching this.

2 Carry out a short survey finding out what use people make of the mass media in their daily lives – for example, for leisure, relaxation, information, background 'wallpaper' while doing other things, exploring and confirming their identities, and so on.

3 Identify four ways that you think you are influenced by the content of what you see or read in the media.

4 Refer to table 8.4. Which approach to the study of the effects of the media on audiences do you find most persuasive? Give reasons for your answer.

5 Explain briefly in your own words what is meant by each of the 'hypodermic syringe', 'two-step flow' and 'uses and gratifications' approaches to the effects of the media on audiences.

6 Explain in your own words, with examples, what is meant by each of 'selective exposure', 'selective perception' and 'selective retention'. The cartoon on page 185 may help you with this.

VIOLENCE AND THE MEDIA

Violent TV news reports, dramas, cartoons, films, videos, some Internet websites (including pornography), and computer games are now part of popular culture, and more people are exposed to such violence than ever before. Estimates suggest young viewers will see around 13,000 murders on television.

Such media violence is often blamed for increasing crime and violence in society. For example, in 1993, 2-year-old James Bulger was murdered by two 10-year-old boys. The judge in the case commented 'I suspect that exposure to violent video films may in part be an explanation.' Similar assertions that media violence generates real-life violence are commonplace, and a lot of research has been carried out to find out whether violent media content does cause people to behave violently themselves. However, despite all the research, there is little reliable and undisputed evidence about whether violence in the media leads to an increase in aggressive behaviour.

Much media violence is fictional, and there is a problem in defining what counts as 'violence'. Boxing and wrestling, fights in TV dramas, parents hitting children, police attacking protesters, shooting, news film of warfare, and many children's cartoons all depict violent scenes, but they are unlikely to have the same effects on every individual. Researchers and audiences may not all view scenes showing real-life violence, fictional violence, and cartoon violence in the same way.

As Tony Giddens has pointed out:

In crime dramas featuring violence (and in many children's cartoons) there are underlying themes of justice and retribution. A far higher proportion of miscreants are brought to justice in crime dramas than happens with police investigations in real life, and in cartoons harmful or threatening characters usually tend to get their 'just deserts'. It does not necessarily follow that high levels of the portrayal of violence create directly imitative patterns among those watching . . . In general, research on the 'effects' of television on audiences has tended to treat viewers – children and adults – as passive and undiscriminating in their reactions to what they see. (Anthony Giddens, *Sociology*, 4th edition, Polity)

1 Suggest a range of ways that people might interpret and respond to seeing violent content in the media – for example, switching the television off, treating it as harmless entertainment, or going out and beating someone up. You might find the approaches in table 8.4 of some use in getting ideas.

2 Do you think violence in the media is of any importance? For example, do you think that media violence over a period of time might make people more tolerant of real-life violence in society?

THE MASS MEDIA AND DEMOCRACY

Much of this chapter has suggested that the mass media act as a conservative influence in society, and give only a biased view of the world. However, some argue that the wealth of information provided by the mass media encourages and promotes a variety of opinions, and this enables the population to be informed on a wide range of issues, which is essential in a democratic society. The page opposite examines briefly some of the competing views on this aspect of the role of the mass media in modern Britain.

DISCUSSION

'That the mass media in Britain are owned by a small group of individuals who control the spread of ideas and information, and who are not elected or answerable to the public, means people's opinions are manipulated by a small minority. Far from promoting democracy, the mass media in Britain are a major threat to it.' Discuss this statement with others in your group, including considering the effects the Internet might have on the spread of alternative ideas and opinions.

INTO THE FUTURE

This chapter has examined only a very limited range of the mass media, but there is a dramatic communications explosion occurring in the early years of the third millennium. Digital broadcasting will potentially lead to hundreds of cable and satellite television channels, with interactive television shows where audiences can participate in what they are watching on television.

The media have become a gigantic international business, with instant news from every part of the globe. International marketing of TV programmes and films to international audiences is backed by huge investments. The Internet has millions more people going 'on line' every year. TV and radio cards and modems for personal computers mean that computers are quite likely to replace televisions in our homes, with instant access to colossal amounts of information and entertainment from the entire globe. Newspaper sales have been steadily declining, and may well continue to do so, as more and more news services (and newspapers) appear in electronic form on the Internet.

The media promote democracy

- Because the media in Britain are not controlled by the state, the risk of censorship by governments is reduced, and free speech is protected. Journalists are free to report and comment – within legal limits.

- The wide variety of privately owned media means a range of opinions are considered and public debates take place. By criticizing the actions of governments, the mass media can play an important 'watchdog' role, and keep governments in touch with public opinion.

- The media give an unbiased account of news. TV news has to be impartial.

- The media accurately reflect public opinions that already exist in society rather than creating new ones. People wouldn't read newspapers or watch TV unless they were providing what their audiences wanted.

- Anyone can put his or her views across, by setting up a website or a newspaper, distributing leaflets, putting up posters, and other means of communicating ideas.

The media restrict democracy

- The media (particularly newspapers) reflect the conservative views of their wealthy owners. While journalists are often critical and expose wrongdoing, they will frequently avoid issues which might cost them their jobs by upsetting newspaper owners.

- The variety of opinion presented is limited. Working-class political views, for example of strikes, are rarely reported. The ideas and actions of the least powerful groups are the most likely to be excluded. Those who in some way present a challenge or threat to the status quo – the existing way society is organized – are presented as irresponsible or unreasonable extremists.

- News values, agenda-setting, norm-setting, and other sources of bias mean only some issues are covered, and these are not presented in neutral ways. The media choose what to report and how to report it, and therefore provide a biased view of the world.

- The media do not simply reflect public opinion, but actively form and manipulate it. People can only form opinions on the basis of the knowledge they have, and the media are primarily responsible for providing this knowledge. The owners of the mass media hold overwhelmingly conservative views, and their ownership gives them the power to defend their position by forming favourable public opinion.

- Only the rich have the resources necessary to publish and distribute a newspaper on a large scale, or to set up a television or radio station. The concentration of ownership of the mass media is a threat to democracy, as a small, powerful group of media owners can control access to ideas, information, and knowledge. Those who wish to put forward alternative views to those presented in the mass media may not be allowed access to the media by their owners, and will therefore be denied any real opportunity to persuade public opinion of their ideas.

The speed of technological change is now so great that the world is said to be rapidly becoming a 'global village'. This means that the whole world has become like one small village, with everyone (at least those who are affluent enough) exposed to the same information and messages through mass media which cut across all national frontiers. It remains to be seen how the media will develop during the twenty-first century, but it seems likely there will be an enormous increase in the power of the already-powerful media companies.

DISCUSSION   How do you think the mass media will develop over the next century? Do you welcome or worry about the changes that might lie ahead, such as a huge increase in the number of TV channels and easier and faster Internet access? How do you think these changes might affect our daily lives?

CHAPTER SUMMARY

After studying this chapter, you should be able to:

- Explain what is meant by the term 'mass media'.

- Describe briefly the ways the law, the government, and other factors might exercise control over the mass media.

- Describe the concentration of ownership of the mass media and explain why this might be of some concern in a democracy.

- Describe the differences between the 'quality' and the 'popular' newspapers, and their relationship to different social classes.

- Explain a variety of ways in which the mass media might form public opinion and exercise social control.

- Explain the terms 'agenda-setting', 'gate-keeping', and 'norm-setting'.

- Explain what is meant by 'bias' in the media, and identify a range of factors influencing the content of the mass media.

- Explain, with examples, what is meant by 'news values'.

- Discuss, with examples, the role of the mass media in stereotyping and scapegoating.

- Explain how the mass media might give false impressions of crime.

- Explain how the mass media might amplify deviance.

- Discuss different views of the effects of the mass media on audiences.

- Explain what is meant by 'selective exposure', 'selective perception', and 'selective retention'.

- Explain the effects of media violence.

- Explain the competing views of the role of the mass media in a democracy.

KEY TERMS

agenda-setting
bias
deviancy amplification
folk devils
gate-keeping
labelling
moral panic
news values
norm-setting
scapegoats
selective exposure
selective perception
selective retention

COURSEWORK SUGGESTIONS

1   Video BBC and ITV news bulletins for a week, or study 'popular' and 'quality' newspapers for a week, and compare their coverage of different events. What evidence is there of agenda-setting?

2   Study some of the 'popular' and 'quality' newspapers for a week and discuss the differences between them, for example by measuring the column inches given to different categories of news, advertising, TV, and photographs.

3   Carry out a study of newspapers, advertisements, or children's comics, looking at the presentation of minority ethnic groups or women.

4   Carry out a survey to find out which of the mass media people see as most reliable in presenting the news. The questionnaire in chapter 17 could be used as a starting point. You could compare your results with those given in table 8.3 earlier in this chapter.

5   Compare two 'quality' and two 'popular' national Sunday or daily newspapers for the same days. Carefully analyse the headlines, types of story, photographs, and cartoons they contain. On the basis of this evidence, draw up a list of the news values you think each newspaper uses to decide which stories to include and which to exclude.

6   Interview the editor and other journalists on a local newspaper to find out how they decide what to print and what not to, what makes a story 'newsworthy', how far they think they exaggerate stories, and so on.

9 Social Control, Deviance, and Crime

KEY ISSUES

- Agencies of social control.
- Crime and deviance.
- The pattern of crime.
- What's wrong with the official crime statistics?
- Is the crime rate increasing?
- Explaining crime and deviance.
- Policy solutions to crime

In order for people to know how to behave in society, to be able to predict how others will behave, and therefore to live together in some orderly way, some shared values and norms are necessary. Without some measure of agreement on the basic ground rules, social life would soon fall into confusion and disorder. For example, imagine the chaos on the British roads if drivers stopped following the rules about driving on the left-hand side of the road, or stopping at red traffic lights.

Norms and values are learnt through socialization, but knowing what the norms are does not necessarily mean people will follow them. Social control is concerned with the various methods used to make sure people continue to obey those social values and norms which have been learnt through socialization. This is achieved by various positive and negative sanctions – rewards and punishments.

Together, socialization and social control help to maintain social conformity – conforming to social values and norms. Deviance is the term given to behaviour which is in some way socially unacceptable or not approved of – non-conformist behaviour.

ACTIVITY

Look at the cartoon opposite:
1 Explain in your own words the point the cartoon is illustrating.
2 List four possible consequences that might face a person who followed a deviant path as an adult.
3 Suggest two reasons why a person might fail to conform to social norms.
4 Identify and explain two ways in which not conforming to social norms might lead to success in society.
5 Much deviance is disapproved of to some extent, but can you think of forms of deviance in any society which might be welcomed by the majority of the public as opening the way for society to change and improve?

AGENCIES OF SOCIAL CONTROL

Social control is carried out through a series of agencies of social control, many of which are discussed in fuller detail in other parts of this book, but it is useful to summarize them here.

Formal social control

Formal social control is that which is carried out by an agency specifically set up to ensure that people conform to a particular set of norms, especially the law. The police, courts, and prisons force people to obey the

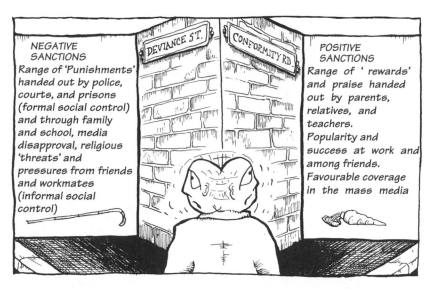

NEGATIVE SANCTIONS		POSITIVE SANCTIONS
Range of 'Punishments' handed out by police, courts, and prisons (formal social control) and through family and school, media disapproval, religious 'threats' and pressures from friends and workmates (informal social control)	DEVIANCE ST. CONFORMITY RD.	Range of 'rewards' and praise handed out by parents, relatives, and teachers. Popularity and success at work and among friends. Favourable coverage in the mass media

Social control: people make rules and then enforce them on the carrot-and-stick principle

law through formal sanctions such as arresting, fining, or imprisoning those who break society's laws.

Informal social control

The following agencies carry out social control in an informal way. This means their primary purpose is not social control, but they play an important role in it none the less.

The family

This is where primary socialization takes place, and children first begin to form their identities and learn about the basic values and norms of

Formal social control
Photo: Ted Fussey

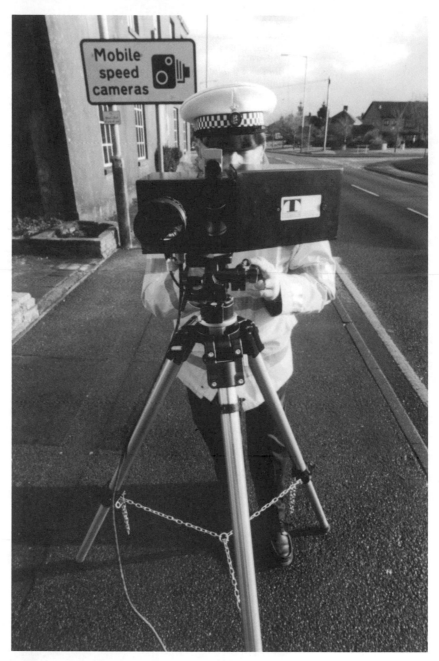

Formal social control
Photo: Ted Fussey

society. For example, children learn the difference between right and wrong, 'good' and 'bad' behaviour, norms governing gender roles, and acceptance of parental authority. Children may become embarrassed or develop a guilty conscience if they break these rules. The approval or disapproval of parents can itself be an important element in encouraging children to conform, along with other sanctions such as praise and rewards, threats, teasing, and physical violence.

The school

This socializes pupils and sets standards of 'correct' behaviour, the forms of dress and so on which are expected by society. This is achieved by sanctions such as detentions, suspensions, exclusions, merit points, and other aspects of the hidden curriculum (see glossary and chapter 11 for a discussion of this). Through the actions of teachers and the way the school is organized, for example through streaming and examinations, pupils are encouraged to accept norms like the competitiveness, the gender roles, the ranking of people with unequal pay and status, and the inequalities in power and authority to which they are expected to conform in the wider society. In this way, the school helps to maintain the way society as a whole is presently organized, such as the inequalities between men and women and between managers and workers.

The peer group

The peer group is very important in providing an individual's view of herself or himself – their sense of identity. The desire for approval and acceptance by peers is itself an important source of social control. The fear of rejection and ridicule by peers may exert an enormous influence on an individual's self-identity and behaviour. Such pressure may promote conformity to the wider norms of society, such as acceptance of traditional gender roles. However, conformity to the peer group may also promote deviance. This is particularly likely among young people, where peer pressure may encourage them to adopt forms of deviant behaviour, such as playing truant from school, taking illegal drugs, or under-age drinking.

The workplace

At work, there are frequently strong pressures from fellow workers to conform to work-related norms, and an individual who is labelled as a trouble-maker or uncooperative may find herself or himself denied promotion opportunities, allocated unpleasant jobs, or even dismissed. Fellow workers may use such negative sanctions as refusing to talk to or mix with workmates, ridiculing them, or playing practical jokes on those who fail to conform to their norms.

ACTIVITY

1 Give examples of three norms in each case to which you are generally expected to conform in *two* of the following: (a) at your school or college, (b) in your peer group, (c) at work.

2 Explain in each case how these norms are enforced, and outline the sanctions applied if you fail to conform to them.

The mass media

The mass media are major sources of information and ideas, and can have powerful influences on people's attitudes, opinions, and behaviour. As discussed in chapter 8, the mass media carry out social control through the processes of norm-setting and agenda-setting. These generally encourage conformist behaviour, such as conformity to gender roles promoted through advertising. Social control is achieved through such devices as the selection and presentation of news items, advertising, sensationalism, stereotyping, and scapegoating. By reporting the serious consequences which follow for those who break society's norms, and telling people what they should be thinking about, norm-setting and agenda-setting are effectively carrying out social control.

Religion

Religion is a belief system which may influence people's ideas about 'right' and 'wrong' behaviour, and this in turn may affect their behaviour. For example, the Christian religion promises rewards (heaven) to those who conform to its teachings, and punishments (an eternity in hell) to those who do not. Religious beliefs and teachings often support and re-inforce the values and norms of society by giving them a 'sacred' quality. The Ten Commandments in Christianity – 'thou shalt not kill . . . steal . . . commit adultery', etc. – reinforce values such as respect for human life, private property, and monogamous marriage. Feelings of guilt (a guilty conscience) may result if religious rules are broken by believers – a sort of inner police officer controlling behaviour.

CRIME AND DEVIANCE

DEFINITION	**THE DIFFERENCE BETWEEN CRIME AND DEVIANCE** ■ Deviance is any non-conformist behaviour which is disapproved of by society or a social group, whether it is illegal or not. It is norm-breaking behaviour, and can range from being eccentric to criminal activity. ■ Crime is the term used to describe behaviour which is against the law – law-breaking. ■ Juvenile delinquency is crime committed by those between the ages of 10 and 17, though the term 'delinquency' is often used to describe any anti-social behaviour by young people, even if it isn't criminal.

The difficulty of defining deviance

Crime is easy to define, as the law states what a criminal act is. However, while deviance appears to be easy to define as any non-conformist behaviour, it is, in fact, quite difficult to pin down what members of any society or group actually regard as deviant behaviour. Deviance covers a very wide range of behaviour, and what is regarded as deviant will depend on the norms of a group or society. These norms differ between societies and between groups within the same society, and they change over time. Whether or not an act is defined as deviant will therefore depend on the time, the place, the society, and the attitudes of those who view the act. The following examples illustrate how definitions of deviance can vary according to a range of circumstances.

Non-deviant crime?

Most people commit deviant and even illegal acts at some stage in their lives, and there are many illegal acts which most people don't regard as particularly deviant. For example, parking and speeding offences, under-age drinking, use of soft drugs like cannabis, pinching office stationery, or making unauthorized personal calls on the office phone are all illegal but extremely common, so it is difficult to see them as deviant. Some offences, like under-age drinking, are often seen as expected behaviour, and those who don't commit the offence may even be seen as deviant by those around them.

The time

Deviance can only be defined in relation to particular norms, and norms change over time. For example, cigarette smoking used to be a very popular and socially acceptable activity, but is increasingly becoming branded as deviant, and smokers are now unwelcome in many places. Attitudes to abortion and homosexuality have also changed dramatically. Homosexuality, for example, is no longer seen as being as deviant as it once was, and it is becoming far more accepted by many people, including many members of Parliament and the Anglican clergy. Fashion, of course, is an obvious example of changing norms – people today would generally be regarded as deviant were they to wear the fashions of seventeenth-century England, or even those of a few years ago (but not if they come into fashion again).

Attitudes to smoking have changed

The society

Norms, and therefore definitions of deviance, differ between societies. For example, consumption of alcohol is often seen as deviant and illegal in many Islamic countries, but is seen as normal in Britain. Topless bathing on a Mediterranean beach is generally acceptable, but not so in a local park in England. Smoking cannabis is regarded as deviant by many people in modern Britain (but see the next paragraph), but is common behaviour in many countries of the Middle East.

The social group

Norms can vary between social groups in the same society, and so what may be acceptable in a particular group may be regarded as deviant in the wider society. For example, smoking cannabis is perfectly acceptable behaviour among Rastafarians in Britain, and among many young people who are not Rastafarians, although it is regarded as deviant by many adults, and it is illegal.

The place

The place where an act takes place may influence whether it is regarded as deviant or not. For example, it is seen as deviant if people have sex in the street, but not if it takes place between couples in a bedroom; fighting in the street is seen as deviant, but not if it takes place in a boxing ring. Similarly, killing may be seen as 'heroic' on a battlefield in wartime, but as murder in peacetime.

ACTIVITY

Apart from the examples given above:

1 Identify and explain two examples of acts which are against the law but are not usually regarded as deviant by most people.

2 Give three examples of deviant acts which are not against the law.

3 Identify and explain two examples of acts which are generally accepted by the majority of people in Britain, but which might be regarded as deviant in some social groups in Britain, for example minority ethnic or religious groups.

4 Explain the circumstances in which the following acts might not be regarded as deviant or illegal:

- Two men having sex together.
- Killing ten people.
- Driving through red traffic lights.
- Deliberately breaking someone's arm.
- Punching someone in the face.
- Breaking into someone's house and removing her or his possessions.
- Taking children away from their parents by force.

Why are some deviant acts defined as criminal while others are not?

Cannabis use in some countries of the Middle East is an extremely common practice, with few laws controlling its use, and yet alcohol consumption is strictly banned by laws which are vigorously enforced. In Britain, the opposite is more or less the case, despite the massive social cost caused by alcoholism in terms of family breakdown, days off work, acts of violence, and costs to the NHS, and little evidence that cannabis has any addictive properties. Why are there such differences in the way some acts are defined as criminal while other, similar acts are not? There are two broadly competing views on this.

Illegal

Legal

The consensus approach

The consensus approach suggests that social rules are made and enforced for the benefit of everyone. The law and the definition of crime represent a consensus – a widespread agreement among most people – that some deviant acts are so serious that they require legal punishments to prevent them occurring. This may seem fairly clear in cases such as murder, rape, and armed robbery, but it is not so clear on other issues, like those of alcohol and soft drug abuse. From the consensus view, this would be explained by the varying norms found in different societies, which mean alcohol and drugs are viewed differently.

The conflict approach: inequalities in power

The conflict approach suggests that the law reflects the interests of the richest and most powerful groups in society, who have managed to impose their ideas and way of thinking on the rest of the population through the agencies of social control. Those in positions of influence in society, such as newspaper editors, politicians, owners of industry, powerful pressure groups, judges, and the police, are much better placed to make their definition of a crime stick than the ordinary person in the street. They also have the power to define some acts as criminal through newspaper campaigns, by passing laws in Parliament, or by treating some offences more seriously than others.

In this way the powerful are able to maintain their own position of power and influence by defining those activities which are against their interests as deviant or criminal. The issue of alcohol raised above could well be explained by the power of the wealthy large brewers and distillers. A further example is the way laws against picketing by trade unionists are much stronger and more rigidly enforced than those imposing health and safety standards on employers. Middle-class crimes such as tax evasion are often neither prosecuted, nor pursued as vigorously, nor punished as severely as a working-class offence such as social security fraud, which is much more likely to result in prosecution and a prison sentence.

DISCUSSION	Which view explaining why some deviant acts are defined as criminal while others are not do you find most convincing? Do you think the law is biased in deciding both which acts are defined as criminal, and which ones get pursued by the police and the courts?

THE PATTERN OF CRIME

Information on the pattern of crime is obtained from the official crime statistics. These are published each year by the Home Office from the records of local police forces.

Figure 9.1 shows a breakdown of the types of offence recorded by the police in 2002–3. It is notable that, despite wide media coverage of

Total offences: 5.9 million
   of which: 16% were car crimes (theft of or from
         vehicles) and 15% were burglaries

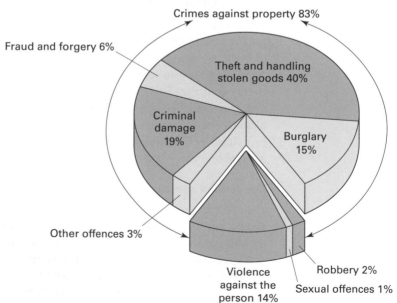

Figure 9.1 Crimes recorded by the police: England and Wales, 2002/3

Source: Adapted from Crime in England and Wales 2002/2003 (Office for National Statistics, 2003)

dramatic incidents such as attacks on the elderly, violence against the person made up only about 14 per cent of all offences in 2002–3. Most recorded assaults and crimes of violence do not result in any serious physical injury, and a half of all violent crime reported to the police in 2002–3 did not result in any injury to the victim. Only a small proportion of such cases need professional medical attention, and in only a few of such cases is the victim admitted to hospital. In fact, as figure 9.1 shows, most crime is fairly small-scale property crime.

Criminal statistics are notoriously unreliable, so the pattern of crime shown in them must be treated with considerable caution. The problem of the crime statistics will be discussed shortly, but for the moment our concern will be with explaining the pattern shown in the official statistics.

The official crime statistics show that most crime is committed:
- In urban areas.
- Against property.
- By:
  - young
  - working-class
  - males.

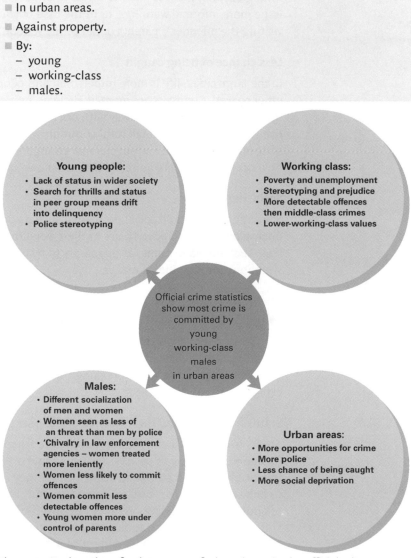

Figure 9.2 Explanations for the pattern of crime shown in the official crime statistics

Why is the crime rate higher in urban areas?

The official crime rate is significantly higher in urban areas than in rural areas. There are four main reasons for this.

More opportunity for crime

Large urban areas provide greater opportunities for crime: more and larger shops, warehouses and business premises, cars, houses, and other typical targets of crime.

Policing

There is a greater police presence in urban areas, so more crime is likely to be detected. Different policing methods also mean the police are more likely to take formal action (arrest and prosecution) in urban areas. In rural areas they are less likely to arrest offenders, preferring merely to issue more informal warnings, or in the case of young people perhaps visiting the offender's parents or her or his school.

Less chance of being caught

In the large cities, life is more impersonal and people do not know each other so well. Strangers are more likely to go unrecognized, and are therefore more able to get away with offences. Potential criminals are less likely to steal within a small rural community where everyone knows almost everybody else and suspicious 'strangers' are likely to be noticed. Any local offenders are quite likely to be known in the community.

Social deprivation

Social deprivation and social problems, such as poor housing, unemployment, and poverty, are at their worst in the inner cities. These have been linked to crime, as people try to resolve their desperate situations through illegal means.

Why are most convicted criminals young?

Official statistics show that roughly half of all those convicted are aged 21 or under, and a 2002 survey found that almost half of Britain's secondary school students admitted to breaking the law. There are several explanations for this.

Status frustration and the influence of the peer group

Status frustration means young people are frustrated at their lack of an independent status in society. Young people are caught in the transition between child and adult status: they are no longer expected to behave as children, but are denied the full rights and responsibilities of adults. They therefore often feel deprived of status in society and suffer from status frustration. The peer group provides some support for an identity and status independent of school or family, and therefore takes on a greater importance among young people than at any other age. Many young people lack the responsibilities involved in having children, in paying rent or mortgage repayments, and often in keeping down a job.

This lack of responsibilities and status, and the search for excitement and peer group status, mean many young people drift into minor acts of delinquency and clashes with the law. Peer group pressure may also give young people the confidence and encouragement to involve themselves in minor acts of delinquency which they would not engage in on their own. The idea of status frustration helps to explain why many young people give up crime as they grow older. Adulthood, marriage, parenthood, their own home, and employment give them a more clearly defined, independent status in society, and the peer group becomes less important for achieving status.

While most young people will break the law at some time, the kinds of offence they commit are usually fairly trivial and peer group related. For example, under-age drinking, vandalism, and shoplifting are the most common offences committed by young people. The reasons most often given for their law-breaking are to impress others, and boredom. Research conducted at the Centre of Criminology at Edinburgh University found that about half the offences committed by 11–15-year-olds involved rowdiness and fighting in the street, with the rest consisting mainly of shoplifting (usually sweets) and vandalism (usually graffiti).

Police stereotyping

The police are likely to see young people as the source of problems, and this stereotype means the police spend more time observing and checking youths. As a result, more get caught, get defined as offenders, and appear in the statistics. In fact, the Edinburgh research referred to above found that young people were far more likely to be the victims of crime than to commit crimes, and these crimes were often committed by adults. The young complained of being followed by 'weirdos', bothered by 'flashers', alcoholics, and junkies, and in fear of rape and other sexual assaults. In 2002, up to half a million 11–15-year-olds were victims of mobile phone thefts. However, the research found that the police often didn't take the complaints of the young seriously, seeing them primarily as trouble-makers. More than half had been moved on, told off, stopped and questioned, or stopped and searched during the previous nine months. This situation discourages young people from reporting offences against them, and reinforces the impression of young people as delinquents rather than the victims of crime.

| DISCUSSION | Do you think the police stereotype young people, and unfairly make them out to be trouble-makers? What evidence do you have to back up your opinions? |

Why are most convicted criminals male?

Males outnumber females by about 7:1 in the official statistics, and only about 5 per cent of the prison population are women. Why is this?

Reproduced by permission of David Haldane

Why do males commit more crime than women?

◼ Owing to gender-role socialization, the tough and dominant behaviour expected of men is more likely to lead to more serious and detectable criminal behaviour, and men are more likely than women to carry out crimes of violence and other serious offences.

◼ The police see men as more likely to be criminals than women, and they are more likely to press charges in the case of men.

◼ Men have more independence and opportunities to commit crime – they are less restricted by the demands of housework and childcare.

Why do females commit less crime than men?

◼ The chivalry thesis suggests that paternalism or sexism on the part of the police and courts means they regard female offenders as a less serious 'threat' than men, particularly for minor offences. The police and courts therefore adopt more informal approaches to their offences, such as unrecorded cautions or simply letting them off. According to the Home Office, women are consistently treated more leniently by the law, with women first offenders about half as likely to be given a sentence of immediate imprisonment as their male counterparts.

◼ Police stereotyping means women who commit crimes may benefit from the police stereotype that they are less likely than men to be criminals, and so are less likely to have their behaviour watched and get caught.

◼ More social control means teenage girls are likely to be more closely supervised by their parents, reducing the chances of their getting into trouble in the first place.

■ The demands of the *housewife/mother role* – caring for husbands, children, and dependent elderly relatives – means adult females may be less likely to get involved in crime as they have less opportunity to do so.

■ Women's offences are more likely to be *less detectable ones*, such as sexual offences like prostitution, or petty theft like shoplifting.

While women are far less likely to commit serious offences than men, those who do are likely to face more severe punishment than men, particularly for violent crime, as it violates socially acceptable patterns of feminine behaviour. Women offenders are more likely to be remanded in custody (put in prison) than men while awaiting trial for serious offences, but in three-quarters of cases, women do not actually receive a prison sentence when they come to trial. Women are about twice as likely as men to be denied bail when charged with drug offences, and three times as likely for offences involving dishonesty. Many women in prison appear to have been sentenced more severely than men in similar circumstances – for example, by being imprisoned rather than given community punishment. Many women prisoners are there for not paying fines, for drug offences (40 per cent of all women prisoners) or for committing theft, fraud, and robbery trying to feed themselves or their children. More than half of women prisoners have children under age 16. Women are over twice as likely as men to be imprisoned for theft, and, in effect, many women are sent to jail for being poor.

In general, then, women might commit less crime, and fewer serious offences, than men, but appear to suffer more serious consequences when they do. This may well be because in our society women are expected to be good and punished if they're not, but men are expected to go off the rails and so are punished less severely when they do.

ACTIVITY

Read carefully the previous section on why most convicted criminals are male:

1 Try to think of any other reasons that you can. Make a list in order of importance of the reasons why women are less likely to be criminals than men.

2 How do you think police attitudes to women and crime could affect the number of female offenders recorded in the official crime statistics? Explain your answer carefully, with examples of particular crimes.

3 Women are more likely to be victims of some crimes than men. Suggest, with reasons, examples of some of these crimes.

Why are most convicted criminals working class?

According to the official statistics, working-class people are more likely to be arrested and charged with crimes than people of other social classes. There are a number of possible explanations for this.

Poverty and unemployment

There is a link between the level of crime and the state of the economy. Property crime in particular seems to rise when people are hard up, when poverty is on the increase and people need to provide for their families.

Such hardship provides an obvious explanation for the most common offences of property crime, and would account for the high proportion of working-class criminals. In a society where there are wide inequalities in wealth and income, some level of crime is to be expected from those who live a more deprived life than others.

Stereotyping and prejudice

Working-class youth fit more closely the police stereotype of the 'typical criminal', and there is therefore a greater police presence in working-class areas than in middle-class ones. This means there is a greater likelihood of offenders being seen and arrested by the police when committing an offence than in middle-class areas. Crime rates will therefore be higher in working-class areas simply because there are more police to notice or respond quickly to criminal acts.

The activities of working-class youth are more likely to be defined by the police as criminal than the same behaviour in the middle class. For example, a case of university students getting drunk and wrecking a restaurant might result in their having to pay for the damage and be dismissed by the police as 'high jinks', but the same behaviour by working-class football supporters would be more likely to be seen as 'hooliganism', with resulting prosecutions for criminal damage. The prejudices of middle-class judges and magistrates may mean that, when working-class people appear in court, they are more likely to be seen as 'typical criminals' and found guilty. The middle class are more likely to be found not guilty. Their offences may be seen more as a temporary lapse in otherwise good behaviour, and so are punished less severely than those of the working class.

Informal social control

Working-class youth are also more likely to be prosecuted if they are caught than the middle class. This is perhaps because they are less likely to benefit from informal processes of social control. For petty offences, middle-class youth are more likely to be dealt with by parents and teachers than by the law, with the police perhaps visiting the parents to give them a warning.

Lower-working-class values

Some have suggested that the values of the lower working class often carry with them risks of brushes with the law. These values are discussed later in this chapter.

ACTIVITY

Most judges and magistrates come from white, upper-middle-class or middle-class backgrounds.

1 Suggest ways this might influence judges and magistrates to give more favourable and sympathetic treatment to some groups and less favourable and unsympathetic treatment to others. Give examples of particular groups.

2 Imagine you are to appear in court on a shoplifting charge. You desperately want to get off lightly. Identify and explain four ways you might try to give a good impression to the judge or magistrate.

3 What might this activity suggest about the real pattern of crime in society?

White-collar and corporate crime

DEFINITION	■ White-collar crimes are offences committed by people in the course of their middle-class jobs. ■ Corporate crimes are offences committed by large companies which directly profit the company rather than individuals.

White-collar crimes include offences such as bribery and corruption in government and business, fiddling expenses, professional misconduct, fraud, and embezzlement. A spectacular example is the case of Nick Leeson, who bankrupted Barings Bank in 1995 after losing the bank £830 million.

Corporate crimes include offences like misrepresentation of products, industrial espionage, breaches of health and safety regulations, and hacking into rival companies' computers to obtain confidential information. British Airways did this in the early 1990s, to obtain confidential information about its rival Virgin Atlantic. In 2003, Argos and Littlewood's were fined a total of £22.6 million for fixing the price on a range of toys so that prices (and profits) were kept artificially high.

White-collar and corporate crimes are substantially underrepresented in official statistics, giving the impression that the middle class commit fewer offences. However, there may be many companies and white-collar criminals who simply don't get caught or even have their crimes detected. The impression gained from the official statistics that most crime is committed by the working class may therefore be quite misleading.

There are several reasons why white-collar and corporate crime are underrepresented in the official statistics:

■ Such crime is often 'without victims' and may benefit both the parties concerned. For example, in cases of bribery and corruption both parties stand to gain something. It is therefore hard to detect.

■ There is often a lack of awareness that a crime has been committed and therefore it is not reported. For example, members of the public may lack the expertise to know if they are being misled or defrauded.

■ Even if these crimes are detected, the people who commit them are often not prosecuted. For example, violations of health and safety legislation often lead only to a reprimand. Crimes such as professional misconduct, medical negligence, industrial espionage, and computer fraud are rarely reported, to protect the interests or reputation of the profession or institution, and avoid the loss of public confidence which the surrounding scandal might cause. A typical example of this occurred in 2002, when it was reported that at least four large Internet banks in Britain had been attacked by computer hackers who had broken into their central computer systems and stolen hundreds of thousands of pounds. The banks concerned were reluctant to report these thefts to the police for fear it would damage public confidence in the banks, and in on-line banking in general. In such circumstances, a private security firm is more likely to lead any investigation rather than it being reported to the police.

In general, the higher up you are in the social class hierarchy:
- The less likely you are to be arrested.
- The less likely you are, if arrested, to be prosecuted.
- The less likely you are, if prosecuted, to be found guilty.
- The less likely you are, if found guilty, to be given a prison sentence.

WHAT'S WRONG WITH THE OFFICIAL CRIME STATISTICS?

The previous section outlined some explanations of the pattern of crime as revealed in the official crime statistics. However, these are not as factual as they might appear, and there is a large percentage of crimes which are not discovered or reported: the 'dark number' of undiscovered crimes. Figure 9.3 from the 2003 British Crime Survey shows a large gap for many offences between the amount of crime committed and that finally recorded by the police. This figure, which could be as much as 80 per cent or more for some crimes, is known as the 'dark figure' of unrecorded and unreported crime.

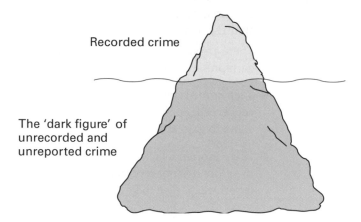

Recorded crime

The 'dark figure' of unrecorded and unreported crime

This survey estimated that overall about four times as many offences are committed as the number recorded by the police, though for some categories of crime, such as vandalism, theft from the person, and theft from motor vehicles, the number is much higher. Many burglaries, rapes, crimes of domestic violence, wounding, and common assaults go unreported. Only about one in five of all crimes reported to the police results in a conviction, so we don't really know who is committing 80 per cent of offences.

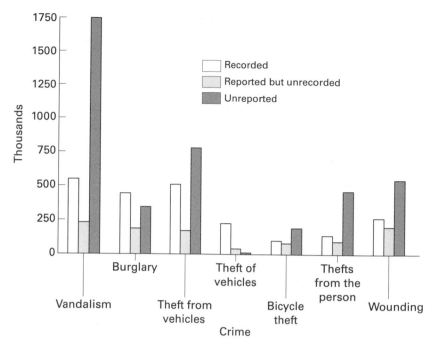

Figure 9.3 Levels of recorded, unrecorded, and unreported crime: England and Wales, 2003

Source: Adapted from *Crime in England and Wales 2002/2003* (Office for National Statistics, 2003)

ACTIVITY

Study figure 9.3 and answer the following questions:

1 Approximately how many crimes of vandalism were recorded in 2003?

2 Approximately how many thefts from vehicles were recorded in 2003?

3 In which offence category was crime most likely to be recorded in 2003?

4 In which offence category was crime most likely to be reported?

5 About how many thefts from vehicles were there in total in 2003?

6 Approximately how many bicycle thefts were reported but unrecorded in 2003?

7 According to the statistics in figure 9.3, a high proportion of crimes of vandalism, thefts from vehicles, wounding, and thefts from the person went unreported. Suggest reasons for this for each offence.

8 Suggest, with examples, reasons why the police may decide not to record a crime (a) which has been reported to them, and (b) which the police themselves have detected.

9 Explain how the information given in figure 9.3 might be used to show that the official crime statistics give a misleading impression of the extent of crime in society. Is there any evidence for the opposite view for particular types of crime? Be sure to give statistical evidence from figure 9.3.

SELF-REPORT STUDIES AND VICTIM SURVEYS

Sociologists know that the number of crimes is far higher than the official statistics suggest, because of the use of self-report studies and victim surveys.

Self-report studies are anonymous questionnaires where people own up to committing crimes, whether they have been discovered or not. (Table 9.1 shows an example of a self-report study.)

Victim surveys involve people admitting to being the victim of a crime, whether or not they reported it. An example of a victim survey is the British Crime Survey, carried out every year by the Home Office. This tries to discover how much crime goes unreported by victims and unrecorded by the police. In this way, it is able to estimate how much crime there really is in society. However, even survey techniques like self-report and victim surveys do not give a full picture of the real levels of crime in society.

In self-report studies:

■ People may exaggerate or understate the number of crimes they've committed.

■ They may not own up to some offences – particularly more serious ones.

In victim surveys:

■ People may forget they were victimized.

■ They may not realize they have been the victims of a crime – particularly white-collar and corporate crimes, where they may not realize that have been duped, 'conned', or, for example, sold dangerous products.

■ Victims may feel embarrassment or guilt at admitting to being a victim, such as in the case of sex offences or domestic violence.

■ Crimes without victims, such as drug offences or white-collar crimes like bribery and corruption where both parties have something to lose, are not recorded.

■ Around a fifth of people refuse to cooperate with victim surveys, possibly making the results inaccurate.

Research from self-report studies and victim surveys suggests that the high proportion of young, urban, working-class males in the criminal statistics gives a misleading impression of the criminal population as a whole. In reality the ratio of working-class to middle-class crime and the ratio of male to female is much more equal than official statistics suggest. Therefore, the extent of crime and the type of people committing it are very different from those which the official statistics suggest. Why are the official crime statistics so inaccurate?

ACTIVITY

1 Work through the self-report study in table 9.1. List any offences you and/or your friends have committed but have not been caught for (no matter how trivial or whether they're on the list or not). What conclusions might you draw from your findings about the levels of undiscovered crime in society?

2 List three crimes which a victim might choose not to report to the police, and explain why in each case.

3 Have you or any of your friends ever been a victim (or suspected you might have been a victim) of a crime that you didn't report to the police? Explain the reasons why you didn't report it. What does this tell you about the real extent of crime in society?

Table 9.1 Example of a self-report study

Acts of delinquency	Acts of delinquency
1 I have ridden a bicycle without lights after dark.	23 I have planned well in advance to get into a house to take things.
2 I have driven a car or motor bike/scooter under 16.	24 I have got into a house and taken things even though I didn't plan it in advance.
3 I have been with a group who go round together making a row and sometimes getting into fights and causing disturbance.	25 I have taken a bicycle belonging to someone else and kept it.
4 I have played truant from school.	26 I have struggled or fought to get away from a police officer.
5 I have travelled on a train or bus without a ticket or deliberately paid the wrong fare.	27 I have struggled or fought with a police officer who was trying to arrest someone.
6 I have let off fireworks in the street.	28 I have stolen school property worth more than about 50p.
7 I have taken money from home without returning it.	29 I have stolen goods from someone I worked for worth more than about 50p.
8 I have taken someone else's car or motor bike for a joy ride, then taken it back afterwards.	30 (Females only) I have had sex with a boy when I was under 16.
9 I have broken or smashed things in public places like on the streets, cinemas, discos, trains or buses.	31 (Males only) I have had sex with a girl when I was under 16 or with a boy when I was under 18.
10 I have insulted people on the street or got them angry and fought with them.	32 I have trespassed somewhere I was not supposed to go, like empty houses, railway lines or private gardens.
11 I have broken into a big store or garage or warehouse.	33 I have been to an '18' film under age.
12 I have broken into a little shop even though I may not have taken anything.	34 I have spent money on gambling under 16.
13 I have taken something out of a car.	35 I have smoked cigarettes under 15.
14 I have taken a weapon (like a knife) out with me in case I needed it in a fight.	36 I have had sex with someone for money.
15 I have fought with someone in a public place like in the street or at a dance.	37 I have taken money from slot machines or telephones.
16 I have broken the window of an empty house.	38 I have taken money from someone's clothes hanging up somewhere.
17 I have used a weapon in a fight, like a knife or a razor or a broken bottle.	39 I have got money from someone by pretending to be someone else or lying about why I needed it.
18 I have drunk alcoholic drinks in a pub under 16.	40 I have taken someone's clothes hanging up somewhere.
19 I have taken things from big stores or supermarkets when the shop was open.	41 I have smoked cannabis or taken pills (ecstasy, speed).
21 I have dropped things in the street like litter or broken bottles.	42 I have got money/drink/cigarettes by saying I would have sex with someone even though I didn't.
22 I have bought something cheap or accepted as a present something I knew was stolen.	43 I have run away from home.

Source: Adapted from A. Campbell, *Girl Delinquents* (Blackwell)

Table 9.2 Reasons for not reporting incidents to the police: by type of offence

Reason for not reporting %	Burglary	Thefts and attempted thefts from vehicles	Other household theft	Other personal theft	Violence	All offences
Too trivial/no loss/police could do nothing	74	81	78	62	46	69
Fear of reprisal	3	1	less than 0.5	less than 0.5	7	2
Police-related reasons[a]	6	2	1	less than 0.5	3	2
Private matter/dealt with ourselves	23	19	20	20	47	26
Reported to other authorities	3	2	3	17	8	6
Inconvenient to report	4	6	6	8	5	5
Other reasons	2	2	2	3	3	2

[a] Police-related reasons include dislike or fear of the police and previous bad experiences with the police or courts.
Source: Adapted from *Crime in England and Wales 2002/2003* (Office for National Statistics, 2003)

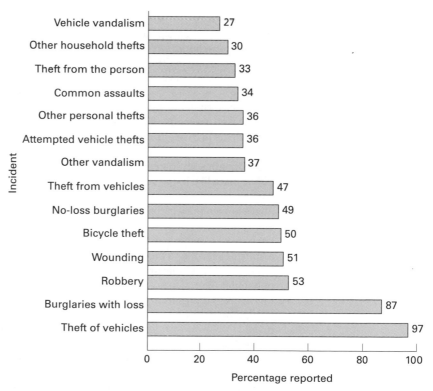

Figure 9.4 Percentage of incidents reported to the police: 2003
Source: Adapted from *Crime in England and Wales 2002/2003* (Office for National Statistics, 2003)

ACTIVITY

1   Refer to figure 9.4. Which offence was (a) most likely to be reported to the police and (b) least likely to be reported to the police? Suggest reasons for this in each case.

Refer to table 9.2:

2   Which offence did 81 per cent of people say they didn't report because it was too trivial, involved no loss, or the police couldn't do anything?

3   Which offence was most likely not to be reported because people dealt with the matter themselves?

4   For all offences, what were the two most common reasons given for not reporting crime to the police?

5   How do you think the evidence in figure 9.4 and table 9.2 might be used to challenge the view in the official crime statistics that most criminals are young, male, and working-class?

The failure to report crimes to the police

As table 9.2 and figure 9.4 suggest, a large number of people who are victims of crime don't bother to report it to the police. There are a number of reasons for this, which you can compare with your own findings in the activity on page 210.

■   The victims may think that the incident is too trivial to report; for example, where the incident involved no loss or damage, or the loss was too small, such as losing a small amount of money, garden tools, or bottles of milk.

■   The victims may think there is little point in reporting the incident as they feel the police could not do anything about it, by either recovering their property or catching the offenders; for example, cases of shoplifting or being pickpocketed.

■   The victims may fear embarrassment or humiliation at the hands of the police or in court. Groups working with rape victims, such as the Rape Crisis Line, estimate two out of three rape victims do not report the crime because of embarrassment, because they think the police won't take them seriously, or because they are made to feel it is their own fault they got raped. Recent rises in the number of reported rapes and crimes of domestic violence are often explained by changing police practice, and the growing willingness of the police to treat such offences in a more serious way and to be more sympathetic to the victim. However, victims may still feel there is little point in reporting a rape, as only about one in thirteen women reporting a rape to the police in 2002 saw the rapist convicted.

■   People may not report offences because they will themselves be in trouble. Some crimes benefit both parties, and there is no obvious victim. The consequence of reporting such offences will harm all concerned. For example, offences such as the illegal supplying of drugs, under-age sex, or giving and accepting bribes involve an agreement between both parties, and both will lose out if the police find out. Similarly, the illegal drug user who gets ripped off is more likely to be charged with an offence than shown sympathy by the police, and is therefore extremely unlikely to report the incident.

■ The victim may fear reprisals if the crime is reported, for example the blackmail victim afraid of the consequences of reporting the blackmailer.

■ Victims may feel it is a private matter they would rather deal with themselves. Examples might include offences such as theft or assault between friends.

■ Victims may not be aware an offence has been committed. 'Lost' property may have been stolen, and while the media often report cases of hoax gas-meter readers, 'dodgy' builders, and so on, there may be many people who never actually realize they have been the victims of such a hoax or been 'conned'.

The failure of the police to record a crime

The police may decide not to record an offence because they may regard the matter as too trivial to waste their time on, such as the theft of a very small sum of money, or the vandalism of a car window. They may not record an incident because it has already been satisfactorily resolved, or because the victim does not wish to proceed with the complaint.

They may regard the person complaining as too unreliable to take his or her account of the incident seriously, as in the case of complaints made by a tramp, a drug addict, or a drunk. The police may think that a report of an incident is mistaken, or that there is simply insufficient evidence to show that a crime has been committed.

In some cases, the police may regard an incident as nothing to do with them, even though an offence has been committed. This has traditionally been true in cases of domestic violence, such as wife-battering and rape within marriage, with such incidents being dismissed as a relatively unimportant 'domestic', and no offence being recorded or charges preferred.

ACTIVITY	The police often have a great deal of work to do, and every arrest they make involves considerable paper work. The police also have discretion over whether to arrest and charge someone for some offences. For example, pub closing time may involve lots of trouble, but the police can choose to move people along rather than arrest them.

1 Suggest three examples of crimes which the police might turn a blind eye to. Give reasons for your answer.

2 Suggest three crimes the police would be forced to record and investigate. Give reasons for your answer.

3 Sometimes the police seem to take some offences more seriously than at other times, and this results in increasing numbers of arrests and prosecutions for these offences, for example drink-driving at Christmas. List, with examples, all the factors you can think of which might make the police occasionally increase their levels of activity against some offences.

IS THE CRIME RATE INCREASING?

Much of what was said in the previous section suggests that the official crime statistics provide no real guide to the type or extent of crime, and must therefore be used with great care. Such care must also be applied to statistics which show increases in the amounts of recorded crime.

Much public and media concern is always expressed at any increase in recorded crime, but such increases need not necessarily mean there are more crimes being committed, or that people are at greater risk of being victims of crime. The increases could be explained by a wide range of factors, which suggest more offences are being discovered, reported, and recorded by the police, but not necessarily that more offences are actually being committed. These factors include:

- *Changing counting rules.* Changing rules for counting crimes can lead to higher numbers of offences being recorded, but not necessarily more crime. For example, before April 2002, theft of a cheque book and using these cheques in shops would have counted as one offence. Changes to the counting rules meant that, after April 2002, there would now be one crime recorded for each cheque that was used. Similarly, a person vandalizing six cars in a street now counts as six separate offences, whereas before it would have counted as one.

- *More sophisticated police training, communications, and equipment,* such as the use of computers, forensic science, and DNA testing, and higher policing levels all lead to increasing detection rates. Neighbourhood Watch schemes may also lead to more crimes being detected.

- *Changing police attitudes and policies* – a stronger desire by the police to prosecute certain offenders due to changing police attitudes and policies towards some offences, such as a crack-down on prostitution, drug dealing, or drink-driving. This may give the impression of an increase in crimes of that type, when it is simply that the police are making extra efforts and allocating more officers to tackle such crimes, and therefore catching more offenders.

- *Changes in the law* make more things illegal, such as rape in marriage.

- *Easier communications,* such as mobile phones and e-mail, make reporting of crime easier.

- *Changing social norms* – for example, changing attitudes to rape among the police and the public may have resulted in more rapes being reported, even though no more have been committed. The same might apply to crimes like domestic violence and child abuse, which are also statistically on the increase.

- *People have more to lose today* and more have household contents insurance cover. Insurance claims for theft need a police crime number, so more crime is reported. For example, nearly all thefts of cars and burglaries with loss are reported today so people can claim the insurance money.

■ *People may be bringing to the attention of the police less serious incidents*. This may be because they have become less tolerant of law-breaking, or simply because they want the police to help them and take more action. An example might be so-called 'nuisance youth', who often are not committing any offences, but are increasingly reported to the police by annoyed adults.

It is an irony of the official statistics that attempts to defeat crime by increased levels of policing, more police pay and resources, and a determination to crack down on offences can actually increase the levels of recorded crime. The more you search for crime, the more you find; and the official crime rate rises.

ACTIVITY

Go to the website of the Home Office (<www.homeoffice.gov.uk>), the Office for National Statistics (<www.statistics.gov.uk>), or <www.crimestatistics.org.uk> and, searching for 'crime statistics':

1 Identify the three most common crimes recorded by the police in England and Wales, or Scotland or Northern Ireland, in the latest year for which statistics are available.

2 Identify what percentage of all crimes in England and Wales were not solved (or 'cleared up') by the police. Try to find the latest clear-up rate for your local police force.

3 Find the latest British Crime Survey, and identify the two offences that are least likely to be reported to the police.

4 On the Home Office site, find out two measures that the Home Office is taking to try and reduce crime.

EXPLAINING CRIME AND DEVIANCE

Deviance covers very wide and varied forms of behaviour, and definitions of deviance and crime vary widely between societies and change over time. It is impossible to be born a criminal or a deviant, because crime and deviance involve legal and social rules, and what counts as deviant or criminal will depend on how society defines these rules. No single explanation can possibly provide an adequate account of all forms of deviance. The following sections briefly cover some of the major theoretical explanations which have been offered by sociologists for deviance, particularly criminal deviance.

Anomie

An American sociologist, Robert Merton, suggests that all societies set goals which people are encouraged to achieve, such as making money and career success. Norms or social rules define the socially approved ways of achieving these goals, such as hard work and educational qualifications. Most people are what Merton calls conformists – they try to achieve society's goals in approved ways.

Merton argues that deviance arises when the approved ways of achieving society's goals don't correspond with the actual situation individuals are in. In these circumstances, anomie results. This is a situation where people face confusion and uncertainty over what the social norms are, as these no longer help them to cope with the conditions they find themselves in. For example, many disadvantaged groups such as the poor and the lower working class have little chance of achieving society's goals by acceptable means, because they face disadvantages in education or are stuck in dead-end jobs with no promotion prospects. A strain is therefore placed on these individuals – they want to achieve the goals but lack the opportunities for doing so by conventional means. Merton suggests people may respond to these difficulties in achieving society's goals by breaking the rules, for example turning to crime or other deviant behaviour. He identifies four different types of rule-breaking: innovation, ritualism, retreatism, and rebellion. Innovators, for example, break the accepted rules for achieving success and turn to illegal means of achieving society's goals, such as theft. The cartoon below illustrates these four types of deviance.

MERTON'S RULE-BREAKERS

INNOVATORS	RITUALISTS	RETREATISTS	REBELS
Try to achieve success by illegitimate means, such as theft	*Continue to work within the system but give up trying for success, for example office workers stuck in a dead-end job and simply 'going through the motions' with no ambition*	*Abandon both the goals and the means of achieving them, and become drop-outs, turning to drink, drugs, or some other deviant behaviour*	*Reject society's goals and the accepted means of achieving them, and replace them with their own, for example revolutionaries*

ACTIVITY

Look at the cartoon on 'Merton's rule-breakers'.

1 Which one of the four types of rule-breaker would those who fiddled their income tax normally be considered as?

2 Explain in what way each of Merton's rule-breakers is deviant, and how each would have to change to become conformist.

3 Classify each of the following acts/groups according to Merton's ideas:
   ■ Someone cheating in exams.
   ■ A teacher who has lost interest in the job, but carries on teaching.
   ■ A heroin addict.
   ■ A terrorist.
   ■ A tramp.
   ■ A lazy student who only pretends to do any work.

4 Suggest two examples of your own for each type of rule-breaking (or deviance), and explain how your examples show each type of deviance.

Sub-cultural explanations

A sub-culture is a smaller culture held by a group of people within the main culture of a society, in some ways different from the dominant culture, but with many aspects in common. Figure 9.5 illustrates, with examples, this idea of a sub-culture. Sub-cultural explanations of crime and deviance suggest that those who commit crime share some values which are to some extent different from the main values of society as a whole.

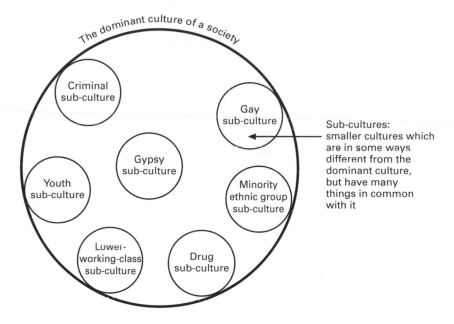

Figure 9.5 Culture and sub-cultures

Status frustration and the deviant sub-culture

While most lower-working-class young people accept the main goals of society, like obtaining wealth, achieving educational success and good incomes, they have little chance of attaining them. This is because they live in deprived areas, with poor schools and the worst chances in the job market. They therefore develop status frustration. This simply means they lack status in society, and feel frustration at being unable to achieve such status by accepted means.

Their response to this sense of status frustration is to develop a set of alternative, deviant values which provides them with alternative ways of gaining status – a deviant sub-culture. Delinquent acts are based on a deliberate reversal of accepted norms. At school, playing truant, messing about in class, and destroying school property may replace the values of studying and exam success. Stealing becomes a means of getting money, replacing career success, and vandalism replaces respect for property. Such acts of delinquency enable some lower-working-class youths to gain a status in their peer group which the wider society has denied them.

Delinquency also gives them a way of getting their revenge on the system which has condemned them to failure.

Relative deprivation, social exclusion and marginality

Social exclusion and marginalization (see glossary) were discussed in chapter 4. Relative deprivation is a related idea. This refers to a sense of lacking things (deprivation) compared to the group with which people identify and compare themselves.

Those who find themselves pushed to the margins of society and excluded from the normal everyday life that most members of society enjoy, and who have a sense of relative deprivation, are vulnerable to committing crime. This is because crime offers one route to resolving the problems of relative deprivation, social exclusion, and marginality that arise when people are denied things that others may take for granted.

The lower-working-class sub-culture

Some suggest that the values of lower-working-class male sub-culture can often lead to crime among young people. This sub-culture encourages men to demonstrate their toughness, their masculinity, and their 'smartness', and to pursue excitement and thrills. These features of working-class life can lead to clashes with the law. For example, the concern with 'toughness' might lead to offences like assault.

These values may become exaggerated in the lives of young males who want to achieve status in their peer group by engaging in delinquent acts to show how tough and smart they are. A 'good night out' might consist of a few drinks, a fight outside the pub, a rampage round the streets with mates, and a run-in with the police, with everyone competing to show they are more 'macho' than the rest.

Labelling

Labelling theory is concerned with two main features:

- The process whereby some people committing some actions come to be defined or labelled as deviant, while others do not.

- The consequences which follow once a deviant label has been applied, and how this may create more deviance or crime.

The first of these issues was discussed earlier in this chapter, so here the emphasis will be on the consequences which follow once a deviant label has been applied.

The deviant 'master status'

Labelling theorists point out that most people commit crimes and other deviant acts at some time in their lives, but not everyone becomes defined as a deviant or a criminal. For labelling theorists, what is important in explaining crime is the consequences of being caught and labelled.

Once someone is caught and labelled as a criminal or deviant, the label attached may become the dominant label or master status which overrides all other characteristics of that person – she or he becomes not someone's wife/husband, mother/father, friend, or business associate, but an 'ex-con' or a 'hooligan'.

Once a person is labelled as 'mad' (mentally ill), as a football hooligan, as a thief, or as a failure at school, the label may have quite serious consequences for his or her life, as people are treated differently according to the label. Each label carries with it a range of prejudices and images – the football hooligan, for example, is often seen as irresponsible, violent, a drunkard, a racist, and a serious threat to society. A person with a conviction for theft may be seen as fundamentally untrustworthy and never to be left alone with valuables, and if things go missing this may automatically reinforce suspicions that they have been stolen by the labelled thief. The bottom-stream pupil in school may be seen as a 'waster', and thoroughly untrustworthy and unreliable. Once labelled, a person's behaviour might be interpreted differently from that of a person not labelled as deviant. For example, teachers may treat some questions from bottom-stream 'delinquents' as red herrings, but regard the same questions from top-stream conformists as intelligent and worthy of discussion. Much the same could apply when different pupils offer excuses for not doing homework, missing games, and so on. Someone with a history of mental illness may have signs of eccentricity interpreted as evidence of his or her mental illness, but the same behaviour might pass unnoticed in a person not labelled as mentally ill.

Deviant careers

Labelling may lead to a deviant career. This simply means people start acting the way they have been labelled. For example, a man caught in an isolated act of stealing may be prosecuted, imprisoned, and labelled as a 'criminal' and later as an 'ex-con' – friends desert him, employers refuse to offer him jobs, and the man may then begin to see himself primarily as a criminal. Since alternative opportunities are closed off to him, and everyone treats him as a criminal anyway, he may then turn to crime as a way of life and follow a deviant career of crime.

In this way, labelling theory suggests that the attachment of a label can actually generate more deviance. For example, adult prisons and Young Offenders' Institutions play a key role in making the label of 'criminal' and, later, 'ex-con' stick. They immerse offenders in a criminal sub-culture, increase the opportunities to learn about crime, and make it extremely hard for offenders to go back to living a 'normal' life when they are released. More crime may therefore result as alternative opportunities are limited.

In each of the cases listed below:

1 Identify a possible label which may be attached to the person concerned as a result of her or his deviant behaviour.

2 Outline how a 'deviant career' might develop by describing the possible consequences of the labelling for the person's future life and relationships.

3 Suggest ways that a person might avoid being labelled even after she or he has committed the deviant act.

- A young woman caught shoplifting.
- A male teacher who publicly declares himself to be gay.
- A person who is temporarily admitted to a mental hospital as a result of a nervous breakdown.
- An 18-year-old man who gets arrested during a fight at a football match.

GOVERNMENT INITIATIVES AND POLICY SOLUTIONS TO CRIME

Over the years, governments have taken a range of measures to tackle crime, but with mixed success. The main deterrent to crime seems to be not the severity of the sentence or punishment, but the risk of getting caught in the first place. However, the police are detecting a smaller proportion of crimes than ever, and just 6 per cent of all crimes result in a conviction. Table 9.3 (on page 222) outlines some of the measures that have been, and are being, tried to tackle crime.

CONCLUSION: DEVIANCE, CRIME, AND SOCIAL CHANGE

This chapter has shown that the definition and explanation of deviance and crime are no simple matter. This is hardly surprising given the very wide range of behaviour that the term 'deviance' covers.

We must recognize that deviance, and even crime, are not by any means always harmful to society. Much crime remains fairly trivial, and the wide range of non-conformist behaviour, its quirks and oddities, add a richness of colour and variety to what might otherwise be a drab existence.

Without deviance, even without crime, there would be no possibility of innovation and change. The rebels and the reformers, the heretics and the inventors, and campaigners for peace and justice have all been labelled as deviants or criminals at one time or another. For example, Jesus Christ was seen as a rebel in his time, and crucified for it. Nelson Mandela was imprisoned in South Africa for thirty years for alleged terrorist offences in fighting a white racist society, but later became president of South Africa and an internationally respected world leader and celebrity. Gerry Adams spent years fighting the British occupation of Northern Ireland, and was often accused of terrorism. He later became a British MP, and something of a celebrity, appearing on the cover of VIP magazine, the Irish equivalent of Hello! magazine.

It is often the non-conformists who have contributed to changes which many would regard as of benefit to all. Deviance should be treated with an open mind, for what is regarded as deviant today is often the accepted behaviour of tomorrow.

Table 9.3 Policies to tackle crime

Policy	Description/comment
Electronic tagging	Electronic tag is fitted to ankle of offenders to monitor and control their movements
Community service	Instead of prison, offenders do work in the community, like painting community centres or digging pensioners' gardens
Curfew schemes and Anti-Social Behaviour Orders	To ban people from specific areas and to keep young tearaways off the streets
More police on the streets, and more efficient policing	Recruiting more police officers, cutting paper work so officers have more time patrolling, monitoring police performance, and taking action where results are poor
Zero-tolerance policing	Tackling *all* crime, including low-level crimes like vandalism and petty theft, where police tolerance and inaction can create an 'anything goes' culture in some communities, leading to more crime
More community involvement in policing, such as Neighbourhood Watch schemes	To promote public confidence in the police, and encourage people to report crime and to volunteer evidence that might help secure convictions
Fast-track justice for young offenders	So punishment follows quickly on the crime
Crime diversion	Divert young offenders from crime, through projects like sport, arts, and car maintenance
Rehabilitation of offenders to stop them reoffending	Rehabilitate criminals, through education and skills training, and help with finding jobs when they leave prison – 56 per cent of criminals reoffend within two years. The present prison regime is not working for most prisoners
Better use of technology	More closed-circuit television cameras, more DNA testing, photos on credit cards, more alarms and better locks on homes and cars, etc., to deter and catch criminals
Tougher sentencing	Heavier sentences for offenders, particularly persistent (repeat) offenders
Decriminalizing drug offences (i.e. stopping drug abuse being a criminal offence) and treating drug addicts	Drug abuse is the single largest cause of crime. Decriminalization and treatment programmes to cure addiction would reduce crime

Nelson Mandela

Gerry Adams

CHAPTER SUMMARY

After studying this chapter, you should be able to:

- Define social control and explain how it is carried out formally and informally through agencies of social control.

- Explain the difference between crime and deviance.

- Explain how and why definitions of deviance vary.

- Explain the link between deviance and power.

- Describe and explain the pattern of crime shown in the official crime statistics.

- Explain why white-collar and corporate crimes often go undetected or unrecorded.

- Explain a range of reasons why the official crime statistics provide no accurate record of the full extent of crime in society.

■ Explain why an increase in the official crime rate might not necessarily mean that there has been an increase in the real amount of crime.

■ Provide a range of sociological explanations of crime, delinquency, and deviance.

■ Describe and explain the ideas of labelling and deviant careers.

■ Outline some policy solutions to crime.

■ Suggest reasons why deviance and crime may not always be harmful to society.

KEY TERMS

anomie
chivalry thesis
corporate crime
crime
deviant career
juvenile delinquency
master status
relative deprivation
status frustration
sub-culture
white-collar crime

COURSEWORK SUGGESTIONS

Using secondary sources (see chapter 17), give an account of the pattern of crime in your own area, and compare it with the national crime statistics. Perhaps interview the local police for information.

Do a survey about attitudes to some deviant or illegal act, such as under-age drinking or drug abuse.

1

Carry out a case study of a Neighbourhood Watch scheme.

Carry out a self-report study (you might use the self-report study included

2   in this chapter as a starting point) or a victim survey (perhaps using the British Crime Survey to help you devise your questions) among a small sample in your school, college, or workplace, and try to discover how much

3   undiscovered and/or unreported crime there is. Compare your results with

4   those in the British Crime Survey.

10 The Family

KEY ISSUES

• What is the family?

• Consensus and conflict approaches to the family.

• Different forms of the family and marriage.

• Changes in the family in Britain.

• Family diversity and the myth of 'cereal packet' families.

• Critical views of the family.

• Alternatives to the family.

• Are marriage and the family declining social institutions?

Most people are raised in families, and so we might think we know all about them. We may make assumptions that people will fall in love with someone of the opposite sex and get married, start having children, and form their own family. We may have the impression that the typical family unit in Britain consists of parents and a couple of children, with Dad out working and Mum staying at home looking after the kids, but with both partners sharing a lot of jobs around the home. We may believe the family is the only place where children can be properly brought up, and that it is a source of unconditional affection – a place to retreat to whenever things get too much or go wrong in the outside world.

On the other hand, you may believe that the family is in decline, pointing to rising rates of divorce, extra-marital sex, and abortion, with rising numbers of lone-parent families. You might point to rising levels of child abuse, violence against women, vandalism and crime, and drug abuse. You would not be alone in holding such a belief – the mass media, politicians, the police, social workers, teachers, and religious leaders have all at some time or another tried to 'blame the family' and lack of parental control for a wide range of problems in society.

There is, whichever way you look at it, a controversy over the family. This chapter will attempt to throw some light on some of these issues, and the variety of forms of marriage and the family.

WHAT IS THE FAMILY?

A family is a group of people who are related by kinship ties: relations of blood, marriage, or adoption. The family unit is one of the most important social institutions, which is found in some form in nearly all known societies. It is a basic unit of social organization, and plays a key role in socializing children into the culture of their society, and forming their identities – how they see themselves and how others see them.

CONSENSUS AND CONFLICT APPROACHES TO THE FAMILY

The consensus approach of Functionalist writers tends to see the family as a vital 'organ' in maintaining the 'body' of society. The family does this through things like the primary socialization of children, and providing food and shelter and an 'emotional refuge' for family members. In this way the family makes a major contribution to social stability, and the creation of a harmonious society. This approach to the family emphasizes the way the family socializes children into a value consensus (shared norms and values) which makes up the culture of the society to which they belong, and helps to keep human personalities stable.

Conflict theorists, like Marxist and many feminist writers, tend to emphasize the way the family reproduces social inequality from one generation to the next, such as the inequalities between social classes and between men and women. Conflict theorists stress the way the nuclear family is concerned not with building value consensus, but with teaching its members to submit to the values and beliefs of the wealthy upper class, and not be critical of the society around them. The family is seen as working to dampen down the inevitable social conflict that is bound to appear in unequal societies. Conflict theorists also emphasize the negative aspects – the 'darker side' of family life – such as violence against partners and children.

DIFFERENT FORMS OF THE FAMILY AND MARRIAGE

Even though the family is found in nearly every society, it can take many different forms. Marriage and family life in earlier times in Britain, and today in many other societies, can be organized in quite different ways from family life in modern Britain. Sociologists use a number of different terms to describe the wide varieties of marriage and the family. Table 10.1 summarizes these varieties.

The nuclear family

The nuclear family means just the parents and children, living together in one household. It is sometimes called the two-generation family, because it contains only the two generations of parents and children. In Britain in 2003, 37 per cent of people lived in this type of family.

The extended family

The extended family is a grouping consisting of all kin. There are two main types of extended family: the classic extended and the modified extended family.

The classic extended family

The classic extended family is made up of several nuclear families joined by kinship relations. The term is mainly used to describe a situation where many related nuclear families or family members live in the same house, street, or area and the members of these related nuclear families see one another regularly. It may be horizontally extended, where it contains just two generations, with aunts, uncles, cousins, etc., or vertically extended, where it contains more than two generations, such as grandparents and grandchildren as well as parents and their own children.

The modified extended family

The modified extended family is one where related nuclear families, although they may be living far apart geographically, nevertheless maintain regular contact and mutual support through visiting, the phone,

Table 10.1 Forms of marriage and the family

Forms of	Description
MARRIAGE	
Monogamy	One husband and one wife
	Found in Europe, the USA, and most Christian cultures
Serial monogamy	A series of monogamous marriages
	Found in Europe and the USA, where there are high rates of divorce and remarriage
Arranged marriage	Marriages arranged by parents
	Found in the Indian sub-continent and the Asian community in Britain
Polygamy	Marriage to more than one partner at the same time
	Includes polygyny and polyandry
Polygyny	One husband and two or more wives
	Found in Islamic countries like Egypt and Saudi Arabia, and (illegally) among some Mormons in the state of Utah, USA
Polyandry	One wife and two or more husbands
	Found in Tibet, among the Todas of southern India, and among the Marquesan Islanders
FAMILY STRUCTURE	
Nuclear family	Two generations: parents and children living in the same household
Extended family	All kin including and beyond the nuclear family
Classic extended family	An extended family sharing the same household or living close by
Modified extended family	An extended family living far apart but keeping in close touch by phone, letters, frequent visits, and e-mail
INHERITANCE	
Patrilineal descent	Property and title passes through the male side of the family
Matrilineal descent	Property and title passes through the female side of the family
RESIDENCE	
Patrilocal	Couple live with or near the man's family
Matrilocal	Couple live with or near the woman's family
Neo-local	Couple set up home apart from either the man's or woman's family
AUTHORITY	
Patriarchal family	Authority held by males
Matriarchal family	Authority held by females
Symmetrical family	Authority shared between male and female partners
RESULTS OF MARRIAGE BREAKDOWN	
Reconstituted family	One or both partners previously married, with children of previous marriages
Lone-parent family	Lone parent, most commonly after divorce or separation (though may also arise from death of a partner or unwillingness to marry)

letters, and e-mail: continuing close relations made possible by modern communications. This is probably the most common type of family arrangement in Britain today.

ACTIVITY

1 Do a brief survey among your friends or workmates and find out how many live in nuclear families, how many live in classic extended families, and how many have modified extended families. You will have to think of suitable ways of measuring the features of these families, such as how near relatives live, how often they see one another, what other relatives live in the household apart from parents and children, and so on.

2 Ask them what it is like living in these different types of family. On the basis of your findings and using also your own experience of family life, make a list of the advantages and disadvantages of living in each type of family.

The lone-parent family

The lone-parent or single-parent family is increasingly common in Western societies. In 2003, 11 per cent of people in Britain lived in this type of family. Although lone-parent families can also arise from the death of a partner, they are today largely a result of the rise in the divorce rate. In 2003 around 25 per cent of all families with dependent children were lone-parent families, and nine out of ten of these lone parents were women. Increasingly, lone-parent families are arising from a simple lack of desire to get married – in 2003 about 45 per cent of lone mothers fell into this category. About three-quarters of lone-parent families receive income support.

The reconstituted family

The reconstituted family is a family where one or both partners have been married previously, and they bring with them children of a previous marriage. This 'reconstitutes' the family with various combinations of stepmother, stepfather, and stepchildren. Such families are increasingly common in Western societies, as a result of rising divorce rates and remarriages. In Britain, more than 40 per cent of all marriages involve remarriage for one or both partners, and more than one in ten children today live in stepfamilies, with parents of one or more previous marriages.

The symmetrical family

The symmetrical family is one where the roles of husband and wife or of cohabiting partners have become more alike (symmetrical) and equal. There are more shared tasks within relationships rather than a clear division between the jobs of male and female partners. Both partners are likely to be wage earners. It remains a popular impression that most families in modern Britain are symmetrical, but evidence which will be discussed later in this chapter suggests this is not the case.

Monogamy

In modern Britain and the rest of Europe, the USA, and most Christian cultures, monogamy is the only legal form of marriage. Monogamy is a form of marriage in which a person can have only one husband or wife at the same time. Monogamy has not traditionally been the most common form of marriage in the world, though it is rapidly becoming so as Western ideas of marriage spread through the world, as societies modernize. In a society where monogamy is the only form of legal marriage, a person who marries while still legally married to someone else is guilty of the crime of bigamy – a serious offence punishable by imprisonment.

Serial monogamy

In modern Britain, most of Western Europe, and the USA there are high rates of divorce and remarriage. Some people keep marrying and divorcing a series of different partners, but each marriage is monogamous. The term serial monogamy is sometimes used to describe these marriage patterns. This form of marriage has been described as 'one at a time, one after the other, and they don't last long'.

Arranged marriages

Arranged marriages are those where the marriages of children are organized by their parents, who try to match their children with partners of a similar background and status. The arranged marriage is more a union between two families than between two people, and romantic love is not necessarily present between the marriage partners. They are typically found among Muslims, Sikhs, and Hindus. The arranged marriage is still common in the Asian community in Britain, where the custom is often more strictly enforced than in the Indian sub-continent. This is because the present generations of parents and grandparents here often still stick to the customs which existed when they left India for Britain many years ago.

DISCUSSION

What are the advantages and disadvantages of arranged marriages? How do you think arranged marriages might be changing in Britain, and what pressures do you think there might be on the survival of the custom in Britain?

Polygamy

Although marrying a second partner while still married to the first is a crime in Britain, in many societies it is perfectly acceptable to have more than one marriage partner at the same time. Polygamy is a general term referring to marriage between a member of one sex and two or more members of the opposite sex at the same time. There are two different types of polygamy: polygyny and polyandry.

Polygyny

Polygyny is the marriage of one man to two or more women at the same time. It is widely practised in Islamic countries such as Egypt and Saudi

Monogamy   Polygyny   Polyandry

Polygamy

Arabia. It is also practised (illegally) among some Mormons in the state of Utah in the USA. The possession of several wives is often seen as a sign of wealth and success and generally only those men who can afford to support several wives practise polygyny. Because of this, even where polygyny is allowed, only a small number of men actually practise it. In any case, the numbers of men and women in most societies are usually fairly evenly balanced, and there are not enough women for all men to have more than one wife. Further information on polygyny, including its practice among people who are not members of minority ethnic groups, can be found at <www.polygamy.com>.

Polyandry

Polyandry is the marriage of one woman to two or more men at the same time. This is rare and is found in only about 1 per cent of all societies. Polyandry appears to arise where living standards are so low that a man can only afford to support a wife and child by sharing the responsibility with other men. It is found among the Todas of southern India and the Marquesan Islanders, and has been reported as occurring in parts of Tibet.

Patterns of family inheritance

As well as the variety of marriage relations, there are also differences in the patterns of inheritance in the family. Patrilineal descent is the system where the inheritance of title, property, and position as family head is passed down through the male side of the family, from father to son. An example of this is the way the succession to the British throne is passed through the male side of the royal family. Matrilineal descent is the system where inheritance is through the female side of the family.

Patterns of residence

Different societies have different traditions about where the newly married should live. Patrilocal residence is the system where a married couple lives by tradition with or near the husband's family. Matrilocal residence is the system where the couple lives with or near the wife's family. In modern Britain, families tend to be neo-local, in that couples are not expected to move near either the husband's or the wife's family.

Patterns of authority

Patriarchy is a term used to describe the dominance of men over women. A patriarchal family is one where the father, husband, or eldest male is usually the chief authority and decision-maker. The family in Victorian Britain was an example of this, but many writers would argue the modern British family remains patriarchal. Matriarchy describes the dominance of women over men. Matriarchal families are where power and authority is held by the most senior woman. These are rare, but there is some evidence of them in rural Japan.

CHANGES IN THE FAMILY IN BRITAIN

The family in Britain has gone through a number of changes since the beginnings of industrialization, and it continues to change today. The extent of some of these changes thought to have occurred in the family has often been exaggerated, and misleading conclusions drawn. Each of these changes will be examined in turn. The key changes which have commonly been thought to have occurred are summarized in Figure 10.1, and then discussed.

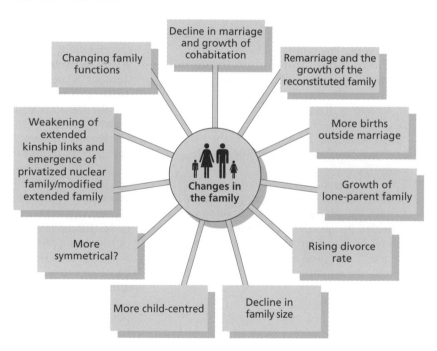

Figure 10.1 Changes in the family

Change 1: the changing role of the family in society

The family in Britain and most other societies has traditionally had a number of responsibilities placed upon it (its functions), primarily connected with its role in the preparation of children to fit into adult society. These tasks of the family, and how they've changed during the course of this century in Britain, are described below.

Traditional responsibilities (or functions) of the family

- *Reproduction of the population* – the reproduction and nurturing of children. Having children was often seen as the main reason for marriage, as a means of passing on family property and providing a future workforce.

- The family and kinship network traditionally played a major role in *maintaining and caring for dependent children* – housing, clothing, and feeding those children who were still unable to look after themselves.

- The family provided most of the *help and care for the young, the old, the sick, and the poor* during periods of illness, unemployment, and other crises. Poverty often meant poor health and poor healthcare.

- The *primary socialization and social control of children*. The family is where society's new recruits first learn the basic values and norms of the culture of the society they will grow up in. For example, it is in the family that children first learn the difference between what is seen as 'right' and 'wrong', 'good' and 'bad' behaviour, and the acceptance of parental and other adult authority.

- The family used to be one of the only sources of *education* for young people in Britain. Before compulsory schooling was provided by the state in Britain from 1880, many children from working-class families were very poorly educated by today's standards, and illiteracy rates were extremely high.

- Before industrialization and the growth of factory production in Britain, the family was a *unit of production*. This means that the family home was also the workplace; the family produced most of the goods necessary for its own survival, and children would learn the skills needed for working life from their parents.

How they have changed

- In Britain since the 1970s, there has been a steady increase in the reproduction of children and sexual relations before and outside of marriage. In 2003, for example, around 40 per cent of children were born outside marriage. These changes are explained later in this chapter.

- The modern nuclear family is less dependent on relatives for help and assistance in maintaining and caring for children. Welfare benefits like social security and child tax credits, and the social services, including social workers working with families, all help parents to maintain their children.

- This has become shared with the state through the NHS and the social services. Homes for the elderly, hospitals, welfare clinics, GPs, old age pensions, benefits during unemployment, and income support reduce the dependence on kin for money and support.

- The family still retains the major responsibility for the socialization of very young children, but the increase in the number of pre-schools and playgroups has meant this is no longer restricted to the family. The state educational system now helps the family with the socialization of school-age children, and the mass media also play an important role.

- The education of children has been mainly taken over by the state, and is now primarily the responsibility of professional teachers rather than parents. All children between the ages of 5 and 16 now have to attend school by law. However, the family continues to play an important socializing and supporting role in preparing a child for school, and encouraging and supporting her or him while at school. The family still has a major effect on a child's level of educational achievement.

- Since the early nineteenth century in Britain, work has been mainly based in factories and offices, not in the home. Families do not generally produce the goods they need any more; they go out and buy them. The skills required for adult working life are no longer learnt in the family, but at the place of work, at colleges, or on government-supported job training schemes.

1 Go carefully through the section opposite on the traditional functions or responsibilities of the family and how they have changed. Make a list summarizing these changes under two main headings: (a) the tasks traditionally performed by the family, and (b) who performs these functions today: family, or government and state, or shared between them.

2 Identify two ways that the family provides for the well-being of its members.

3 Do you think the changes that have occurred in the family's functions have made it more or less important in society today? Back up your viewpoint with evidence.

4 Imagine all families were banned by law tomorrow. What tasks currently carried out in your own family would someone else have to perform? Who would do these tasks, do you think?

5 Consider all the ways you can think of that the family a child is born into might affect the chances she or he gets in life, such as in health, education, and job opportunities. Be sure you explain the connection between family background and the life chances you identify.

Change 2: the emergence of the privatized nuclear family and the modified extended family

A traditional view in sociology was that the main form of the family in Britain changed from the classic extended family before industrialization to the privatized nuclear family in the late twentieth century. However, research has shown that both nuclear and extended families were common in pre-industrial Britain, with the nuclear family perhaps being the most common. The family in Britain can be said to have developed through three basic stages.

The pre-industrial family

At this stage, the family was a unit of production which produced most of society's goods in small family workshops based in houses and farms (the domestic system), where all family members, including children, would live and work together. The nuclear family was the most common form.

The early industrial classic extended family

With industrialization in nineteenth-century England, factory production replaced the domestic system, and the family ceased to be a unit of production. People began to go outside the home to work in factories, offices, and mines. Early industrialization strengthened the extended family, especially in the working class. This was because in the new industrial towns wages were low, unemployment was high, housing conditions and health were very poor, and working-class poverty was widespread. Relatives often provided the only sources of help and support against the insecurity and hardship of poverty and unemployment, so most working-class people strengthened links with kin through the formation of extended families.

The twenty-first century privatized nuclear family

Over about the last hundred years, a traditional view has been that the extended family has largely disappeared in modern Britain, with the typical family form in Britain becoming the privatized nuclear family. This means the nuclear family is separated and isolated from its extended kin, and has become a self-contained, self-reliant, home-centred unit. Life for the modern privatized nuclear family is largely centred on the home – free time is spent doing jobs around the house and leisure is mainly home- and family-centred. DIY, gardening, watching television, or going out as a family to pleasure parks like Alton Towers are typical family activities. The modern nuclear family has thus become a very private institution, isolated from wider kin and often from neighbours and local community life as well.

The following explanations have been offered for this decline of extended family life and the process of privatization:

■ Industrial societies require a geographically mobile labour force, with people able and willing to move to other areas of the country to find work, improve their education, or gain promotion. This often involves leaving relatives behind, thus weakening and breaking up traditional extended family life. The small size of the modern isolated nuclear family and its lack of permanent roots in an area (such as wider kin) mean that it is geographically mobile, which some sociologists argue makes it ideally suited to life in an industrial society.

■ Industrial societies have become more meritocratic – the jobs people get are mainly achieved on the basis of talent, skill, and educational qualifications, rather than whom they know. Extended kin therefore have less to offer family members, such as job opportunities, reducing reliance on kin.

■ Educational success and promotion often involve upward social mobility and this leads to differences in income, status, lifestyle, and attitudes and values between kin. Kin have less in common, and this contributes to the weakening of extended family ties.

■ With the development of higher standards of living and the provision of welfare services by the state for security against ill-health, unemployment, and poverty, people have become less dependent on kin for help in times of distress. This further weakens the extended family.

The modified extended family

While there is evidence that nuclear families have become the most common form of the family in industrial society, geographical separation does not necessarily mean all links with kin are severed. Often, in the age of mass communications and easy transportation, the closeness and mutual support between kin, typical of classic extended family life, are retained by letter writing, telephone, e-mail, and visiting. It has therefore been suggested that the typical family today in Britain is not simply the isolated nuclear family, but this modified form of the extended family.

The continued existence of the classic extended family

While the most common type of family found in modern Britain is the nuclear family or the modified extended family, there is evidence that the classic extended family still survives today in modern Britain in two types of community:

■ *Traditional working-class communities.* These are long-established communities dominated by one industry, like fishing and mining, in the traditional working-class industrial centres of the north of England, and in inner-city working-class areas. In such communities, there is little geographical or social mobility, and children usually remain in the same area when they get married. People stay in the same community for several generations, and this creates a close-knit community life – it is the type of community shown in TV 'soaps' such as *Coronation Street* or *EastEnders*. Members of the extended family live close together and meet frequently, and there is a constant exchange of services between extended family members, such as washing, shopping, and baby-sitting between female kin, and shared work and leisure activities between male relatives. Such extended family life declined in the 1980s and 1990s, as traditional industries closed down and people were forced to move away in search of new employment.

■ *The Asian community.* There is evidence that the extended family is still very common among those who came to Britain in the 1960s and 1970s from India, Pakistan, and Bangladesh. The extended family usually centres on the male side of the family, with grandfathers, sons, grandsons, and their wives, and unmarried daughters. Such a family life continues to be an important source of strength and support in such communities.

The 'Beanpole' family: the return of the extended family?

Britain's ageing population (which is discussed in chapter 15) means that a growing number of people are reaching old age, and often living well into their eighties and many into their nineties. At the same time, couples are having fewer children and nuclear families are getting smaller. This means that there is an increase in the number of extended three- and four-generation families. There are fewer children in families, but more of them are growing up in extended families alongside several of their grandparents and even great-grandparents. This new shape of the extended family is sometimes called the 'beanpole' family. This is because the family tree is 'thinner' and less 'bushy': fewer brothers and sisters in

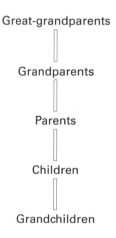

Great-grandparents

Grandparents

Parents

Children

Grandchildren

The 'beanpole' family

one generation leads to fewer aunts and uncles in the next. It is also longer, with several generations of older relatives, as people live longer. This trend towards a new emerging 'beanpole' form of the extended family can only be expected to increase with the growing numbers of the elderly, and fewer children being born.

Change 3: the emergence of the 'symmetrical' family?

There is a common belief that the relations between male and female partners in the family in Britain became more equal in the second half of the twentieth century. The assumption has been that there was a change from segregated to integrated conjugal roles, and the emergence of a more 'symmetrical' or equally balanced family, with male partners becoming 'New Men' and taking more responsibility for housework and childcare (see pages 93–4). Conjugal roles are simply the roles played by male and female partners in marriage or in a cohabiting couple. There are said to be two main types:

■ Segregated conjugal roles, where male and female partners have very different tasks in the family, with a clear division and separation between the male's role and the female's role.

■ Integrated (or joint) conjugal roles, where there are few divisions in the jobs done by male and female partners.

Some of these differences are identified below.

Segregated conjugal roles
■ Partners in a married or cohabiting relationship have clearly separated roles.

■ Men take responsibility for bringing in money, major decisions, and doing the heavier and more technical jobs around the home, such as repairing household equipment and doing repairs. Women are mainly housewives, with responsibility for housework, shopping, cooking, childcare, etc. Women are unlikely to have full-time paid employment.
■ Partners are likely to have separate friends and different leisure activities.

Integrated conjugal roles
■ Partners in a married or cohabiting relationship have interchangeable and flexible roles.

■ Both partners are likely to be either in paid employment or looking for a job. Household chores and childcare are shared, with males taking on traditional female jobs like housework, cooking, shopping, etc., and female partners taking on traditional male jobs, such as household repairs, looking after the car, etc.

■ Partners share common friends, leisure activities, and decision-making.

The change from segregated to integrated roles

The supposed change from segregated to integrated roles is thought to have occurred for a number of reasons.

■ The improved status and rights of women have forced men to accept women more as equals and not simply as housewives and mothers.

■ The increase in the number of working women has increased women's independence and authority in the family – where the female partner has her own income, she is less dependent on her male partner, and she has more power and authority. Decision-making is therefore more likely to be shared.

■ The importance of female partners' earnings in maintaining the family's standard of living may have encouraged men to help more with housework – a recognition that the women cannot be expected to do two jobs at once.

■ Improved living standards in the home, such as central heating, TV, videos and stereos, and 'all mod cons', have encouraged men to spend more time at home, and share home-centred leisure with their female partners.

■ The decline of the close-knit extended family and greater geographical mobility in industrial society have meant there is less pressure from kin on newly married or cohabiting couples to retain traditional roles – it is therefore easier to adopt new roles in a relationship. There are often no longer the separate male and female networks (of friends and especially kin) for male and female partners to mix with. This increases their dependence upon each other, and may mean men and women who adopt new roles avoid being teased by friends who knew them before they got married or began cohabiting.

ACTIVITY

How far is there equality between partners in a household you know well? It could be your own home, or any household where there are children. Put the following questions to the male partner of the household:

1 Have you ever ironed your partner's blouse?
2 What foods do your children refuse to eat?
3 What do the following cost: a loaf, a jar of instant coffee, a packet of tea, a packet of butter, a tin of baked beans, a packet of washing-powder/liquid, and a packet of toilet rolls?
4 How does the washing machine work?
5 What would you use to clean the kitchen floor?
6 How do you empty the vacuum cleaner bag?
7 What days are the bins emptied?
8 What brand of washing powder/liquid do you normally use?
9 When did you last do the family shopping alone?
10 When did you last draw up the shopping list alone?
11 When did you last clean the loo?
12 What is the children's favourite meal?
13 How many hours a week do you spend on housework?
14 When did you last clean the bathroom or kitchen taps?
15 When did you last clean the bath or shower, or the kitchen/bathroom sinks?

Compare your findings with others in your group. What conclusions do your findings suggest about the apparent change towards growing equality between men and women in the family?

Have conjugal roles really changed?

The myth of integrated roles

The Office for National Statistics suggested in the late 1990s that rising numbers of men were choosing to become 'house-husbands' and raise children rather than work outside the home, leaving their female partner to become the family breadwinner. This reversal of traditional roles reflects the growing earning power of women at work, and provides some evidence of changing attitudes among some men towards childcare and housework. However, this trend appears to be mainly happening only in those relatively few families where the woman earns more than the man, and it is financially practical to swap roles. Evidence from a number of surveys shows that, in most cases, traditional segregated roles still remain:

Table 10.2 Percentage who never do selected household tasks: United Kingdom, 2001

Activity	Does not do activity	
	Men	Women
Cooking a meal	15	3
DIY repair work	16	46
Gardening	20	22
Non-food shopping	7	3
Food shopping	33	10
Cooking a meal (special occasion)	18	27
Decorating	12	5
Tidying the house	13	4
Helping children with homework	66	60
Washing clothes	39	5
Ironing clothes	42	8

Source: Adapted from UK Time Use Survey, Office for National Statistics

■ Women still perform the majority of domestic and childcare tasks around the home, even when they have paid jobs themselves. Cooking the evening meal, household cleaning, washing and ironing, and caring for sick family members are still mainly performed by women (see figure 10.2), and women spend on average nearly twice as long as men each day (five hours) cooking, cleaning, shopping, washing, and looking after the children. Housework is the second largest cause of domestic rows, after money.

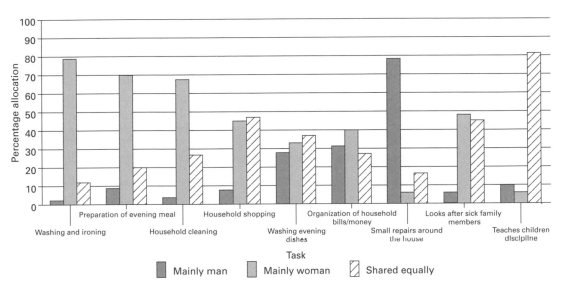

Figure 10.2 Household division of labour among married or cohabiting couples: Great Britain, 1990s

Source: Data from British Social Attitudes Survey, 1992, 1994; Social Trends, 1997; British and European Social Attitudes Report, 1998

ACTIVITY

Refer to figure 10.2 and table 10.2. These show the results of surveys which were conducted through the 1990s and in 2001. Then answer the following questions:

1 Which three household tasks were the most likely to be performed mainly by women?

2 Which two household tasks were the most likely to be performed mainly by men?

3 Who is most likely to look after sick family members?

4 Which household task is the least likely to be performed mainly by men?

5 Which three household tasks are most likely to be shared equally?

6 Who is most likely to prepare the evening meal, and either to be solely responsible for washing evening dishes or to share it with their partners?

7 What percentage of men never iron clothes?

8 What percentage of women never do DIY repair work?

9 Outline all the evidence in figure 10.2 and table 10.2 which suggests that it is largely a myth that the family is a 'partnership of equals' today.

■ It is women who are most likely to make sacrifices to buy the children clothes, and to make sure other family members are properly fed.

■ Women are less likely than men to have the final say on the most important decisions in the family.

■ Men are still often the major or sole earners, and this puts men in a stronger bargaining position than women, and often puts their female partners in a position of economic dependence.

■ Women's continuing responsibility for housework and childcare often means their careers suffer. Surveys suggest many working women are limited in the jobs they can do and the hours they can work because they are still expected to take the main responsibility for housework and childcare, and to be at home for the children leaving for and returning from school. Women consequently have less pay, less security of employment, and poorer promotion prospects than men, and this reinforces men's economic superiority and greater authority in the family.

■ It is mainly women who give up paid work (or suffer from lost/restricted job opportunities) to look after children, the elderly, or the sick.

■ Women still take the major responsibility for 'managing' the emotional side of family life. This refers to things like the emotional aspects of childcare, such as talking to, listening to, understanding, and supporting children, including older children. It also involves liaising between family members when there are rows, and acting as the family mediator.

WOMEN'S TRIPLE SHIFT

The points above mean many female partners now often have three jobs (paid work, domestic labour and childcare and emotional work) to their male partner's one.

While there does seem to be evidence of more role integration in leisure activities and decision-making, housework and childcare remain predominantly 'women's work'. While men are perhaps more involved in childcare than they used to be, this would appear to be in the more enjoyable activities like playing with the children and taking them out. The more routine jobs such as bathing and feeding and taking children to the doctor are still done predominantly by women, and it is still mostly women who get the blame if the house is untidy or children are dirty or badly dressed.

While men might be doing marginally more around the home in recent years, this change would appear to have been massively exaggerated. In a majority of marriages and cohabiting relationships, the traditional roles of women and men remain.

Change 4: the changing position of children in the family

During the course of the twentieth century, families became more child-centred, with family activities and outings often focused on the interests of the children. The amount of time parents spend with their children has more than doubled since the 1960s, and parents are more involved with their children, taking an interest in their activities, discussing decisions with them, and treating them more as equals. Often, the children's welfare is seen as the major family priority, frequently involving the parents in considerable financial sacrifice and cost.

The causes of child-centredness

■ Families have got smaller over the last century, and this means more individual care and attention can be devoted to each child.

■ The typical working week has got shorter. This means parents have more time to spend with their children.

■ Increasing affluence, with higher wages and a higher standard of living, has benefited children, as more money can be spent on them and their activities.

■ The welfare state provides not only a wide range of benefits designed to help parents care for their children, but also a range of measures, such as Sure Start, to give children a good start in life through early-years education. There are now increased demands on parents to look after their children properly: social workers, for example, have a wide range of powers to intervene in families on behalf of children who are at risk, and have the ultimate power to remove children from families if parents fail to look after them properly.

■ Paediatrics, or the science of childhood, has developed over the last century, with a wide range of research and popular books suggesting how parents should bring up their children to encourage their full development. 'Parenting skills' have now been recognized as a very important aspect of children's educational and social development.

■ Compulsory education and more time spent in further education and training have meant young people are dependent on their parents for longer periods of time. 'Childhood' has itself become extended.

■ Children have more legal rights through the Children Act 1989, and there is now a government minister for children. The government was proposing to establish a Children's Commissioner in 2005 to protect and promote the rights of children.

■ Children's lives have become more complex, with more educational, medical, and leisure services for them. This frequently involves parents in ferrying children to schools, cinemas, friends, and so on.

■ Growing traffic dangers and parental fears (largely unjustified) of assaults on their children have meant that children now travel more with parents rather than being left to roam about on their own as much as they used to.

■ Large businesses have encouraged a specific childhood consumer market. Businesses like Mothercare, Toys R Us, Nike, publishers, and the music industry aim at the childhood consumer market, encouraging children to consume – and parents to spend, to satisfy their children's demands. 'Pester power', where advertisers target children to pester their parents into buying them CDs, clothes, toys, and so on, is now an important feature of the advertising business.

Change 5: the decline in average family size

Over the last century or so, the birth rate has been declining in Britain. This has meant that average family size has been dropping, from around 6 children per family in the 1870s to an average of around 1.8 children per family in 2003. The reasons for this change include:

■ More effective and cheaper methods of contraception, and easier and safer access to abortion.

■ Compulsory education. Children have become an economic liability and a drain on the resources of parents, as they have to be supported for a long period in compulsory education, and often in post-16 education and training.

■ The changing position of women. Women today have less desire to spend long years of their lives bearing and rearing children, and many wish to pursue a career of their own.

■ The decline in the infant mortality rate (the number of deaths of babies in the first year of life per 1000 live births per year) and the death rate (the number of deaths per 1000 of the population per year). Fewer children are dying before adulthood, so parents no longer have many children as security against only a few surviving.

■ The range of welfare state agencies which exist to help the elderly today. People are less reliant on care by their children when they reach old age.

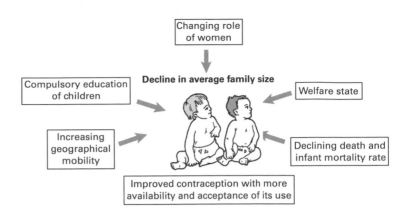

Figure 10.3 The reasons for smaller families

■ Industrial societies' need for a geographically mobile workforce. This means a workforce that can easily move to other areas for work or promotion. This may have been a factor in encouraging smaller families, as they can more easily pack up and move elsewhere.

Change 6: the rising divorce rate

One of the most startling changes in the family in Britain over the last century has been the general and dramatic increase in the number of marriages to end in divorce, as shown in figure 10.4 on page 244. The number of divorces in England and Wales rose from 29,000 in 1951 to 148,000 in 2002, almost doubling during the 1970s. Although the number has now stabilised and is no longer increasing, this is because fewer people are marrying – relationships continue to break up, but fewer of them are marriages. Britain still has one of the highest divorce rates (numbers divorcing per thousand married people) in the European Union, and estimates have suggested more than 40 per cent of marriages in the early 2000s were likely to end in divorce.

DEFINITION	**DIVORCE AND 'BROKEN HOMES'**
	Divorce is the legal termination of a marriage, but this is not the only way that marriages and homes can be 'broken'. Homes and marriages may be broken in 'empty shell' marriages, where the marital relationship has broken down, but no divorce has taken place. Separation – through either choice or necessity (like working abroad or imprisonment) – may also cause a broken home, as may the death of a partner. So homes may be broken for reasons other than divorce, and divorce itself is often only the end result of a marriage which broke down long before.

Who gets divorced?

While divorce affects all groups in the population, there are some groups where divorce rates are higher than the average. Teenage marriages are twice as likely to end in divorce as those of couples overall, and there is a

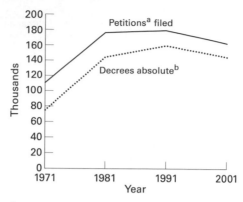

ᵃ A request to a court for a divorce
ᵇ The final divorce

Figure 10.4 Divorce: England and Wales, 1971–2001

Source: Data from Populations Trends, Office for National Statistics

ACTIVITY

Study figure 10.4 and answer the following questions:
1 Approximately how many divorce petitions were filed in 1971?
2 How many decrees absolute were there in 2001?
3 In what year was there the highest number of decrees absolute?
4 About how many more decrees absolute were there in 1991 than in 1971?
5 Figure 10.4 shows there is a large difference between the number of divorce petitions (requests to a court to grant a divorce) and the number of decrees absolute (the final divorce) granted. Suggest explanations for this.

high incidence of divorce in the first five years of marriage and after about twelve to fourteen years (when the children are older). The working class, particularly semi- and unskilled, has a higher rate of divorce than the middle class. Childless couples and partners from different social class or religious backgrounds also face a higher risk of divorce.

ACTIVITY

Go through the groups above, and suggest explanations why each of them is more at risk of divorce than most of the rest of the population. Can you think of other groups who might have a higher risk of divorce than most people?

Explanations for the rising divorce rate

Rising divorce rates must be treated with considerable caution, and assessed against changing legal, financial, and social circumstances, if misleading conclusions about the declining importance of marriage and the family are to be avoided. The increase may simply reflect easier and cheaper divorce procedures enabling the legal termination of already unhappy 'empty shell' marriages rather than a real increase in marriage breakdowns. It could be that people who in previous years could only separate are now divorcing as legal and financial obstacles are removed.

There are two broad groups of reasons for the increase in the divorce rate. First, there have been changes in the law which have gradually made divorce easier and cheaper to get. Each change in the divorce law has

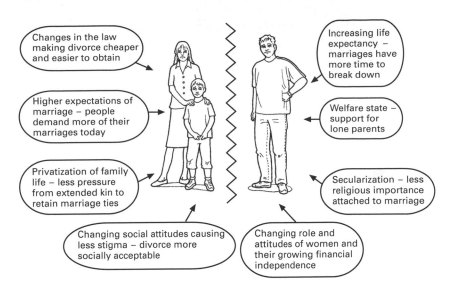

Figure 10.5 Causes of the rising divorce rate

increased the divorce rate. However, legal changes alone do not explain the increasing divorce rate – legal changes often reflect changing social attitudes and norms. The second group of explanations is therefore made up of those changes in society which have made divorce a more practical and socially acceptable way of terminating a broken marriage.

Changes in the law

Two major types of legal changes have occurred over the last century or so. First, the costs of obtaining a divorce have reduced. Second, the divorce laws have changed to make it easier to get a divorce, and created equal rights for men and women.

Changes in society

THE CHANGING ROLE OF WOMEN   This is a very important explanation for the rising divorce rate. Around three-quarters of divorce petitions (requests to a court for a divorce) are presented by women, and nearly three out of four of all divorces were granted to women in 2002. This suggests more women than men are unhappy with the state of their marriages, and are more likely to take the first steps in ending a marriage. This may well be because women's expectations of life and marriage rose during the course of the twentieth century, and they are less willing to accept a traditional housewife/mother role, with the sacrifices of their own lives, independence, and careers this involves.

The employment of married/cohabiting women has increased over the last century. For example, in 1931, only 10 per cent of married/cohabiting women were employed, but this had gradually risen to about 75 per cent in 2003. This has increased their financial independence, and reduced the extent of dependence on their husbands. This makes it easier for women to escape from unhappy marriages, and in the event of marriage breakdown,

SOME RECENT CHANGES IN THE DIVORCE LAWS

The *Divorce Law Reform Act of* 1969 This came into effect in 1971, and was a major change. Before the 1969 Act, a person wanting a divorce had to prove before a court that his or her spouse had committed a 'matrimonial offence', like adultery, cruelty, or desertion. This frequently led to major public scandals, as all the details of unhappy marriages were aired in a public law court. This may have deterred many people whose marriage had broken down from seeking a divorce. Also, marriages may have broken down – become 'empty shell' marriages – without any matrimonial offence being committed.

The 1969 Act changed all this, and made 'irretrievable breakdown' of a marriage the only grounds for divorce. It is now no longer necessary to prove one partner 'guilty' of a matrimonial offence, but simply to demonstrate that a marriage has broken down beyond repair. After 1971, one way of demonstrating 'irretrievable breakdown' of a marriage was by two years of separation. This change in the law led to a massive increase in the number of divorces after 1971.

The *Matrimonial and Family Proceedings Act of* 1984 allowed couples to petition for divorce after only one year of marriage, whereas previously couples could normally divorce only after three years of marriage. This led to a record increase in the number of divorces in 1984 and 1985.

The *Family Law Act of* 1996 came into effect in 1999. This increased the amount of time before a divorce could be granted to eighteen months, introduced compulsory marriage counselling for a 'period of reflection', and required children's wishes and financial arrangements to be agreed before a divorce was granted. This was an attempt to stem the rising number of divorces by increasing the time for 'cooling off'. The compulsory counselling sessions were abandoned in 2001 as it was found that these were more likely to encourage people to go through with a divorce, even when they were initially uncertain about whether they really wanted to get divorced.

there is a range of welfare state benefits to help divorced women, particularly those with children.

More women are postponing marriage until they have established their careers. The age at which people marry has therefore increased, and so has the average age at which people get divorced, as the length of marriage of couples divorcing has changed little since the 1960s. The average age at which people divorce has risen from about 39 years for men and 37 for women in 1971 to about 41 and 39 years in the early twenty-first century.

HIGHER EXPECTATIONS OF MARRIAGE   People's expectations of what marriage should be like have risen over the past century, and couples (especially women) expect and demand far more from their relationships today than their parents might have settled for. The mass media (especially television) often emphasize the romantic aspects of marriage, and they also provide us with images of and insights into other people's relationships which earlier generations didn't have. People therefore have come to expect more companionship, understanding, and sexual compatibility in their relationships, rather than the financial security which seemed more important in the past. Consequently couples are more likely to end a relationship which earlier generations might have tolerated.

This view of the higher expectations of marriage is reflected in the fairly high rate of remarriage among divorced people. In other words, families split up to reform happier families – a bit like 'old banger' cars failing their MOT test, being taken to the scrap yard and replaced with a better-quality car, and thereby improving the general quality of cars on the road.

CHANGING SOCIAL ATTITUDES Divorce has become more socially acceptable, and there is less social disapproval and condemnation (stigmatizing) of divorcees. Divorce no longer hinders careers through a public sense of scandal and outrage. As a result, people are less afraid of the consequences of divorce, and are more likely to seek a legal end to an unhappy marriage rather than simply separating or carrying on in an 'empty shell' marriage.

GROWING SECULARIZATION Secularization – the decline in religious belief, influence, and power – has meant that divorce is not seen so much today as breaking solemn vows or morally wrong, and over half of first-time marriages today do not involve a religious ceremony. Many people today therefore probably do not attach much religious significance to their marriage.

INCREASING LIFE EXPECTANCY People live to a greater age than they did in the early years of the last century, and this means the potential number of years a couple may be together, before the death of a partner occurs, has increased. This gives more time for marriages to 'go wrong' and for divorces to occur. It has been suggested that the divorce courts have taken on the role in finishing unhappy marriages that the undertaker once had.

THE GROWTH OF THE PRIVATIZED NUCLEAR FAMILY This has meant that, during marital crises, it is no longer so easy for marriage partners to seek

ACTIVITY

1 Go through all the reasons suggested above for the rising divorce rate, putting them in what you think is their order of importance.

2 Study television advertisements or television 'soaps' for a few days. What kind of overall impressions are given of married life today? Refer to particular advertisements or 'soaps' as evidence for your findings. Do you agree or disagree with the view that these create higher expectations of marriage today? Explain the reasons for your answer.

3 Of men and women marrying today, well over half had lived with their partners beforehand, and living together before marriage was seen as one of the major social changes of the late twentieth century. However, many of these people eventually marry. What social pressures are there that push people towards conforming to the norm of marriage? Write down all the reasons you can think of why so many people continue to marry eventually, despite the high divorce rate and previous experience of living together outside marriage. Discuss your reasons with others in your class.

advice from or temporary refuge with relatives, and there is also less social control from extended kin pressuring couples to retain marriage ties.

Change 7: the emergence of the lone-parent family

One of the biggest changes in the family has been the growth of the lone-parent family (also known as the single-parent or one-parent family). Britain now has one of the highest proportions of lone-parent families in Europe, and the percentage of such families has tripled since 1971. About 25 per cent of all families with dependent children were lone-parent families in 2003 – nine out of ten of them headed by women. Nearly one in four (23 per cent) of dependent children now live in such families, compared to just 7 per cent in 1971.

Why are there more lone-parent families?

The rapid growth in the number of lone-parent families can be explained by a number of factors, some of which have already been discussed earlier in explaining the rising divorce rate and in the chapter on gender. These include:

- *The greater economic independence of women.* Women have greater economic independence today, both through more job opportunities and through support from the welfare state. This means marriage, and support by a husband, is less of an economic necessity today compared to the past.

- *Improved contraception, changing male attitudes, and fewer 'shotgun weddings'.* With the wider availability and approval of safe and effective contraception, and easier access to safe and legal abortion, men may feel less responsibility to marry women should they become pregnant, and women may feel under less pressure to marry the future father. There are therefore fewer 'shotgun weddings'.

- *Reproductive technology* available to women, enabling them to bear children without a male partner, through surrogate motherhood and fertility treatments like IVF (in vitro fertilization).

- *Changing social attitudes.* There is less social stigma (or social disapproval and condemnation) attached to lone parenthood today. Women are therefore less afraid of the social consequences of becoming lone parents.

The growth in lone parenthood has been seen by some as one of the major signs of the 'decline' of conventional family life and marriage. Lone-parent families – and particularly lone never-married mothers – have been portrayed by some of the media and conservative politicians as promiscuous parasites blamed for everything from rising juvenile crime to housing shortages, rising drug abuse, educational failure of children, and the general breakdown of society. However, the never-married lone mother only accounts for about 40 per cent of all lone parents, with most lone parenthood arising from divorce, separation, or widowhood. Even among the never-married lone mothers, the vast majority previously cohabited with the father and had registered his name on the birth certificate.

One in four families with dependent children are lone-parent families, 90 per cent of them headed by women

Photo: Ted Fussey

Nailing the myths

The Home Office has reported no difference in the crime rates between youngsters from lone- and two-parent families. Even if there were such a link, it would probably be caused by poverty rather than lone parenthood, as lack of childcare facilities means many lone parents have to depend on state benefits to live. This is likely to explain other factors linked in the popular imagination to lone parenthood, such as lower educational achievement. A misleading myth is that of single teenage mothers getting pregnant to jump the queue for social (council and housing association) housing. There is very little evidence for this. The average age of a lone parent is 34, and at any one time, less than 3 per cent of all lone parents are teenagers. Research by the Economic and Social Research Council found that only 10 per cent of the small minority of women who became mothers prior to any partnership with the father were living alone with their child in social housing six months after the birth. Many live with their parents, and many single, never-married parents have been in cohabiting relationships which break down. In effect, this is no different from marriages that break down.

ACTIVITY/
DISCUSSION

1 Try the following websites, and identify five issues that seem to be of particular concern to lone parents. Describe each issue briefly, and outline any solutions that are suggested.
   ■ <www.lone-parents.org.uk>
   ■ <www.oneparentfamilies.org.uk>
   ■ <www.gingerbread.org.uk>

2 Do you believe that a lone parent can bring up his or her child as well as a married (or cohabiting) couple? Do you believe that people who want children ought to get married? Do you believe that to grow up happily, children need a home with both their mother and father? Is it better for a child to grow up with one loving, caring parent, or with two who don't get on very well? Do you believe young single mothers deserve help and support from society, or should they be condemned for being irresponsible?

Change 8: the decline in marriage and the growing incidence and acceptance of cohabitation

The decline of marriage and the rise in cohabitation – living together before or outside of marriage – have been two of the major social changes at the turn of the twenty-first century. Marriage rates are declining in Britain, and there are more and more couples cohabiting rather than seeking official recognition of their relationships through marriage. In 2002, there were 250,000 marriages in England and Wales – 19 per cent fewer than in 1991, and the lowest number ever. Over a quarter of non-married males and females are cohabiting, and this proportion is rising. By the early 2000s, the majority of people in first marriages had lived with their partner beforehand, and cohabitation before marriage is now the norm rather than the exception. There are well over a million and a half cohabiting couples who have refused to tie the marriage knot – more than one in ten of all couples. Around 11 per cent of dependent children are now being brought up by unmarried, cohabiting couples. Many cohabiting relationships eventually end up in marriage – about 60 per cent of first-time cohabitations turn into marriages.

The reasons for the decline of marriage and growing cohabitation have been considered earlier (see pages 245–8), including:

■ The changing role of women, whose growing economic independence has given them more freedom to choose their relationships.

■ The growing divorce rate, and the message that is sending out to potential marriage partners.

■ Growing secularization.

■ Changing social attitudes and reduced social stigma. Young people are more likely to cohabit than older people, and this may in part reflect the evidence that older people are more likely than younger people to think that 'living together outside marriage is always wrong'. This reveals more easy-going attitudes to cohabitation among the young, showing the reduced social stigma attached to cohabitation.

■ The greater availability of, and more effective, contraception.

■ Higher expectations of marriage.

Change 9: remarriage and the growth of the reconstituted family

More than two-fifths of marriages now involve a remarriage for one or both partners, mainly reflecting the increase in the divorce rate. A lot more divorced men remarry than divorced women, reflecting women's greater dissatisfaction or disillusionment with marriage.

These trends have meant that there are more reconstituted families (sometimes called 'stepfamilies') with step-parents, stepchildren, and stepbrothers and sisters arising from a previous relationship of one or both partners. Nearly nine out of ten of these reconstituted families consist of a couple with at least one child from a previous relationship of the woman, as it is nearly always women who gain custody of children in the event of a relationship breakdown. There are estimated to be around half a million stepfamilies with dependent stepchildren in Britain, and about one in ten children today live in stepfamilies, with parents of one or more previous marriages.

Change 10: more births outside marriage

Around four in every ten births in 2003 were outside of marriage – about four times more than the proportion in 1977. Despite the record numbers of children being born outside of marriage, more than three-quarters of those births were registered jointly by the parents. Both parents in three out of four of these cases gave the same address. This suggests the parents were cohabiting, and that children are still being born into a stable couple relationship, even if the partners are not legally married.

The explanations for the increase of births outside of marriage are very similar to those for the increase in the divorce rate, the decline in marriage and the increase in cohabitation, which were discussed above.

ACTIVITY   Read the sections above, and explain carefully the reasons why there are more births outside marriage today.

FAMILY DIVERSITY AND THE MYTH OF 'CEREAL PACKET' FAMILIES

The 'cereal packet' family

The popular image of the family in Britain in the early twenty-first century has been described as the 'cereal packet' family. This is the image often promoted in advertising, with 'family size' breakfast cereals, toothpaste, family holidays, and a wide range of other consumer goods. This popular 'happy family' image often gives the impression that most people live in a 'typical family' with the following features:

- It contains two parents and about two dependent children, who are the natural offspring of both parents.
- These parents are married to one another, and neither of them has been married before.
- The husband is the breadwinner, with the wife staying at home and primarily concerned with housework and childcare.

This 'cereal packet' image of the 'typical family' is very mistaken, and there is a wide diversity, or range, of family types and household arrangements in modern Britain.

The 'cereal packet' family, with a working father in a first marriage to a home-based mother, caring for their own two natural children, makes up only about 5 per cent of all households

Households and families

Figure 10.6 shows the different types of household in Britain in 2003, and the types of household people were living in (a household is simply either one person living alone or a group of people living together at the same address). In 2003, only 23 per cent of households contained a married/cohabiting couple with dependent children, and only 37 per cent of people lived in such a family. This alone shows that the 'cereal packet' image of the nuclear family does not represent the arrangement in which most people in Britain live.

Families with dependent children

Figure 10.7 examines families with dependent children. This shows that in 2003, 25 per cent of such families were lone-parent families, with nine out of ten of them headed by women. Although 75 per cent of families with dependent children were headed by a married or cohabiting couple, this doesn't mean that most of these families conformed to the 'cereal packet' image.

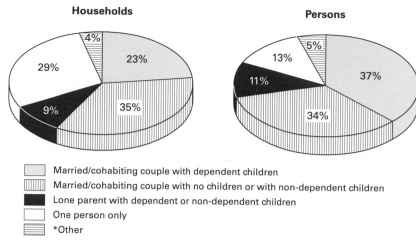

Figure 10.6 Households and people: by type of household, Great Britain, 2003

Source: Data from Labour Force Survey, Office for National Statistics

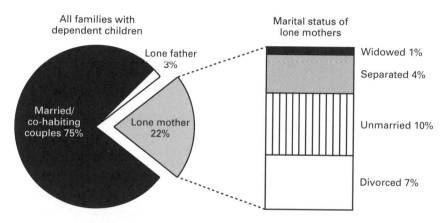

Figure 10.7 Families with dependent children: by family type and, for lone mothers, by marital status, Great Britain, 2003

Source: Data from Labour Force Survey

ACTIVITY

Refer to figure 10.6:

1 What percentage of households in 2003 consisted of one person only?

2 What percentage of people in 2003 were living in households consisting of a married or cohabiting couple with no children or with non-dependent children?

Refer to figure 10.7:

3 In 2003, what percentage of all families with dependent children were lone-parent families?

4 What percentage of families with dependent children were headed by a lone mother who was widowed?

5 What was the main cause of lone motherhood?

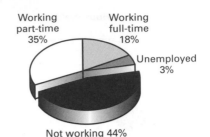

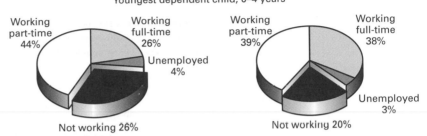

Figure 10.8 Working patterns of women with young children: Great Britain, 2003
Source: Data adapted from Labour Force Survey

■ A number of these families were reconstituted families, in which one or both partners were previously married. About 8 per cent of all families with dependent children were stepfamilies in the early 2000s.

■ A number were headed by cohabiting, rather than married, couples. Twelve per cent of women with dependent children were cohabiting in 2001.

■ Most of these families were dual-worker families, where both parents were working. In 2003 well over half of married or cohabiting couples with children had partners who were both working. As figure 10.8 shows, large numbers of mothers with dependent children work in paid employment, with the numbers increasing as children get older. In 2003, about 65 per cent of all women with dependent children were working.

■ The 'cereal packet', 'happy family' stereotype, of a working father first-time married to a home-based mother, caring for their own two small children, in 2003 made up less than 5 per cent of all households.

ACTIVITY

Refer to figure 10.8:

1 What percentage of mothers whose youngest child was aged 0–4 years were not working in 2003?

2 Identify two trends which occur as the youngest dependent child gets older.

3 What does figure 10.8 suggest might be the main restriction on mothers with young children going out to work? Suggest ways this restriction might be overcome.

4 Suggest reasons why so many people seem to believe that the 'cereal packet' family is the most common type of family.

Other forms of family diversity

Other forms of family diversity include the following.

Ethnic diversity

This refers to differences in family life styles between ethnic and religious groups.

- *South Asian families*. Extended family relationships are more common in minority ethnic groups originating in South Asia, from Pakistan, Bangladesh, and India. Such families are commonly patriarchal in structure, with seniority going to the eldest male, and males in general. In many ways, the traditional British 'cereal packet' family stereotype of a working male married to a home-based female is more likely to be found among Pakistani and Bangladeshi households than any other ethnic group. Divorce rates are low in such families because of strong social disapproval, and a wide support network of kin for families under stress. Arranged marriages are still common in such communities.

- *African-Caribbean families* are often centred on the mother, who is in many cases the main breadwinner. Lone parenthood is higher among African-Caribbean mothers than any other ethnic group – over half of African-Caribbean families with children are lone parents, and there are low marriage rates. This partly reflects a cultural tradition in such communities.

Social class diversity

Social class diversity refers to differences between upper-, middle-, and working-class families. For example, extended families are still often found in traditional working-class communities, and the nuclear family may be more common in middle-class families. Differences in income and wealth will also lead to differences in lifestyle between families from different social classes.

Life-cycle diversity

This refers to the way families may change through life, as partners have children, as the children grow older and eventually leave home, when divorces and remarriage occur, when partners retire, or when the difficulties of old age arrive. All these factors mean the family will be constantly changing, for example with changing levels of family income as children move from dependence to independence, with differing levels of domestic labour and childcare, and with different levels of participation in paid employment, particularly by women, arising from the absence or presence of children and their age.

Regional diversity

This refers to the way family life varies in different geographical locations around the country. There are distinctive patterns of family life in different areas of Britain. For example, on the south coast, there is a high proportion of elderly couples, while older industrial areas and very traditional rural communities tend to have more extended families, and the inner cities have a higher proportion of families in poverty and lone-parent families.

Figure 10.9 Family and household diversity

Conclusion

This section has suggested that it is very misleading to assume that the 'cereal packet' image of the family represents the reality of family life in Britain. Only a small minority of families are of this type. It is much more realistic to recognize that there is a wide diversity, or variety, of family types and household relationships in modern Britain, and trends suggest there will be growing numbers of extended, dual-worker, reconstituted, cohabiting, gay and lesbian, and lone-parent families. Figure 10.9 summarizes a range of different family and household relationships which are to be found in Britain.

ACTIVITY

1 Either using an imaginary family or one that you know, identify the various ways that housework (domestic labour), childcare, conjugal roles, and employment might all change during the life-cycle of your chosen family.

2 Suggest ways that the lifestyles of upper-class and lower-working-class families might differ.

3 Suggest reasons why the 'cereal packet' family is most likely to be found in the Pakistani and Bangladeshi communities.

CRITICAL VIEWS OF THE FAMILY

The 'cereal packet' image of the 'typical family' has already been questioned earlier in this chapter, but the view of the warm and supportive 'happy family' which is often presented in the mass media has been questioned on a more fundamental level by many writers.

The 'darker side' of family life

While the family is often a warm and supportive unit for its members, it can also be a hostile and dangerous place. The growing privatization of family life can lead to emotional stress in the family. Family members are thrown together, isolated from and lacking the support of extended kin, neighbours, and the wider community. Tempers become easily frayed, emotional temperatures and stress levels rise, and – as in a pressure cooker without a safety valve – explosions occur, and family conflict is the result. This may lead to violence, divorce, psychological damage to children, perhaps even mental illness and crime.

The breakdown of marriages which leads to divorce is often the end result of long-running and bitter disputes between partners. The intense emotions involved in family life often mean that incidents that would appear trivial in other situations take on the proportion of major confrontations inside the family. The extent of violence in the family is coming increasingly to public attention, with rising reports of the physical and sexual abuse of children, the rape of wives by their husbands, and wife- and baby-battering. One in four murders takes place in the family. This is the darker side of family life.

Because of the private nature of the family, accurate evidence on the extent of violence and abuse inside the family is difficult to obtain, and fear or shame mean that it is almost certain that most of such incidents are covered up.

The abuse of children

The sexual, physical, and emotional abuse of children, and their neglect, is increasingly brought to everyone's attention through the mass media, though much child abuse is likely to remain 'hidden' because of the private nature of the family. A 2000 report from the National Society for the Prevention of Cruelty to Children (NSPCC) found around 10 per cent of children suffered serious abuse or neglect at home, with most committed by natural parents. In 2003, Department of Health statistics showed there

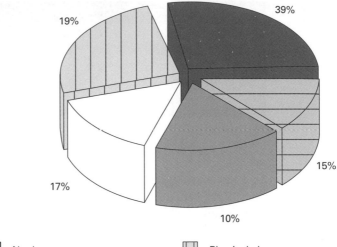

19%   39%

17%

10%   15%

Neglect   Physical abuse
Emotional abuse   Sexual abuse
More than one category of abuse

There were 25,700 children and young people on child protection registers in England on 31 March 2002

Figure 10.10 Children and young people on child protection registers: by category of abuse, England, year ending 31 March 2003

Source: Department of Health

were 25,700 children and young people under the age of 18 on child protection registers in England for various forms of abuse. Twenty-nine per cent were registered for physical abuse or sexual abuse alone, 39 per cent for neglect, and a further 17 per cent for emotional abuse. Fifteen per cent suffered more than one category of abuse, for example sexual and physical abuse (see figure 10.10). These figures were for England alone, and only for abuse which was brought to the attention of social services departments. It is very likely that much abuse goes on that is undiscovered.

**ACTIVITY/
DISCUSSION**

Suggest reasons why the number of child abuse cases recorded in the Department of Health statistics in 2003 might not give a true picture of the extent of child abuse. Do you think the increase in the number of reported cases of child abuse means the problem is growing? What other explanations might there be for the increasing reporting of child abuse?

Violence in the family

There is widespread evidence of violence by men and women against their partners. It is estimated one in four women, and one in six men, will suffer some form of domestic violence at some point in their relationships, though most of the physically most violent incidents are committed by men against their female partners. Each year about 150 people are killed by a current or former partner, and 80 per cent of them are women. Domestic violence accounts for an estimated 30 per cent of all violent crime, and about 650,000 incidents are recorded by the police each year, with around four out of five of the victims being women. Around 45 per cent of all violent crime experienced by women is domestic, and estimates suggest there may be as many as six and a half million incidents each year. It is women who are most likely to experience domestic violence, to experience repeated violence, and to sustain injuries that require medical treatment. For many women, home is neither a secure nor a safe place to be.

Such violence is often not taken very seriously by the police or courts, being dismissed as a 'domestic dispute' – which seems to suggest violence in the family, and particularly against women, is seen in some quarters as an acceptable and normal part of a relationship. Certainly the type of physical violence carried out in the family, mainly by male partners, would quite probably result in prosecution and imprisonment if it was carried out against a stranger outside the family. None the less, an estimated two-thirds of victims of domestic violence do not seek help because they are afraid, are ashamed, or see it as a private matter, and only about a quarter of all domestic violence incidents are reported to the police.

Statistics such as these, and the widespread growth of refuges for battered women since the 1970s (in 2003 there were around 500 refuges in England and Wales), reflect the extent and seriousness of the problem of violence in the home, much of which goes unreported and undiscovered.

'Can I have a black eye, too, Ma?' asks the little girl. 'Wait till you're old enough to get married, pet,' says her mother.

This cartoon from 1896 shows domestic violence was the norm then, but are things really much better today?

Rape in marriage

Rape is when someone is forced to have sex against her or his will, often accompanied by the actual or threatened use of violence. Estimates suggest more than one in four women has been raped, with most rapes being committed by husbands on their wives. Nearly half of these rapes within marriage are accompanied by the actual or threatened use of violence, and one in five wives suffers physical injury.

Such sexual violence in the family, then, would appear to be disturbingly common, but only as recently as 1991 was rape within marriage confirmed as a criminal offence by the Court of Appeal.

ACTIVITY

Go to <www.womensaid.org.uk> (the Women's Aid site), and find out what steps are being taken to combat domestic violence.

Feminist criticisms of the family

Feminist writers – those concerned with establishing equal rights for women – have been responsible for highlighting much of the violence against women in the family. However, they also have a range of other criticisms of the family, arguing that it is an institution that serves men's needs better than women's, and that it particularly oppresses and exploits women. Many of these criticisms are covered in other chapters, and the following is simply a brief summary of them.

■ Far from the popular impression of growing equality between male and female partners in the family being correct, inequalities continue. As seen earlier in this chapter, women still have most of the responsibility for housework, even when they are in full-time employment. Most women work both outside the home in paid employment and inside the home as housewives and mothers, and take the major responsibility for managing family emotions and conflicts. They have three jobs (the 'triple shift') to the man's one.

■ Feminists emphasize that housework is, in fact, unpaid labour. The government's New Earnings Survey put the value of work done by women in the home at £313 a week.

■ It is still mainly women who give up paid work (or suffer from lost/restricted job opportunities) to look after children, the old, the sick, and male partners. Women still take most of the responsibility for childcare and child rearing, and are most likely to get the blame from society if these tasks are not performed 'properly'.

■ As seen in chapter 5, women's position in the family remains a primary source of discrimination and disadvantage in the labour market. Employers are often unwilling to employ or promote married women, particularly in jobs with high levels of pay and responsibility. Marriage poses no such problem for men.

■ The family is a major source of gender-role socialization, which causes women to underachieve (do less well than they are able) in a wide range of areas, and which keeps women in a secondary position to men in many areas of social life.

Looked at from these points of view, women have much to lose from the present organization of the family.

DISCUSSION	Discuss the view that men have much to gain, and women much to lose, from marriage and the family.

ALTERNATIVES TO THE FAMILY

Most societies in the world have some established arrangements for the production, rearing, and socialization of children, and the nuclear family is probably the most common one. However, it would be wrong to assume that the conventional nuclear family is a universal institution, and that arrangements for bringing up children always or necessarily involve the prime responsibility resting on the family or both biological parents. This is particularly the case today, where new forms of relationship are developing, and where the idea of a lifetime relationship is increasingly diminishing as people have a series of partners during their lifetimes, and abandon traditional styles of family living.

The following examples help to illustrate some alternative arrangements which suggest the family is not always the main way of bringing up children, nor does it necessarily have to be the family that does this.

The Nayar

Among the Nayar of south-west India before the nineteenth century, there was no nuclear family. A woman could have sexual relations with any man she wished (up to a maximum of twelve) and the biological father of children was therefore uncertain. The mother's brother, rather than the biological father, was responsible for looking after the mother and her children. Unlike our society, where in most cases the biological parents marry, live together, and are responsible for rearing their children, among the Nayar there was no direct link between having sexual relations, child bearing, child rearing, and cohabitation.

Gay and lesbian families

Same-sex couples are becoming more common, though they are still relatively rare. Most same-sex couples with children tend to be lesbian couples. However, there are more cases emerging of gay male couples adopting children or having children through surrogate mothers. Gay and lesbian couples in 2004 were set to gain the same legal rights as married couples in Britain. You might therefore argue that these are families like any other, but they do offer an alternative to more conventional views of the nuclear family.

Foster care and children's homes

It is worth remembering that a considerable number of children – around 80,000 in 2002 – are brought up by foster parents or in children's homes. This does demonstrate that the link between natural parents and the rearing of children can be, and sometimes is, separated.

Communes

Communes are self-contained and self-supporting communities. They developed in Western Europe, Britain, and the USA in the 1960s, among groups of people wanting to develop alternative lifestyles to conventional society because of the political or religious beliefs they held.

Communes often try to develop an alternative style of living and a kind of alternative household, with the emphasis on collective living rather than individual family units. A number of adults and children all aim to live and work together, with children being seen as the responsibility of the group as a whole rather than of natural parents. Many communes tended to be very short-lived, and only a few remain in Britain today.

The kibbutz

The Israeli kibbutz is a form of commune, and is one of the most famous and successful attempts to establish an alternative to the family. Here, the emphasis is on collective child rearing, with the community as a whole taking over the tasks of the family. In the early kibbutzim, children were kept apart from their natural parents for much of the time and brought up in the Children's House by metapelets – a kind of 'professional parent' combining the roles of nurse, housemother, and educator. Children were seen as the 'children of the kibbutz' – they were the responsibility of the community as a whole, which met all of their needs.

In recent years, the more traditional family unit has re-emerged in the kibbutzim, with natural parents and children sharing the same accommodation, but the kibbutz remains one of the most important attempts to find an alternative to conventional family structures.

ARE MARRIAGE AND THE FAMILY DECLINING SOCIAL INSTITUTIONS?

Arguments that the family is in decline

■ Around 40 per cent of marriages in the early 2000s will end in divorce, and about one in four children will experience a parental divorce by their sixteenth birthday.

■ In Britain today, about a quarter of families with dependent children have just one parent.

■ About 40 per cent of births are outside of marriage, and the proportion is growing every year.

■ There are well over a million cohabiting couples who have refused to tie the marriage knot – one in twelve of all couples. This is expected to rise to 1.7 million by 2020, making up around one in seven of all 'couple' households.

■ Rising rates of divorce, cohabitation, lone parenthood, and reconstituted families shows a picture of the family in decline. This has been blamed for a wide range of social ills, such as declining moral standards, social disorder, drug abuse, crime, vandalism, anti-social behaviour, football hooliganism, and increasing levels of violence in society.

Arguments that it isn't

■ The rising divorce rate is caused by easier divorce laws, reduced social stigma, and more sympathetic public attitudes, rather than more marriage breakdowns. In the past, many couples may have been condemned, by legal and financial obstacles and social intolerance, to suffer unhappy 'empty shell' marriages or to separate without divorcing. Making divorce harder to get would simply mean couples would separate without divorcing. Marriages today are more likely to be based on love and companionship than on the custom and financial necessity of the past. Of all divorced people, 75 per cent remarry, a third of them within a year of getting divorced. This shows that what they are rejecting is not the institution of marriage itself, but a particular marriage partner – they divorce hoping to turn an unhappy marriage into a new, happier one. Marriages that exist today are therefore probably much stronger and happier than ever, since unhappy relationships are easily ended by divorce.

■ Lone parenthood arises from a variety of reasons (see earlier in this chapter) and lone parents are as able to provide care and security for children as two-parent families, and can probably provide better care than two parents who don't get on.

■ Despite the record numbers of children being born outside of marriage, nearly 80 per cent of those births are registered jointly by the parents, with the same address given by both parents in three out of four of these cases. This suggests they are cohabiting, and that most children are still being born into a stable relationship, and live in families with concerned parents who are simply reluctant to tie the legal marriage knot. Most dependent children still live in families headed by a married or cohabiting couple.

■ Many of those who cohabit eventually marry – about 60 per cent of first-time cohabitations turn into marriages – and about 54 per cent of the population over age 16 consists of married people. It would appear that marriage remains an important social institution, even in the light of the high divorce rate and previous experience of living together outside marriage.

■ The causes of these social problems all too often blamed on the family are many and complex, and those who blame the family are often searching for simple solutions to complex problems.

The box on the previous page examines some arguments about whether or not the family is in decline. These arguments suggest that what really seems to be happening is not so much that the family and marriage are in decline as that they are changing. There are more lone-parent families, more reconstituted families, more gay and lesbian families, more experiments in living together before marriage, and fewer people prepared to marry simply to bring up children. Nevertheless, marriage remains an important social norm, and strong pressures from parents, peer groups, and the responsibilities brought about by the birth of children continue to propel most people into marriage.

But perhaps it doesn't really matter whether or not couples are married or have been married before, or whether there is one parent or two, or whether they are of the same or opposite sexes. Though the form of the family will keep on changing, the importance of the family lies in its role as a stable and supportive unit for one or two adults and their dependent children. In that sense, the ideal of the family perhaps still remains intact.

DISCUSSION	Is the family of less importance in society today than it used to be? Do you think the family is in decline?

CHAPTER SUMMARY

After studying this chapter, you should be able to:

- Describe consensus and conflict approaches to the family, and explain the differences between them.

- Describe the different forms of marriage and the family.

- Describe how the role of the family in society has changed.

- Explain why the privatized nuclear family, or modified extended family, became the most common form of families, and provide evidence for the continued existence of the classic extended family.

- Explain the link between the nuclear family and industrial society.

- Explain the apparent change from segregated to integrated conjugal roles, and criticize the view that marriages and cohabiting couples have become partnerships of equals.

- Explain why families have become more child-centred.

- Explain why families have become smaller.

- Explain the reasons for the rising divorce rate and identify the groups most at risk of divorce.

- Explain why there has been a large increase in the number of lone-parent families.

- Explain why there has been a decline in the numbers of people getting married, and increased cohabitation.

■ Explain why remarriage and reconstituted families have become more common.

■ Explain why there are now more births outside of marriage.

■ Explain why the 'cereal packet' image of the family is an inaccurate stereotype of the family in modern Britain.

■ Describe the diversity of families and households in contemporary Britain.

■ Explain, with examples, what is meant by the 'darker side' of family life.

■ Describe alternatives to the family.

■ Identify some arguments and evidence for and against the view that the family and marriage are of declining social importance.

KEY TERMS

arranged marriage
bigamy
classic extended family
communes
conjugal roles
death rate
divorce rate
extended family
feminist
household
infant mortality rate
integrated conjugal roles
kibbutz
kinship
matriarchy
matrilineal descent
matrilocal residence
modified extended family
monogamy
neo-local residence
nuclear family
patrilineal descent
patrilocal residence
polyandry
polygamy
polygyny
privatized nuclear family
reconstituted family
secularization
segregated conjugal roles
serial monogamy
symmetrical family

COURSEWORK SUGGESTIONS

1   Investigate how far conjugal roles have really become more integrated, by carrying out a series of interviews with five or six families in the community to discover how work is divided between men and women in the home. Use equal numbers of middle-class and working-class families and/or different age groups and/or different ethnic groups to discover whether there are any social class, age, or ethnic differences. You might use the questions on page 237 in this chapter, and figure 10.2 and table 10.2 on equality of partners in the home, as a basis for your research.

2   Using secondary sources (see chapter 17), carry out a study of the variety of family types in Britain today. Alternatively, carry out a survey in your school, college, or workplace about the types of family people live in and how family life differs between nuclear and extended families. Take into account different class, ethnic, or religious backgrounds.

3   Carry out a survey of attitudes towards arranged marriages among different age groups or males and females in the Asian community.

4   Carry out a study among lone-parent families, finding out the major problems they encounter.

5   Carry out a survey on attitudes to divorce among a small sample of people from different religious, ethnic, or age groups.

11 Schooling in Britain

Education is a major social institution, and schools in Britain command a captive audience of virtually all children between the ages of 5 and 16. During this period of compulsory schooling, children spend almost half of their waking hours at school during term time – about 15,000 hours of their lives.

The sociology of education covers a vast area, and it is impossible in this book to cover all aspects. This chapter therefore takes as its main focus the school system, rather than further and higher education, and concentrates on two main aspects of this: the main features and changes which have occurred in the school system in about the last thirty years, and what the purposes of education are.

KEY ISSUES

• Education in Britain before the 1970s.

• Comprehensive schools and selection.

• The key aims of educational change.

• Recent developments in education.

• The role of education in society.

EDUCATION IN BRITAIN BEFORE THE 1970S

Until the 1960s, all children went first to primary schools (as they do now) but then were selected by a test of their ability at age 11, known as the 11+ examination, to go to one of three types of secondary school – grammar, technical, or secondary modern. These three types of secondary school became known as the tripartite system.

During the 1960s, the tripartite system came under increasing attack. The 11+ exam was seen as an unfair, unreliable, and inaccurate selection test, which disadvantaged children from working-class homes, and damaged the self-esteem and educational opportunities of children who failed to win a place at a grammar school. Secondary modern schools were seen as inferior, second-rate schools, with grammar schools having higher status and offering better life chances to their pupils.

Research in the 1950s and 1960s suggested that the talent, ability, and potential of many children in the secondary modern schools were being wasted. It was felt that this wasted talent could be better developed in

Photo: Michael Dyer LRPS

comprehensive schools, which accept pupils of all abilities. As a result, in the 1960s the tripartite system was abolished in most of the country, and by the 1970s most children attended comprehensive schools.

COMPREHENSIVE SCHOOLS AND SELECTION

Comprehensive education abolished both selection at age 11 by the 11+ exam and the three types of secondary school. Children in most areas now, regardless of their ability, generally transfer to the same type of school at the age of 11, with no selection by examination. Around nine out of ten young people in 2003 were attending some form of comprehensive school, with just 164 grammar schools remaining.

'True' comprehensive schools have no selection by ability at all, and children of all abilities are admitted to the same types of school and taught in mixed-ability classes. While most schools are now comprehensive schools in that they do not select the majority of the pupils they admit by ability, there are different types of comprehensive school, and some selection by ability does continue in the education system and, through streaming, in many comprehensive schools as well.

The case against selection and the advantages of 'true' comprehensive schools

■ The possibility of educational success and obtaining qualifications remains open throughout a child's school career, since moving between streams and classes within one school is easier and more likely to happen than moving between different types of school where selection takes place for secondary school.

■ Late developers, whose intelligence and ability improve later in life, can be catered for better in the comprehensive system, rather than having their opportunities limited at an early age.

■ The large size of many comprehensive schools, as they contain all pupils in an area, means there are more teachers teaching a wider range of subjects to meet the needs of pupils of all abilities, with a wide variety of equipment and facilities. This benefits all pupils and gives them greater opportunities to develop their talents, to reach their full potential and gain some educational qualifications.

■ As all children attend the same type of school, there is more social mixing between students from homes of different social class and ethnic backgrounds, and this helps to overcome divisions between different social groups. Selection by ability in education often benefits the middle class, which dominates selective schools and the top streams in streamed comprehensive schools. This is discussed in the next chapter.

■ Fewer children leave school without any qualifications in the comprehensive system, and more obtain higher standards than under selective systems, such as where grammar schools continue to exist.

■ Children are less likely to be branded as 'failures' at an early age, which avoids both lowering their self-esteem (how they feel about themselves and their ability) and the damaging effects of the self-fulfilling prophecy. This is discussed further in the next chapter.

■ Where all pupils of the same age, regardless of their ability, are taught in the same type of school and in the same classroom (mixed-ability teaching) the more intelligent pupils can have a stimulating influence on the less able, and the problems created by the self-fulfilling prophecy are easier to avoid. Recent research has shown that mixed-ability teaching has no negative effect on the 'high-flyers', improves the performance of the 'less able', and makes no difference to a school's overall examination performance.

Selection by ability can have harmful effects on the self-esteem of students, and create a self-fulfilling prophecy

The self-fulfulling prophecy is the process whereby the prediction that children won't do well as a result of testing and selection by ability actually comes true, due to the low expectations of teachers, and students' consequent poor image of their own ability.

The case for selection and criticisms of comprehensive schools

The lack of selection by ability is not without its critics.

■ The large size of many comprehensive schools may make it impossible for staff to know all pupils personally. This may create discipline problems and the talents of individuals may not be noticed and developed.

■ Because these schools contain pupils of all abilities, brighter children are held back by the slower pace of learning of the less able. Critics argue this wouldn't happen with selection, as 'high-flyers' are taught in the same selective school or streams within a school.

■ Where selective (grammar) schools continue to exist, they 'cream off' the most able pupils, so the so-called comprehensives are not really 'true' comprehensives containing all abilities, and are little different from the secondary moderns of the tripartite system.

■ Selection by ability through streaming or setting (rather than mixed-ability teaching) in the same school means brighter students can be 'stretched' rather than held back by slower learners taking up the teacher's time, and who may be disruptive because they are unable to cope with the work. Many so-called comprehensive schools are not true comprehensives, as they stream or set pupils, and this is really a form of selection in the same school.

DEFINITION

Setting puts pupils into different groups or sets for a particular subject according to their ability in that subject, while streaming involves putting them into the same group for all subjects according to their ability.

Table 11.1 The effects of streaming on children's recorded ability between the ages of 8 and 11 years

Measured ability at 8 years of age: test scores	Average change in test scores between 8 and 11 years	
	Children in an upper stream	Children in a lower stream
41–5	+5.67	−0.95
46–8	+3.70	−0.62
49–51	+4.44	−1.60
52–4	+0.71	−1.46
55–7	+2.23	−1.94
58–60	+0.86	−6.34

+ indicates improvements in score, − indicates deterioration in score.
Source: Adapted from J. W. B. Douglas, The Home and the School (Panther/Grafton Books)

ACTIVITY

Study table 11.1 and answer the following questions:

1 What average change occurred in the test scores of children in a lower stream whose test score at 8 years of age was 55–7?

2 What average change occurred in the test scores of children in an upper stream whose test score at 8 years of age was 46–8?

3 Which ability group in which stream showed (a) the greatest deterioration in test scores, and (b) the greatest improvement in test scores?

4 What does table 11.1 suggest about the effects of streaming on children's educational performance? List all the factors you can think of which might explain this, drawing on your own experiences at school.

5 With reference to table 11.1 and the arguments over selection, outline the arguments for and against selection by ability in education, drawing on examples from your own experiences at school.

6 Do you think streaming and setting or mixed-ability teaching is better for pupils' progress? Give some evidence to back up your view from your own experiences at school.

7 Have you had any experience of the self-fulfilling prophecy in your own schooling? How do you know whether teachers think you are 'bright' or not, and how do you think this has affected your progress?

8 Suggest measures that could be taken to make comprehensive schools better for all pupils.

THE KEY AIMS OF EDUCATIONAL CHANGE

The move to comprehensive schooling, and more recent changes in the education system, have been driven by four main aims:

■ Economic efficiency: developing the talents of young people to improve the skills of the labour force so Britain maintains a successful position in the world economy.

■ Making the education system meet the needs of industry and employers through more emphasis on vocational education.

■ Raising educational standards.

■ Creating equality of educational opportunity in a meritocratic society, and establishing a fairer society by opening up opportunities for secondary and further/higher education to the working class and other disadvantaged groups.

DEFINITION

■ Equality of educational opportunity is the idea that every child, regardless of his or her social class background, ability to pay school fees, ethnic background, gender, or disability, should have an equal chance of doing as well as his or her ability will allow.

■ A meritocracy (or meritocratic society) is a society where occupational positions (jobs) and pay are allocated on the basis purely of people's individual talents, abilities, qualifications, and skills – their individual merits. In Britain today, this nearly always means educational qualifications.

RECENT DEVELOPMENTS IN EDUCATION

While the comprehensive system has succeeded in improving overall educational standards, it came under increasing criticism in the 1980s and 1990s for not meeting the needs of employers and industry closely enough, for not reaching high enough standards, and for failing to benefit the most disadvantaged, poorest groups in society. As a result, attempts have been made to tie all parts of the education system more closely to the needs of industry and business, to raise standards, and to target the most disadvantaged groups.

ACTIVITY

Go to <www.standards.dfes.gov.uk> and find measures that the government is taking to tackle educational underachievement by more deprived social groups, minority ethnic groups, and males. Find four actions for each group, and explain how each measure might raise standards and improve levels of achievement.

Making schools more aware of industry and the needs of employers: vocational education

Attempts to produce a more flexible labour force, fitting education more to the needs of employers, have included:

- Sending teachers from schools (and further education) into industry to develop their understanding, which they can then apply in their teaching.

- Work experience programmes for year 10 and 11 pupils in schools to ease the transition from school to work.

- New educational courses, and government training schemes for those leaving school, which are more closely related to the world of work and concerned more with learning work-related skills. For example, work-based NVQs (National Vocational Qualifications) and school/college-based GNVQs (General National Vocational Qualifications) were developed to provide nationally approved and recognized qualifications for vocational courses. Vocational GCSEs and AVCEs (Advanced Vocational Certificates in Education) were intended as vocational alternatives to academic GCSEs and A-levels (AVCEs from 2005 will be known as GCEs, with 'applied' added to subjects that already exist at A-level).

- The introduction of key skills in the use and application of number, communication, and information technology. These are the skills that most employers find that school leavers lack, with poor communication skills mentioned by almost two-thirds of employers in 2004 as one of the most frequent problems they face in recruiting staff (as shown in figure 11.1).

Criticisms

- Vocational education and qualifications are often seen as having lower status than more traditional academic subjects and courses. Vocational

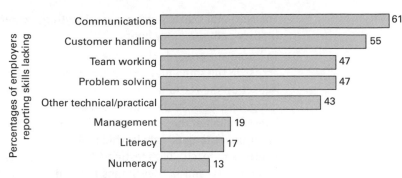

Figure 11.1 The key skill areas that employers found lacking in their employees
Source: Data from Learning and Skills Council, 2004

qualifications are, in general, less likely to lead to university entry, and are more likely to lead to lower-status, lower-paid jobs as adults.

- Work experience is often seen by school students as boring and repetitive, involving little development of their skills and little to do with their future ambitions.

- Post-school training schemes are often criticized for providing little development of skills, for being used as a source of cheap labour by employers, and for not leading to 'proper' jobs at the end of the training.

DISCUSSION

What should the aims of schooling be? Should schools be concerned mainly with meeting the needs of business and industry, and fitting people into the job market? Or should they be concerned with the development of individuals, allowing them to pursue and develop their interests?

Raising standards

More money for schools

The Labour government, first elected in 1997, allocated huge amounts of extra money to schools, to enable them to provide the staff, materials, buildings, and facilities to enable them to provide a high-quality learning environment for children, and thereby improve standards.

Activity-based learning

Teaching has become more student-centred and activity-based, with the aim of developing students' skills and understanding. GCSEs, AS- and A-levels, GNVQs and AVCEs now have more activity- and skills-based exams, and involve students doing more coursework. This has led to much better exam results among 16–18-year-olds. Modular exams (which students can take in parts) aim to ensure that all students can obtain some qualifications by allowing them to resit parts of a course. AS-levels aim to encourage 16–18-year-olds to study a broader range of subjects, and make them more flexible and less specialized.

The National Curriculum, national testing, target-setting, and the literacy and numeracy hours

To improve standards across the country, and ensure all students had access to the same high-quality curriculum, the 1988 Education Reform Act set up the National Curriculum, a range of subjects and set 'programmes of study' that must be followed by all school students. The latest version of the National Curriculum is shown below. There are 'attainment targets' (goals which all teachers are expected to enable students to reach), with testing (the Standard Assessment Tests or 'SATs') at ages 7, 11, and 14 (Key Stages 1, 2 and 3) in mathematics, English, and science to ensure these targets are met. All schools are now set targets for improvement by the government – standards they are expected to achieve and improve on every year. In addition, all primary schools (Key Stages 1 and 2) must have a literacy hour and a numeracy hour each week, to improve basic skills in these areas.

The National Curriculum: 2004

Key Stage	Ages	Compulsory ('statutory') subjects
1	5–7	English, mathematics, science, history, geography, art and design, music, information and communications technology (ICT), design and technology (D&T), and physical education (PE)
2	7–11	Same as Key Stage 1
3	11–14	Same as Key Stages 1 and 2, plus modern foreign language and citizenship
4	14–16	English, mathematics, science, modern foreign language, ICT, D&T, PE, and citizenship

At all key stages, pupils must study sex education and religious education (though parents have the right to withdraw their children from lessons), and at Key Stages 3 and 4 students must also receive careers education.
Source: Department for Education and Skills

National 'league tables'

Schools and colleges are now required to publish tables of testing (SATs) and exam (GCSE/AS-/A-level/AVCE, and GNVQ) results. These have become known as 'league tables' and are designed to give parents and students an idea of how well schools and colleges are doing so they can choose the best. By encouraging competition for students between schools and colleges, these league tables aim to raise overall standards.

Local management of schools (LMS)

Local management of schools (LMS) gives schools rather than the local education authority (county and city councils in most areas) much greater control of their budgets, and a wide range of other aspects of the school. Further education and sixth-form colleges have also become completely independent of the local education authority. This is designed to make schools and colleges more responsive to local needs and the wishes of parents.

Formula funding

Schools and colleges are funded by a formula which is largely based on the number of students they attract. It was thought this would drive up standards by rewarding 'successful' schools and colleges that attracted students (and hence money), giving less successful schools and colleges the incentive to improve.

Open enrolment and parental preference

Parents are now allowed to express a preference for the school of their choice, and a school cannot refuse a pupil a place if it has vacancies. This was designed to raise the quality of teaching and exam results by encouraging competition between schools. Unpopular schools run the risk of losing pupils and therefore money, and the government has taken steps to close what it sees as 'failing' schools which are unpopular with parents and where exam and test results, and standards of behaviour, are poor.

More information for parents

To help parents to choose the 'best' schools and encourage schools to improve their standards and performance, schools now have to provide, by law, a range of information for parents, This includes:

- A governors' report every year, sent to all parents, including the standards achieved, examination and National Curriculum test results, details of the school budget, the amount of authorized and unauthorized absence, and what school leavers do after they leave school.

- A written report on each child's progress at least once a year.

- A school prospectus or brochure, giving details of the aims of the school, the subjects and other activities offered, and the school's exam results compared with local and national results.

In addition, all schools have to hold an annual meeting between parents and school governors if parents request it, though in most cases very few parents attend these meetings.

Specialist schools and selection by ability

Since the early 2000s, there has been a huge growth in the number of 'specialist schools', the highest-status of which are the city academies. These schools have a special focus on their chosen subject area, such as technology, languages, arts, sports, business and enterprise, engineering, science, mathematics and computing, humanities, or music. These are an attempt to move away from what were called 'bog standard' comprehensives. Before being granted 'specialist' status, these schools have to raise money from private business, but they then get extra money from the government and are allowed to select up to 10 per cent of their pupils by 'aptitude' (ability). It is thought that by specializing these schools will raise standards in their specialist subjects, and that selection by ability will raise standards not just in the specialist subjects, but across the whole school curriculum.

The Office for Standards in Education (Ofsted)

The Office for Standards in Education (Ofsted) was established to conduct inspections of all state schools, further education colleges, and local education authorities at least once every six years. This aimed to ensure schools, colleges, and local education authorities were doing a good job, by publishing their inspection reports and requiring action to be taken on any weaknesses identified.

Criticisms

Many of the attempts to raise standards discussed above have been very controversial, and there are many criticisms of them. Some of these criticisms are outlined below.

The National Curriculum and testing

The National Curriculum has been criticized for not giving teachers enough opportunity to respond to the needs of their pupils, as teachers are told what they have to teach and when they have to teach it. Testing (the SATs) has been criticized, particularly at Key Stage 1 (age 7), for putting too much pressure on young children, and possibly giving them a sense of failure early in their schooling. More generally, teaching may become too focused on the content of the tests, to get the good test results needed for a high position in the league tables, at the expense of the wider school curriculum.

Parental choice and open enrolment

In most cases, parents don't really have much choice of school, as places are usually filled up by those living in the school's 'priority area' (the area from which children are admitted first). Middle-class parents have been able to make the greatest use of parental choice and open enrolment, and it is they who generally make the most effective use of the education system. The reasons for this are discussed in the next chapter, but include the fact that their own higher levels of income and education means they are better placed than many working-class parents to:

- Shop around and find the best schools.

- Understand and compare schools in the league tables.

- Know more about how to assess school OFSTED inspection reports and what constitutes a 'good school'.

- Afford more easily to move into the priority areas of the 'best' schools.

- Make more effective use of appeals procedures should they be refused a place at their chosen school.

This means that those who have already benefited from education the most will gain more, while those who are more disadvantaged may become further disadvantaged.

Formula Funding and Competition between schools and colleges

Competition between schools and colleges for students, and therefore for money, may make it harder for some schools and colleges to improve. The emphasis on exam results, and presenting a good 'image' to parents, may have the effect of making it even harder for poorer schools or colleges to improve, as students go elsewhere. Such schools and colleges may therefore lack the resources to improve their performance – the opposite of what was intended from the reforms.

League tables

League tables of test and exam results don't really reveal how well a school is doing. This is because, as the following chapter shows, the social class background of students can affect how well they perform in education. Schools and colleges in more deprived working-class areas may produce results which are not as good as those in middle-class areas, but where the students have actually made much more progress than middle-class students compared to what they started school with. For example, a sixth form or college where students enter with four GCSEs grade C cannot reasonably be expected to get as good AS- and A-level results as one where students enter with seven GCSEs grade *A, A, and B. The latter sixth form or college might get better results and a higher league table position than the first one, but the students in the first one might have actually made greater progress compared to what they started with, despite having a lower position in the league tables.

League tables therefore do not show how much value has been added by the educational institution (the 'value-added' approach), and could conceal underperforming schools and colleges in advantaged middle-class areas, where results should be much better given their social class intake, and successful schools and colleges in more deprived working-class areas.

Student needs at risk and social divisions increased

The needs of students have been replaced by the needs of the school or college to achieve a good position in the league tables of results. Brighter students, or those, for example, on the C/D grade borderline at GCSE, are likely to get more resources spent on them, disadvantaging weaker students who are less likely to deliver the prestige results, such as grades A–C at GCSE and AS/A-level, necessary to gain or maintain the image of a 'good' school or college. Weaker students, who are more likely to come from working-class backgrounds (as the next chapter explains), may find their needs are neglected. As a result, social divisions between the middle class and the working class are widened.

Specialist schools and selection by ability

As seen earlier, and in the next chapter, selection by ability can lead to a lowering of the self-esteem of those not selected, and may lead to lower expectations by teachers and the self-fulfilling prophecy. Specialist schools are seen as being 'better' schools, and therefore given higher status, by parents and pupils, than other schools, and are given extra resources giving them advantages over other schools. As schools compete for pupils, specialist schools may increasingly select their pupils by ability (up to 10 per cent of their intake). This will create unfair competition between schools, and increase inequality between them. Middle-class parents are likely to gain most from this, and the working class to lose out, for reasons mentioned above and in the next chapter. This will add further to social divisions between social classes.

Equality of educational opportunity and helping the most disadvantaged groups

The Labour government, first elected in 1997, emphasized the need to create equality of educational opportunity for all, particularly focusing on the most deprived and most disadvantaged areas where educational results were poor. This was carried out through a number of measures, including more money and better-paid teachers for schools in the poorest areas, through schemes such as Excellence in Cities and Education Action Zones. According to a 2003 Ofsted report, these schemes had only mixed success, and seemed more successful in improving standards among primary, rather than secondary, school students. These measures are considered a little more in the following chapter.

The last thirty years or so have been a period of frenzied change in education, all aimed at improving standards, and making education more responsive to the needs of industry and business. How effective and successful these changes prove to be will only be discovered in the years ahead, and there will undoubtedly be more changes to come in the schooling system as Britain progresses through the twenty-first century and adapts to the demands of a rapidly changing world.

ACTIVITY/ DISCUSSION

1 Do you think the recent changes in education will succeed in raising standards? Go through each of the changes, and explain in each case why it might or might not improve standards.

2 Do you think schools alone can be held responsible for exam results and truancy rates? What other factors might influence how good a school's exam results are, and whether pupils play truant or not?

THE ROLE OF EDUCATION IN SOCIETY

The provision of education is an incredibly expensive business, eating up over £50 billion a year in Britain in 2003 – about 17 per cent of government spending. Why is such importance attached to the provision of education in modern industrial society? What does education contribute to society? Why are schools necessary in industrial societies and why is education to the age of 16 compulsory? The answer to these questions lies in the *functions* that education performs in society.

ACTIVITY

1 List all the reasons you go/went to school. What benefits (if any!) do you think going to school has brought you?

2 How do you think your life would differ if you didn't have/hadn't had to go to school?

3 Now read the following sections (to the end of the chapter) on the role that education plays in society, and compare them with your own reasons for going to school. Which do you think are the more important, from your point of view?

4 What problems might there be for individuals and society if compulsory education were to be abolished tomorrow?

Socialization: preparation for adulthood and citizenship

The school is an important agency of secondary socialization, continuing the process of primary socialization which begins in the family. Consensus theorists argue schools transmit from one generation to the next the culture and shared values of a society, though conflict theorists argue this is the culture and values of the dominant and most powerful groups in society. For example, the school curriculum hands on knowledge about history, geography, science, English language and literature, and so on. Children also learn how to develop relationships with others, including sex education, and to adopt many of the norms of the society to which they belong. Citizenship courses, concerned with the rights and responsibilities of people living in a democratic society, are now part of the National Curriculum for 11–16-year-olds (Key Stages 3 and 4), and aim to encourage young people to play a full, active, and responsible part in running the society to which they belong. As children move from primary school to the end of secondary schooling, they are gradually encouraged to take on more responsibilities, to become more independent and to stand on their own two feet, as they will have to when they leave school. Much of this preparation for adult life takes place through the hidden curriculum, which is discussed below. As a result of schooling, society is reproduced and each new generation is integrated into society.

Education and the economy: preparation for working life

In a complex industrial society, the education system plays an important role in preparation for working life in two respects:

- *Producing a labour force with the skills needed for working life.* A literate and numerate workforce is more or less essential in an industrial society, and, as discussed earlier, the key skills of use and application of number, communication, and information technology are much in demand by employers. There is also the need for specific skills related to particular jobs, such as computing, engineering, technical drawing, and science. The things learnt at school will generally affect the kind of job and training opportunities open to people after school.

■ *Selecting people for different occupations. Consensus theorists* see modern industrial societies as generally meritocratic, with most social positions being achieved on the basis of experience and exam qualifications. In schools and colleges, people are graded and receive different qualifications, which are used by employers and other educational institutions to select suitable people for work and further courses.

Through exams, schools sort pupils out, and decide the kinds of occupation they will eventually get – for example, who will become middle-class professionals or skilled or unskilled workers. Education will therefore influence the individual's eventual social class position as an adult. In a few cases, education can be a means of upward social mobility into the middle class for children from a working-class family. Figure 11.2 illustrates this link between education and the class structure.

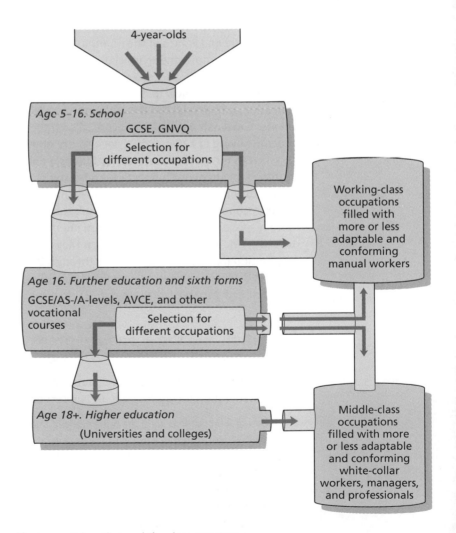

Figure 11.2 Education and the class structure

Conflict theorists question whether society is really meritocratic at all as, in most cases, the education system is not a means of upward social mobility, but seems to be sending children from working-class homes into working-class jobs as adults, and children from middle-class homes into middle-class jobs. The education system, from this point of view, is simply reproducing and justifying the inequalities that already exist in society. Exam results and qualifications give the impression that those who fail in the education system do so because of their lack of ability and effort, and have only themselves to blame. In this way, people are encouraged to accept the positions they find themselves in after schooling. However, in most cases it is not lack of ability and effort, but disadvantages arising from social class and family background that cause failure. The reasons for this are discussed in the next chapter.

Social control

Schools act as important agencies of social control, which encourage children to learn and conform to the values and norms expected by society (though the *conflict view* suggests these are those of the dominant groups in society). This is mainly carried out through what is known as the hidden curriculum.

DEFINITION	The hidden curriculum is the teaching of values, attitudes, and behaviour through the school's organization and teachers' attitudes, but which are not part of the formal timetable.

This teaching is 'hidden' because there are no obvious, organized courses in 'obedience and conformity' as there are in mathematics or English, though citizenship courses may be an exception. Citizenship courses may carry out social control, by encouraging young people to be responsible conformists and not 'rock the boat' as adults; on the other hand, they may encourage young people to become critical adults, challenging the inequalities and conflicts which divide society.

The hidden curriculum is present throughout schooling, and those who conform to it are likely to be rewarded, while those who don't are likely to be branded as non-conformists by the school and may find themselves getting into trouble. Some features of this hidden curriculum, and what is being taught, are shown on the next page.

ACTIVITY/ DISCUSSION

1 Drawing on your own experiences at school, what features of your education do you think prepared you/will prepare you most for adult and working life after school? Think of the particular subjects studied and activities undertaken. To what extent do you think these were successful?

2 What other things do you think should be taught at school to enable people to play a full and responsible part in adult and working life?

Features of the hidden curriculum	What is being taught
■ Privileges and responsibilities given to older pupils	■ Respect for elders, and acceptance of adult responsibilities
■ School rules, detentions and suspensions, rewards like merit badges, prizes, good marks, etc.	■ Conformity to society's rules and laws, whether you agree with them or not
■ School assemblies	■ Respect for religious beliefs and the dominant moral values
■ Pupils' lack of power and control about the subjects taught, how the school is run or the school day organized	■ Workers' lack of power and control at work
■ The authority hierarchy of the school involving pupils fitting into a complex organization of heads, deputies, heads of department, year heads, etc.	■ Learning about their place in the hierarchies of power and control in society and accepting it – for example, in the authority hierarchy at work
■ Males and females often having different dress rules, being expected to conform to different standards of behaviour, and being counselled into different subjects, further education courses, and careers	■ Males and females being expected to conform to gender stereotypes
■ Respecting the authority of teachers regardless of what they say or do	■ Respect for those in authority, such as bosses at work and the police
■ Punctuality/being on time	■ Good time-keeping at work
■ Streaming and setting by ability, with rewards and prizes given for hard work and exam success	■ Accepting that the different levels of the job market, such as professional, managerial, skilled, semi-skilled, and unskilled manual occupations, and the differences in power, status, and pay between social classes, are natural and justified, as those higher up have worked harder and are more intelligent and better qualified

ACTIVITY

1 Describe in detail three features of the hidden curriculum found in your school, or the one you once attended, which reflect the values of society outside school.

2 Identify three features of the hidden curriculum in your school, or the one you once attended, which might be regarded as discriminating against students from minority ethnic groups or either boys or girls.

3 Are/were there any features of the hidden curriculum in your school which you think might encourage students to take more power and control in their lives, such as democratic decision-making, free choice of dress, or school councils? Explain your answer.

Implementing government policy

Schools have often been used as a means of carrying out government policies. For example, comprehensive schools were originally established by a Labour government in an attempt to create both more equal opportunities in society and greater social equality. Some schools in areas where there is widespread poverty have been given extra teachers and more resources than other schools in an attempt to relieve the disadvantages faced by the poor in education. Multicultural courses are also organized in many schools in an attempt to stop the spread of racist ideas, and encourage respect for people from different cultural backgrounds. Equal opportunities policies have been adopted to reduce the effects of gender stereotyping, by encouraging girls to go into subjects like science and computing, which have been traditionally dominated by boys.

Preparing for social change

As well as encouraging people to accept traditional ideas which will lead to order and stability in society, schools and colleges also prepare students for a rapidly changing industrial society. Since the 1970s there has been a massive expansion of computer courses and the use of computers in schools and colleges, in an attempt to prepare young people for a world after school in which information and communications technology (ICT) plays a central role. ICT is now a compulsory National Curriculum subject at all Key Stages, and every state school in the country is now connected to the Internet through the National Grid for Learning (NGfL). Attempts to make pupils more adaptable and aware of the world of work, and to make schools more closely related to the needs of the economy, are partly due to the demands of a rapidly changing industrial economy.

This chapter has shown that one of the most important consequences of education is the influence it has on people's life chances, and for most people it affects in a very direct way their job opportunities – and social class position – as adults. This important result of education has been reflected in the attempts to establish equality of opportunity in education, so that all children can have the best educational opportunities in life. However, despite these attempts, inequality in educational opportunity remains. This continuing inequality is the theme of the following chapter.

CHAPTER SUMMARY

After studying this chapter, you should be able to:

- Outline briefly the education system before the 1970s.

- Explain what is meant by a meritocracy and equality of educational opportunity.

- Outline the main arguments for and against comprehensive schools and selection in education.

- Explain what is meant by streaming, setting, the self-fulfilling prophecy, and mixed-ability teaching, and the problems associated with each of them.

- Explain how the government has tried in recent years to improve standards in schools and make schools more aware of the needs of industry and business.

- Describe some steps taken to establish equality of opportunity in education.

- Outline and criticize recent changes in the education system.

- Describe and explain the role of education in society.

- Explain what is meant by the 'hidden curriculum', and how it reflects the values of society outside schools.

KEY TERMS

equality of educational opportunity
self-fulfilling prophecy
tripartite system

COURSEWORK SUGGESTIONS

1   Do interviews with a sample of people from three different age groups (such as 16–25, 35–50, and over 60) asking them about their views and experience of schools today compared to the past, and whether they think standards have fallen or not.

2   Do a study of work experience schemes in a local school, perhaps interviewing pupils and teachers about the aims and usefulness of such schemes.

3   Do a survey asking a range of people (parents, school leavers, people in jobs, current students, etc.) about what they think the purposes of schooling should be, such as getting qualifications, getting a job, being able to think for themselves, etc. Compare the results from the different groups you ask.

12 Inequality in Education

KEY ISSUES

- Social class and underachievement.

- Compensatory education.

- Ethnicity and underachievement.

- Gender differences in education: the underachievement of boys.

- Private education: the independent schools.

- Is equality of educational opportunity possible to achieve?

The development of the education system in Britain aimed to secure equality of educational opportunity for all children, regardless of their social class, ethnic background, or sex. However, despite these efforts, sociological evidence has made it clear that not all children of the same ability achieve the same success in education, and inequalities in educational opportunity remain. The failure of pupils to do as well in education as they should, given their ability, is called underachievement. The evidence suggests that social class origins (the social class of a child's parents), ethnicity, and gender continue to have an influence on how well people do in education, even when they are of the same ability, and these factors appear to be more important than innate (inborn) ability in affecting the level of educational achievement or success. This chapter will look at the patterns of inequality remaining in education, and some of the explanations for them.

SOCIAL CLASS AND UNDERACHIEVEMENT

The facts

Social class is one of the key factors that determine whether a child does well or badly at school. There are major differences between the levels of achievement of the working class and middle class, and, in general, the higher the social class of the parents, the more successful a child will be in education. The degree of social class inequality in education begins in the primary school and becomes wider as children move through the education system, with the higher levels of the education system dominated by middle-class students.

Lower-working-class children, compared to middle-class children of the same ability:

- Are more likely to start school unable to read.

- Do less well in National Curriculum SATs (Standard Assessment Tests).

- Are more likely to be placed in lower streams.

- Generally get poorer exam results. For example, around three-quarters of young people from upper-middle-class backgrounds get five or more GCSEs *A–C, compared to less than a third from lower-working-class backgrounds.

- Are more likely to leave school at the minimum leaving age of 16, many of them with few or no qualifications of any kind. Only about half of young people from unskilled manual working families stay on in post-16 full-time education, compared to about nine in every ten from managerial and professional families.

In addition, a high proportion of AS- and A-level students and sixth-formers, and those entering further and higher education, are from the middle class: a much higher proportion than is justified by the proportion of the middle class in society as a whole. Even when the working class do enter further education, they are more likely to take lower-status courses than students from middle-class backgrounds, such as vocational courses rather than A-levels leading to higher education.

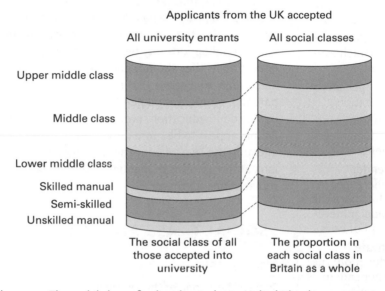

Applicants from the UK accepted

Figure 12.1 The social class of university students: United Kingdom, 2003
Excludes those whose social class was unknown
Source: Data adapted from UCAS, 2003

The working class is underrepresented in higher education. As figure 12.1 shows, in 2003 about 77 per cent of university students came from middle-class backgrounds, even though only just over half of the population was middle class. Young people from unskilled backgrounds are less than a quarter as likely to enter higher education as those from upper-middle-class professional backgrounds.

Explaining working-class underachievement

There is a range of factors that explain social class differences in educational achievement, which can be grouped into three main categories:

- Material explanations, which put the emphasis on social and economic conditions.

- Cultural explanations, which focus on values, attitudes, and lifestyles.

- Factors within the school itself.

Material explanations

Although schooling is free, material factors like poverty and low wages, diet, health, and housing can all have important direct effects on how well individuals do at school, and after leaving school.

Poverty and home circumstances

- Poor housing conditions such as overcrowding and insufficient space and quiet can make study at home difficult.

- Higher levels of sickness in poorer homes may mean more absence from school and falling behind with lessons.

- Low income or unemployment may mean that educational books and toys are not bought, and computers are not available in the home. This may affect a child's educational progress before or during her or his time at school. There may also be a lack of money for out-of-school trips, sports equipment, calculators, and other 'hidden costs' of free state education.

- It may be financially difficult for parents on a low income to support students in education after school leaving age, no matter how bright their prospects might be. This is particularly the case in further education, where there are few grants available and there may be travel costs involved. In higher education, student grants have been replaced by student loans, and these are likely to be a source of anxiety to those from poorer backgrounds, deterring them from going to university.

- Young people from poorer families are more likely to have part-time jobs, such as paper rounds, baby sitting, or shop work. This becomes more pronounced after the age of 16, when students may be combining part- or full-time work with school or college work. This may create a conflict between the competing demands of study and paid work.

The effects of these material factors tend to be cumulative, in the sense that one aspect of social deprivation can lead to others. For example, poverty may mean overcrowding at home *and* ill-health *and* having to find part-time work, making all the problems worse.

The effects of social deprivation on educational achievement are cumulative

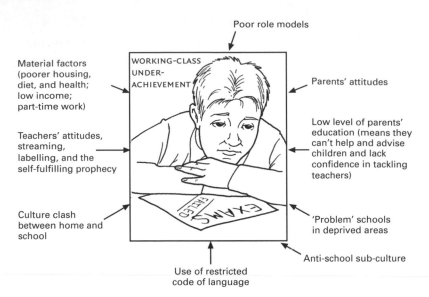

Poor role models

Material factors (poorer housing, diet, and health; low income; part-time work)

WORKING-CLASS UNDER-ACHIEVEMENT

Parents' attitudes

Teachers' attitudes, streaming, labelling, and the self-fulfilling prophecy

Low level of parents' education (means they can't help and advise children and lack confidence in tackling teachers)

Culture clash between home and school

'Problem' schools in deprived areas

Anti-school sub-culture

Use of restricted code of language

Figure 12.2 Social class and educational underachievement

The catchment area and role models

Catchment areas (or priority areas) are the areas from which primary and secondary schools draw their pupils. In deprived areas, where there may be a range of social problems such as high unemployment, poverty, juvenile delinquency, crime, and drug abuse, there are often poor role models for young people to imitate. The accumulated effects of the environment on children's behaviour mean schools in such areas are more likely to have discipline problems and hence a higher turnover of teachers. This may mean that children from the most disadvantaged backgrounds have the 'worst' schools. In contrast, schools in middle-class neighbourhoods will probably have stronger and more conformist role models for young people, have fewer discipline problems, and therefore have a better learning environment. Additionally, schools in middle-class areas will have more active and wealthy parent teacher associations able to provide extra resources for the school. Parents in poorer areas may find it difficult to make financial contributions to school funds, and therefore the schools in such areas may lack the 'extras' found in schools in wealthier, middle-class areas.

Cultural explanations

Cultural explanations suggest that the values, attitudes, language, and other aspects of the life of working-class groups act as a barrier to success in education. The blame for underachievement in education is placed on young people's socialization in the family and community, and on the cultural values with which they are raised.

Parents' attitudes to education

Middle-class parents on the whole seem to place a higher value on their children's education and take more interest in their progress at school than working-class parents. Evidence suggests middle-class parents visit the school more frequently to discuss how their children are getting on, and this interest grows as the children reach the more critical stages of education as they get older, when exam options are selected and career choices loom. Middle-class parents are also more likely to encourage their children to stay at school beyond the minimum leaving age.

These differences between working-class and middle-class parents, however, do not necessarily indicate that working-class parents have a 'poor attitude' to education, or that they don't care about their children's progress. Working-class parents are more likely to work longer hours, doing shiftwork and overtime, and are less likely than the middle class to get paid for time off work. This may mean it is more difficult for working-class parents to visit schools, rather than that they don't care about their children's progress. Middle-class parents also, of course, can more easily afford to continue to support their children in education after the age of 16. The interest shown by middle-class parents may be due to the importance of educational qualifications in obtaining their own middle-class occupations. By contrast, working-class parents may see education as of less importance because they may have found their own education had little relevance to their working-class jobs. This may lead to poor motivation of some working-class children in school and therefore lower levels of achievement, regardless of ability. Parental attitudes can also affect the child's learning by the lower value placed on books or educational toys in many lower-working-class homes.

Parents' level of education

Because they are generally themselves better educated, middle-class parents tend to understand the school system better than working-class parents. Lower-working-class parents may feel less confident in dealing with teachers at parents' evenings, and in dealing with subject options and exam choices. Middle-class parents know more about schools, the examination system, and careers and so are more able to advise and counsel their children on getting into the most appropriate subjects and courses. They can hold their own more in disagreements with teachers (who are also middle class) about the treatment and education of their child. They know what games and books to buy to stimulate their children's educational development both before and during schooling (and have the money to buy them), and can help their children with school work generally. As a consequence, even before they get to school, middle-class children may have learned more as a result of their socialization in the family. These advantages of a middle-class home may be reinforced throughout a child's career at school.

Language use: the restricted and elaborated codes

Success at school depends very heavily on language – for reading, writing, speaking, and understanding. Bernstein argues that there is a relationship between language use and social class, and that the language used by the middle class is a better instrument for success at school than the language used by the working class. His view is that the language used by the lower working class has a restricted code while the language used by the middle class has an elaborated code.

THE RESTRICTED CODE   The restricted code of language is used by both middle-class and working-class people, but is more characteristic of working-class people. It is the sort of language which is used between friends or family members – informal, simple, everyday language (such as slang), with limited explanation, sometimes ungrammatical and limited in vocabulary. This form of language is quite adequate for everyday use with friends because they know what the speaker is referring to – the context is understood by both speakers and so detailed explanation is not required. Bernstein argues that lower-working-class people are mainly limited to this form of language use.

THE ELABORATED CODE   The elaborated code of language is used mainly by middle-class people. It is the language of strangers and individuals in some formal context, where explanation and detail are required – like an interview for a job, writing a business letter, writing an essay or examination answer, or in a school lesson or textbook. It has a much wider vocabulary than the restricted code.

Bernstein argues that the language used in schools is the elaborated code of the middle class, and that it is the middle-class child's ability to use the elaborated code that gives her or him an advantage at school over working-class children. The elaborated code of the middle class is more suited to the demands of school work, since understanding textbooks and writing essays and examination questions require the detail and explanation which is found mainly in the formal language of the elaborated code. Middle-class children who are used to using the elaborated code at home will therefore find school work much easier and learn more in school than those working-class children whose language is limited only to the restricted code. In addition, the teacher may mistake the working-class child's restricted use of language for lack of ability, and therefore expect less from the child. The self-fulfilling prophecy (discussed later in this chapter) may then come into effect.

The culture clash

Schools are mainly middle-class institutions, and they stress the value of many features of the middle-class way of life, such as the importance of hard work and study, making sacrifices now for future rewards, the 'right' form of dress, behaviour, manners, and language use, 'good' books, good TV programmes, 'quality' newspapers, and so on. This means that middle-class children may find that school greets them almost as an extension of their home life, and they may start school already familiar with and 'tuned in' to the atmosphere of the school, such as the subjects that will be explored there, seeking good marks, doing homework, good behaviour, a cooperative attitude to teachers, and other features of middle-class culture. Consequently, they may appear to the teacher as fairly intelligent and sophisticated.

For the working-class child, the atmosphere and values of the school may be quite unfamiliar and different to those of his or her home. This is likely to result in a culture clash between home and social class background and the middle-class culture of the school. This culture clash may partly explain working-class underachievement.

Factors inside the school

The material and cultural explanations discussed so far are mainly concerned with factors outside the school that influence children's education. However, there is also a range of factors in the school itself that can affect how well children perform in education, apart from the obvious ones like the amount of money schools have to spend on their pupils. See, for example, the box below.

DO SCHOOLS MAKE A DIFFERENCE?

Michael Rutter, Barbara Maughan, Peter Mortimore, and Janet Ouston, in their book *Fifteen Thousand Hours: Secondary Schools and their Effects on Children*, reported research they had carried out in twelve schools. This study attempted to show, in the face of much previous research suggesting the opposite, that 'good' schools can make a difference to the life chances of all pupils. Rutter et al. suggest that it is features of the school's organization which make this difference. These features are summarized below.

- Teachers are well prepared for lessons.
- Teachers have high expectations of pupils' academic performance, and set and mark class work and homework regularly.
- Teachers set examples of behaviour; for example, they are on time and they use only officially approved forms of discipline.
- Teachers place more emphasis on praise and reward than on blame and punishment.
- Teachers treat pupils as responsible people, for example by giving them positions of responsibility looking after school books and property.
- Teachers show an interest in the pupils and encourage them to do well.
- There is an atmosphere or ethos in the school which reflects the above points, with all teachers sharing a commitment to the aims and values of the school.
- There is a mixture of abilities in the school, as the presence of high-ability pupils benefits the academic performance and behaviour of pupils of all abilities.

ACTIVITY

Refer to the box above.

1 Explain how you think each of the features of a 'good' school which Rutter et al. describe there might help pupils of all backgrounds and abilities to make more progress.

2 Are there any other features that you would expect to find in a 'good' school?

3 List at least six characteristics, based on your own opinions, of a 'good' teacher'. How important do you think the role of the teacher is in the educational progress of pupils compared to the home, the neighbourhood, and the pressures of friends?

Teachers' attitudes, streaming, labelling, and the self-fulfilling prophecy

Evidence suggests that teachers' judgements of pupils' ability are influenced by factors other than ability alone. For example, teachers seem to take into account things like standards of behaviour, dress, speech, and the types of home children come from, including the social class background of pupils. Teachers are middle class, and children from middle-class homes who share the same standards and values as the teacher are often likely to be seen by teachers as 'brighter' and 'more cooperative' than those from working-class homes.

Streaming or banding is a system used in schools to separate pupils into different groups according to their predicted ability. Even if children really are of equal ability, teachers are more likely to think working-class children are 'less intelligent' because of the assumptions they hold about their home backgrounds. This may explain why working-class children tend to be found more in the lower streams of streamed comprehensive schools. Streaming therefore seems to divide pupils along social class lines and reflects the class divisions in society, with many children from lower-working-class homes placed in lower streams. This is illustrated in figure 12.3. Streaming has been shown to be unfair and harmful to the self-esteem and educational performance of bottom-stream pupils, as teachers expect less from children in lower streams and give them less encouragement than those in higher streams.

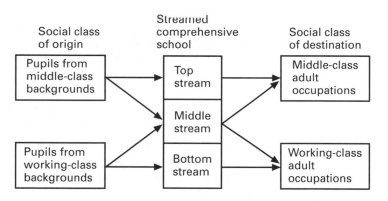

Figure 12.3 Social class divisions and streaming

Much research has suggested that predicting whether a child will be a 'success' or 'failure' through testing, teachers' judgements, and streaming, and labelling him or her as 'bright' or 'slow', can actually make that child a success or failure. Such predictions and labelling can affect an individual's view of himself – or herself – their self-esteem – and the individual may act in accordance with the prediction made and the label attached. This process of predicting that something will happen, and of pupils acting in the way teachers expect them to act in accordance with the label they have been given, is known as the self-fulfilling prophecy. Figure 12.4 illustrates this process.

Once placed in bottom streams, pupils may become victims of the self-fulfilling prophecy – those pupils labelled as 'bottom-stream material' may take on the characteristics expected of them by teachers. Because more working-class children tend to be put into bottom streams by teachers, and middle-class children continue to dominate the higher streams, streamed comprehensive schools may actually create working-class underachievement in education, adding to the material and cultural difficulties working-class children already face there.

ACTIVITY/ DISCUSSION

1 In a streamed school, the best and most qualified teachers are often kept for the upper-stream classes. Why do you think this is the case? How might it affect the progress of those facing the greatest difficulties in the lower streams?

2 List all the reasons you can think of to explain why pupils from lower-working-class homes are more likely to be placed in lower streams than those from middle-class homes.

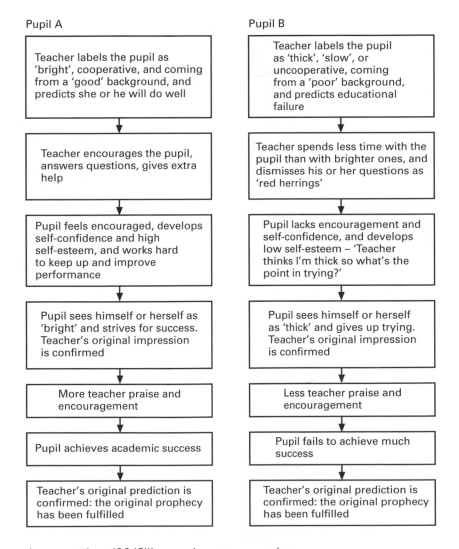

Pupil A

Teacher labels the pupil as 'bright', cooperative, and coming from a 'good' background, and predicts she or he will do well

↓

Teacher encourages the pupil, answers questions, gives extra help

↓

Pupil feels encouraged, develops self-confidence and high self-esteem, and works hard to keep up and improve performance

↓

Pupil sees himself or herself as 'bright' and strives for success. Teacher's original impression is confirmed

↓

More teacher praise and encouragement

↓

Pupil achieves academic success

↓

Teacher's original prediction is confirmed: the original prophecy has been fulfilled

Pupil B

Teacher labels the pupil as 'thick', 'slow', or uncooperative, coming from a 'poor' background, and predicts educational failure

↓

Teacher spends less time with the pupil than with brighter ones, and dismisses his or her questions as 'red herrings'

↓

Pupil lacks encouragement and self-confidence, and develops low self-esteem – 'Teacher thinks I'm thick so what's the point in trying?'

↓

Pupil sees himself or herself as 'thick' and gives up trying. Teacher's original impression is confirmed

↓

Less teacher praise and encouragement

↓

Pupil fails to achieve much success

↓

Teacher's original prediction is confirmed: the original prophecy has been fulfilled

Figure 12.4 The self-fulfilling prophecy: two examples

The anti-school sub-culture

Most schools generally place a high value on things such as hard work, good behaviour, and exam success. One of the effects of streaming and labelling is to divide pupils into those in the top streams who more or less conform to these aims and therefore achieve high status, and those in the bottom streams who are labelled as 'failures' by the school and are therefore deprived of status. In response to this, bottom-stream pupils often rebel against the school and develop an alternative set of values, attitudes, and behaviour in opposition to the aims of the school. This is called an anti-school sub-culture, and provides a means for bottom-stream pupils to achieve some success and status in their peer group. Among such pupils, truancy, playing up teachers, messing about, breaking the school rules, and generally disrupting the smooth running of the school become a way of getting back at the system and resisting a schooling which has labelled them as 'failures' and denied them status.

The anti-school, or counter-school, sub-culture

Because of all the factors discussed above causing the under-achievement of working-class pupils in schools, bottom-stream pupils are very often working class and such pupils will often be found in this anti-school sub-culture. They then themselves reject the school which has already rejected them as 'failures' and 'thick'. This almost guarantees their failure in education, as they look forward to leaving school at the earliest possible opportunity, often before taking any GCSEs or other formal qualifications.

The 'double test' for working-class children

Taken together, the factors in the home, social class background, and the school help to explain why working-class students do less well at school than middle-class students of the same ability. Schools test all pupils when doing subjects like mathematics, English, or science. However, for the working-class student there is a double test. At the same time as coping with the academic difficulties of school work which all students face, working-class youngsters must also cope with a wide range of other disadvantages and difficulties.

These problems on top of the demands of academic work explain working-class underachievement in schools. These disadvantages start in the primary school and become more and more emphasized as children grow older, as they fall further and further behind and become more disillusioned with school. In this context, it is perhaps not surprising that a large majority of those who leave school at age 16 every year, with few or no qualifications, come from lower-working-class backgrounds.

ACTIVITY

1 Put the following explanations for working-class underachievement in what you think is their order of importance: home circumstances; parents' attitudes to education; parents' level of education; the catchment area; role models; language use; the culture clash; teachers' attitudes, streaming, labelling, and the self-fulfilling prophecy; the anti-school sub-culture. Give reasons why you put them in that order.

2 In the light of your list, suggest ways that schools and teachers might improve the performance of pupils who face social class disadvantages in education.

3 Do you think schools can make up for problems that begin outside of school, such as in the home and the neighbourhood? Give reasons for your answer.

COMPENSATORY EDUCATION

Because of the disadvantages in education arising from social class background, positive discrimination has been attempted as a solution to working-class underachievement. This means that schools in deprived areas, where home and social class background are seen as obstacles to success in education, are singled out for more favourable treatment. They are given more resources than schools in other areas, in terms of better-paid teachers and more money to spend on buildings and equipment. This is an attempt to compensate for the problems of disadvantage faced by the poorer sections of the working class in schooling (hence the term compensatory education).

The idea of positive discrimination is based on the idea of equality of opportunity, since it is argued children from disadvantaged backgrounds and poor homes can only get an equal opportunity in education to those who come from non-disadvantaged backgrounds if they get unequal and more generous treatment to compensate.

The policy of positive discrimination and compensatory education was put into practice by the government setting up Educational Priority Areas in the 1970s. These were areas where unemployment was high and there were poverty, overcrowding, many children whose home language was not

English, and large concentrations of unskilled and semi-skilled working-class people. Schools in these areas were given extra money and teachers. Compensatory education didn't really succeed, and educational priority areas were abandoned in the early 1980s. Nevertheless, the Labour government in 1997 took a very similar approach with its Education Action Zones. These are aimed at targeting money and other resources at areas where educational performance is poor, in an attempt to improve standards. However, an Ofsted report in 2003 found that the achievements in Education Action Zone secondary schools were often 'very low and gave continuing cause for concern', and that education action zones had little effect on student achievements. Schools have, so far, not been able to overcome or compensate for the disadvantages arising from home and social class background.

| ACTIVITY | Go to <www.standards.dfes.gov.uk/eaz> and identify five measures that are being taken in Education Action Zones to improve the educational achievements of the most disadvantaged social groups. |

ETHNICITY AND UNDERACHIEVEMENT

The facts

Many children from ethnic minority backgrounds tend to do as well as and often better than many white children. For example, Indian Asians – particularly girls – are more likely to get better GCSE and A-level results, to stay in education post-16, and to enter university than many white students. However, those of Pakistani and Bangladeshi origin, and particularly males from African-Caribbean homes, tend to do less well than they should given their ability. There is some evidence that African-Caribbean males may actually be falling further behind, and they are at the bottom of the heap by the time they reach GCSE. Most of what follows focuses mainly on the African-Caribbean group, though some of the points also apply to the Pakistani and Bangladeshi minority ethnic groups as well.

- They appear to have below average reading ability.

- The tend to get fewer and poorer GCSE results than children of white or Indian origin.

- Male African-Caribbeans are overrepresented (that is, there are more than there should be given their numbers in the population as a whole) in special schools for those with learning difficulties and in special units for children with emotional and behavioural difficulties.

- African-Caribbean pupils are between three and six times more likely to be permanently excluded from schools than white students of the same sex, and to be excluded for longer periods for the same offences.

- They are overrepresented in lower streams. Evidence suggests they are put in lower streams even when they get better results than pupils placed in higher streams.

■ They are more likely than other groups to leave school without any qualifications.

■ They are less likely to stay on in education post-16, and when they do, they are more likely to follow vocational courses rather than the higher-status academic courses.

■ Relatively fewer obtain AS- and A-levels and go on to higher education at universities (though African-Caribbean females do better than both African-Caribbean and white males).

■ In the population as a whole, they are generally less qualified than those of white or Indian origin.

Explaining the underachievement of some ethnic minorities

The pattern of underachievement of Pakistani, Bangladeshi, and African-Caribbean school students has a number of explanations.

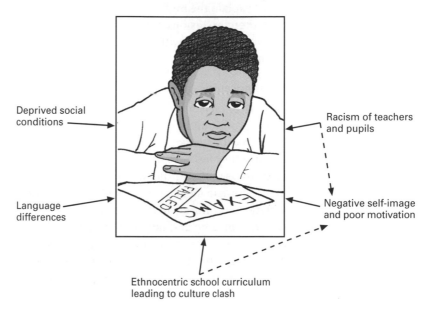

Figure 12.5 Ethnicity and educational underachievement

Social conditions

Young people from minority ethnic backgrounds often face a series of disadvantages in social conditions, such as poor-quality housing, overcrowding, and higher rates of unemployment in their homes, which contribute to difficulties in coping with school work. More than four out of five Pakistani and Bangladeshi households are living below the poverty line. Such material disadvantages are a major obstacle to success in education, and many of the factors discussed above explaining working-class underachievement also affect some minority ethnic groups, as they tend to be mainly working class.

Racism

Although all schools are now legally obliged to have an anti-racist policy, and teachers are trained in equality legislation, research in primary and secondary schools has found an unusually high degree of conflict between white teachers and African-Caribbean pupils. Teachers often hold stereotypes, with more positive expectations of Asians (as relatively quiet, well-behaved, and highly motivated) than of African-Caribbeans, whom they often expect to be trouble-makers. This may mean teachers label African-Caribbeans and take swift action against them. African-Caribbean students, unlike whites and Asians, are often punished not for any particular offence but because they have the 'wrong attitude'.

Although racism is not as widespread in teaching as in some professions, like the police and legal professions, and teachers have often been among the first to tackle racism, there is racism among teachers and pupils, as there is in the rest of society. African-Caribbean male pupils, in particular, are more likely to fight racism and form anti-school peer groups, reinforcing their labelling by teachers as trouble-makers. This might explain the high level of black exclusions from school, since most permanent exclusions are for disobedience of various kinds, such as refusing to comply with school rules, verbal abuse, or insolence to teachers.

An ethnocentric curriculum

Because of racism in both the school and the wider society, minority ethnic group children in Britain, particularly African-Caribbeans, may grow up with a negative self-image – a lack of self-respect and confidence because they feel they are in some ways rejected. The school curriculum tends to be ethnocentric, which may contribute to this low self-esteem. Ethnocentrism means that school subjects concentrate on a particular society and culture – in this case white British society and culture – rather than recognizing and taking into account the cultures of different ethnic communities. This may cause a culture clash between home and school for African-Caribbean pupils. Textbooks still frequently carry degrading stereotypes of people from non-white races. This may lead to low motivation in school and poor educational achievement.

ACTIVITY/ DISCUSSION

1 What evidence can you think of, if any, from your own experiences at school which suggests that the cultures of minority ethnic groups are either ignored or treated in a degrading way? Think about the subjects you studied, the textbooks you used, and the kinds of activity you undertook.

2 Many schools today are trying to include the cultures of minority ethnic groups in school subjects and activities. What evidence is there of this happening in your experience? Give examples.

3 Discuss the following statements: (a) 'Cultural differences between people of different ethnic groups are very important and should be recognized and welcomed in schools', and (b) 'Anti-racism should only be discussed in schools which have a mix of different ethnic groups.'

Language

Some African-Caribbean children speak a different dialect of English, Creole or 'Caribbean English', and children from other ethnic groups may have a language other than English used in their homes. This language difference may cause difficulties in doing some school work and communicating with the teacher, and may cause disadvantages at school. Teachers may mistake language difficulties for lack of ability (leading to the self-fulfilling prophecy), and because Caribbean English is non-standard English, it may be unconsciously penalized in the classroom, because most teachers are white and middle class. The same may apply to Bangladeshi pupils, who may be seen as 'low ability' because they may speak English as a second or additional language rather than as their first. Such cultural difficulties may present obstacles to motivation and progress at school.

ACTIVITY

1 Go through the explanations above for the underachievement of some ethnic minorities, putting them in what you think is their order of importance. Give reasons why you have put them in that order.

2 For each of the explanations, suggest changes that could be made in both school and society which might help to improve the educational performance of these ethnic minorities.

3 Go to <www.standards.dfes.gov.uk/ethnicminorities> and identify five measures that are being taken to improve the educational achievements of minority ethnic groups.

GENDER DIFFERENCES IN EDUCATION: THE UNDERACHIEVEMENT OF BOYS

There are marked differences between the sexes in education. Until the late 1980s, the major concern was with the underachievement of girls. This was because, while girls used to perform better than boys in the early years of their education (up to GCSE), after this they tended to fall behind, being less likely than boys to get the three A-levels required for university entry and less likely to go into higher education. However, since the early 1990s girls have outperformed boys in all areas and at all levels of the education system. The main problem today is with the underachievement of boys, although there are still concerns about the different subjects studied by boys and girls.

The facts

▪ Girls do better than boys at every stage in National Curriculum SAT results in English, maths, and science.

▪ Girls are now more successful than boys at every level in GCSE, and in every major subject (including traditional boys' subjects like design, technology, maths, and chemistry) except physics. In 2003, 57 per cent of girls got five GCSEs (grades *A–C) compared to 46 per cent of boys (see figure 12.6 on page 301). In English at GCSE, the gender gap is huge, with 67 per cent of girls getting a grade *A–C, compared to 52 per cent of boys.

■ A higher proportion of females stay on in post-16 sixth-form and further education, and post-18 higher education.

■ Female school leavers are now more likely than males to get two or more A-level passes (see figure 12.6).

■ More females than males now get accepted for full-time university degree courses.

Refer to table 12.1:

1 In which qualification was there the largest gap between the pass rates of males and females?

2 In which qualification was there the largest gap between male and female entries?

3 In which qualification did females achieve the best pass rate?

Refer to figure 12.6:

4 What difference was there between the percentage of female and male students obtaining five or more GCSE grades *A–C in 2003?

5 What percentage of 17-year-old males achieved two or more GCE AS/A-levels or VCEs in 2003?

6 Which difference showed the largest gap in the achievements of males and females?

Refer to figure 12.7:

7 In which GCSE subjects were there more female than male entries in 2003?

8 In which three GCSE subjects was the gap between the percentage of male and female entries the greatest?

9 In which A-level subjects were there more male than female entries in 2003?

10 In which three A-level subjects was the gap between the percentage of male and female entries the greatest?

11 Which subject showed the greatest gap between the percentage of male and female entries at both GCSE and A-level?

12 Suggest explanations for the difference in subjects males and females choose to study at GCSE and A-level.

Table 12.1 GCSE, AS- and A-level, and AVCE achievements of males and females in all subjects: United Kingdom, 2003

	Male entries	Pass rate %	Female entries	Pass rate %
GCSE[a]	2,833,611	55	2,899,876	62
A-level[b]	345,682	94	404,855	96
AS-level[b]	471,137	84	559,782	89
Advanced VCE[b]	19,892	80	21,022	87
AS VCE[b]	7,970	75	8,006	85

[a] Grades *A–C
[b] Grades A–E
Source: Joint Council for General Qualifications, 2003

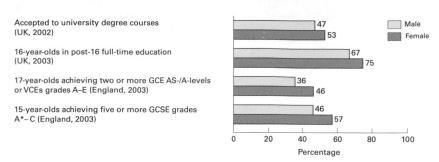

Figure 12.6 Some male and female differences in educational achievement: 2002–3

Source: Data from Department for Education and Skills; UCAS; Joint Council for General Qualifications

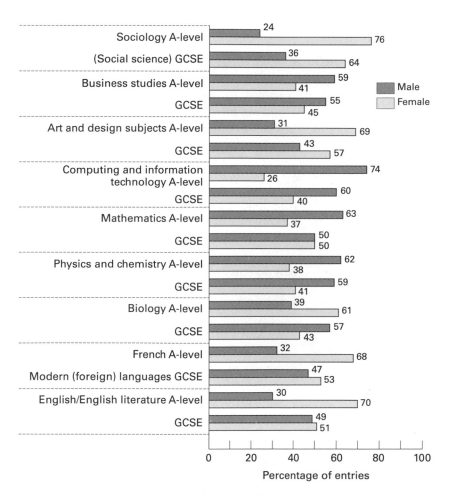

Figure 12.7 Percentage of entries by subject and sex, GCSE and A-level: United Kingdom, 2003

Source: Joint Council for General Qualifications, 2003

Problems still remaining for females

■ Females and males still tend to do different subjects, which influence future career choices. Broadly, arts subjects are 'female', science and technology subjects 'male'. This is so at GCSE, and becomes even more pronounced at A-level and above. Girls are therefore less likely to participate after 16 in subjects leading to careers in science, engineering, and technology.

■ Girls achieve fewer high-grade A-levels than boys with the same GCSE results.

■ There is little evidence that girls' better results at 16 and above have yet led to improved post-school opportunities in terms of training and employment. As discussed in chapter 5, women are still less likely than men with similar qualifications to achieve similar levels of success in paid employment.

■ In the 16–59 age group in the population as a whole who are in employment or unemployed, men tend to be better qualified than women. However, this gap has decreased among younger age groups, and can be expected to disappear if females keep on outperforming males in education.

Explaining gender differences in education

What follows are some explanations for the huge improvement in the performance of girls since the late 1980s, the underachievement of boys, and the subject choices that continue to separate males and females.

Why do females now do better than males?

■ *Equal opportunities.* The work of sociologists in highlighting the educational underperformance of girls in the past led to a greater emphasis in schools on equal opportunities. This was to enable girls to fulfil their potential more easily. These policies included things like monitoring teaching and teaching materials for sex bias to help schooling to meet the needs of girls better. Teachers are now much more sensitive about avoiding gender stereotyping in the classroom, and this may have overcome many of the former problems which girls faced in schools.

■ *More employment opportunities.* The number of 'male' jobs has been declining in recent years, while there are growing employment opportunities for women.

■ *Changing female attitudes and ambitions.* Growing opportunities for women in the world of work may have made girls more ambitious and less likely to see having a home and family as their main role in life. Many girls growing up today have mothers working in paid employment, and this provides more positive role models for them. Many girls now recognize that the future involves paid employment, often combined with family responsibilities. Sue Sharpe found in *Just like a Girl* in 1976 that girls' priorities were 'love, marriage, husbands, children, jobs, and careers, more or less in that order'. When she repeated her research in 1994, she found these priorities had changed to 'job, career and being able to support themselves'. These factors may all have provided more incentives for girls to gain qualifications.

■ *The women's movement.* The women's movement (discussed in chapter 5) has achieved considerable success in challenging the traditional stereotype of women's roles as housewives and mothers. This means many women now look beyond the housewife/mother role as their main role in life.

■ *Girls work harder.* There is mounting evidence that girls work harder and are better motivated than boys:
   - They put more effort into their work.
   - They spend more time on doing their homework properly.
   - They take more care with the way their work is presented.
   - They concentrate more in class (research shows the typical 14-year-old girl can concentrate for about three or four times as long as her fellow male students).
   - They are generally better organized – for example, in bringing the right equipment to school and meeting deadlines for handing in work.
   It has been suggested that the above factors may have helped girls to take more advantage of the increasing use of coursework in GCSE, AS- and A-level, AVCEs, and GNVQs. Such work often requires good organization and sustained application, and girls appear better in these respects.

■ *Girls mature earlier than boys.* By the age of 16, girls are estimated to be more mature than boys by up to two years. Put simply, this means girls are more likely to view exams in a far more responsible way, and recognize their seriousness.

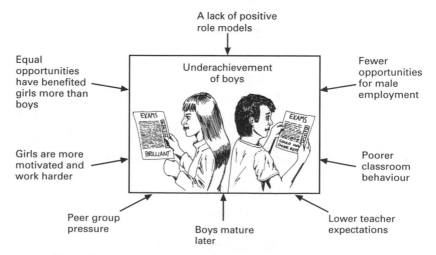

Figure 12.8 Gender and educational underachievement

Why do boys underachieve?

Many of the reasons given above also suggest why boys may be underachieving. However, there are some possible additional explanations.

- *Teacher expectations.* There is some evidence that staff are not as strict with boys as with girls. They are more likely to extend deadlines for work, have lower expectations of boys, are more tolerant of disruptive, unruly behaviour from boys in the classroom, and accept more poorly presented work.

- *Poorer behaviour.* Boys are generally more disruptive in classrooms than girls. They may lose more classroom time learning things because they are sent out of the room or sent home. Four out of every five permanent exclusions from schools are of boys – most of these are for disobedience of various kinds, and usually come at the end of a series of incidents.

- *A lack of positive role models.* Teaching is often seen as a mainly female profession, and there is a lack of male role models, especially in primary schools. Learning has therefore come to be seen as a 'feminine' and 'girly' activity.

- *Peer pressure.* Boys appear to gain 'street cred' and peer group status by not working, and some develop almost an anti-education, anti-learning, 'laddish' sub-culture, where school work is seen as 'unmacho'. This may explain why they are less conscientious and lack the persistence and application required for exam success, particularly in new coursework styles of assessment.

- *The decline in male employment.* The decline in traditional male jobs may be a factor in explaining why many boys are underperforming in education. They may lack motivation because they may feel that getting qualifications won't get them anywhere anyway, so what's the point in bothering?

ACTIVITY/ DISCUSSION

1 Go through the reasons suggested above for why girls outperform boys in education. List the explanations in what you think is their order of importance and explain why you have put them in that order.

2 Drawing on your own experiences at school or college, try to think of any other explanations for the underachievement of boys.

3 Discuss the steps that might be taken in schools to improve the performance of boys.

4 Go to <www.standards.dfes.gov.uk/genderandachievement> and identify five measures that are being taken to reduce gender differences in educational achievement.

Why do males and females still tend to do different subjects?

As you will have discovered from the earlier activity on table 12.1 and figures 12.6 and 12.7, there is still a difference between the subjects that males and females do at GCSE and above. Females are still more likely to take arts and social science subjects, like English literature, history, foreign languages, and sociology, and males are more likely to take scientific and technological subjects, particularly at A-level and above (even though girls generally get better results when they do take them). This is despite the National Curriculum, which makes maths, English, and science compulsory for all students. However, even within the National Curriculum, students can choose different options, and there are gender differences within these option choices. For example, girls are more likely to take home economics, textiles, and food technology, while boys are more likely to opt for electronics, woodwork, or graphics.

These differences might be explained as follows:

- Gender socialization (discussed in chapter 5) may encourage boys to develop more interest in technical and scientific subjects.

- In giving subject and career advice, teachers may be counselling girls and boys into different subject options, according to their own gender stereotypes of 'suitable' subjects.

- Science and the science classroom are seen as 'masculine' because gender stereotyping is still found in textbooks, with the 'invisibility' of females particularly obvious in maths and science textbooks, where examples are often more relevant to the experience of males than females. This reinforces the view that these are 'male' subjects.

- Boys tend to dominate science classrooms, grabbing apparatus first, answering questions directed at girls, and so on. This all undermines girls' confidence and intimidates them into not taking up these subjects.

ACTIVITY/
DISCUSSION

The following comments are from year 11 boys talking about doing English and science:

'I hate it! I don't want to read books.'

'Science is straightforward. You don't have to think about it. There are definite answers. There are no shades to it.'

'In science, everything is set out as a formula, and you have the facts. All you have to do is apply them to the situation.'

'When you read a book, it's like delving into people's lives. It's being nosey.'

'English is about understanding, interpreting . . . you have to think more. There's no definite answer . . . the answer depends on your view of things.'

'I don't like having discussions – I feel wrong . . . I think that people will jump down my throat.'

'That's why girls do English, because they don't mind getting something wrong. They're more open about issues, they're more understanding . . . they find it easier to comprehend other people's views and feelings.'

'You feel safe in science.'

Source: Adapted from Eirene Mitsos, 'Boys and English: classroom voices', English and Media Magazine, no. 33, Autumn 1995

What points do you think are being made about English and science? Do you agree? Why do you think males and females tend to do different subjects? How do you think these choices might be linked to gender-role socialization in society as a whole?

PRIVATE EDUCATION: THE INDEPENDENT SCHOOLS

A final problem for the principle of equality of educational opportunity in Britain is the continued existence of a fee-paying private sector of education – the independent schools. Pupils at these schools are largely the children of wealthier upper-middle- and upper-class parents who have decided to opt out of the free, state-run comprehensive system and can afford to pay for a private education.

The public schools are a small group of independent schools belonging to what is called the 'Headmasters' Conference'. These are long-established private schools, many dating back hundreds of years, which charge fees often running into thousands of pounds a year. For secondary age students, annual fees varied from £6000 to £21,000 per year in 2003. The two most famous boys' public schools are probably Eton (boarding fee £20,961 a year in 2003) and Harrow, and many of the 'top people' in this country have attended these or other public schools. A public school education means parents can almost guarantee their children will have well-paid future careers bringing them power and status in society.

Founded in 1495, *Loughborough Grammar School is one of the oldest schools in the independent sector*

The case for independent schools

The defenders of private education point to the smaller class sizes and better facilities of the public schools than those found in the state system, which means children have a better chance of educational success. Many teachers are paid more, examination results are often better, and pupils have a much higher chance of getting into university. Many defend private education on the grounds that parents should have the right to spend their money as they wish, and improving their children's life chances is a sensible way of doing so.

The case against independent schools

Many remain opposed to private education, arguing that most people do not have the money to purchase a private education for their children, and it is wrong that the children of the well-off should be given more advantages in education than the poor. Many of these schools have charitable status, which entitles them to receive various tax benefits on gifts of money and investments. This charitable status has been estimated to be worth around £2000 per pupil each year. Until 1997, they also received a state subsidy in the form of the Assisted Places Scheme, which paid for poorer children with ability to attend private schools. This means public schools were and are effectively subsidized by the taxpayers, the vast majority of whom can't afford to attend them. The taxpayer also pays the cost of training the teachers in these schools, since they attend state-run universities and colleges. The existence of private schools undermines the principle of equality of educational opportunity, because wealth and income rather than simply ability become the key to success in education. Not all children of the same ability have the same chance of paying for this route to educational success.

There are many poor-quality schools in the private sector of education, and the quality of teaching in independent schools is often no better than in state-run comprehensives. However, their pupils may obtain better results because classes tend to be smaller than in comprehensives, allowing more individual attention, and the schools often have better resources and facilities. For example, Eton College in 2003 had assets estimated at £162 million, with the added advantage of charitable status. These investments and fee income allow Eton to spend around £20,000 per year on each student, compared to about £2,900 for the average state school student in 2003. The opponents of private education argue more money should be spent on improving the state system rather than subsidizing the private sector, so everyone has an equal chance in education.

ACTIVITY

Go to <www.etoncollege.com>, the website of Eton College, and explore how the educational facilities and lifestyle of Eton College differ from those of the school you go/went to.

Research has shown that even when children who go to private schools, especially the public schools, get worse examination results than children who go to comprehensive schools, they still get better jobs in the end. This suggests that the fact of attending a public school is itself enough to secure them good jobs, even if their qualifications are not quite as good as those of pupils from comprehensives.

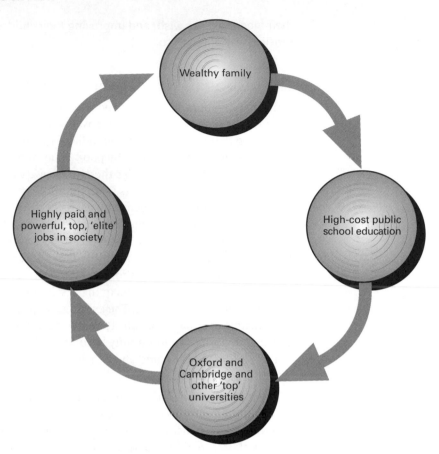

Figure 12.9 The old boys' network

Elite education and elite jobs

A public school education remains an essential qualification for the elite jobs in society – that small number of jobs in the country which involve holding a great deal of power and privilege. Although only about 7 per cent of the population have attended independent schools (and public schools are only a proportion of these schools), many of the top positions in the Civil Service, the courts, the Church of England, the armed forces, industry, banking, and commerce are held by ex-public school pupils.

In many cases, even well-qualified candidates from comprehensive schools will stand a poor chance of getting such jobs if competing with public school pupils. The route into the elite jobs is basically through a public school and Oxford and Cambridge universities (where nearly half of students come from public schools). This establishes the 'old boys' network', where those in positions of power recruit others who come from the same social class background and who have been to the same public schools and universities as themselves. This shows one aspect of the clear relationship which exists between wealth and power in modern Britain, and how being able to afford a public school education can lead to a position of power and influence in society.

DISCUSSION

Should private education be abolished? It might be useful to think at the same time about whether private medicine should be abolished – there are many similarities.

IS EQUALITY OF EDUCATIONAL OPPORTUNITY POSSIBLE TO ACHIEVE?

Despite attempts to secure equality of educational opportunity, children of equal ability but from different social classes, different ethnic backgrounds, and different sexes are still not achieving the same success in education. Compensatory education, such as Education Action Zones, has not overcome the disadvantages faced by many pupils in education.

We live in an unequal society, where different groups and classes do not start the educational race on equal terms. In such a society, the combined effects of socialization, home and social class background, teachers' attitudes, the white, middle-class language and culture of the school, and the continued existence of a privileged private sector of education will mean the realization of the ideal of equality of educational opportunity will remain an impossible dream.

DISCUSSION

It has been suggested that reforming schools is about as worthwhile an exercise as rearranging the furniture on the *Titanic* – the luxury liner that sank on its first voyage. This is because in terms of improving life chances, schools often do not make much difference to social class, gender, or ethnic inequalities in society as a whole, so reforming schools is basically a pointless exercise. Do you agree?

CHAPTER SUMMARY

After studying this chapter, you should be able to:

- Explain what is meant by educational underachievement.

- Describe, and give a range of explanations for, the differences in achievement in relation to social class, ethnicity, and gender.

- Explain what is meant by the self-fulfilling prophecy, and the problems associated with selection, streaming, and labelling in education.

- Explain what is meant by positive discrimination and compensatory education.

- Discuss the arguments for and against the existence of the private sector of education.

- Explain the obstacles to the achievement of equality of educational opportunity.

KEY TERMS

anti-school sub-culture
compensatory education
education action zones
educational priority areas
elaborated code
ethnocentrism
positive discrimination
restricted code
underachievement

COURSEWORK SUGGESTIONS

1   Observe classroom activities and try to see if boys and girls behave
    differently in class and are treated differently by teachers. For example, do
    they sit separately? Are boys asked more questions? Are boys more
    troublesome? Does this vary in different subject classes and between male
    and female teachers? Draw conclusions about the hidden curriculum and
    gender socialization in schools.

2   Make a study of class, ethnic, or gender differences in educational
    achievement in a local school or college. For example, examine subject
    choices and exam results.

3   Interview a sample of school students from different class or ethnic
    groups, and/or of different sexes, asking them what the major influences
    are on their subject choices and on whether they stay at school after 16 or
    not.

4   Interview a group of people who have left school but who were in the
    bottom stream when they were there. Try to discover whether there was any
    evidence of the self-fulfilling prophecy at work. For example, find out
    whether they felt as valued and encouraged by teachers as those in higher
    streams. Was there any evidence of the emergence of an anti-school sub-
    culture?

13 Religion

KEY ISSUES

- Defining religion.
- The role of religion in society.
- Religion, social conflict, and social change.
- Religious organizations.
- New religious movements.
- The secularization thesis.

Sociologists are not generally concerned with whether religious belief is 'true' or not. In many ways this does not matter, for the fact is that millions of people hold religious beliefs, and these beliefs have given rise to powerful movements and institutions. In modern Britain, there are millions of followers of the main religions of Christianity, Islam, Hinduism, and Sikhism. Religious belief is therefore certainly real enough in its consequences. Sociologists are mainly interested in these consequences, or the role and significance of religion in society.

DEFINING RELIGION

There are two main types of definition of religion, outlined below.

The inclusive definition

This is a very broad definition of religion that includes a wide range of beliefs which people give a religious quality to, but may not include beliefs in a supra-human, supernatural being (a being superior to humans and beyond scientific explanation). As well as conventional religions, this wide definition might include phenomena like football, music, and royalty, which for some people have almost a religious status and play a similar role in their lives to conventional religions, even though most people would not regard these as 'religions'.

The exclusive definition

This refers to beliefs which involve a supernatural, supra-human element, and is the definition that includes what most people would regard as 'religion', such as Islam, Christianity, Buddhism, Sikhism, and Hinduism. This would include non-conventional beliefs like witchcraft and Satanism. It is this exclusive definition which will be mainly used in this chapter.

Organized religions and religious beliefs are likely to include all or some of the following features:

- *Religious beliefs* – beliefs in the supernatural (some sort of belief in God or gods) or in symbols which are in some way regarded as sacred, such as a cross or totem pole.

- *Theology* – a set of teachings and beliefs, usually based on some holy book, such as the Bible or the Koran.

- *Religious practice* – a series of rituals or ceremonies to express these beliefs, either publicly or privately. For example, most religions contain rituals such as getting on your knees to pray, church services, singing, fasting, or lighting candles.

- *Religious institutions* – some form of organization of the worshippers/believers, such as priests, churches, mosques, and temples.

- *Religious consequences* – a set of moral values which guide or influence the everyday behaviour of believers, such as the ten commandments in Christianity.

THE ROLE OF RELIGION IN SOCIETY

Consensus approaches: religion providing individual support, socialization and social integration

Consensus theorists emphasize the way religion can act as a source of support for individuals, and as an agency of socialization, integrating them into a society based on value consensus.

Individual support

Religion can play an important role for individuals in a number of ways.

- Religion can provide a source of comfort, explanation, and meaning for individuals when faced by strains and crises in their lives, such as war, death, accidents, and natural disasters. Funeral services, for example, act as a source of comfort for the bereaved – either with beliefs in life after death, or through the support gained in such moments of stress through the gathering of friends and relatives. Church attendances soar during wartime.

- Religious ceremonies can give believers a feeling of identity and security and a sense of belonging to a group that cares about them, and unite them around a shared moral code of behaviour.

- Religion can provide a source of explanation and understanding of questions such as the meaning of life and death, or an explanation or justification for an individual's social position. For example, in the Indian caste system (see chapter 2), the Hindu religion provides an explanation for an individual's position in the social hierarchy.

■ Religious groups still carry out some important welfare roles for individuals, even though many of these have been taken over by the welfare state. For example, the Salvation Army remains the largest provider of sleeping accommodation for homeless single men in the country, and its work with 'down and outs' is renowned.

Socialization and social integration

Religion is part of the culture or way of life of a society, and it helps to maintain cultural traditions. Society can only survive if people share some common beliefs about right and wrong behaviour. Durkheim, writing in the nineteenth century, saw religion as a kind of social glue, binding society together and integrating individuals into it by encouraging them to accept basic social values. For example, he saw worshipping together as a means of reinforcing a sense of solidarity in a social group, and it is partly through religion that an individual is socialized into the values of a society. The dominant Christian culture of Britain maintains traditions like Christmas, baptism, and monogamous marriage, and tries to encourage conformity to society's norms. For example, monogamous marriage is seen as 'God-given', and the ten commandments, with their rules about stealing, murder, adultery, and so on, in many ways reinforce society's norms.

This set of moral beliefs and values may have been so deeply ingrained through socialization that it may have an effect on the everyday behaviour of believers and non-believers alike. For example, if the rules about killing, stealing, and adultery are broken, most individuals will experience a guilty conscience about doing something 'wrong', and this is a powerful socializing and controlling influence over the individual.

In minority ethnic communities in Britain, religious beliefs and customs are often a means for these groups to maintain their own cultural identity and traditions. Sikh and Hindu temples and Muslim mosques often play an important role in integrating such communities, acting as focal points of community life as well as religious life.

Conflict approaches: religion as social control

Conflict theorists emphasize the role of religion in social control – keeping people in their places, obeying the rules, and supporting and justifying inequalities in a society based on conflict.

Karl Marx, writing in the nineteenth century, described religion as 'the opium of the people' – an hallucinatory and pain-relieving drug. This is

Religion is the sigh of the oppressed creature, the heart of a heartless world, and the soul of soulless conditions. It is the opium of the people.

Karl Marx, 1844

because he saw religious belief as an illusion, attempting to justify existing arrangements in society and encouraging people to accept them. He saw religion doing this in two ways.

First, religion justifies existing inequalities in income and power in society, by explaining the position of the rich and poor as 'the will of God'. For example, the Hindu religion provides a religious justification for the inequalities of the Indian caste system, and the Bible is riddled with quotations such as 'It is easier for a camel to pass through the eye of a needle, than for a rich man to enter the Kingdom of Heaven.' Poverty, and acceptance of it, therefore become, in themselves, virtues. As a result, the poor are more likely to accept their position in society.

Second, Marx believed religion provided comfort for the poor, and drew their attention away from their present misery and the inequalities and injustices of this world with promises of a future, golden life after death. In this way, the poor are encouraged to put off the pursuit of personal happiness and rewards in this life for some future reward in heaven.

These two aspects of religion, Marx believed, could only benefit the privileged and powerful, since the poor are encouraged to find 'salvation' through religion rather than challenging the position of the rich and powerful.

Religion: the opium of the people?

ACTIVITY

1 Explain what point the cartoon above is making.
2 'Religion mainly encourages people to accept the way things are.' Suggest evidence both for and against this view.

RELIGION, SOCIAL CONFLICT, AND SOCIAL CHANGE

As well as acting as a stabilizing and integrating force in society, religion can also be a source of social change and conflict, causing divisions and instability in society. For example, in Northern Ireland, competing religious beliefs between Catholics and Protestants have been partly responsible for massive social unrest for centuries, with lengthy armed conflict with the British army over many years throughout history – the latest phase erupting in 1969 and only finishing in the early 2000s. In the Indian sub-continent, warfare between Muslims and Hindus was in part responsible for the division of a once united India into two separate countries, India and Pakistan. In the 1980s and 1990s, these divisions were added to by conflicts between Hindus and Srikhs. In the 1990s, the former Yugoslavia disintegrated into warring factions of Serbs, Croats, and Bosnians, often aligned on religious lines.

Religion has been responsible for major social change. For example, in South America, Roman Catholic priests – followers of a doctrine mixing Communism and Catholicism, called liberation theology – have played major roles in fighting against political dictatorships and poverty. In Iran, an Islamic revolution led to the overthrow of the monarchy (the shahdom) and the establishment of an Islamic republic in 1978–9. Islam became a major international force for social change in the late twentieth century, and the present spread of Islamic fundamentalism (a return to the literal words of holy texts) has attempted to forge social changes in much of the Islamic world based on literal interpretations of the Koran. This generally involves the removal of 'decadent' Western cultural influences, changes in the position of women (such as the wearing of veils, being banned from driving and going out in public unaccompanied, and being refused access to some education and occupations), and the establishment of legal punishments which to most Western eyes are barbaric, such as public flogging, beheading, or the amputation of the hands of persistent thieves. Islamic fundamentalism has also played important roles in early twenty-first century wars in Afghanistan and Iraq, in resisting Western occupation and influence.

RELIGIOUS ORGANIZATIONS

Sociologists have tried to put religious organizations into one of four main categories, based on factors like their relationship to the state, their attitudes to other religious beliefs, their attitude to society, their size and type of membership, and how well organized they are. These categories are church, denomination, sect, and cult, and are described in table 13.1 on page 317.

A further classification of religious groups is based on how they view existing society around them, and their response to it.

■ World-rejecting groups, mainly religious sects, are in opposition to the world, reject many of the dominant norms and values of society, and replace them with alternative beliefs and practices.

■ World-accommodating groups, mainly churches and denominations, generally accept the dominant norms and values, and they are more concerned with spiritual behaviour and everyday morality than 'other-worldly' activities.

■ World-affirming groups, often called cults, accept society as it is, and they offer individuals the opportunity to be successful in terms of existing values through providing access to spiritual or supernatural powers.

No religious group will conform exactly to the categories outlined in table 13.1, and, for example, the terms 'sect' and 'cult' are often used interchangeably, particularly by the mass media when they try to produce sensationalized stories about some of the more horrific new religious sects. Similarly, 'churches' and 'denominations' have relatively minor differences between them, other than their size, influence, and relationship to the state. However, table 13.1 gives a rough guide to the main features of each type of organization.

ACTIVITY

Refer to Table 13.1 and the section above. Mark the following statements as true or false:

1 Churches are world-rejecting institutions.
2 Cults are world-affirming movements.
3 Denominations have close links with the state.
4 Sects are large, world-accommodating organizations.
5 Sects are often controlled by people with powerful personalities.
6 Churches are intolerant of other religions and beliefs.
7 Cults often appeal to the more 'well off' sections of society.
8 Sects are often hostile to or suspicious of those not belonging to the sect.
9 Cult members can carry on with their existing religious beliefs if they want to.
10 Denominations tend to be a bit more critical than churches of the present state of society.

NEW RELIGIOUS MOVEMENTS

New religious movements are those which have emerged in the period since 1945, and particularly since the 1960s. These are mainly sects and cults, and many have little in common with established churches and denominations.

The features of new religious movements

Eileen Barker suggests new religious movements have some or all of the following features.

■ They are religious in so far as they are often concerned with spirituality and/or the supernatural, and with similar questions shared with mainstream religions, like: Why am I here? What is the meaning of life? Is there a God? Is there life after death?

Table 13.1 Churches, denominations, sects and cults

Feature	Churches	Denominations	Sects	Cults
Example	Church of England, Roman Catholic Church	Methodists, Baptists	Jehovah's Witnesses, Mormons, Moonies, Heaven's Gate, Hare Krishnas	Scientology, Transcendental Meditation
Organization	Large organizations, with hierarchy of clergy and paid officials	Like churches, but smaller	Often small, tight-knit groups, with no hierarchy of paid officials, but often under the control of a single charismatic (magnetic) leader	Open to everyone who can afford to participate. Often lack some features associated with a religion, e.g. belief in supra-human being or religious ceremonies
Attitude to wider society	*World-accommodating* Generally accept and support dominant norms and values of existing society	*World-accommodating* Generally accept dominant norms and values of existing society, though perhaps more critical than churches	*World-rejecting* Many (but not all) reject many dominant norms and values of existing society, and replace them with alternative beliefs and practice	*World-affirming* Accept society as it is, offering individuals access to spiritual or supernatural powers to help them be happier and more successful in existing society
Members/ supporters	Members come from all sections of society, and are not expected to withdraw from society or change their lifestyles	Like churches, but sometimes attract disillusioned members of churches or sects	Members often come from those who are disillusioned or dissatisfied with life in some way; expected to withdraw from or make sharp break with conventional life outside sect	Membership open to all, but members often have above-average incomes, necessary to buy into activities
Attitude to other religions/ beliefs	Intolerant, as they claim to have the only true beliefs	Tolerant, as don't claim to have the only true beliefs, and see themselves as one denomination among many	Intolerant and often hostile, as they claim to have the only true beliefs, and only the group of believers will be 'saved'	Tolerant, and exist alongside other more established beliefs
Relationship to the state	Often close and formal links with the state, e.g. Britain's queen is head of the Church of England	Often no formal links with the state	Critical of, and often hostile to, the state and existing society	No link

■ They are most likely to find supporters among young adults who are first-generation converts, rather than born into the sect or cult. The fact that young adults often lack the responsibilities of work, paying rent or a mortgage, or children gives them the time and freedom to get involved should they so choose.

■ There is a high turnover of members, suggesting that the need new religious movements fulfil is temporary.

■ They are likely to be led by a charismatic leader – a person with a powerful, imposing, and 'magnetic' personality that gives them power over other group members. As Barker says, 'they may be seen as gurus, prophets, teachers, messiahs, gods, goddesses or God'.

- They are certain that they hold the only correct 'truth', and that they are the 'chosen' ones.

- There is frequently a sharp divide between 'us' – the 'good and godly' group – and 'them' – the 'bad and, perhaps, satanic' outsiders.

- There is often suspicion or hostility from wider society, particularly the mass media.

- Many are short lived, particularly world-rejecting sects, as the heavy commitment required is hard to maintain, and younger people grow older and look to more 'normal' lives, or support dwindles when the leader dies.

There are many new religious movements, with wide differences in beliefs, membership, organization, and rituals. Some embrace distorted or extremist versions of existing religions, like Christianity or Hinduism, or blend different religions. Some new religious movements hold totally obscure and bizarre beliefs, which have little to do with established religions. Some adopt weird, sometimes sinister, and sometimes violent rituals and attempt to brainwash members.

Eileen Barker summarizes the range or diversity of new religious movements in the following way:

> Leaders may be rich or poor, Members may be old or young, black or white, rich or poor. Some live in communes in remote rural areas, some in semidetached houses in the suburbs, and others in inner-city apartments. They may indulge in sexual orgies or lead ascetic lives of strict celibacy. Practices range from chanting, prayer, meditation or dance to ritual sacrifice. The size of the movement may be hundreds of thousands or no more than a handful. (Eileen Barker, 'An Introduction to New Religious Movements')

Why do people join new religious movements?

Practical reasons

- *The key to success.* World-affirming movements, like Transcendental Meditation and Scientology, claim to offer people knowledge and techniques enabling them to unlock spiritual powers within themselves. This self-development promises individuals wealth, power, success, and personal happiness within their existing careers and lives.

- *Escape.* A short-term practical solution for those escaping from some difficult family, personal or work circumstances.

Secularization

Secularization (discussed in the next section) is the decline in the importance of religion in society. Science seems to try to explain everything, and established religions have been watered down, seem boring, and lack commitment. In such circumstances, some people may experience a lack of spiritual or emotional fulfilment, and 'shop around' for alternative new religious groups that better meet their needs.

Marginality

New religious movements often arise within groups which are marginal in society – on the margins of society, and outside the mainstream of social life. Reasons for this might include, for example, poverty, homelessness, unemployment, being in trouble, being lonely, having personal or family problems, and disillusionment with wider society. New religious movements may offer a 'quick fix', providing security with other individuals experiencing a similar range of problems.

Relative deprivation

Relative deprivation refers to the feeling by individuals that they are not receiving the economic rewards or personal fulfilment they feel they deserve and see in those around them. New religious movements may provide the security and spiritual experiences to overcome these feelings of relative deprivation.

Status frustration

Status frustration simply means people are frustrated at their lack of status in society. This term is particularly used in relation to young people going through the long period of transition from childhood to full independent adult status, brought about by longer periods in education and their lack of work and family commitments. New religious movements can provide some support for an identity and status independent of school or family, and overcome the sense of status frustration.

Social change

Rapid social change may create uncertainty and insecurity, and membership of a new religious movement, particularly close-knit sects, may provide clear answers and security.

ACTIVITY

Refer to the box on page 320, the features of new religious movements identified on pages 316–18, and the differences between world-accommodating, world-rejecting, and world-affirming organizations on pages 315–16.

1 Explore two of the new religious movements, or two of your own choosing, on one or both of the following websites:
   ■ <www.religioustolerance.org>
   ■ <http://religiousmovements.lib.virginia.edu>

2 Identify those aspects of each group which fit the features of a new religious movement. For example, do they have a charismatic leader? Are they treated with suspicion by outsiders?

3 Give reasons why each might be seen as world-accommodating, world-rejecting, or world-affirming. For example, are they hostile to the outside world, and do members have to change their normal lives?

SIX NEW RELIGIOUS MOVEMENTS

■ *Heaven's Gate* is a *world-rejecting sect*, combining elements of Christianity and science fiction. Its followers believe that UFOs contain extra-terrestrial beings, and by committing suicide together at the correct time, they will be reborn as extra-terrestrials. Thirty-nine men and women voluntarily committed suicide in March 1997, when the Hale Bop comet, which they believed had a spaceship behind it to offer them rebirth, was at its nearest to earth.

■ *The International Society for Krishna Consciousness (the Hare Krishnas)* is a *world-accommodating sect* with around one million members worldwide, and follows, with some exceptions, much of conventional Hinduism. Hare Krishna monks are often seen in public places, and are highly visible when spreading their message – dressed in brightly coloured robes, chanting, playing drums, selling their literature and incense, and the men have distinctive shaven heads.

■ *The Church of Scientology*, a *world-affirming cult*, claims a membership of about 8 million worldwide. It has been widely persecuted, but has now become more accepted. It believes individuals can improve their lives through 'auditing' by a member of the clergy using an 'e-meter'.

■ *The Unification Church (the 'Moonies')* is a *world-rejecting, Christian-based sect*, founded by Rev. Sun Myung Moon, (hence the nickname the 'Moonies'). They have hundreds of thousands of members in over 150 countries. Many of their beliefs are similar to those of other Christian groups, though the Moonies also believe the Rev. Moon has been asked by God to complete the work that Jesus Christ started, and to unite all Christians into a single body.

■ *Transcendental Meditation (TM)* is a *world-affirming cult*, founded by Maharishi Mahesh Yogi. TM has merged a simplified form of Hinduism with science. It believes that meditation can develop human potential and intelligence, provide better health and career success, and eventually individuals can develop paranormal powers, such as levitating or flying in mid-air (yogic flying). Well over a million people have taken basic TM courses, and there are estimated to be tens of thousands of members worldwide.

■ *The Branch Davidians* were a *world-rejecting Christian sect*, led by David Koresh, which believed in the imminent 'second coming' of Christ to earth. This would only occur when at least a small group of Christians had been 'cleansed' by David Koresh, who was sent by God to do this. Koresh and 75 followers, including 21 children, died in a shoot-out with the FBI in 1993 in Waco, Texas, USA, believing that the Apocalypse and the final 'battle of Armageddon' mentioned in the Bible were beginning at their compound.

Hare Krishnas

THE SECULARIZATION THESIS

The word 'secular' means 'non-religious', and the secularization thesis is simply the suggestion that religion and religious beliefs are of declining importance both in society and for the individual.

| DEFINITION | **Secularization** is the process whereby religious belief, practice, and institutions lose social significance. |

Secularization can then be examined in terms of three aspects:

■ *Religious belief* – the influence of religion on people's beliefs and values.

■ *Religious practice* – such as the levels of church membership and church attendance.

■ *Religious institutions* – the extent to which churches and other religious institutions have maintained their social influence and wealth.

| ACTIVITY | 1 Take each of the three aspects of secularization – religious belief, religious practice, and religious institutions – and in each case suggest two ways you might measure whether secularization is occurring. |
| | 2 Using the measures you have drawn up, suggest how, in each case, the indicators may, or may not, provide reliable evidence of a decline of religion in society. |

The problem of measuring secularization

The previous activity may have shown you that the main difficulty with deciding whether secularization has taken place is how religion and religious belief are defined and measured. For example, is attendance at religious institutions, like churches, mosques, temples or synagogues, a good way of measuring how much religious belief there is in a society? Does going to one of these mean you really believe in God? Can you be religious without attending religious ceremonies?

Church membership figures are very unreliable as sources of evidence for secularization because different denominations have different ways of defining membership. For example, the Catholic Church decides membership on the basis of those who are baptized as Catholics, but this tells us nothing about their beliefs as adults. The Methodists decide on the basis of those attending a membership service, while the Church of England may use indicators such as baptisms, confirmations, or those attending key services such as Easter Communion.

Table 13.2 on page 323 shows the results of a number of surveys carried out between 1985 and 2003 on people's religious beliefs in Britain. Sociologists would want to ask what the indicators used actually mean. For example, what do people mean by 'God', 'sin', the 'soul', and that 'Religion is important in my life' (in what ways?)? If people say they believe in God, does this mean it influences their everyday behaviour?

Because of these problems of interpreting and measuring the extent of religious belief and practice, there is no clear agreement among sociologists over whether and to what extent secularization has occurred.

ACTIVITY/
DISCUSSION

Refer to table 13.2 while you do this activity. This gives some indicators of religiously based moral values, religious beliefs, and commitment. Some of these indicators refer mainly to the Christian religion. If you come from another religious background, replace the Christian indicators with others that apply to your religious group. For example, replace 'Ten commandments' with rules your own religion might expect you to obey, and substitute 'mosque', 'temple', 'synagogue', etc., for 'church'.

1 List the ten most important indicators of religious commitment in table 13.2 which, in your opinion, show that Britain has become a secular society. Explain the reasons why you think these indicators are important.

2 Are you a religious person? How many of the forty-one indicators in table 13.2 would you answer 'yes' to? How many would you answer 'no' to?

3 Do you think the religiously based moral values (1–12) are necessarily good indicators of religious commitment? Do religious people have to support them? Does not supporting them mean a person is not religious? Discuss this with others if you are in a group.

Despite the problems in measuring secularization, there does seem to be a general decline in participation in organized religion in modern Britain. Table 13.2 suggests that while many people claim to continue to hold some religious beliefs and values, most people do not have much attachment to religious institutions. In the 2001 census, 77 per cent of people identified themselves with some religion, yet only 60 per cent said they believed in God, only about 18 per cent of the population were practising members of an organized religion, and just 20 per cent went to church once a year or more (excluding weddings and funerals), while 90 per cent went just once a year or even less or never. Less than a half of marriages involve a religious ceremony, and less than a quarter of all English babies are now being baptized, compared with two-thirds in 1950.

The reasons for growing secularization

The apparent growth of secularization would seem to be the result of the combination of a number of factors.

■ Advances in science and technology now provide scientific explanations for questions traditionally answered by religion, such as the origin of the universe and the causes of famine and disease. The 'miracles' of yesterday have become today's scientific discoveries. The development of scientific knowledge and explanation tends to undermine religious belief.

■ The growth of the welfare state has removed many of the tasks that used to be performed by religious institutions, such as the provision of education, and financial aid in times of distress. This reduces the significance of religion in people's lives.

Table 13.2 Indicators of religious/moral values, beliefs, and commitment: Great Britain, 1985–2003

Indicator	% of sample	Indicator	% of sample
1 Absolute guidelines exist about good and evil	28	24 Spirit or life force	39
2 Often regret doing wrong	8	25 Christ rising from the dead	52
Fully accept commandments prohibiting:		26 Define self as religious person	58
3 Killing	90	27 Draw comfort/strength from religion	46
4 Adultery	78	28 Religious teachings have the most influence on my views and outlook on life	17
5 Stealing	87		
6 Unrestricted sex	23	29 Religion is important in my life	33
Following acts never justified:		30 Identify with some religion	77
7 Claiming unentitled benefit	78	31 Great confidence in church	19
8 Accepting a bribe	79		
9 Homosexuality	47	*Church answers:*	
10 Euthanasia	30	32 Moral problems	30
11 Greater respect for authority is good	73	33 Family problems	32
12 Willing to sacrifice life	34	34 Spiritual needs	42
13 Never think life meaningless	50	*Attend church:*	
14 Often think about death	15	35 At least once a year	20
15 Often think about meaning/purpose of life	34	36 Only once a year or less/ never	90
16 Have had a spiritual experience	19		
17 Believe in paranormal activity e.g. ghosts, near-death and out-of-body experiences, premonitions	70	37 Practising member of an organized religion	18
		Believe religion will become:	
		38 More important in future	21
		39 Less important in future	40
Believe in:			
18 God	60	40 Believe in one true religion	21
19 Sin	69	41 Religious faith an important value to develop in children	14
20 Soul	70		
21 Life after death	45		
22 The devil	30		
23 Ten commandments	68		

Source: Adapted from M. Abrams, D. Gerard, and N. Timms (eds), *Values and Social Change in Britain* (Macmillan); Census 2001, Office for National Statistics; Mori and Gallup polls; British Social Attitudes Survey; Nunwood Consulting; Christian Research

■ The development of the mass media, particularly television, has replaced the church as the main source of authority and knowledge for many people. People are now more likely to form their opinions on the basis of what they read in the newspapers or watch on TV rather than what religion or the church has to say.

Religious beliefs have been replaced by scientific explanations

1 Explain in your own words the point being made in the cartoon above.
2 Look at the following religiously based explanations. Suggest a scientific explanation for each event.
   (a) God made the walls of Jericho come tumbling down.
   (b) 'Mad' people are possessed by evil.
   (c) AIDS is God's vengeance for immorality.
   (d) Witches cure people by casting magic spells.
   (e) 'And the Lord sent a sign . . . and all the land of Egypt was corrupted by a swarm of flies.'
   (f) 'And the Lord appointed a set time . . . and all the cattle of Egypt died: but of the cattle of the children of Israel died not one.'
   (g) Lazarus was dead, and 'when Jesus came, he found that he had lain in the grave four days already . . . it was a cave and a stone covered the entrance . . . Jesus said "Take ye away the stone" . . . and "Lazarus, come forth." And he that was dead came forth, bound hand and foot with grave-clothes.' Christ had made Lazarus rise from the dead.

Competing evidence on secularization

Much of the secularization debate has been focused on the mainstream Christian churches and denominations in Britain, and there would appear to be little evidence of secularization occurring in smaller Christian groups, ethnic minority religions, or other non-Christian religions. On the contrary, such religious beliefs are perhaps growing in strength, particularly in the Muslim community. The following section, therefore, primarily concentrates on some of the competing arguments and evidence both for and against the view that secularization is occurring in the main Christian churches and denominations in modern Britain.

Evidence for secularization

The decline of religious belief

Religious beliefs have become less important to individuals in guiding their morals in everyday life. A MORI poll in 2003 found only 60 per cent of people believed there was a god. Various churches' traditional disapproval of divorce, contraception, abortion, sex outside of marriage, illegitimacy, and homosexuality appears to have little impact on people's behaviour. The rising number of divorces, lone-parent families, children born outside marriage, and couples living together without getting married, as well as the growing acceptance of gays and lesbians, extra-marital sex, and the widespread use of contraception among Catholics in direct opposition to Catholic teachings, and rising levels of drug abuse, pornography, and violent crime might all be used as evidence for the declining importance of religious morals and beliefs in people's lives.

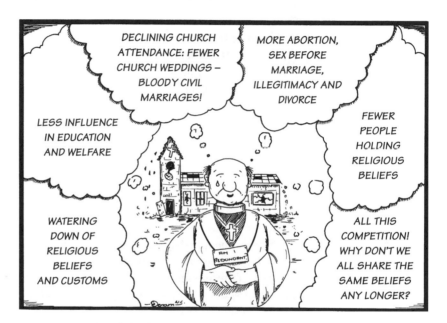

Some indicators of secularization

The fragmentation of belief

The fragmentation of belief means that there is no longer one set of beliefs which most people share, but fragments of different types of belief. Many people continue to hold religious beliefs of some kind, but drawn from a wide area. Christianity now has to compete with tarot cards, paganism, American Indian religious beliefs, self-help therapies, spiritual healing, New Age mysticism, palmistry and horoscopes, astrology, witchcraft, and beliefs in the paranormal (like extra-sensory perception). This is on top of the growing adoption by some outside of the ethnic minority communities of Hinduism, Buddhism, and Islam. Each person can now mix his or her own personal, do-it-yourself religious cocktail. Instead of everyone uniting around one religion, traditional religious thinking has been replaced by a kind of pick-and-mix religion chosen, after shopping around, from the wide range of beliefs available in the 'spiritual supermarket'.

Do you think Christian religious thinking is in decline in modern Britain? Do you think there is a fragmentation of religious belief? Try to think of evidence both for and against these views.

The decline of religious practice

There has been a decline in church membership and church and Sunday school attendance in all the major Christian denominations. Traditional churches have lost one member every six minutes since 1975.

In 2003, only around 2 per cent of the population went to Church of England services on most Sundays, compared to about 40 per cent in 1851. As seen earlier, only about 20 per cent go once or more a year (excluding weddings and funerals), and half of them go only once, mostly at Christmas. Ninety per cent of the population either go only once a year or less or never to any religious service. In 2003, the Church of England had the lowest attendance at Sunday services in more than twenty years, with less than a million people attending, and there are declining attendances at Christmas and Easter. The Catholics, too, are losing support, with around 50,000 fewer people attending mass each year. This makes Britain one of the most irreligious countries in the Christian world. Many of those who attend may do so for reasons other than religious belief, such as family pressure or because friends or relatives are being buried or married. The picture may, therefore, be even worse for religious practice.

While many people do still make use of religious ceremonies for the 'rites of passage' marking significant stages in life – such as baptism, marriage, and funerals – the ceremonies may only be used to give a sense of occasion, and for most people they may have little religious significance. Most people never attend a church apart from these occasions, and in any case the numbers of these ceremonies are declining. For example, more than half of all marriages are now civil marriages (non-religious ceremonies).

The decline of religious institutions

The power and influence of the church in society have declined. The status of the clergy is steadily declining, they are hard to recruit, and they often have lower pay than unskilled manual workers. Church buildings are closing and crumbling today, with over 1250 churches being closed since 1970. In the much poorer society of the past they were built, expensively decorated, well maintained, and repaired. There is likely to be a greater social protest at the closure of a branch of McDonalds than there is at the closure of a Christian church.

The church used to have great influence in the state and society, in terms of law-making (such as on divorce and abortion), education, politics, and social welfare. Today, the welfare state has taken over many of these roles, with free state education, the social services, the NHS, state benefits, old people's homes, and so on to care for the sick, the poor, the unemployed, and other disadvantaged groups.

Answer the following questions yourself, and perhaps do a small survey, to see how much you and other people in modern Britain know about religion.

1 In how many days does the Bible say the earth was created?

2 What was the name of the garden where Adam and Eve were tempted?

3 Who killed Goliath?

4 Whom did God tell to build an ark?

5 Who was thrown into the lion's den?

6 Who was turned into a pillar of salt?

7 Who was the father of Cain and Abel?

8 What were the gifts the three wise men brought to the baby Jesus?

9 In what town did Jesus grow up?

10 What feast was prepared for the prodigal son?

11 Which disciple betrayed Jesus for thirty pieces of silver?

12 When Jesus was crucified, who was the Roman governor of Jerusalem?

13 Name the first book of the Bible.

14 Give five of the ten commandments.

15 Who gave the Sermon on the Mount?

16 Complete the following: 'Blessed are the meek, for . . .'.

17 Who turned water into wine?

18 How many days did Jesus spend in the wilderness?

19 In which religion is Bar Mitzvah a ceremony?

20 By what name are members of the 'Society of Friends' often known?

21 Which religion has the Koran as its sacred book?

22 Which is the holy book of the Sikh faith?

23 Who was the founder of Islam?

24 Which is Islam's holiest city?

25 Members of which religions in Britain normally worship in a temple?

26 Name three Hindu gods.

27 In which country was Buddha born?

28 Which religion has its laws set out in the Talmud?

29 Which is the oldest, and which the newest, of these faiths: Buddhism, Hinduism, Islam, Christianity, Sikhism?

30 Which religion celebrates Divali?

(Answers are at the end of the chapter.)

Religion is fighting a losing battle to survive, by uniting in the ecumenical movement. This seeks to achieve greater unity between different Christian churches, such as the Church of England, the Roman Catholic Church, and the Methodist Church. This could be seen as a classic example of religion – drowning in a sea of apathy, indifference, and empty churches – desperately clutching at straws trying to save itself. Ecumenism might therefore be interpreted as a sign of the weakness of the churches, as they are no longer able to stand on their own feet.

ACTIVITY

Study table 13.3 and answer the following questions:

1 How many people belonged to Anglican churches in 1995?
2 By how many did the membership of the Catholic Church decline between 1990 and 2002?
3 What percentage of the population belonged to a Trinitarian church in 1995?
4 Identify two trends shown in the membership of non-Trinitarian Christian churches in table 13.3.
5 Which three churches or religions are estimated to increase membership most between 1990 and 2005?
6 How might the evidence in the table be used to show that religion is not necessarily declining in the United Kingdom?
7 There has been a decline in the number of religious marriages in Britain, and over half of all marriages today are civil ceremonies. Do you think this necessarily means there is a decline in religious belief? What other explanations might there be?

The growing number of competing religions, churches, and sects means there is no longer one main church or body of shared religious belief around which people are united. Religion can no longer attract people without packaging itself in many different guises, to appeal to a whole variety of consumer tastes. It has become like washing powder on supermarket shelves, with all the rival manufacturers competing desperately to sell the same product to a declining market.

Religion itself is becoming secularized. It no longer provides a lead for people and seems to follow trends rather than set them. The only way religion can maintain any support is by repackaging itself and watering down or abandoning traditional beliefs and customs – by itself becoming 'less religious'. Take, for example, trendy 'happy-clappy' and 'rave-in-the-nave' services (mixing loud rock music, disco lights, and dancing), the acceptance of easier divorce laws and allowing divorced people to remarry in churches, the growing acceptance of abortion, the abolition of Latin in Catholic services, the ordination of women priests, and the growing acceptance of lesbians and gay men by the church (though the ordination of a gay Anglican bishop in the United States, and the near-ordination of a British gay bishop, in 2003 were threatening to tear the Church of England apart). These might all be seen as evidence of this collapse of traditional beliefs. In October 1997, the *Sunday Times* reported that a majority of the forty-four diocesan bishops of the Church of England no longer believed cohabiting couples, traditionally regarded as 'living in sin', were necessarily committing a sin. So it would appear that even the clergy are becoming secularized and abandoning their traditional beliefs.

Evidence against secularization

The continuing importance of religious belief

Religious belief of various kinds remains very widespread. Surveys show that, although around 70 per cent of the population thinks religion is losing its influence, between 60 and 70 per cent of people still claim in

Table 13.3 Membership of churches and other religions: United Kingdom, 1990–2005

Church or religion	1990	1995	2002	2005[a]
Trinitarian churches:[b] thousands				
Anglican	1728	1785	1495	1549
Catholic	2205	1921	1712	1631
Presbyterian	1214	1099	933	856
Methodist	450	403	334	306
Baptist	232	224	214	209
Pentecostal	167	209	261	280
Other Trinitarian	638	663	729	767
Total Trinitarian	6634	6304	5678	5598
% of population	11.6%	10.9%	9.6%	9.4%
Non-Trinitarian churches (active members): thousands				
Mormon (Latter-day Saints)	160	170	180	188
Jehovah's Witnesses	117	131	128	130
Spiritualism	45	40	34	30
Church of Scientology	75	122	155	165
Other non-Trinitarian	61	55	52	50
Total non-Trinitarian	458	518	549	563
% of population	0.8%	0.9%	0.9%	0.9%
Other religions: thousands				
Islam	495	632	823	905
Sikhism	125	145	172	184
Hinduism	210	242	286	305
Judaism	101	94	86	83
Buddhism	31	52	80	92
Other (includes new religious movements)	71	87	113	124
Total other religions	1033	1252	1560	1693
% of population	1.8%	2.2%	2.6%	2.8%
All religions: thousands	8125	8074	7787	7854
% of population	14.2%	14%	13.1%	13.1%

[a]Estimate.
[b]Trinitarian churches are Christian churches which believe God consists of three persons: father, son, and Holy Spirit.
Source: Data adapted from UK *Christian Handbook Religious Trends 2003/2004* (Christian Research)

surveys to believe in God, 69 per cent in sin, and 52 per cent in Christ rising from the dead (see table 13.2 earlier in this chapter). There is still widespread belief in the supernatural; many remain superstitious and believe in horoscopes, ghosts, and so on. (See, for example, the range of religious activities discussed earlier under 'The fragmentation of belief'.)

Rising rates of crime, divorce, births outside marriage, and so on have a wide range of causes, and cannot be explained as simply arising from declining religious beliefs. Religious beliefs still play an important role in underpinning many social values and social welfare policies. Table 13.2 shows that many people in Britain still support religiously based moral values, such as attitudes to stealing, killing, and adultery.

The widespread acceptance of religiously based beliefs such as the importance of caring for the poor may have forced the state to take over many of the social welfare responsibilities formerly carried out by the church.

ARSES ON PEWS!

A controversial vicar is calling for dramatic changes in the way churches operate. For unless drastic steps are taken, he fears we could soon be witnessing the end of Christianity itself.

And vicar Dennis Randall believes that unless Holy men are prepared to move with the times, they will soon be left preaching to rows of empty pews.

'That's what churches need' says controversial vicar

Could churches like this soon be closing their doors for the last time. (Inset) Rev. Randall yesterday.

PACKED

Christmas has traditionally meant big business for the churches, with standing room only in packed houses throughout the country. But all that is changing, and this year vicars are bracing themselves for record low attendances.

FALL

Over the last few years there has been a dramatic fall in the number of people going to church. And religious chiefs fear that unless action is taken to stop the rot, thousands of churches around Britain could soon go under.

STEEPLES

Rev. Randall believes several factors are responsible for the fall in attendances. 'There's been a lack of investment' he told us. 'Too much money has been spent on steeples, and not enough on the churches themselves. We're stuck with old, outdated buildings. Most of them lack even basic toilet facilities.'

FORMAL

'Hymns are also outdated. Some of them are literally hundreds of years old. And I'm sure many young people are put off by the formal dress code. For instance, a church is probably the only place in Britain where you aren't allowed to wear a hat.'

SHORTCOMING

Failure to compete in an increasingly competitive Sunday morning environment has been another major shortcoming, according to Rev. Randall. 'DIY superstores and Garden Centres are pulling in the punters in their thousands', he told us.

'They offer shopping, refreshments, play areas for the kids and free car parking. And all we have to offer is a cold seat, a couple of hymns and a few stories about God you've probably heard a hundred times before. It's no wonder we're losing out.'

OUTSKIRTS

Among many suggestions he has put forward is the construction of new, out-of-town 'super-churches'. 'The whole idea of the little church on the corner is completely outdated. We should be building big, new churches on the outskirts of town, with late opening, seven nights a week, and free car parking.'

SPACE

Steps should also be taken to attract people to church. 'Prime land is wasted on cemeteries. We could use this space to have attractive garden displays, fun fairs for kids, and car washes. Everyone washes their car on a Sunday.'

FINAL

Rev. Randall believes a huge commercial opportunity exists in the form of Sunday lunches. 'If we served up good, basic, traditional nosh, at reasonable prices, we'd have the punters queuing up for it', he told us.

The Reverend also dreams of the day when churches will be granted drinks licenses. 'It's ridiculous', he told us. 'You can buy a drink in any pub in the country. But if you're in a church you can't. Britain must be the only country in the world that has such outdated licensing laws. God only knows what tourists make of it all.'

FRONTIER

Rev. Randall believes the key to future success will be attracting young people back to church. 'We must try to get families back. It's all well and good the old folks turning up – they're always welcome – but a lot of them are only interested in the free cup of tea afterwards. And they're not exactly the most generous people in the world when the collection plate comes round.'

BISHOP

So far Rev. Randall's suggestions have met with a cautious response from the Archbishop of Canterbury. 'He hasn't actually replied yet', Rev. Randall admitted, 'but he's been very busy lately.'

ROOK

Meanwhile, the Reverend tells us that he hopes to attract a bumper congregation to his church on Christmas Day, by lining up a troup of exotic dancers to top the bill. 'There's nothing in the Bible to say thou shalt not have strippers on', he joked yesterday. 'And besides, anything that puts arses on pews is good business in my book.' To overcome the drinks ban Rev. Randall will be inviting parishioners to bring along their own bottle of wine.

An article from Viz

Reproduced with permission of Fulchester Industries/JFG

Read the spoof article from *Viz* magazine. The article is intended to be amusing, but how far do you think it highlights the kinds of thing that are happening to religious institutions today?

1   Do you think religious institutions are becoming less religious in the face of competing demands from DIY superstores, garden centres, and the lure of television? What evidence can you think of to back up your view?

2   Do you think religious institutions should follow some of the suggestions (somewhat adapted!) of the 'Rev. Randall', and water down traditional beliefs and practices in order to get 'more arses on pews'?

3   Make a list of your own suggestions for ways religious institutions might attract more people.

The strength of religious practice

Believing in God does not necessarily mean going to church, and going to church does not necessarily mean believing in God. In the past many people may have attended church regularly only because church-going was seen as necessary to achieve respectability in the community. The decline in church attendance today therefore may not necessarily mean that there has been a decline in belief, only a decline in the social pressure to attend church.

The desire for religious belief and commitment is still very strong today. People are simply disillusioned with the traditional churches and are expressing their beliefs in different ways. For example, declining church attendance may simply mean that people prefer to practise their religion more in the privacy of their own homes, in 'house groups', or with services on TV and radio, rather than going to church.

As table 13.3 shows, there has actually been an increase in membership of other Christian groupings, such as the Mormons and the Jehovah's Witnesses, and of other religions. New religious sects and cults are constantly emerging, and these may be responding to a deep-seated spirituality that people find lacking in existing religious institutions and faiths.

Despite an overall decline in church attendance, the fact that many people continue to make use of religious ceremonies for the 'rites of passage', such as baptism, marriage, and death, may show they still believe it is important for religion to 'bless' the important stages in their lives. About 90 per cent of funerals involve a religious ceremony.

The decline in the number of people marrying in churches and the increase in civil weddings could be because many involve second marriages for one or both partners, or because of the cost, not because of a lack of religious belief.

The continuing influence of religious institutions

Although the power and influence of religious institutions, particularly the Church of England, may have declined since the nineteenth century, they remain important in a number of ways.

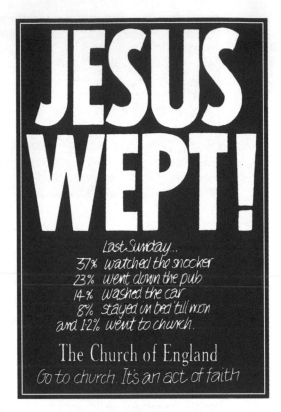

JESUS WEPT!

Last Sunday...
37% watched the snooker
23% went down the pub
14% washed the car
8% stayed in bed till noon
and 12% went to church.

The Church of England
Go to church. It's an act of faith

The church fights back: a draft advertisement prepared for a Church of England media conference, to promote the church when religious advertising on TV became legal in the 1990s

- The monarch must be a member of the Church of England, is crowned by the Archbishop of Canterbury, and since the time of Henry VIII has been Head of the Church of England, and 'Defender of the Faith'.

- Church of England bishops continue to have seats in the House of Lords (the 'Lords Spiritual'), despite extensive reform of the House of Lords in the early 2000s.

- The Church of England remains the established (or 'official') church in England.

- The Church of England is extremely wealthy, with investment funds of £3.5 billion in 2002, and it is one of the largest land owners in the country.

- Since the 1944 Education Act, all schools have been legally obliged to hold a religious ceremony each day, and the 1988 Education Reform Act reaffirmed and strengthened the requirement to hold assemblies of a broadly Christian nature and teach Christian beliefs for at least 51 per cent of the time allocated to religion in schools. Religious education is a part of the National Curriculum.

- Religious institutions still provide many schools, such as Catholic and Church of England schools.

- There remains a religiously defined 'day of rest' on Sundays, and many people still regard this as their day off (albeit for shopping, leisure, and pleasure – rather than religion – in many cases).

- Churches can still wield a lot of political influence. A political row erupted in 1997 when a report on unemployment and poverty, backed by bishops and leaders of all the twelve main Christian churches, attacked the Conservative government's record and, in effect, supported Labour party policies just before a general election. Similarly, religious leaders of all the main faiths in Britain opposed the government when, with America, it invaded Iraq in 2003.

- Religious groups can still act as powerful pressure groups influencing those in positions of power in society. For example, LIFE and SPUC (the Society for the Protection of the Unborn Child) are mainly Catholic organizations seeking to make abortion completely illegal, and have been very effective (though unsuccessful) in raising the issue of abortion in the House of Commons over the years. In Northern Ireland, the Presbyterian Church (in its various forms) and the Catholic Church play major political roles.

- Religion remains very important in the minority ethnic communities. Mosques, temples, and synagogues are often a focus of social and cultural life as well as religious life. Minority ethnic group religious leaders are becoming increasingly influential, particularly in Muslim communities.

It is unrealistic to expect religion not to change with the times. 'Rave services' and the like are simply trying to make the church more 'seeker-friendly' – accessible and attractive to people who before had no contact with the church. The wide variety of churches today simply represents different ways of expressing belief.

Evangelical Christianity is the fastest growing form of Christianity in Britain. Evangelicalism is a broad collection of Christians sharing a fundamentalist belief in the Bible – accepting that the Bible is God's literal word and should be followed strictly. Many evangelicals believe in the second coming of Christ, faith healing, speaking in tongues, miracles, casting out of demons, and possession by evil. They campaign against witchcraft, satanism, black magic, any form of occult activity, smoking, drinking, sexual promiscuity, and homosexuality. The religious fundamentalism this involves cannot be regarded as 'watered-down' religion. Much the same may be said of the commitment required by Islamic fundamentalism and many new religious movements.

CONCLUSION: BELIEF WITHOUT BELONGING?

This chapter has shown that, while religion can play an important role for the individual and in society, there does seem to be evidence that religion is of declining significance in Britain. However, whether secularization is judged to have taken place or not will be influenced by the indicators of religious commitment which are used. Grace Davie described the position of the Christian religion in the UK as one of 'belief without belonging' – while many people still claim to hold religious beliefs, there is little evidence of their belonging to or attending religious institutions, or involving themselves in any religious activities.

| DISCUSSION | Has religion a future in Britain? |

CHAPTER SUMMARY

After studying this chapter, you should be able to:

- Give a definition of religion.
- Explain, with examples, the role of religion for the individual and society according to the consensus approach.
- Explain how religion can act as an agency of social control, using the conflict approach.
- Explain, with examples, how religion can influence social change and conflict.
- Outline briefly the differences between a church, a denomination, a sect, and a cult.
- Explain what is meant by a 'world-affirming', a 'world-rejecting', and a 'world-accommodating' religious organization.
- Explain what a new religious movement is, and suggest reasons why people might join one.
- Explain what is meant by the term 'secularization'.
- Explain some of the problems with measuring religious belief, particularly the difficulties of using church membership and attendance statistics.
- Explain the reasons why society may have become more secular.
- Provide a range of arguments and evidence both for and against the secularization thesis.

KEY TERMS

church
cult
denomination
ecumenical movement
evangelicalism
fundamentalism
liberation theology
new religious movement

sect
world-accommodating group
world-affirming group
world-rejecting group

COURSEWORK SUGGESTIONS

1 Carry out a study of church attendance figures over time in some local church(es). Are people becoming less religious as measured by church attendance? Try to discover some reasons for this.

2 Interview some local clergy from a variety of denominations and faiths – or members of the public – about whether and in what ways religion is or is not becoming less important.

3 Study the role of a church, mosque, or temple in the local community, including interviews with religious leaders.

4 Ask a sample of people of different ages about what, if any, religious beliefs they hold. Table 13.2 or the questions on religious knowledge on page 327 may give you some ideas for a questionnaire. Relate your findings to the secularization debate.

5 Using secondary sources, investigate a new religious movement or an evangelical group, exploring their beliefs, the commitment required, and the occupations (social class), sex, and ages of those involved.

Answers to questions on p. 327

1 Six.

2 Eden.

3 David.

4 Noah.

5 Daniel.

6 Lot's wife.

7 Adam.

8 Gold, frankincense, and myrrh.

9 Nazareth.

10 The fatted calf.

11 Judas Iscariot.

12 Pontius Pilate.

13 Genesis.

14 Not to: have any other gods but me, make any graven image, worship any graven image, take the name of God in vain, kill, steal, commit adultery, bear false witness, covet neighbour's wife/house, etc.; to: keep the Sabbath holy.

15 Jesus.

16 'they shall inherit the earth'.

17 Jesus.

18 Forty.

19 Judaism.

20 Quakers.

21 Islam.

22 Guru Granth.

23 Mohammed.

24 Mecca.

25 Sikhism, Hinduism, and Buddhism.

26 Shiva, Vishnu, Krishna, Ganesh.

27 India.

28 Judaism.

29 Hinduism is the oldest, Sikhism the newest.

30 Hinduism.

14 Work and Leisure

KEY ISSUES

- The importance of work.
- Attitudes to work.
- Work and identity.
- Unemployment.
- Craft production, industrial society, and the division of labour.
- Fordism and post-Fordism.
- The effects of changing technology on society.
- Alienation and job satisfaction.
- The changing occupational structure and patterns of employment.
- Trade unions.
- Leisure.

Without work, it is difficult to see how society could survive in the form to which we have grown accustomed. The building of roads, houses, hospitals, schools, shops, and factories, the education of children, the production of food and consumer goods, the provision of services, health, welfare, and leisure activities all involve people working. Even when most of us relax from work by watching television, going to a sports centre or a cinema, going out for a meal or to the pub, someone else is working to provide these services.

In this chapter, the major issues covered are the importance of work, the factors which influence whether or not work may be an enjoyable experience, and the role of trade unions in the workplace. The changes that have occurred in employment patterns in modern Britain, the changing nature of technology and its consequences for the individual and society, and the patterns of leisure are other key themes.

THE IMPORTANCE OF WORK

Work is the production of goods and services that usually earns a wage or salary or provides other rewards. This may be in the *formal* or *informal* economy.

- The *formal economy* is the officially approved economy, where people's earnings are subject to National Insurance and the payment of income tax.

- The *informal economy* is the unofficial cash economy – sometimes called the *black economy* – where people's earnings are paid in cash to avoid paying income tax, national insurance, or VAT.

While work is usually paid, some is unpaid, such as housework and voluntary work for groups like community organizations, charities, and political parties.

Work is an important element in occupying, directing, and structuring the individual's time – the demands of working life involve a high degree of self-discipline if jobs are to be kept. It is, for most people, the single biggest commitment of time in any week, and it is perhaps one of the most important experiences affecting people's entire lives.

Work influences:

- *Status and social class.* The work a person does is generally the most important single factor deciding status in modern societies – most people categorize themselves and others by the job they do. Work is therefore central to the individual's sense of identity and self-esteem. For most people, the work they do provides their sole or major source of income and a person's occupation is a major factor deciding her or his social class.

■ *Life chances.* How money is earned, how much, in what working conditions, and how long it takes decide in many ways the kind of life a person will lead. For example, income from work – and future possibilities for promotion and therefore increasing income – will affect the kind of housing and mortgage a person can afford, and therefore the residential area he or she will live in. The hours worked and whether working conditions are good or bad can have major effects on health. Shiftwork, nightwork, long hours of overtime, and work carrying risks of industrial disease, accidents, and stress can have serious consequences for a person's health and life expectancy.

■ *Friendship and community life.* Work is a major place for meeting people and for making friends. The nature of the work situation can affect how much 'social mingling' there is at work and therefore how easily friendships can be made. In the case of traditional working-class communities which are dominated by one industry for generation after generation, such as traditional coal-mining and fishing communities, relationships formed at work are likely to be the basis for community life, as workmates are often neighbours, kin, and childhood friends.

■ *Values and attitudes.* Work is an important socializing experience that shapes the individual's values and attitudes. Attitudes to trade unions, for example, are likely to be formed by people's experiences at work and the solidarity which develops there. The extent to which people can adopt future planning will frequently depend on how secure their employment is, and whether they can look forward to promotion and increased pay.

■ *Family life.* Work will affect the amount of money and time available for family life. Full-time working married or cohabiting women generally have less time for leisure, as they are often expected to do two jobs – their paid work and unpaid housework inside the home.

■ *Leisure activities.* The number of hours spent at work, how much overtime has to be worked, the amount of shiftwork and nightwork, and the income earned will obviously affect the time and money available for leisure activities. However, a person's occupation and her or his experiences at work, such as the amount of independence and satisfaction she or he has at work, can have a direct effect on how leisure time is spent. This is considered in the opposition, neutrality, and extension patterns included in the 'Leisure' section towards the end of this chapter.

ATTITUDES TO WORK

The *extrinsic or instrumental attitude to work* is one in which the most important thing about a job is high wages. This attitude is usually found in uninteresting and repetitive jobs such as assembly line work, where high wages are a means of compensating for otherwise boring work, and of achieving satisfaction outside work in leisure time.

The *intrinsic attitude to work* is one in which the most important feature of a job is the amount of pleasure, fulfilment, and satisfaction it offers. High pay is not seen as the only, or most important, reason for doing the job. This attitude is found in professional jobs such as nursing and teaching, and among craft workers.

WORK AND IDENTITY

When we meet people for the first time, one of the first things we usually find out about them is what they do for a living. In fact, it is quite likely that most people we do meet as adults are a result of contacts made through work. Work is therefore central to the individual's sense of identity – how they see themselves and how others see them. Work influences the kinds of leisure pursuit we follow, and the time available to enjoy them, and enables us to obtain the income necessary to buy the consumer goods and services – including leisure goods and services – which support the lifestyles which are also important aspects of our identity.

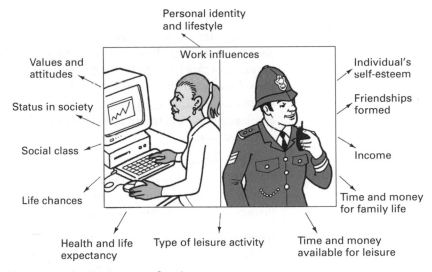

Figure 14.1 The importance of work

ACTIVITY

Imagine you were to lose your job, or left school or college and were unable to find work while your friends were working. List all the ways this would affect or change your life. What conclusions can you draw about the importance of work in the lives of individuals?

UNEMPLOYMENT

Nothing shows the importance of work more than the loss of a job, or not being able to find one. Being made redundant is nearly always a shattering experience for the individual, particularly for older people who stand poorer chances of finding another job than those who are younger.

Measuring unemployment

The definition of unemployment used will affect the numbers counted as unemployed. For example, the method of defining and counting the unemployed changed about thirty times between 1982 and 1998, with each change creating a drop in the numbers counted as unemployed. In 2003, the two main measures used were:

■ The *claimant count*. This defines the unemployed as those who are available for and actively looking for work, and who are in receipt of the jobseeker's allowance or other unemployment-related benefits. In August 2003, there were 930,800 unemployed in the United Kingdom according to the claimant count.

■ The *ILO (International Labour Organization) count*. This includes those who are available for and actively looking for work, whether or not they are in receipt of unemployment-related benefits. This count therefore includes more people than the claimant count. In August 2003, there were 1,490,000 unemployed in the United Kingdom according to the ILO count.

The problems of unemployment statistics

Unemployment figures have a number of problems that mean they often underestimate the real numbers of unemployed, as they exclude a number of groups:

■ Those in part-time work who are really looking for full-time work – a form of disguised unemployment.

■ Those on government job training schemes, who can't find a proper job but don't count as unemployed.

■ Those reluctantly staying on at school or college because they can't find jobs.

■ Some married women who can't claim unemployment-related benefits as they don't have enough national insurance contributions to qualify.

■ Those under 18 and men over 60, who aren't counted as unemployed.

The causes of unemployment

There are various causes of unemployment:

■ The development of new technology, with fully automated work processes using computers and microelectronics, requires fewer workers.

■ The increase in the working population, including more married women working and more people working to retirement age, reduces the number of unfilled job vacancies.

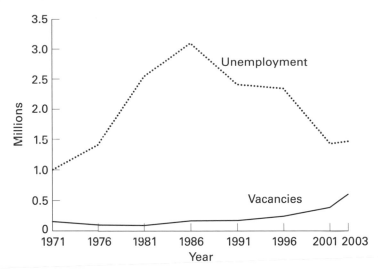

Figure 14.2 Unemployment and Jobcentre vacancies: United Kingdom, 1971–2003

Just over half of all vacancies are notified to Jobcentres.

Source: Data from *Labour Market Trends*

■ Foreign competition from cheaper manufactured goods, such as Japanese cars and electrical goods, and the decline of older manufacturing industries have led to many factory closures.

■ The skills workers possess may become redundant or obsolete, and they may lack the skills required for the jobs available. This may mean that, despite unemployment, those job vacancies that are available may remain unfilled. It is also possible job vacancies may not be in the same area of the country as the unemployed.

Attempts to reduce unemployment

Attempts to reduce unemployment include measures such as:

■ 'Welfare to work' schemes, to enable disadvantaged groups like lone mothers to get off welfare benefits and into paid employment.

■ More retraining opportunities for older workers with redundant skills.

■ Government job training schemes for the unemployed, to provide them with the skills to find work.

■ More vocational education, including key skills (see chapter 12), so school leavers have more of the skills required by business and industry, making them more employable.

■ Effective management of and investment in the economy, enabling British industry and British goods to remain competitive in the world economy, protecting British jobs.

Who is most at risk of unemployment?

Neither all groups in the population nor those in different areas of the country face the same risks of unemployment. Some groups and areas are far more likely to face unemployment than others.

■ Young people (18–24), because they lack training and experience, and cannot compete with those already trained.

■ Older people (over 55), as they have a limited working life. Employers are reluctant to retrain them if they have redundant skills, or to offer them jobs if unemployed.

■ Non-white people more than white people – an effect of racism and educational underachievement (see chapters 6 and 12). In 2003, about 4 per cent of white people were unemployed, compared to 5 per cent of Indians, 14 per cent of African-Caribbeans and Pakistanis, and 21 per cent of Bangladeshis.

■ Semi-skilled and unskilled manual workers more than skilled manual and non-manual workers, since they are more disposable and more easily replaceable.

■ Men more than women, because men are more likely than women to be in higher-paid, full-time employment in the manufacturing industries which are hardest hit during periods of economic recession.

■ The north, which tends generally to be hit harder when unemployment strikes than the more prosperous south. (This is sometimes referred to as the north–south divide.) As figure 14.3 on page 342 shows, with the exception of London, the unemployment rate gradually rises moving from the south to the north of the United Kingdom.

The consequences of unemployment

The importance of paid work for individuals and society is shown by the effects of its loss – unemployment.

Consequences for individuals

■ Loss of the identity, status, and self-esteem which are obtained through work, which may undermine a person's self-confidence. The endless search for work and the stigma of dependence on welfare benefits and

Figure 14.3 Unemployment rate, June 2004

Source: Data from *Labour Force Survey*, September 2004

social services are likely to undermine self-esteem further and contribute to growing demoralization and despair.

■ Poverty, mounting debts, and hardship arising from the loss of an adequate regular income, which may create stress and anxiety in coping with daily life. The loss of a home may result for home-owners or tenants if mortgages or rent cannot be paid.

■ Social isolation, with the loss of friendships formed through work, particularly as there is little money to spend on leisure activities, such as going to the pub with friends. More free time, but with little money to enjoy it, may result in boredom.

- More ill-health, brought on by a poorer diet, stress, and depression arising from a loss of a sense of purpose and identity.

- Increasing stress in the family. There may be confusion over roles in the family, for example the 'role swapping' which may occur with working wives and unemployed husbands. 'Getting under one another's feet' may be a problem, particularly if both partners are unemployed.

Consequences for society

- More discipline at work, with declining influence and membership of trade unions and fewer strikes, as people worry about their jobs.

- More dissatisfied people, as they have less opportunity to change jobs they no longer enjoy or want.

- An increase in political unrest. The high levels of unemployment in the 1980s in Britain were accompanied by periodic outbreaks of rioting in many of the inner cities.

- More racism and scapegoating, as people try to find easy answers to their unemployment and try to lay the blame on vulnerable groups such as minority ethnic groups, young people, and asylum seekers.

- More social problems such as poverty, homelessness, mental illness, and rising rates of crime, suicide, alcoholism, and drug abuse.

- Rising levels of stress in the family. These may cause more family breakdowns, higher divorce rates, and more violence in the home, such as wife and child abuse.

CRAFT PRODUCTION, INDUSTRIAL SOCIETY, AND THE DIVISION OF LABOUR

Craft production

Before industrialization, work was mainly agricultural but with some small-scale craft production based in the home. In craft production, a worker has full control of the production process, and makes a complete product from start to finish using manual skills and hand tools. An example would be hand-making and finishing a pair of shoes.

DEFINITION

INDUSTRIAL SOCIETY

An industrial society is one which has the following features:

- The production of goods is mainly carried out by machines rather than using craft skills.
- The workforce is urban-based, in industrial towns and cities, rather than rural-based, in agriculture in the countryside.
- Work is based in factories and offices, rather than the home.
- The workforce is dependent for its livelihood on earnings gained through working for others, rather than self-produced goods and foodstuffs.

The division of labour

In industrial society, work becomes factory-based, and the division of labour develops very rapidly. This is a term referring to the way work is divided up into a large number of specialized tasks, each of which is carried out by one worker or group of workers. In modern industrial society, the division of labour has been developed so highly that most jobs have been reduced to a few simple tasks requiring very little skill – they have been deskilled. Today, most workers make only one small part of a finished product. This often leads to little satisfaction and pride for the worker, compared to the craft worker who used to make an entire product, and many craft skills have been taken over by machinery today.

FORDISM AND POST-FORDISM

Mechanization and automation

■ Mechanization involves the production of goods by machines, which take over the manual skills involved in craft production. This removal of skills from work by the application of machinery which simplifies tasks is known as *deskilling*.

■ *Assembly line production* is a further development of mechanization. Here, as products travel along a moving conveyer belt, each worker uses machines to carry out the same small task until the product is finished at the end of the line. Because the tasks required of each worker are so routine and simple and require little skill or training, such work is often boring, repetitive, and unsatisfying.

■ Automation is the process whereby machinery and computers not only make goods, but also control the speed of production, the input of raw materials, and the correction of any mistakes, with very little human supervision. Automation has become very widespread in many industries and offices at the beginning of the twenty-first century because of the development of the microchip and computer technology.

Craft   Mechanization   Assembly line   Automation
production   production

ACTIVITY

1 Identify three jobs or industries where you think the application of machinery might have deskilled, or reduced the skills needed by, workers doing those jobs or working in those industries. Give reasons for your answer.

2 In what ways do you think office work has been changed by the application of computer technology?

Car assembly line production
Source: Peugeot Talbot

Assembly line production and Fordism: 'Any colour you like, as long as it's black'

From the employer's point of view, assembly line production is fast, cheap and efficient, because workers can be cheaply and quickly trained, as there are so few skills involved in the work; they can easily be replaced; and labour costs are therefore relatively low. Mass production of standardized goods using assembly lines became known as Fordism. This was because Henry Ford, founder of the Ford Motor Company, was one of the first to use assembly line production to mass produce cheap, standardized cars in the 1920s. Ford's first car – the Model-T – cost only about half the price of ones that were produced previously using craft skills, but there was little choice of model, style, or colour. Ford famously summed up this

Computers play a key role today in car design and engineering development
Photo: Jeffrey Berger, Fin-el LLC and Solid Edge design

mass-produced, standardized car when he said his Model-T was available in 'any colour you like, as long as it's black'. By 1929, over 15 million Model-T cars had been produced on assembly lines using mainly unskilled labour. Fordist assembly line techniques were rapidly adopted internationally for the mass production of a whole range of consumer goods, and are still widely used in many manufacturing industries today.

THE MAIN FEATURES OF FORDISM

■ Single, standardized, products are mass produced on assembly lines – there is little consumer choice.

■ Work is broken down into the smallest, simplest, and most easily learnt tasks possible.

■ The speed of work is controlled by the speed of the assembly line.

■ Workers lack skills and control and are closely supervised by managers.

Post-Fordism

During the later years of the twentieth century, Fordist mass production assembly line methods began to be abandoned in some industries for some goods. While Fordism was effective for producing a very limited range of relatively cheap products on a mass scale, consumers have become more demanding and want more personalized, or customized, specialized, and higher-quality goods, rather than the 'Any colour you like as long as it's black' approach of Fordism.

Multi-purpose computer-controlled machinery now provides the opportunity for firms to produce higher-quality, more customized, specialized goods and change product lines quickly to satisfy changing consumer demands. The emphasis is now on flexibility to satisfy consumer choice, and on *flexible workers* who have a wider range of skills necessary to produce a wider range of specialist goods than found in the 'bog standard' mass production techniques of Fordism. This system of production, involving computer-controlled multi-purpose machinery, specialized products, and a multi-skilled, flexible workforce able to do a range of jobs, is called post-Fordism.

Table 14.1 on the next page summarizes the main differences between Fordism and post-Fordism, and the box on the Ford Focus illustrates these differences in the changing patterns of car production.

ANY COLOUR YOU LIKE: THE FORD FOCUS

A good example of post-Fordist flexible production, which contrasts markedly with Henry Ford's original Model-T Ford of the 1920s, is production of the Ford Focus – Britain's best-selling car in 2004. The Ford Focus in 2004 was available in ten different models, of varying engine sizes and type. There was a choice of three- and five-door models, plus an estate version. There were six body designs, and three choices of interior design. There was a variety of 'styling packs' available, four types of optional alloy wheels, and a range of 'comfort' options, such as air deflectors, sound systems, sensors, climate control, sunroofs (manual and electric), and sunblinds. There was a choice of twelve colours, with options for metallic or non-metallic finishes. This vast range of options and possible combinations meant each car could be built uniquely customized to the individual tastes of consumers. Customers could even build their own personalized car on the Internet <www.fordjourney.com/build.asp>).

The changing nature of car production is illustrated below.

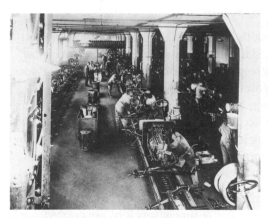

Production of the original Ford Model-T in the 1920s

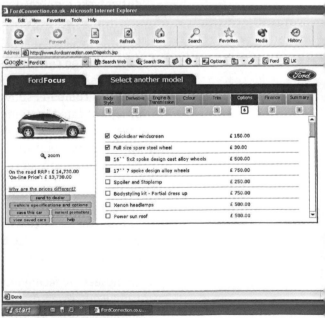

Table 14.1 Fordism and post-Fordism

Area of production	Fordism	Post-Fordism
Technology	Assembly-line production, with machines producing one product	Computer-controlled, multi-purpose machines
Products	Relatively cheap, standardized products for mass market, with little consumer choice	Specialized range of products, offering choice of options to consumers, changing with styles and fashions
Work	Repetitive, limited number of tasks, workforce with few skills	Wider range of tasks and skills, multi-skilled, flexible workforce able to do range of jobs

THE EFFECTS OF CHANGING TECHNOLOGY ON SOCIETY

The development of technology has had important effects on the way people experience their work, and there are wider effects on society.

■ As technology changes, new skills are needed and old skills become redundant. Retraining or *reskilling* (giving workers new skills) is becoming increasingly important. As discussed in chapter 11, vocational education and new vocational qualifications are increasingly important to meet the demands of industry for changing expertise, with flexible workers able to adjust to rapidly changing technology.

■ The numbers of unskilled and semi-skilled workers have been reduced, as machines have taken over the more repetitive, more physical, and dirtier tasks formerly done by people.

■ Technology removes or deskills jobs. For example, the typesetting and printing of newspapers used to be a highly skilled process, but is now carried out on computer screens and by automated printing processes. Clerical skills have been removed by word-processing and voice-activated computer software; bank clerks have been deskilled by the use of sophisticated computer accountancy programs; cash-point machines have removed many banking jobs; shop workers have been deskilled by bar-code checkouts and computerized tills; and robot technology has taken over the jobs of car assembly-line workers.

■ While new technology threatens existing jobs, it also creates new ones. More skilled manual and white-collar supervisory jobs are created, such as those for technicians, computer system analysts, and programmers to maintain and service the new technology, and administrators to organize production.

■ Employees are facing more flexible work patterns, with more shiftwork, night work, seven-day working, and overtime, to keep complex automated processes and customer call centres running twenty-four hours a day, seven days a week, all the year round (see pages 356–7).

■ New technology enables consumers to have a much wider choice of more personalized and customized products to support their lifestyles, and these are becoming both cheaper and of better quality, and available in a shorter space of time.

■ New technology is revolutionizing our lifestyles. For example, the major supermarkets now offer twenty-four-hour shopping via the Internet. On-line banking services and cash dispensers mean we are no longer tied by banking hours, and call centres – often located in places as far away as India – increasingly mean we can make telephone enquiries twenty-four hours a day. Information and communications technology, with the Internet used as a key learning tool and information source, has transformed learning in schools and colleges.

Does automation threaten all jobs?

1 In what ways do you think information and communications technology has changed the way students study?

2 Outline all the ways you can think of that changes in technology have affected, and are affecting, your lifestyle. Think about things like mobile phones, the Internet, computer technology generally, and the mass media.

3 Do you think that technological change will have good or bad effects on society generally and on the individual's experience of work? Give reasons for your answer.

ALIENATION AND JOB SATISFACTION

■ *Job satisfaction* is concerned with how much enjoyment, involvement, and pleasure people get from their work. Sociologists have attempted to measure the degree of job satisfaction by looking at factors such as how much absenteeism there is at work, how much involvement there is in work-based social clubs and similar activities, and how many strikes there are.

■ Alienation is the condition where workers have no job satisfaction or fulfilment from their work. Work becomes meaningless and workers have an extrinsic or instrumental attitude to their job.

Two views of alienation

The Marxist view

Karl Marx, writing from a conflict approach, believed alienation came about because the workers lacked power and were exploited at work. The workers have little control over the work they do, and they own neither the products they produce nor the means of producing them, with all the products and the profits going to the factory owner – the capitalist. In many cases, the workers cannot even afford to buy the products they spend all day producing. Marx believed that only in a communist society, where industry was owned by all the people rather than private individuals, could work be really satisfying and fulfilling. (See chapter 2 for a fuller discussion of Marx's ideas.)

Blauner's view

Blauner described four main aspects of alienation:

■ *Powerlessness.* The worker has no control over decisions that are made at work; for example, a lack of control over working conditions or management decisions.

■ *Meaninglessness.* Work is seen as pointless and boring, as it often involves making only one small part of a finished product.

■ *Isolation.* The worker feels isolated from fellow workers. Friendships are hard to form and the worker feels like a cog in a machine.

■ *Self-estrangement.* The worker feels his or her full potential is not being fulfilled, with no personal creativity or self-expression in the work – a feeling that anyone could do the job.

The type of technology used and the way it is used can have an effect on how much alienation or job satisfaction workers derive from their work. For example, craft production often involves a high level of job satisfaction. This is because the craft worker is responsible for the production of a complete product, and the work involves a high level of skill in using hand tools, and demands creativity and judgement. The skills of craft workers often give them independence, responsibility, and control in the work situation. By contrast, assembly line work often involves high levels of alienation. Here, the speed of the assembly line decides how fast the worker must work, and each worker makes only a small part of the finished product. Such work requires little skill and is very boring and repetitive. The worker lacks control over the speed of work, and the speed and noise of the assembly line often prevent the development of any real social contact with other workers.

Figure 14.4 illustrates the range of factors which can influence the amount of satisfaction found in work.

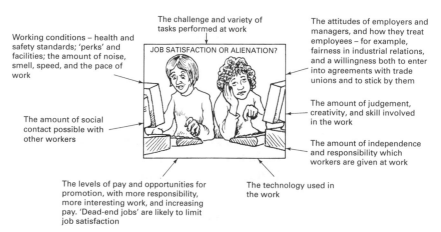

Figure 14.4 Factors influencing job satisfaction and alienation

ACTIVITY

1 Study figure 14.4 and look at the following list of jobs. Based on your own opinions, list each of them as having either 'high', 'medium', or 'low' levels of job satisfaction. In each case identify the features of each job which explains your answer.

Nurse	Office worker (clerical work)
Social worker	Car assembly line worker
Refuse collector	Painter and decorator
Child minder	Police officer
Receptionist	Bricklayer
Teacher	Airline pilot
Senior company manager	Housewife
Pub/bar worker	Shop assistant
Taxi driver	Fire fighter

2 It is often thought that people in non-manual work are more likely to have higher levels of job satisfaction than those in manual jobs. Explain, with reference to particular jobs, why this might be the case. How and why do you think this might be changing?

Responses to alienation

Workers do not take alienating work lying down, and there is a wide range of methods used to resist it. Some typical responses of workers to alienating work include:

- Producing poor-quality, faulty goods, or providing a poor service to customers.

- Taking unofficial breaks ('going to the toilet'), and extending official ones to get some relief.

- High levels of absenteeism and 'skiving off', with large numbers of workers 'off sick'.

- Leaving the job because it is so boring. A high turnover of workers is common in alienating work.

- Conflict with management, with workers using trade unions to 'get back' at management, through actions such as lack of cooperation, strikes, and working to rule.

- Attempts to achieve more creativity outside work in leisure time to compensate for the lack of meaning in work, such as DIY activities or gardening.

- Industrial sabotage. This concerns actions aimed at destroying the workplace, machinery, or goods produced – literally putting a spanner in the works – to get some temporary relief from alienating work. Laurie Taylor and Paul Walton describe this process graphically:

> They had to throw away half a mile of Blackpool rock last year, for, instead of the customary motif running through its length, it carried the terse injunction 'Fuck Off'. A worker dismissed by a sweet factory had effectively demonstrated his annoyance by sabotaging the product of his labour . . . Railwaymen have described how they block lines with trucks to delay shunting operations for a few hours. Materials are hidden in factories, conveyor belts jammed with sticks, cogs stopped with wire and ropes, lorries 'accidentally' backed into ditches. Electricians labour to put in weak fuses, textile workers 'knife' through carpets and farmworkers cooperate to choke agricultural machinery with tree branches. (Laurie Taylor and Paul Walton, 'Industrial sabotage: motives and meanings', in Stanley Cohen (ed.), *Images of Deviance*, Penguin)

Attempts to reduce alienation

In the face of declining work satisfaction and the consequences of this for the efficient running of industry, a number of attempts have been made to overcome feelings of alienation among the workforce, by making work more interesting and increasing employees' involvement in their work.

- *Teamwork* involves a group of workers carrying out a complete operation, to give them a sense of control.

- *Job rotation* involves swapping around jobs to give more variety.

- *Job enlargement* involves making each particular job cover a wider range of activities.

- *Worker participation in management decision-making* aims to give employees a greater sense of control.

■ *Flexitime* gives employees more independence and choice over when they work, such as some long days and some short ones at their own discretion, provided they work the total hours each week and they are completed between certain times each day, such as between 8 a.m. and 7 p.m. This practice is more likely to be found in office-based work than factory production, as there are fewer pressures to keep machinery running.

■ *Profit-sharing schemes* aim to motivate workers by promising them a share in the firm's profits if they work harder, and to identify themselves as having a stake in the firm's success.

**ACTIVITY/
DISCUSSION**

1 Go through the list of measures to reduce alienation, explaining to what extent you think that each might be successful.

2 Suggest two additional measures of your own that might help to overcome alienation at work.

3 Do you agree or disagree that most work today is basically unsatisfying? What could be done to make work a more fulfilling experience for people?

Who gets job satisfaction today?

Industrialization, the division of labour, and changing technology have meant that most jobs today require little skill or creativity, and work for many people has become a boring, mind-numbing experience. There are probably only a minority of people today who really enjoy their work. Craftworkers, artists, and those in professional and managerial occupations are likely to find some intrinsic job satisfaction. Professional caring jobs such as those in medicine, nursing, social work, and teaching are often personally satisfying jobs because of the responsibility and commitment involved in caring for people. However, many workers lack the independence and responsibility found in such occupations, and it is likely that the majority of workers have an instrumental attitude to work. It is not something they enjoy or identify with. Work is primarily and simply a means of getting the money to enjoy 'real life' outside work, rather than an enjoyable and satisfying activity in its own right.

THE CHANGING OCCUPATIONAL STRUCTURE AND PATTERNS OF EMPLOYMENT

The themes which have been discussed in much of this chapter so far have contributed to quite dramatic changes in the pattern of employment in Britain over the past two centuries. The key changes, which are all related to each other, are summarized in the box below, and then discussed.

> ## MAJOR CHANGES IN THE OCCUPATIONAL STRUCTURE AND PATTERNS OF EMPLOYMENT
>
> 1 The growth of the service economy.
>
> 2 The decline of manual occupations and the increase in non-manual occupations.
>
> 3 The decline of semi- and unskilled manual work and the increase in skilled manual work.
>
> 4 The division of the workforce into core and periphery workers, the casualization of employment, and the rise of the 'flexible worker'.
>
> 5 The growing employment of women.

Change 1: the growth of the service economy

The pattern of work has shifted from a predominantly agricultural economy before industrialization, when most people were working in agriculture (this is often referred to as the *primary sector* of the economy). With the beginning of the Industrial Revolution about two hundred years ago, most people began to move into manufacturing industries (known as the *secondary sector*) in the nineteenth century, concerned with the production of goods. The second half of the twentieth century saw a decline in manufacturing, with most people working in the service sector (or *tertiary sector*) of the economy. The service sector is concerned with administration, information, communication, catering, the leisure industry, sales, finance and insurance, transport and distribution, and the running of government services such as the health, welfare, and education services. This shift in employment patterns between the three sectors of the economy is often referred to as the change to a service economy. Table 14.2 illustrates this change between 1981 and 2003.

This change has meant that the numbers of people employed in different industries has changed, as figure 14.5 shows.

Table 14.2 Workforce jobs: by industry, United Kingdom, 1981–2003

Industry	1981	2003	% change
Agriculture, hunting, forestry, and fishing	639,000	408,000	−36
Manufacturing	6,120,000	3,748,000	−39
Services	16,712,000	23,366,000	+40

Source: Derived from Labour Force Survey, Office for National Statistics

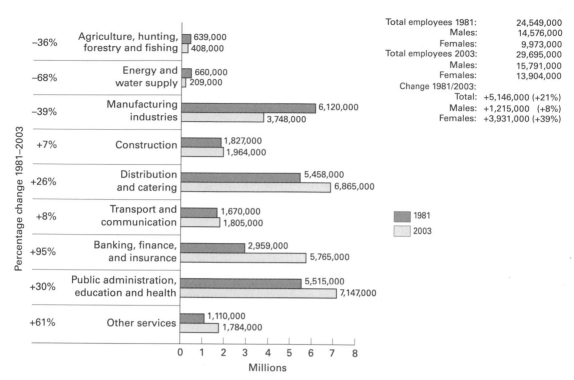

Figure 14.5 Workforce jobs by industry: United Kingdom, 1981–2003
Source: Calculated from Labour Force Survey, Office for National Statistics

ACTIVITY

Read the section on the growth of the service economy opposite, study figure 14.5, and answer the following questions:

1 How many jobs were there in manufacturing industries in 1981?

2 Which industry had 2,959,000 jobs in 1981?

3 Which two industries employed the most workers in 2003?

4 How many more people were employed in banking, finance, and insurance in 2003 than in 1981?

5 Which industry employed the smallest number of workers in 2003?

6 Which two industries showed the greatest percentage decline between 1981 and 2003?

7 How many more female employees were there in 2003 than in 1981?

8 What percentage change was there between 1981 and 2003 in the number of male employees?

9 Classify each of the following jobs as either 'manufacturing' or 'services':

Carpenter	Bank clerk
Car assembly line worker	Lorry driver
Teacher	Shop assistant
Assistant in burger bar	Tool maker
Shipbuilder	Baker

Change 2: the decline of manual occupations and the increase in non-manual occupations

The change towards a service economy has meant there has been a decline in the proportion of the labour force working in manual occupations, and a rapid increase in the percentage engaged in non-manual occupations, especially in routine clerical and sales work, and in managerial and professional work. The percentage of people working in non-manual occupations has increased by about 30 per cent since the 1980s.

Change 3: the decline of semi- and unskilled manual work and the increase in skilled manual work

Traditional industries such as shipbuilding, mining, and the iron and steel industries have declined. These employed many semi- and unskilled workers. This, combined with the speed of technological change, has meant that many semi- and unskilled manual jobs have disappeared, as machinery has taken over tasks that were previously carried out by labourers. New, skilled workers are required to operate new machinery and to maintain computerized industries.

Change 4: core and periphery workers, the casualization of employment, and the rise of the 'flexible worker'

One of the biggest changes in recent times has been the division of the workforce into core workers and periphery workers. Core workers are the well-paid and qualified people who make up the full-time, permanent workers in a workplace. Periphery workers are those who are often part-time, employed on a casual, temporary basis. They tend to be low-paid, and companies will often have little obligation to them. Increasingly, the numbers of core workers are reducing, and more firms are ceasing to employ staff directly themselves, and sub-contracting the work to self-employed individuals or other firms instead. For example, a company may no longer employ its own cleaning and catering staff, but contract the work out to another, cheaper specialist firm.

There is therefore much less security of employment, as companies try to increase their flexibility by cutting the number of core employees, and relying more on periphery workers, who have much less job security. Full-time permanent jobs have been disappearing, to be replaced by part-time or temporary work. This means many workers today face job insecurity (the fear of losing their job), and increasingly people no longer find themselves with secure, full-time, permanent, long-term employment. In 2003, about one in four people in employment were working part-time, and there were over 1.5 million temporary workers in the UK. According to the 2003 Labour Force Survey, about 41 per cent of temporary employees were temporary because they could not find a permanent job, and about one in six men were working part-time because they could not find a full-time job.

The ending of the traditional 'job for life' and the *casualization* of the workforce – that is, people being employed by companies only as and when required, on temporary or part-time contracts to do specific short-term tasks – was one of the main changes in the labour market in Britain in the late twentieth century. This trend appears likely to continue, with growing numbers of people facing temporary or part-time work, varied working hours spread across all times of the day and across all seven days of the week, and with several changes of job in their lifetimes, requiring retraining in new skills as old ones are made redundant. This is what is meant by the rise of the 'flexible worker'.

A flexible workforce?

Change 5: the growing employment of women

There has been a large increase in the numbers of women in paid employment, contrasting with a decline in the numbers of men employed. There are several points worth noting about the employment patterns of women:

■ A large proportion of the increase in the numbers of women working outside the home has been among married women. Far more women work part-time than men, as table 14.3 on page 358 shows, and in 2003 about 43 per cent of women in employment were in part-time work, though this rose to 60 per cent among women with dependent children.

■ Women generally work in different types of jobs to men:
- They are more likely than men to be in non-manual work, though this is usually in the more 'menial' non-manual occupations, such as routine clerical work and sales assistants. Even those women in the professions are most commonly found in the lower ones such as teaching, nursing, and social work.
- They are most likely to be employed in the service sector of the economy. Ninety per cent of working women were employed in this sector in 2003.

The position of women in paid employment was discussed extensively in chapter 5. You should refer to this for further detail on the employment patterns of women, and explanations for it.

Table 14.3 Employees in employment: by sex and full- or part-time status, United Kingdom, 1971–2003

	1971 000s	1981 000s	1991 000s	2003 000s
Women in employment[a]	8,943	9,973	11,635	11,848
Full-time	5,545 (62%)	5,585 (56%)	6,632 (57%)	6,730 (57%)
Part-time	3,398 (38%)	4,388 (44%)	5,003 (43%)	5,118 (43%)
Men in employment[b]	15,577	14,576	14,799	12,564
Full-time	15,421 (99%)	13,993 (96%)	14,059 (95%)	11,392 (91%)
Part-time	156 (1%)	583 (4%)	740 (5%)	1,172 (9%)

[a]Women aged 16–59.
[b]Men aged 16–64.
Source: Adapted from Labour Force Surveys

ACTIVITY

Study table 14.3 and answer the following questions:

1 How many women were in employment in 1991?

2 How many women were in part-time employment in 1971?

3 By how many did the number of part-time women workers increase between 1971 and 2003?

4 According to table 14.3, state whether each of the following statements is true or false:
  (a) There were more men in employment in 1971 than in 2003.
  (b) Between 1971 and 2003, the numbers of women working full-time increased more than the numbers of women working part-time.
  (c) The numbers of men working part-time increased by over a million between 1971 and 2003.
  (d) The numbers of women in full-time employment increased between 1981 and 2003.
  (e) More women work part-time than full-time.
  (f) The table might be misleading because the men included come from a wider age range than the women.

5 Suggest reasons why women are more likely to work part-time than men.

TRADE UNIONS

Trade unions are organizations of workers formed for the protection of their members' interests. A trade union is an example of a protective pressure group (these are discussed in chapter 7). Most larger workplaces today will have a union representative to advise and assist union members. The strength of trade unions lies in the fact that they represent the interests of large numbers of workers, who can act together as one force to negotiate with management. The unity of workers is the union's strength.

About 29 per cent of the employed workforce belonged to a trade union in 2003. Growth in trade union membership has been greatest among white-collar workers in recent years, partly due to the expansion of these occupations. However, the process of proletarianization of white-collar workers, which was discussed in chapter 3, has certainly contributed to their turn to trade unionism.

What do trade unions do?

Individuals have little power on their own to improve or change things in the workplace, and uniting together with other workers is the most effective way for workers to defend their interests. Individuals join unions to benefit from the wide range of activities which unions carry out. These activities include:

- Bargaining with employers for better wages, overtime rates, and bonuses.

- Improving the working hours and terms and conditions of employment of their members. These might include a shorter working week, longer paid holidays, maternity benefits, better pension and sick pay schemes, improved promotion prospects and training schemes, improved health and safety at work, and better canteen and sports facilities.

- Fighting against unfair dismissal and reducing the risks of redundancy, and protecting and promoting the rights of workers in areas such as health and safety at work and employment law.

- Providing legal and financial assistance to members, such as taking an employer to court for causing injury due to negligence in safety standards, and providing strike pay.

- Acting as pressure groups, putting pressure on those with political power in society to reform employment and health and safety legislation, and campaigning on other general issues of interest to their members.

The methods unions use to protect their members' interests

Negotiation with management is one of the most common everyday activities of unions, over grievances such as pay and working conditions. Legal action is sometimes taken against employers; for example, because the employer is to blame for an industrial accident or disease, or because the employer has broken the employment laws in some way.

Overtime bans, 'going slow', or working to rule are frequent forms of industrial action used by trade unions to put pressure on an employer during an industrial dispute. By banning overtime and by working strictly to the employer's rulebook and to agreements reached between a trade union and the employer, workers can slow down production and therefore bring pressure to bear on an employer by eating into his or her profits.

By refusing to work at all, by going on strike, workers can bring production to a standstill. The strike weapon is generally used by unions only as a last resort when all negotiations with employers have broken down. Official strikes are those approved by the union leadership after a 'yes' vote in a secret ballot of members; unofficial strikes are not.

ACTIVITY

1 According to figure 14.6, approximately how many trade union members were there in 1985?

2 In what ten-year period was there the steepest drop in trade union membership?

3 According to figure 14.7, about what percentage of the employed workforce belonged to trade unions in 2002?

4 Describe the trend shown in figure 14.7 (giving figures).

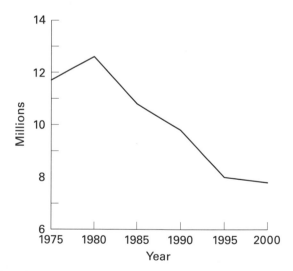

Figure 14.6 Trade unions in decline: membership figures, Great Britain, 1975–2000

Source: Data from Certification Officer's annual reports

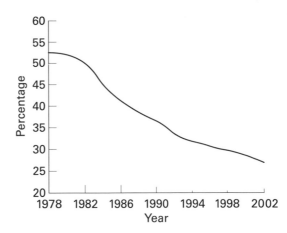

Figure 14.7 Trade union members as a percentage of the employed workforce: Great Britain, 1978–2002

Source: Data from *Employment Market Analysis and Research,* Department of Trade and Industry

The declining membership and influence of trade unions

In recent years the power and influence of trade unions in both society and the workplace have declined. As shown in figures 14.6 and 14.7, both the number of trade union members and the percentage of the employed labour force belonging to trade unions have declined since their peaks in the 1970s.

There are three broad explanations behind the decline in the influence and membership of trade unions.

■ *Changes in the law* have made it more difficult for trade unions to take swift and effective industrial action against employers. For example, secret ballots have to be held among all union members a long time before a strike can be called, and the right to picket has been limited (picketing is trying to persuade fellow workers not to work during a strike by meeting them outside the workplace).

■ *Changing patterns of employment*, with a fall in traditional, secure full-time employment and an increase in part-time and temporary workers, who are less likely to join unions. There has also been an increase in the proportion of the workforce employed in small companies, where it is often difficult for unions to organize.

■ *The decline in the traditional working class*, in the disappearing heavy industries, such as mining and shipbuilding in the north of England, where trade unions were traditionally very strong, has weakened unions. The 'new' working class are less likely to be union members. (See chapter 3 for a discussion of the 'traditional' and 'new' working classes.)

Do employers and workers have different interests?

ACTIVITY/
DISCUSSION

1 What does the cartoon suggest might be some of the causes of strikes?

2 Suggest other issues at work which might provoke trade unions into taking strike action.

3 Discuss the following statement: 'Workers should have the right to join together in trade unions to protect their interests, and should be allowed to take any non-violent action they choose in order to do so, provided the majority of the members support it. Any attempts by the government to limit the power of trade unions undermines workers' rights and can only benefit the employer.'

LEISURE

What is leisure?

Leisure time is not simply time not spent at work, because activities like travelling to work, personal care, housework, shopping, childcare, and sleeping are all essential commitments of time which most people would not regard as leisure. Leisure time and activity generally involve:

■ Time free of practical commitments, such as work (including housework, childcare, etc.) and study.

■ Activities which are self-imposed and freely chosen.

■ Activities which the individual considers to be personally enjoyable.

The distinction between 'work time', 'committed time', and 'leisure time' is sometimes difficult to make, and some activities are not easy to separate. For example, cooking for a family every day may be seen as a real work chore by a housewife, but it might be seen as an enjoyable leisure pastime by those who are not compelled to do it every day. The same activity may be work for one person and yet not work for another. The following examples illustrate this.

■ Decorating your own home yourself is not generally seen as work, but would be for the painter you employed to do it for you. Similarly, some people may not see this as 'committed time' but as an enjoyable leisure activity.

■ Watching a professional football match would be leisure for most people, but not for the newspaper reporter who has to write a report on the game, or for the players.

■ People in professional and managerial work might use their leisure time to carry out work-related activities, such as business people entertaining clients at home or playing golf with them, or teachers going on school trips with pupils.

■ Some jobs involve work-related responsibilities at all times, as in the case of doctors or the police.

■ Some people may enjoy their work so much that they take it up as a leisure activity, such as professional musicians.

ACTIVITY

1 Keep a record for one week of the time you spend on all your various activities. Classify them under the headings 'work time', 'committed time', and 'leisure time'. (Count studying as 'work time' if you are in full-time education.) Keep a record of those activities which you find difficult to classify under any of these headings.

2 Present your findings in the form of a pie chart (there are 168 hours in a week), with a category 'other' for activities which don't really fit under the main headings.

3 Explain why you found the activities in 'other' difficult to classify.

4 What do your findings tell you about:
   (a) the amounts of real leisure time you have?
   (b) the restrictions on expanding your leisure time?
   (c) the difficulties of distinguishing between work and leisure?

The changing pattern of leisure

In pre-industrial Britain, the division between work and leisure was more blurred than it is today. People worked in the family home, which was a unit of production, and they had greater control over when to work and when to enjoy their leisure. Work and leisure were also more closely linked. For example, people might mix business and pleasure, by going to a country fair not only to enjoy themselves but also to sell a few of their goods.

With industrialization, work moved outside the home to factories, and people lost control over their work and leisure time: they had to work for employers who decided the length of the working day and the length of holidays. Leisure therefore became clearly separated from work.

Over the last century the basic working week has been shortened, reduced to an average of about 38 hours a week for full-time employees in 2003, compared to around 46 hours a week in 1961, though a quarter still work more than 45 hours a week. This means people have more time for leisure today, even though many people work much longer hours than the basic working week. Longer holidays and more part-time work have also increased leisure time. All this has meant that the leisure industry, including travel and tourism as well as leisure and fitness centres and so on, was one of the fastest growing industries of the late twentieth century.

Paid holidays have increased, and higher incomes have raised standards of living. This has enabled people to take advantage of increased leisure time to pursue more varied and ambitious activities. Widespread car ownership, for example, has opened up a range of leisure activities, and more working-class people have access through package holidays to places like Greece, Turkey and Spain that were once only available to the rich.

Rapid changes in technology have occurred, which have affected the nature of leisure activities. Increased alienation at work, with deskilling through new technology, has meant that many people are trying to achieve satisfaction and creativity outside work through creative leisure pursuits. The massive growth of the DIY industry and the prolific spread of garden centres illustrate this.

Leisure has itself become a highly organized and commercialized business. The mass production methods employed in manufacturing industry have been applied to leisure activities, such as the mass production of stereo systems and video/DVD recorders to cater for the products of the music and media industries. Mass entertainment such as spectator sports, television, the cinema and video, the package holiday industry, the DIY industry, and spectacular (and expensive) developments such as Alton Towers, Thorpe Park, and Disneyland are very big business indeed. Fewer people make their own entertainment today, and large businesses make huge profits organizing leisure activities for the 'masses'.

Leisure and identity

While work is a major factor in defining individuals' personal identities – how people define themselves and how others see and define them – our leisure activities and lifestyles are also important in defining our identities. People now often express themselves and their individuality through their adoption of different leisure activities. Their choices in music, the places they go on holiday, the shops they buy from and the type of consumer goods and clothes they buy, and the pubs and clubs they go to can establish different identities. For example, going clubbing in Ibiza or Faliraki gives others a quite different impression of who you are from having a week in Blackpool, and bungee jumping, surfing, or 'extreme' sports suggests a different identity from knitting or being a 'couch potato' television viewer.

While there is a vast range of leisure activities and consumer goods available today from which people can choose to establish an identity and image for themselves and to project to others, there are a number of factors which influence people's choice of leisure activity. These are discussed below.

1 To what extent are your own personal identity and the way others see you defined by your leisure activities? Give examples from your own leisure activities.

2 What are the main factors that limit your choice of leisure activities?

Factors influencing the choice of leisure activity

Social class

Social class differences in leisure have been exaggerated, but differences in income, car ownership, educational qualifications, and working hours mean that middle- and working-class people often follow different leisure activities. For example, they are likely to read different books, magazines, and newspapers, watch different TV programmes and films at the cinema, join different organizations, eat and drink in different pubs, wine bars, and restaurants, and travel to different holiday destinations. Some leisure activities are denied to the working class simply because of the high costs involved. For example, the high membership fees of private golf clubs, and the expense of activities such as flying, parachuting, and motor racing, effectively bar such activities to the working class, and much of the middle class.

Figure 14.8 Influences on choice of leisure activity

Age

Age has an obvious influence on the choice of leisure activities. The leisure of young single people tends to be spent outside the home in the company of their peer group. They may gain some economic independence from either a wage packet or benefits obtained on training schemes, but lack the financial commitments and responsibilities of household bills, children, and the burden of paying rent or a mortgage. This means young people are more leisure-centred than perhaps any other age group except the retired. The most common leisure activities among the young are going to the cinema, pubs, and clubbing, as well as listening to music.

Young couples tend to be more home based, as they have little spare money for leisure, after buying or renting a home, buying furniture, and starting a family. DIY, home and car maintenance, and watching the TV or video are likely to be typical activities.

Middle-aged people tend to have the most money available for leisure. Children have grown up, the mortgage is nearly paid off, and there is more disposable income to spend on leisure activities like holidays and eating out.

Older retired people are more likely to be home based than any other group, through either choice, ill-health, pressure of declining income, or poverty. Reading, gardening, television, and other inexpensive pursuits are likely to be typical activities. However, many older retired people are very fit and active, and many are quite well off, and holiday companies like SAGA are developing to provide holidays for older people.

Gender

A person's sex has an important influence on the choice of leisure activity. As a result of gender-role socialization, men and women show different leisure interests and some leisure activities are more associated with one sex than another. For example, dancing, horse-riding, aerobics, and keep-fit are more likely to be pursued by women; car maintenance, DIY, watching or playing football, and weight-training by men. As table 14.4 shows, women generally have less time available for leisure activities than men, with women spending more time on essential activities. Table 14.4 refers to all men and women, and women in full-time employment have substantially less time available for leisure. For many women, so-called leisure activities are often combined with aspects of childcare, such as driving the children to leisure centres and going swimming with them.

Table 14.4 Time use in a typical week: United Kingdom, 2000–1

Weekly hours spent on:	Males	Females
Employment, study, and travel to and from work	40	28
Essential activities[a]	25	38
Entertainment, culture, sports, outdoor activities, social life	27	25
Sleep	59	60
Other	16	18

[a]Household and family care, shopping, childcare, cooking, eating, washing, getting up and going to bed, household maintenance, etc.
Source: Adapted from UK 2000 Time Use Survey, Office for National Statistics

ACTIVITY

Study table 14.4 and answer the following questions:

1 How many hours a week did females spend on essential activities?

2 Who spent the most time each week on employment, study, and travel to and from work?

3 Which category of time use showed the greatest difference between males and females?

4 List all the explanations you can think of for the differences between the weekly time use by males and females shown in the table.

5 What restrictions are there on the leisure activities of women which men don't usually face? Think about things like women going alone into pubs or clubs, going home alone at night, and responsibilities for elderly relatives, husbands, and children.

Occupation and work experience

A person's occupation can have important effects on leisure activities. The hours worked, how much overtime has to be worked, the amount of shiftwork and night work, and the income earned can all restrict leisure opportunities.

People's experience of work, such as the amount of independence and satisfaction they have there, is perhaps one of the most important factors influencing non-work behaviour and leisure. Parker saw three patterns in the link between work and leisure, which he calls the opposition, neutrality, and extension patterns. These are shown in table 14.5.

Table 14.5 Patterns of relationship between work and leisure

Work-leisure pattern	Nature of work	Typical occupations	Nature of leisure
Opposition	Physically hard and dangerous male-dominated occupations; hostility to work	Mining, deep-sea fishing, steelworking	Opposition to work. Leisure is a central life interest – a sharp contrast in opposition to work, and an opportunity to escape from the hardships of work.
Neutrality	Boring and routine work, with little work satisfaction, leading to apathy and indifference to work	Routine clerical work, assembly-line work, supermarket work	Nothing much to do with work (neutral). Leisure is for relaxation with home and family, like DIY and going out with the family.
Extension	Work involving high levels of personal commitment, involvement, and job satisfaction	Professions and management – doctors, teachers, social workers, and business executives	Because work is so interesting and demanding, leisure is work-related, and there is a blurring of the distinction between work and leisure. Work extends into leisure time, and may be used to improve work performance – for example, business executives playing golf or eating out with clients, teachers using their own time to run school trips/holidays with students, preparing lessons or surfing the web for subject information at home.

ACTIVITY

1 List all the ways you can that our working lives might influence our leisure activities. Explain in each case the influences you identify.

2 Parker (see table 14.5) suggests work can extend into and become merged with leisure because some people find their work so satisfying. Suggest examples of occupations (apart from those in table 14.5) where you think this might be the case, giving your reasons.

3 What other reasons, apart from enjoyment at work, might there be for work extending into leisure time?

CHAPTER SUMMARY

After studying this chapter, you should be able to:

- Describe and explain the importance of work, and the range of ways it can affect a person's life and identity.

- Identify the differences between the formal and informal economies.

- Explain the difference between an instrumental and an intrinsic attitude to work.

- Describe some problems of measuring unemployment and the use of unemployment statistics.

- Describe and explain a range of causes and consequences of unemployment.

- Describe and explain the groups most at risk of unemployment.

- Suggest ways unemployment might be reduced.

- Describe the main features of an industrial society.

- Explain what is meant by craft production, mechanization, assembly line production, and automation.

- Explain what is meant by 'Fordism' and 'post-Fordism'.

- Describe and explain the possible effects of changing technology on society.

- Explain what is meant by job satisfaction and alienation, and outline Marx's and Blauner's views of alienation.

- Describe and explain a range of factors which might influence the amount of job satisfaction a worker enjoys.

- Describe how workers respond to alienation.

- Describe attempts to increase job satisfaction.

- Describe and explain how the occupational structure and patterns of employment have changed in Britain up to the beginning of the twenty-first century.

- Explain what is meant by 'core' and 'periphery' workers, and the 'flexible worker'.

- Explain what trade unions are and why individuals join them.

- Describe the methods unions use to protect their members' interests.

- Explain why the membership and influence of trade unions have declined in recent years.

- Explain what is meant by leisure, and why it is sometimes difficult to make the distinction between work and leisure activities.

- Describe how leisure has changed through the twentieth and early twenty-first centuries.

- Explain the link between leisure and identity.

- Outline a range of factors which influence the choice of leisure activity.

KEY TERMS

alienation
automation
core workers
craft production
division of labour
Fordism
mechanization
periphery workers
post-Fordism
work

COURSEWORK SUGGESTIONS

1   Interview a sample of people in different types of work, or in the same work, asking them about the kinds of thing they like or dislike about their job. Try to draw conclusions about the factors influencing job satisfaction and alienation.

2   Carry out a survey among some unemployed people, asking about how they spend their time, the problems they encounter, whom they feel is to blame for their unemployment, etc.

3   Using secondary sources (see chapter 17), carry out a study of the pattern of unemployment in your area, such as the age, sex, and ethnic background of the unemployed.

4   Carry out a study of the introduction of new technology into a workplace, its advantages and disadvantages and workers' attitudes towards it. You could study, for example, the introduction of bar-code checkouts into supermarkets or of computers into district nursing, office work, or other workplaces.

5   Carry out a study of the structure and activities of a local trade union branch.

6   Carry out a survey of people involved in several different leisure activities to see if patterns emerge in terms of social class, age, gender, etc.

15 Population

The study of population is known as demography. Evidence about the size and composition of Britain's population is obtained mainly through the census. This is a survey which asks questions of the entire population of a country. Censuses have been carried out every ten years since 1801, with the exception of 1941, when the Second World War made it impractical to hold one. Censuses are carried out by the Office for National Statistics.

The 2001 census was carried out at a cost of £250 million, and asked questions about age, sex, marital status, ethnic group, religious identity, country of birth, relationships within the household, housing, change of address within the last year, employment, higher qualifications, having the use of a car, general health, long-term illness, and other topics. Questions about general health and religion were asked for the first time in 2001.

Other information on population is obtained through the compulsory registration of births, marriages, and deaths at local Registry Offices, and through national surveys like the Office for National Statistics' General Household Survey and the Labour Force Survey.

In this chapter, the main changes in the population of Britain over the last century will be considered, together with some of the social consequences of these changes.

KEY ISSUES

- The importance of information on population.
- Key terms used in the study of population.
- Population size.
- Population change in the United Kingdom.
- Urbanization.
- Rural and urban life.

ACTIVITY

Go to <www.statistics.gov.uk/census2001> and, following the link for local authority profiles, identify six features of the population in the area in which you live, such as ethnic make-up, population numbers, numbers of lone parents, religion, and so on.

THE IMPORTANCE OF INFORMATION ON POPULATION

In order for a government to plan its policies with regard to social policy, the allocation of scarce resources, land, housing, education, and finance, it is necessary to have accurate information and estimates of future trends in population size and distribution. It is important to know whether the population is increasing or decreasing, and what proportion of the population will be at school, working (or possibly unemployed), and retired in fifteen or twenty years' time. Such information will influence, for example, the number of schools, hospitals, and houses that will need to be built, the number of teachers, doctors, and nurses to be trained, the number of jobs that will be required, and the number of welfare benefits to be paid out. Details about employment help government and businesses to plan jobs and training, and transport information makes possible future planning on road building and public transport. Details on ethnic groups help to identify racial disadvantage, and to allocate resources and plan programmes to meet the needs of minority groups. Health information enables health authorities to plan services and facilities for long-term sick and elderly people. These changes cannot be made overnight, and so governments need this information to plan for the future.

KEY TERMS USED IN THE STUDY OF POPULATION

- The birth rate is the number of live births per 1000 of the population per year.

- The general fertility rate is the number of live births per 1000 women of child-bearing age (15–44) per year.

- The death rate (or mortality rate) is the number of deaths per 1000 of the population per year.

- The infant mortality rate is the number of babies who die in their first year of life per 1000 live births per year.

- Life expectancy is an estimate made about the number of years the average person can be expected to live. It is based on information about existing patterns of infant mortality and death. Estimates of life expectancy can be based on any age, but the most common are life expectancy at birth and at one year. Generally, the older you get, the more life expectancy increases, as early childhood diseases and accidents of youth are overcome.

- Migration is the term used to describe the movement of people from one area to another. Emigration is movement out of a country or area on a permanent basis, and immigration is movement into a country or area on a permanent basis. Net migration is the term used to describe the *difference* between immigration and emigration, and therefore whether the population of a country or area has gone up or gone down when both emigration and immigration are taken into account. Net migration is usually expressed in terms of a net gain (+) or a net loss (−) of population. For example, in 2001 in the UK there were 480,000 immigrants and 308,000 emigrants. The net migration figure is obtained by subtracting the number of emigrants (308,000) from the number of immigrants (480,000), giving a net migration figure of +172,000 (a net gain or increase in population through migration).

- A *natural increase* (+) or *decrease* (−) in population is the term used to describe changes in the size of a population due to changes in the number of births and deaths, but it excludes migration. A *net natural change* is the term used to describe the difference in population size after both births and deaths are taken into account. As for net migration, a *net natural increase* should be preceded by a + sign, and a *net natural decrease* by a − sign. For example, in 2002 there were 668,800 births and 608,000 deaths. The net natural change in population size was therefore +60,800 (the difference between the 668,800 births and the 608,000 deaths).

■ Population projections are attempts to predict future changes in population size. These involve complex calculations based on past and present trends in the fertility rate, the birth rate, the infant mortality rate, the death rate, average life expectancy, and migration patterns. Accurate population projections are very difficult to make because of the wide range of economic, social, and political factors which might influence future developments in any of these areas.

■ The dependent population is that section of the population which is not in work and is supported by others. This includes the under-16s (who are still at school); the over-60/65s (who have retired); housewives; many lone-parent families; the unemployed; the chronically sick and handicapped; prisoners; and students in full-time education.

■ The dependent age groups are those under age 16 and over retirement age (60 for women and 65 for men). These have increased over the last century because of the raising of the school leaving age and more people reaching old age.

■ The dependency ratio is the proportion of those working compared to those who are dependent.

■ Age distribution refers to the percentage of the population which falls into the various age groups.

■ Sex distribution refers to the proportion of males and females in the population. The sex ratio of a population is the proportion of males to females, expressed as the number of males per 1000 females in the population.

■ Regional distribution is the percentage of the population which lives in different geographical areas (such as urban and rural areas).

■ Occupational distribution is the percentage of the population working in different occupations.

ACTIVITY

At the beginning of 1981 the population of the United Kingdom was approximately 56,352,000. There were 731,000 births and 658,000 deaths. The population gained 153,000 people from outside the United Kingdom, and lost 233,000 who left the United Kingdom.

By the beginning of 2001, the population had risen to 58,643,000. In that year there were 669,000 births, 602,000 deaths, 480,000 immigrants, and 308,000 emigrants (based on data from *Population Trends*, no. 113, Office for National Statistics, 2003).

Use the information above to complete the following table:

Year	Population at start of year	Births	Deaths	Net natural change	Immi-grants	Emi-grants	Net migration	Total population change	Population at end of year
1981									
2001									

POPULATION SIZE

There are three main factors which can affect the size of a population, and whether it increases or decreases. These factors are the birth rate, the death rate, and migration.

Population trends are often derived from natural changes in population size (changes in the number of births and deaths) as migration patterns are quite difficult to predict. The basic rules for interpreting figures and graphs showing natural changes in population size are:

- Whenever the birth rate *equals* the death rate, there will be no natural change in population size: for every baby born, someone dies.

- Whenever the birth rate is *higher* than the death rate, there will be a natural increase in population size: more babies are being born than there are people dying. This means that even if there is a falling death rate and a falling birth rate, but the birth rate still remains higher than the death rate, the size of the population will continue to increase.

- When the birth rate is *lower* than the death rate, there will be a natural decrease in population size: the number of births is simply not enough to replace the numbers who die.

POPULATION CHANGE IN THE UNITED KINGDOM

The population of the United Kingdom rose from about 10.5 million in 1801 (the first census) to 58.8 million in the 2001 census. This increase was not a gradual process. Between 1801 and 1851, for example, the population doubled from 10.5 million to 22.3 million, and nearly doubled again in the second half of the nineteenth century, to 38.3 million by 1901. The major reasons for this growth were the falling death and infant mortality rates, while the birth rate remained relatively unchanged. In the last hundred years, a continuing fall in the death rate as well as a falling birth rate has slowed down population growth, and there has been greatly improved life expectancy.

Figure 15.2 on page 375 illustrates the main changes in population through the twentieth century, with projected changes for the twenty-first century.

Changes in the death rate, infant mortality rate, and average life expectancy

The overall increase in the population of the UK since 1870 has been caused by the gradual decline in the death rate. In the late nineteenth century it was 22 per 1000; in 1902 it was 18 per 1000; and in 2003 it was around 11 per 1000. The infant mortality rate has also fallen, from around 142 per 1000 live births in 1902 to just under 6 per 1000 in 2003. Average life expectancy has consequently risen, as shown in figure 15.3 on page 376.

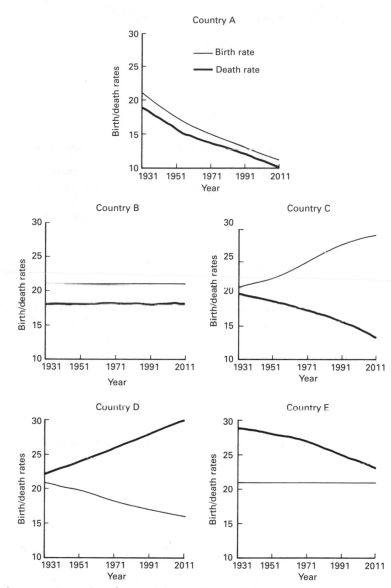

Figure 15.1 Examples of natural changes in population size

Study figure 15.1 and answer the following questions, assuming there is no migration:

1 What is happening to the population size of country A?

2 What is happening to the population size of country B?

3 In which countries is there a natural decrease in population size?

4 In which country is population size increasing the fastest? Explain your answer.

5 In which country is population size decreasing the fastest?

6 Suggest two possible reasons for both the rising death rate and the falling birth rate in country D.

7 Suggest three possible consequences for society of a falling birth rate.

ACTIVITY

Study figure 15.2 and answer the following questions:

1 Approximately how many births were there in 1921?

2 In what year was there the lowest number of deaths?

3 Between what years was there the largest natural increase in population size?

4 What trend is shown in the number of births between 1921 and 1941?

5 Approximately how many deaths are there projected to be in 2011?

6 Suggest three social factors which might make the population projections for births and deaths made in 2001 inaccurate.

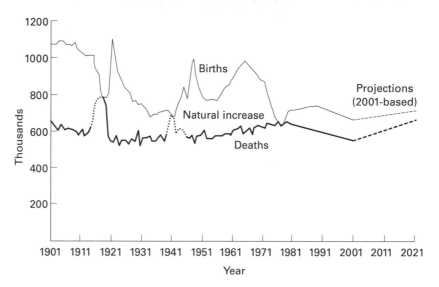

Figure 15.2 Population changes and projections: United Kingdom, 1901–2021

Source: Data from *Annual Abstract of Statistics*, 2003; Government Actuary's Department

Explanations for changes in the death rate, infant mortality rate, and life expectancy

Improved hygiene, sanitation, and medicine

Public hygiene and sanitation have improved enormously since the early nineteenth century, with the construction of public sewer systems and the provision of clean running water. These changes, together with improved public awareness of hygiene and the causes of infection, have contributed to the elimination in Britain of the great epidemic killer diseases of the past, such as cholera, diphtheria, and typhoid, which were spread through infected water and food. These improvements in environmental conditions were more important than medical advances in wiping out the epidemic diseases. The importance of these changes is shown by the scale of death caused by epidemic diseases in the past. For example, between 1337 and 1351 the Black Death, a plague carried by black rats, is estimated to have wiped out about one-quarter of the British population, and in 1918 flu killed about 250,000 people.

ACTIVITY

Study figure 15.3 and answer the following questions:

1 What was the life expectancy of females in 1931?

2 What was the difference between the life expectancy of males and females in 1961?

3 Identify three trends shown in figure 15.3 between 1906 and 2001, and suggest reasons for them.

4 Using the data given in figure 15.3, draw a line graph to show the same information.

5 Suggest three reasons why life expectancy is greater for women than for men.

6 Suggest reasons why life expectancy has increased more for women than for men in the period between 1906 and 2001.

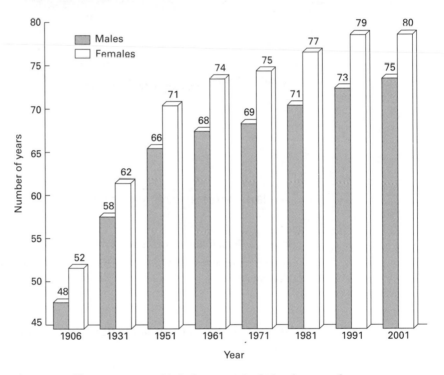

Figure 15.3 Life expectancy at birth: by sex, United Kingdom, 1906–2001

Source: Data from Population Trends

Advances in medicine and science, such as vaccines and the development of penicillin, antibiotics, and other life-saving drugs, and advances in surgery and medical technology, such as transplant surgery, have further contributed to the decline in the death rate. More sophisticated medical care means that people now survive illnesses that would have killed them even in the recent past. Before the twentieth century, the highest mortality rates were among babies and young children, but today death rates rise the older you get. The major causes of death today in Britain are from the non-infectious degenerative diseases, such as cancer and heart disease.

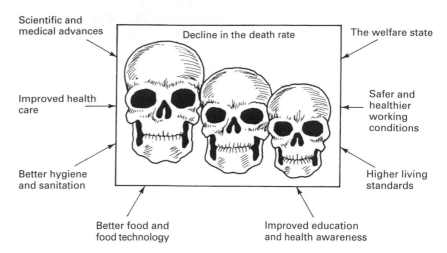

Scientific and medical advances

Decline in the death rate

The welfare state

Improved health care

Safer and healthier working conditions

Better hygiene and sanitation

Higher living standards

Better food and food technology

Improved education and health awareness

Figure 15.4 Reasons for the decline in the death rate

Higher living standards

Rising standards of living have further assisted in reducing death rates. Higher wages, better food, more amenities and appliances in the home, and greatly improved housing conditions, with inside toilets, less damp, and running hot water, have all assisted in improving the health and life expectancy of the population. Because of improved transportation and food technology, a wider range of more nutritious food is available, with improved storage techniques (such as freezing), making possible the import of a range of foodstuffs, including more affordable fresh fruit and vegetables all the year round.

Public health and welfare

There has been a steep rise of state intervention in public welfare, particularly since the establishment of the welfare state in 1945. The NHS has provided free and comprehensive health care, and there is much better ante-natal and post-natal care for mothers and babies. More women have children in hospitals today, and there are health visitors to check on young babies, which helps to explain the decrease in the infant mortality rate. The wide range of welfare benefits available helps to maintain standards of health in times of hardship, and old people in particular are cared for better today, with pensions and a range of services like home helps, social workers, and old people's homes.

Health education

Coupled with these changes has been a growing awareness of nutrition and its importance to health. Improved educational standards generally, and particularly in health education, have led to a much better informed public, who demand better hygiene and public health, and welfare legislation and social reforms to improve health. Bodies like the Health Education Authority seek to improve the health of the public by education, such as emphasizing the benefits of regular exercise, giving up smoking, and eating a balanced diet. The public outcries in the 1980s and 1990s over risks of food poisoning, such as salmonella in eggs, BSE ('mad cow disease') in beef, listeria in cook-chill foods, and the E. coli food poisoning outbreak in 1996–7 (which killed twenty people), and the public's rejection of genetically modified crops and foods in the early 2000s are all evidence of this growing health awareness.

Improved working conditions

Working conditions improved dramatically in the twentieth century. Technology has taken over some of the more arduous, health-damaging tasks, and factory machinery is often safer than it was a hundred years ago. Higher standards of health and safety at work, shorter working hours, more leisure time, and earlier retirement ages have all made work physically less demanding and therefore have reduced risks to health.

Sex differences in life expectancy

In chapter 3, major social class differences in health and life expectancy were discussed, but such differences also exist between men and women. These issues are discussed in more depth in the next chapter.

In most younger age groups, the population is roughly evenly divided between the sexes, but in the older age groups there are far more women than men. In 2001, about two-thirds of people aged 75 or over, and nearly three-quarters aged 85 or over, were women. There are therefore slightly more women than men in the population as a whole. This is because there is a higher death rate among men and life expectancy for women is longer: in 2001, average life expectancy was 80 for women, but only 75 years for men. Figure 15.3 on p. 376 shows these differences in life expectancy between 1906 and 2001.

Why do women live longer than men?

■ Evidence suggests that boys are the weaker sex at birth, with a higher infant mortality rate, and women seem to have a better genetic resistance to heart disease than men.

■ The process of gender-role socialization means men are more likely to be brought up to shrug off illnesses; they drink and smoke more, and use more illegal drugs, with all the consequences these have for health; they are more aggressive and take more risks; they are less careful in what they eat; and they are not socialized to show their emotions as much as women, and so have less outlet for stress. Women are socialized to 'take care of themselves' more than men, and they are more likely to visit doctors, which may mean they receive better health care.

■ Men generally live more hazardous lives than women. The more dangerous occupations are more likely to be done by men, such as construction work, and men are therefore more at risk of industrial accidents and diseases. In the home, men are more likely to do the dangerous and risky jobs, such as jobs using ladders and climbing on the roof. Men also make up the majority of car drivers and motor-cyclists, and are therefore more at risk of death through road accidents.

■ Men are more likely to work full-time and to work longer and more unsociable hours, such as overtime working and shiftwork, which can be harmful to health.

■ Jobs carrying high levels of responsibility are more commonly done by men, which may cause higher levels of health-damaging stress.

■ Men retire later than women (age 65 compared to 60). Evidence suggests that the later retirement age of men could be an important factor in reducing their life expectancy. (Note: women's retirement age is planned to increase to 65 in the period between 2010 and 2020.)

ACTIVITY/ DISCUSSION

1 Which of the reasons given for women living longer than men do you think is most important? Give your reasons.

2 Do you think that men's 'macho' behaviour is an important factor in shortening their lives? Suggest evidence for this from your own experiences.

3 'The growing equality of women with men is a threat to women's health.' Explain this statement. Do you agree? How might this situation be avoided (apart from stopping women becoming more equal!)?

Changes in the birth rate

Over the past hundred years, the birth rate has been declining in the UK, from 28 per 1000 in 1902 to about 11.3 per 1000 in 2003. The only major exceptions to this trend were the post-war 'baby booms' of 1920 and 1947, as men and women started families delayed by separation during the two world wars. There was a further baby boom in the late 1950s and 1960s, when increases in the standard of living and low unemployment meant some parents felt they could afford more children, and improved welfare services and payments made having extra children less of a hardship. However, with increasing unemployment and hardship in the 1980s and early 1990s, birth rates declined once again. A decline in the birth rate has meant that the average family has been getting smaller, from about 6 children per family in the 1870s to about 1.8 in 2003. Despite the declining birth rate, the population has continued to grow slowly, because the birth rate has remained slightly higher than the death rate.

Explanations for the falling birth rate and smaller family size

Contraception

More effective and cheaper methods of contraception were developed in the last century, and society's attitudes to the use of contraception have changed from disapproval to acceptance. This is partly because of growing secularization, and the declining influence of the church and religion on people's behaviour. The availability of safe and legal abortion since 1967 has also helped in terminating unwanted pregnancies. Family planning is therefore easier.

ACTIVITY/ DISCUSSION

1 What sort of pressures might influence governments either to promote or to restrict the use of contraceptive devices?

2 What are the social pressures which influence whether or not individuals choose to use contraception?

The compulsory education of children

Since children were barred from employment, and education became compulsory in 1880, they have ceased to be an economic asset that can contribute to family income through working at an early age. They have therefore become an economic liability and a drain on the resources of parents, as children have to be supported for a prolonged period in compulsory education. Parents have therefore begun to limit the size of their families, to secure for themselves and their children a higher standard of living. The move to a more child-centred society has assisted in this restriction of family size, as smaller families mean parents can spend more money and time on and with each child.

The changing position of women

The changing position of women, particularly since the second half of the twentieth century, has involved more equal status with men and greater employment opportunities. Women today have less desire to spend long years of their lives bearing and rearing children, and many wish to pursue a career of their own. While most women do eventually have children, there is a growing proportion who are choosing not to do so. For example, 25 per cent of 35-year-old women in 2000, and 15 per cent of 45-year-old women, were childless, compared to 11 and 12 per cent in 1980.

The declining infant mortality rate

In the nineteenth century, the absence of a welfare state meant many parents relied on their children to care for them in old age. However, many babies failed to survive infancy, and it was often uncertain whether children would outlive their parents. Parents therefore often had many

Figure 15.5 Reasons for the decline in the birth rate

children as a safeguard against some of them dying. The decline in the infant mortality rate and death rate has meant fewer children are dying before adulthood and old age, so parents need no longer have many children as security against only a few surviving. In addition, the range of agencies which exist to help the elderly today mean people are less reliant on care by their children when they reach old age.

A geographically mobile labour force

Industrial societies generally require a geographically mobile workforce, which means a workforce that can easily move to other areas for work or promotion. This may have been a factor in encouraging smaller families, as they can more easily pack up and move elsewhere.

The ageing population

Britain, like most Western industrialized countries, today has an ageing population. This simply means the average age of the population is getting higher, with a greater proportion of the population over retirement age, and a smaller proportion of young people.

The high birth and death rates of the nineteenth century meant that the majority of the population was young – people didn't live long enough to grow old. The decline in the death rate and increased life expectancy have meant that more people are living longer, and more are reaching old age.

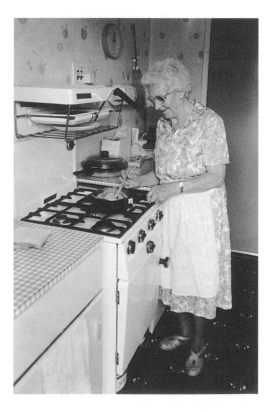

Photo: Ted Fussey

However, the decline in the birth rate has meant that fewer children are being born as well, and this has changed the overall age structure of the population. For example, in 1901, about 33 per cent of the population were under age 15, 63 per cent were between the ages of 15 and 65, and only about 4 per cent were over 65. By 2001, about 20 per cent were under 16, 64 per cent were between 16 and 64, and 16 per cent were over 65. This changing age structure of the population is shown in the pyramids in figure 15.6, and figure 15.7 shows the growing numbers of the elderly.

ACTIVITY

Look at figure 15.6 and answer the following questions:

1 About what percentage of females were in the 80+ age group in 1931?
2 About what percentage of males were aged between 20 and 29 in 1981?
3 By approximately how much did the percentage of females in the 70–9 age group increase between 1901 and 2001?
4 What evidence is there in figure 15.6 that women live longer than men?
5 About what percentage of females are expected to be over the age of 80 by 2021?
6 Explain briefly how figure 15.6 shows that Britain has an ageing population.

The growing proportion of elderly people in the population creates a growing burden of dependence, or an increasing dependency ratio. This simply means that an increasing number of old people have to be supported by a decreasing proportion of the working population. This could mean higher taxes on those working to pay the costs of benefits for the elderly, such as the costs of income support payments for board and lodging of elderly people in residential and nursing homes. Figure 15.8 on page 385 summarizes the processes involved in the ageing population, and some of the consequences are outlined below.

Some consequences of an ageing population

Consequences for individuals

- Enjoyment of retirement, with more time for leisure interests and travel, and more time to spend with grandchildren.

- Loss of income from work, possibly leading to poverty if on an inadequate pension.

- Loss of status obtained from work.

- Loss of social contacts with workmates and friends, and growing isolation and loneliness as friends and partners die.

- Deterioration in health, and growing dependence on others.

- Fear of crime, especially as television and newspapers are often the main source of information for the housebound elderly, and the mass media often give an exaggerated view of how much crime there is.

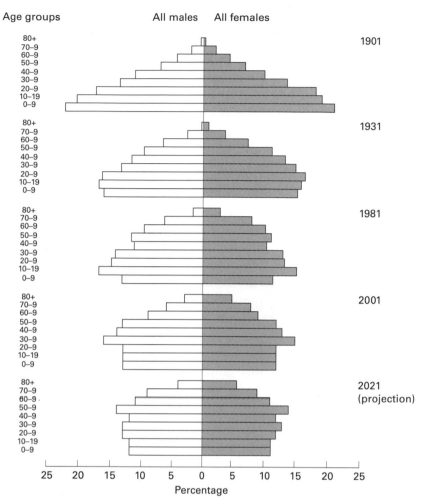

Figure 15.6 The ageing population: United Kingdom, 1901–2021

Source: Data from Census 2001; Government Actuary's Department; *Population Trends*

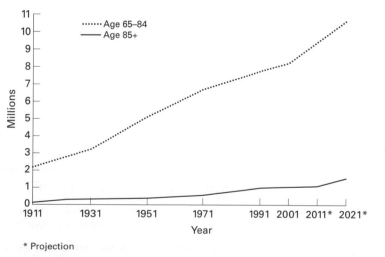

Figure 15.7 The growing numbers of the elderly: United Kingdom, 1901–2021

Source: Data from Census 2001; Government Actuary's Department; *Population Trends*

Consequences for the family

- Elderly relatives can help with childcare and babysitting, and maybe financially (especially in the middle class).

- Emotional strain and overcrowding if an elderly, and possibly infirm, relative moves in with his or her child's family. This might cause conflict between couples, or between children and grandparents.

- Extra work for women. The practical burdens of caring for the elderly often tend to fall mainly on women in the family.

- Problems for planning holidays and moving for work or promotion caused by the care needs of an elderly dependant.

- Financial hardship, as people may increasingly face having to support not just themselves and their children, but also their parents and possibly grandparents too. Loss of income may result if one partner has to give up work to care for elderly dependants on top of the financial burden of extra food and heating bills.

- Difficulties (like stress and their own ill-health) for relatives who have to devote large amounts of time to caring for infirm or disabled elderly relatives. Increasingly, with longer life expectancy, many of these carers are themselves elderly and infirm, for example 65-year-olds caring for their 90-year-old parents.

Consequences for society

- An increased burden of dependency. This may mean more taxes on the working population to pay for higher levels of government spending on welfare benefits, state pensions, health, and social services. Nearly half of all benefit spending goes to elderly people – 48 per cent in 2000 – and without welfare reforms, this is expected to keep on rising. An alternative approach involves cutting pensions and services to the elderly, or charging for services that were formerly free.

- Less money available for other areas, such as schools.

- Pressures on the NHS, such as cash shortages and longer waiting lists for treatment, as the elderly suffer more illness, particularly long-term illnesses.

- More poverty, as the elderly often fall below the poverty line.

- Housing shortages as people occupy their homes for longer.

- Youth unemployment and fewer promotion opportunities at work, as more people survive and work until retirement age.

- More day centres and day hospitals, both to care for the elderly and to provide respite care (facilities to enable relatives looking after elderly infirm relatives to have some time off).

- More demands on social services departments, to provide support to enable older people to continue to live in their own homes.

- More demands for holiday packages, leisure facilities, and transport suited to the needs of older people.

■ More 'pensioner power' as older people make up a larger proportion of the voting population, influencing the decision making of governments and local councils.

A 1990s British Gas report on ageing in Britain asked a representative sample of retired people over the age of 55 about what they thought were the good things about getting older in Britain, and what they thought were the main problems facing older people. Figure 15.9 on page 387 shows the results of the survey.

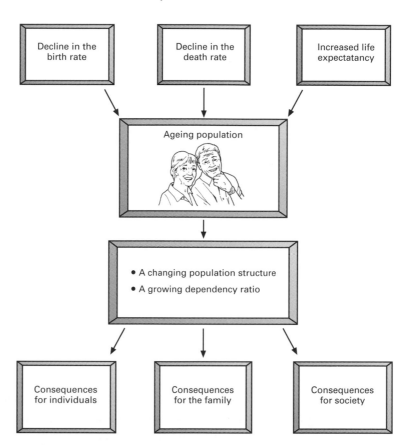

Figure 15.8 The causes and consequences of an ageing population

Migration: immigration and emigration

A further influence on Britain's population size and composition has been migration. Migration to and from Britain has usually occurred because of 'push' factors, such as poverty, unemployment, or persecution, and 'pull' factors, such as the search for jobs and a higher standard of living, more political freedom, and joining relatives.

The pattern of migration

The peak period of immigration in the nineteenth century was in the 1830s and 1840s, when over half a million Irish fled the effects of the potato famine in Ireland. The Irish still remain the single largest immigrant group

ACTIVITY

Study figure 15.9 and the section on 'Some consequences of an ageing population' (see pages 382–5):

1 Explain fully two problems for society of an ageing population, and the possible consequences of these problems.

2 When elderly and infirm relatives move in with their adult children, it is usually the female who gives up paid work. Why do you think this is?

3 Look at figure 15.9:
   (a) What percentage of retired people thought there was nothing good about getting older?
   (b) What was the main problem most retired people faced in getting older?
   (c) What percentage of retired people thought lack of respect from society was a main problem of getting older?
   (d) Identify two good things about growing older.

4 Why do many of the elderly live in poverty?

5 What welfare services are available to help the elderly? List all those you can think of, explaining in each case the kind of help provided.

6 If you have, or were to have, an elderly parent, grandparent, or great-grandparent living with you, what advantages and problems are or might be created for family life? Discuss these with others if you are in a group.

7 Go to <www.helptheaged.org.uk> (Help the Aged) and/or <www.ageconcern.org.uk> (Age Concern) and identify five issues that these organizations for the elderly are campaigning on.

in Britain. The peak periods of emigration from Britain were in the 1880s and the first quarter of the twentieth century, when many left to go to places in the British Empire.

In the twentieth century, there were two peak periods of immigration. During the 1930s and up until about 1945, several hundred thousand refugees fled to Britain from Europe to escape the effects of Nazi occupation and persecution. In the late 1950s and 1960s, widespread immigration from the black Commonwealth (mainly India, Pakistan, and the West Indies) was actively encouraged by the British government, which sent out recruiting teams to these countries to solve labour shortages in unskilled and poorly paid occupations in Britain.

Large-scale black immigration has been effectively ended by a series of racist Immigration Acts since 1962. These have taken away many of the rights to residence in Britain of black British people living in former British colonies, while at the same time preserving those of white people.

ACTIVITY

Go to <www.cre.gov.uk/publs/connections/conn_03sum_wwc.html> and identify as many reasons as you can why people originally emigrated to Britain from other countries.

Overall, the pattern of net migration shows that from about 1870 to the 1930s there were more emigrants than immigrants; that is, a net loss of population through migration. In the periods between about 1931 and 1951, and 1955 and 1962, immigration exceeded emigration (that is, a net gain). In the 1960s and 1970s, more people left the country each year than

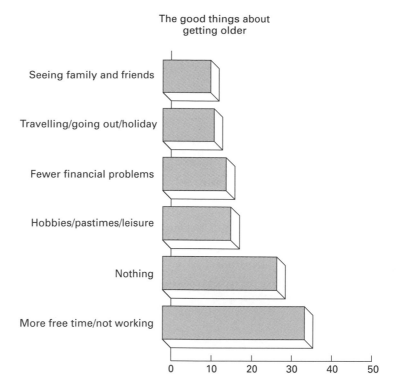

The good things about
getting older

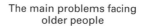

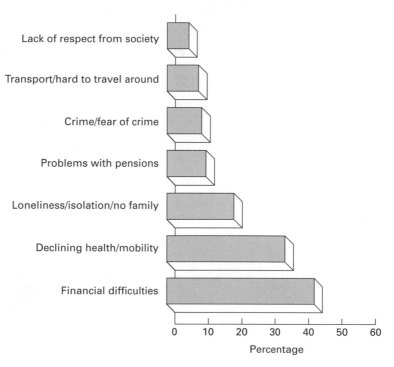

The main problems facing
older people

Figure 15.9 Growing older in Great Britain in the 1990s: the good and the bad

Source: Data from *The British Gas Report on Attitudes to Ageing*

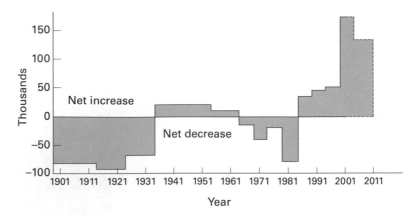

Figure 15.10 Net migration: United Kingdom, 1901–2011

Source: Data from *Annual Abstract of Statistics*; *Population Trends*; Government Actuary's Department

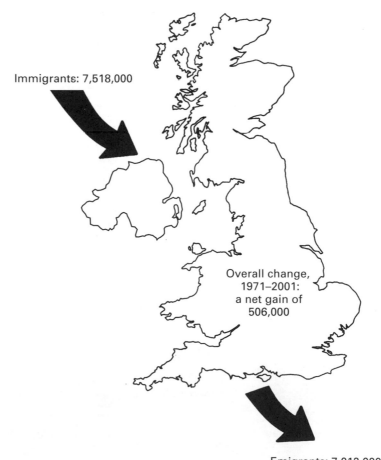

Immigrants: 7,518,000

Overall change, 1971–2001: a net gain of 506,000

Emigrants: 7,012,000

Figure 15.11 International migration into and out of the United Kingdom: 1971–2001

entered it, but since the 1980s more people have entered the country than have left it. Figures 15.10 and 15.11 show net migration between 1901 and 2001 and projections to 2011; they summarize immigration, emigration, and net migration between 1971 and 2001.

It is now extremely difficult to enter Britain as a legal or illegal immigrant, and those seeking asylum from persecution abroad are very unlikely to be granted it. In 2002, for example, about three-quarters of asylum seekers had their applications rejected, and they are very carefully controlled by the authorities while they are waiting for their cases to be considered. The harsh government regulations governing asylum can be viewed at <www.ind.homeoffice.gov.uk>.

URBANIZATION

Urbanization is the process of the movement of people from rural (country) areas to urban areas (towns and cities), with the corresponding growth in towns and cities, which become the major centres of population in a society. An urbanized society is one where most of the population lives in towns and cities.

In Britain, urbanization really began with the beginnings of industrialization in the late eighteenth and early nineteenth centuries. For example, in 1800 about 15 per cent of the population lived in towns and cities, and by 1900 this had increased to about 77 per cent of the population of England and Wales. In 2001, about 72 per cent of the population of England lived in urban areas. About one-third of the UK population is concentrated in seven large conurbations (large, densely populated urban areas including a number of towns). These conurbations are Greater London, Greater Manchester, Merseyside (around Liverpool), Strathclyde (around Glasgow), Tyne and Wear (around Newcastle upon Tyne), the West Midlands (around Birmingham), and West Yorkshire (around Leeds).

The reasons for urbanization

Urbanization is linked to two basic factors: the mechanization of agriculture and the industrialization process. The movement to larger farms and the increasing mechanization of agriculture reduced the number of farm workers required. In the absence of any form of social welfare, these rural unemployed generally had no alternative but to seek work in the towns and cities. Industrialization in the nineteenth century led to the development of industrial centres in urban areas, and people moved to these centres for employment.

De-urbanization

Since the 1960s, there has been a gradual reversal of the process of urbanization, with a decline in the population living in cities. Between 1961 and 1981, for example, the population of the six largest conurbations fell by about two million. This movement of people away from living in cities towards rural areas, the suburbs, and new towns (like Milton Keynes) is known as de-urbanization or urban dispersal.

Why has de-urbanization occurred?

■ Industrial firms have moved from the cities. This is because land prices, rent, and rates tend to be higher in city areas, and firms can cut costs by moving out. This has been assisted by central and local government incentives in terms of rent and rate concessions for firms which relocate in rural areas or in new towns.

■ Improved road networks and bus services, and fast rail services, have enabled industry to operate just as efficiently outside the cities, and have also enabled people to commute to work rather than having to live within walking or cycling distance. The increase in private and company car ownership has helped in this.

■ People have moved to get a better environment and cheaper housing. Often life in the suburbs and in new towns is generally more pleasant than in the cities. With the move towards more home-ownership, house prices in the more pleasant areas of cities are too expensive for many people, and housing is more modern and generally cheaper in the suburbs and new towns. There are usually more parks and open spaces, newer leisure facilities, and less noise and pollution there. General costs of living are lower, and there also tend to be fewer social problems like crime, vandalism, and violence in these areas.

■ As firms have left the cities, employees following these firms can cut down travelling time and costs in getting to work.

■ Many inner-city slum areas have been redeveloped, and this has often meant the people living there have been rehoused in large new social (council and housing association) housing estates in the suburbs or in new towns.

ACTIVITY

1 People often move around the country today, and there may be people in your school or college class, your neighbourhood or workplace, who have moved into your area, rather than being born there. Do a small survey of these people, finding out (a) why they left the area they came from, and (b) why they chose to move to your area.

2 On the basis of your findings, what seem to be the principal factors influencing the movement of people around the country?

The inner cities

The inner cities have undergone a rapid decline in recent years as firms either close down or move out to the suburbs and new towns. Often the only people left in the inner cities are those who can't afford to move out, such as the old, the unemployed, and low-paid unskilled and semi-skilled workers. Many inner-city residents are among the most deprived sections of the population in Britain. These areas have proven to be 'flashpoints' of social conflict, with riots breaking out in the 1980s in the St Paul's area of

The inner cities have often been flashpoints of social conflict

Photo: Sean Smith, *Guardian*

Bristol, the Toxteth area of Liverpool, the Southall, Brixton, and Tottenham areas of London, the Handsworth area of Birmingham, and other inner-city areas.

The inner cities have become centres of deprivation and flashpoints of conflict for a number of reasons.

Poverty and unemployment

Unemployment is particularly high in the inner cities. Many of the sorts of work which are available for inner-city residents without paying expensive travelling costs have been declining. Traditional industries such as docking, shipbuilding, textiles, and clothing have been disappearing, partly because of cheaper foreign competition, and new firms have not opened up in these areas. The demand for semi-skilled and unskilled labour has in any case been declining with increasing mechanization.

Poor housing

The inner cities are likely to have the worst and oldest housing, with fewer facilities, more overcrowding, and a higher level of rented accommodation (often at exorbitantly high rents for the quality of the accommodation) than other areas. Tenants often can't afford to look after their homes properly, and private landlords frequently refuse to do so. Even owner occupiers may have few extra resources to maintain their homes adequately.

Crime

Those who can afford to move out of the inner cities have done so, and only the poor are left. Petty crime is more likely as a necessity for surviving daily life. The redevelopment and slum clearance that have gone on have broken up extended kin networks and traditional communities, and this has weakened informal social controls. The anonymity this creates means delinquency and 'street crime' are therefore more common, as people can get away with them. This rise in the crime rate is frequently fuelled by police activity, as the inhabitants of inner-city areas fit their stereotype of potential criminals. Policing is therefore heavier in these areas, which may cause resentment among those living there, and consequently more confrontations with the police.

Racism and racial tension

Some inner-city areas have high concentrations of minority ethnic groups, since they are often among the poorer sections of the population and live where they can best afford. The white population in such areas may scapegoat these minority ethnic groups by blaming them for their problems of housing and unemployment, which may create racial tension. There is also evidence of racism in the police force, especially in the Metropolitan Police in London, and this often generates hostility and resentment among black people against the police for harassing them, for example by stopping and searching them without good cause.

Poor schools

Schools in inner cities are often in dilapidated buildings. There is frequently a high turnover of teachers in such schools because of the stress caused by having to deal with the complex social problems they encounter in the classroom. Parents do not have the money to provide support for the schools, as parents do in many middle-class areas.

General social problems

The inner cities are more likely to have a concentration of other general social problems, as a result of the stresses and strains caused by the accumulation of the points mentioned above. For example, the inner cities have higher levels of family breakdown and deprived lone-parent families, drug addiction, drug abuse, and prostitution than found in other areas.

Improving the inner cities

Some attempts have been made to redevelop and improve (regenerate) the inner cities in recent years, but often these have not resolved the underlying problems. For example, the redevelopment of London's Docklands in the late 1980s simply meant a massive increase in property prices, and a takeover of the area by highly paid young professionals. Such redevelopment means life for the remaining local residents is made ever more expensive and difficult to cope with. Often these residents are forced to move out by such circumstances, and the 'problem' simply moves elsewhere.

RURAL AND URBAN LIFE

One of the consequences of the urbanization process is thought to be the loss of the 'sense of community' which exists in rural life. This is because rural and urban areas are thought to involve quite different lifestyles and relationships, with the most extreme contrasts being between living in a large city and living in a small village. These differences are summarized and contrasted on the next page.

Criticisms of the distinction between rural and urban lifestyles

The distinction between rural and urban lifestyles presented over the page really represents two extremes. It is unlikely that all the features will be found In any particular area, and there may be more 'blurring' of the differences between urban and rural life in real life. Nevertheless, the general suggestion is that the quality of rural life is generally much 'better' than urban life, with a focus on the more unpleasant aspects of urban living, such as pollution, noise, social isolation, and higher levels of crime and violence. However, it is easy to exaggerate and oversimplify these differences. Research by the Countryside Agency in 2003 found that people in rural areas worried about many of the same things, like crime, housing, money, and world problems, as people in urban areas. While living in towns and cities may bring its own problems, there is also a downside to life in rural communities.

- Poverty is found widely in rural areas, with farm workers traditionally among the most poorly paid sections of the workforce, and losing their jobs could also mean eviction and homelessness.

- The close-knit community can be extremely narrow-minded and oppressive – the village gossip network, for example, can be vicious and spiteful about anyone who fails to conform in even the slightest way.

- Rural communities lack facilities and public services found in towns, like shops, local schools, restaurants, surgeries, libraries, banks, post offices, and public transport. Those without a car are likely to face serious social exclusion.

- There is often a lack of jobs in rural areas, as industry, business, and jobs tend to be concentrated in towns and cities.

- The sense of community in rural areas is disappearing, as well-off people from urban areas are moving into rural villages to live, while continuing to travel (commute) to work every day in the cities. Often there is hostility or conflict between the 'locals' and the wealthy newcomers, especially because the newcomers can afford to pay much higher house prices, which means local people can't afford to live in the communities into which they were born, and often have to leave them. In some cases, villages are often little more than a retreat for affluent 'townies' who work and travel to towns for many of their activities.

Photo: Keith Roberts

Photo: Alison Hallam

Rural life

- *A strong sense of belonging to a close-knit community* – there are relatively small numbers of people; everyone knows everyone else; they share interests; relationships are personal; and people meet and know one another face to face. People will have a 'sense of belonging', support community events, and feel responsibility towards others.

- *Status is ascribed* – who you are, such as the family you come from, is likely to be a more important factor in deciding your status in the community than what you have achieved.

- *There is little geographical or social mobility* – people ('the locals') have lived for several generations in the same place, rarely changing their social class.

- The long periods of residence of inhabitants mean that *extended family networks will be more common*.

- *Informal social control* – because everyone knows everyone else, the family, school, and church are likely to be the most important agencies of social control, crime rates are low, and deviant behaviour, and those committing it, are likely to be spotted quickly. Public opinion through the village gossip network can exert pressure on potential deviants to conform, and strangers will be picked out easily.

Urban life

- *Little sense of belonging to a community* – there are large numbers of people; people don't know many others; relationships are impersonal and loose-knit; and people have wide differences in interests and lifestyle. People will have little identification with the area they live in, and little sense of responsibility to those they don't know.

- *Status is achieved* – what you do, such as your job or lifestyle, is likely to be more important in deciding your status, as many don't know anything else about you or your background.

- *There are high levels of geographical and social mobility*, as people move around in search of work or promotion, with a much higher turnover of people.

- The relatively short periods of residence of inhabitants and high levels of geographical mobility *break up extended family networks*.

- *Formal social control* – because the population is so large and people don't know everyone else, social control is more likely to be formal. Crime rates are high, acts of deviance are more likely to be ignored, or passers-by are more likely to call the police to deal with problems since they are unlikely to know the offenders.

It is also worth noting that community life like that in traditional rural areas is still found in urban areas, particularly in minority ethnic communities and traditional working-class communities. These are the sorts of community life which are shown in Albert Square in the TV series *Eastenders* and in *Coronation Street*, and there is much evidence that such communities continue to exist in urban areas.

ACTIVITY

1 Suggest two reasons why participation in public events might be higher in rural villages than in urban areas.

2 Suggest two reasons why the experience of poverty and deprivation in rural areas may be worse than in urban areas.

3 Identify and explain three differences between living in a large city and living in a small village.

4 Suggest and explain reasons why there is less crime in rural areas.

5 Suggest two ways in which the distinction which is sometimes drawn between rural and urban lifestyles might be misleading.

6 Suggest and explain two disadvantages of living in a large city compared to living in a small village.

7 How might social control differ between a small village and a large city?

8 Go to one of the following sites, and identify three of the major difficulties that are facing traditional rural life at the present time: <www.countryside.gov.uk> (the Countryside Agency); <www.countryside-alliance.org> (the Countryside Alliance); <www.rru.org.uk> (a rural regeneration site).

CHAPTER SUMMARY

After studying this chapter, you should be able to:

■ Explain why governments need to collect information on population trends, and some ways they do this.

■ Define the key terms used in the study of population.

■ Explain the factors which influence the size of a country's population.

■ Explain why death and infant mortality rates have fallen in Britain, and why life expectancy has increased.

■ Explain sex differences in life expectancy.

■ Explain why the birth rate has fallen in Britain.

■ Describe and explain the causes and some consequences of an ageing population.

■ Explain briefly the reasons for immigration and emigration.

■ Explain why urbanization and de-urbanization have occurred in Britain.

■ Identify and explain the major problems of the inner cities.

■ Identify some differences between living in a rural village and living in a city.

KEY TERMS

birth rate
death rate
demography
dependency ratio
dependent age groups
dependent population
de-urbanization
emigration
general fertility rate
immigration
infant mortality rate
life expectancy
migration
net migration
population projections
sex ratio
urbanization

COURSEWORK SUGGESTIONS

1   Using secondary sources (see chapter 17) – such as the census – give an account of the major features of the population of your area, including the balance of the sexes, age distribution, ethnic origins, and the occupations that people work in.

2   Interview a sample of elderly people (over retirement age) asking them about the advantages and disadvantages/problems of being elderly. Figure 15.9 earlier in this chapter may give you some ideas for a questionnaire. Compare your findings with those in figure 15.9.

3   Interview a sample of people living in either an urban or rural community and ask them what advantages and disadvantages they see in either urban or rural life.

4   Interview a sample of elderly people who have lived in a rural community for all or most of their lives, and try to discover how rural life has changed during their lifetimes.

16 Health and Illness

KEY ISSUES

- What is meant by 'health', 'illness', and 'disease'?
- The medical and social models of health.
- Becoming a health statistic.
- Medicine and social control: the sick role.
- How society influences health.
- The food industry.
- Inequalities in health.

In Britain, more people are suffering and dying prematurely of preventable diseases than perhaps ever before. We hear more and more stories of people with cancer, heart disease, asthma, and eczema. If progress towards a civilized society can be measured by the health of a nation, we might sometimes be forgiven for thinking Britain is going in reverse. And if the health of the population is a measure of social justice, then Britain is as divided now as it has ever been. But it is not simply the hand of nature or fate that makes us sick. Poor health and premature death are not random lightning bolts that strike us out of the blue. Disease and premature death are not evenly or randomly distributed throughout society. Official statistics reveal a pattern of social class, gender, and ethnic inequalities in health. These differences in disease and death provide strong evidence that sickness and health are not simply matters of fate or bad luck, but a product of the society in which we live.

While the message in the past has been that medicine can cure us, all the major advances in health occurred before medical intervention. In Britain, the elimination of the killer infectious diseases of the past, such as TB, pneumonia, flu, cholera, typhoid, and diphtheria, all took place before the development of modern medicine. It was social changes such as better diet, clean water supplies, sewage disposal, improved housing, and general knowledge about health and hygiene that improved health, rather than medical improvements like antibiotics and vaccines, which proved less effective than the social changes because of malnutrition. This is

Getting healthier is important to many people today – but what makes us unhealthy in the first place?

Photo: Ted Fussey

shown most noticeably in the Third World, where the major advances in health have come about as a result of simple preventative measures such as clean water and sewage control.

Given the newspaper stories we read about medical breakthroughs, 'miracle cures', organ transplants, and so on, we would expect doctors and nurses soon to be out of business, as the health of the population improves. Surprisingly, perhaps, the opposite is the case. The financial demands of the NHS have rocketed, and more and more people are going into hospital, or are on waiting lists for treatment.

WHAT IS MEANT BY 'HEALTH', 'ILLNESS', AND 'DISEASE'?

ACTIVITY

1 Write your own definitions, with examples, of 'health', 'illness', and 'disease'. Discuss, with examples, what your definitions might mean for promoting health and eliminating disease.

2 Try to think of ways in which your view of 'being healthy' might vary between (a) a rich country like Britain and a poor African country, and (b) a person who lives in poverty in Britain and a wealthy member of the upper class.

The definitions of 'health', 'illness', and 'disease' are no simple matters. What counts as health and illness varies between different groups within a single society, such as between men and women, and between societies. Views of acceptable standards of health are likely to differ widely between the people of a poor African country and Britain. Even in the same society, views of health change over time. At one time in Britain, mental illness was seen as a sign of satanic possession or witchcraft – a matter best dealt with by the church rather than by doctors. Similarly, what were once seen as personal problems have quite recently become defined as medical problems, such as obesity, alcoholism, hyperactivity in children, and smoking.

There is no simple definition of illness, because for pain or discomfort to count as a disease it is necessary for someone to diagnose it as such. There are also subjective influences on health: some of us can put up with or ignore pain more than others; some feel no pain; and many of us will have different notions of what counts as 'feeling unwell'.

- Health is probably most easy to define as being able to function normally within a usual everyday routine.

- Disease generally refers to a biological or mental condition that usually involves medically diagnosed symptoms.

- Illness refers to the subjective feeling of being unwell or ill-health. It is possible both to have a disease and not feel ill, and to feel ill and not have any disease.

The United Nations World Health Organization defines health as 'a state of complete physical, mental, and social well-being, and not merely the absence of disease or infirmity'. Some have argued that this definition goes far beyond a realistic definition of health, as it implies not simply the absence of disease, but also a personally fulfilling life.

1 Discuss how the World Health Organization might view the health of the long-term unemployed in Britain.

2 Using the World Health Organization's definition, how might 'good health' differ between (a) people who live in a poor African country and those who live in modern Britain, and (b) people in Britain who live in an isolated village in the country and those who live in a town?

3 Discuss the view that 'good health is simply a state of mind'.

THE MEDICAL AND SOCIAL MODELS OF HEALTH

As seen above, there are different meanings attached to 'health'. There are two main approaches, arising from different views of what the causes of ill-health are. These are often referred to as the medical and social models of health.

The medical model of health

The medical model has two main features:

- Disease is seen as mainly caused by biological factors, and recently by personal 'lifestyle' factors such as smoking and diet. The sick person is treated in the same way as a car that has broken down. People become objects to be fixed by 'body mechanics' (doctors).

- The causes of ill-health are seen as arising either from the moral failings of the individual (such as smoking too much, eating junk food, or not getting enough exercise) or from random attacks of disease. This is a bit like blaming car breakdowns on poor maintenance and lack of proper servicing, or on bad luck.

The social model of health

This model differs in two ways from the medical model:

■ A strong emphasis is placed on the social causes of health and ill-health, and on how society influences health and causes disease.

■ Health and illness are not seen simply as medical or scientific facts. A choice exists whether people see themselves as ill or not, and those with power can choose whether or not to classify someone as ill. In most cases, 'those with power' means doctors and other medical experts.

BECOMING A HEALTH STATISTIC

The process of becoming ill is not as simple and straightforward as it might seem. People may respond to the same symptoms in different ways. While some may seek medical help, others may choose to ignore their symptoms. They may look for alternative non-medical or less serious explanations for them: bronchitis may become simply a 'smoker's cough', and possible brain tumours may be dismissed as 'headaches'.

For people to be labelled as 'sick' – and to be recorded as a health statistic – there are at least four stages involved:

1 Individuals must first recognize they have a problem.
2 They must then define their problem as serious enough to take to a doctor.
3 They must then actually go to the doctor.
4 The doctor must then be persuaded that they have a medical or mental condition capable of being labelled as an illness requiring treatment.

ACTIVITY

1 List all the factors you can which might influence each of the four stages involved in becoming a health statistic, which lead some people to visit the doctor and others not to. For example, in stage 1, you might consider a person's ability to continue her or his responsibilities to friends and family, pressure from relatives, friends, and employers, etc. Draw on your own experiences of what makes you decide whether you are ill, and whether or not to go to the doctor.

2 Discuss in a group what you think the most common influences on going (or not going) to the doctor might be.

MEDICINE AND SOCIAL CONTROL: THE SICK ROLE

Social control is concerned with maintaining order and stability in society. Sickness is really a form of deviance. When people are ill, they generally want to avoid normal responsibilities because these are too demanding or stressful. The sick role – the pattern of behaviour associated with someone who is ill – is an escape route for the individual. This is because, when you are sick, you can quite reasonably and blamelessly abandon normal everyday activities, and often others will take over your responsibilities.

Allowing individuals to 'opt out' into the sick role is potentially dangerous because the smooth workings of society may be upset if too many people adopt it. Imagine the disruption that would be caused in a school or factory where the teachers, students, managers, or workers were always off ill.

Doctors play a key role in the social control of the sick by acting as gatekeepers of entry to the sick role, and preventing people becoming hypochondriacs and skiving on the grounds of illness. For example, they can stop people taking more than a few days off work on the grounds of illness by refusing to issue sick notes.

Features of the sick role

Rights

- Depending on the illness, individuals are excused normal social activities (for example, they are excused school or work). This requires approval by others such as teachers, employers, and family members. The doctor often plays a key role in this process, by diagnosing the person as 'really ill', and issuing sick notes.

- Individuals are not seen as personally to blame for their illness: relatives, friends, and doctors are often very critical of those they do see as responsible for their own illness. Those who engage in excessive drinking, for example, often don't get much sympathy for their hangover the morning after.

Responsibilities

Individuals have a responsibility – an obligation – to want to 'get well'. When necessary, they are expected to seek and accept medical help and cooperate in their treatment. In other words, sick people are expected to do what the doctor orders, and they cannot expect sympathy and support if they don't try to get well. Even if people don't want to call in the doctor because they don't see their illness as serious enough to do so, they are still expected to stay in bed or take it easy in an effort to recover.

HOW SOCIETY INFLUENCES HEALTH

Figure 16.1 suggests a number of ways that social factors influence health. That health is the product of society rather than simply of biology or medicine is shown by historical evidence that patterns of disease change over time. Changes which occurred during the nineteenth century and the first half of the twentieth century illustrate this well.

ACTIVITY

With reference to figure 16.1, make a list of as many environmental, political, social, and economic factors leading to poor health as you can think of, such as unemployment, pollution, or poor housing. Explain in each case how the factors you identify might influence health.

Improvements in health during the nineteenth and early twentieth centuries

In the nineteenth century, adult and child mortality started to fall, and since then there has been a large and rapid population increase. For a long time this was thought to be due to the development of medicine. However, it is now agreed that it was due to a number of social and economic changes and the general improvement in living standards. These changes included:

■ *Public hygiene.* The movement for sanitary reform and public hygiene in the nineteenth century helped to develop a clean and safe environment and higher standards of public hygiene. Pure drinking water, efficient sanitation and sewage disposal, and paved streets and highways all helped to reduce deaths from infectious diseases.

■ *Better diet.* Being well fed is the most effective form of disease prevention, as shown in the Third World today, where vaccination programmes are not as successful as they should be because children are poorly nourished. The high death rates of the past were mainly due to hunger or

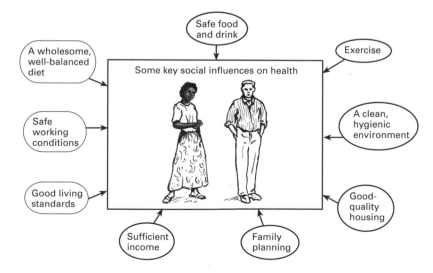

Figure 16.1 Some key social influences on health

malnutrition, which led to poorer resistance to infection. The nineteenth and early twentieth centuries saw improved communications, technology, and hygiene, making possible the production, transportation, and import of more and cheaper food. Wages improved, and higher standards of living meant better food and better health.

- *Contraception.* This led to smaller families, making possible a better diet and healthcare for children. This also improved the health of women, who spent less time child-bearing.

- *Housing legislation.* This increased public control over standards of rented housing, which helped to reduce overcrowding and the spread of infectious diseases between family members.

- *The war effort.* During the First World War (1914–18) unemployment was virtually eliminated. As part of the war effort, rents were controlled, food rationing was introduced, and minimum wages were established in agriculture. The resulting decline in poverty cut childhood deaths, especially among the families of unskilled workers in urban areas.

- *General improvements in living standards.* Higher wages, better food, clothing, and housing, laws improving health and safety at work, reduced working hours, and better hygiene regulations on the production and sale of food and drink all improved health.

All the above suggest that good health is more the result of government policy decisions and of economic development than simply of individual initiative or medical intervention.

The new 'disease burden'

The infectious diseases of the nineteenth century were often called the 'diseases of poverty', since most victims were malnourished and poor. These have been replaced by 'diseases of affluence' – a result of eating too much poor-quality food, a lack of exercise, smoking and drinking too much, and so on.

A well-balanced diet is necessary for good health, and the lack of one makes people more vulnerable to disease. Despite the wealth of modern industrial societies, there is a problem of malnutrition in the form not of too little food, as you find in less developed countries, but of too much of the wrong sort. As a result, advanced industrial societies experience health problems rarely found in simpler rural societies. The new 'disease burden' includes obesity, and degenerative (worsening) diseases like cirrhosis of the liver, certain cancers, heart disease, respiratory diseases, diabetes, stomach ulcers, and varicose veins. These kill or disable more people than they did in the past, and many more people are becoming chronically ill for longer periods in their lives than they did in the past.

Around 20 per cent of men and women in the UK are now officially classified as obese, and the World Health Organization predicts that almost 50 per cent of adults in Britain could be obese by 2025 through a combination of junk food and lack of exercise.

One in five people are now officially classified as obese

What are the causes of these new diseases?

It is generally accepted that the causes of these new diseases of affluence are mainly social and environmental, and therefore preventable. Public concerns over the food supply have been rising. There were major scares over BSE ('mad cow disease') in beef in the 1990s, and the linked human equivalent vCJD (variant Creutzfeldt-Jakob disease) had killed 147 people in the UK up to August 2004. Between 1982 and 1997, cases of food poisoning serious enough to be reported to a doctor rose by 600 per cent, and E.coli food poisoning outbreaks killed twenty people in 1996–7. A Food Standards Agency survey in 2002 found that around 12 per cent of the population – around five and a half million people – had experienced food poisoning in the previous twelve months as a result of food eaten in the UK. Many worry about GM (genetically modified) crops and foods, and the effects on health of the use of growth-promoting drugs in chickens was of continuing concern in the early 2000s. Some doctors have linked the rise in asthma to poor diet, with insufficient fruit and vegetables. The rise in heart disease has been blamed on factors such as smoking, stress, an inactive life style (too many couch potatoes!), and a diet high in sugar, salt, and fats but low in fibre. A 1997 British government report, *Nutritional Aspects of the Development of Cancer*, estimated that up to 70 per cent of cancer cases were linked to the type of food people ate. Diet was seen as ten times more important than the effects of job-related causes and of smoking on all cancers. The *Lancet* medical journal reported in 2003 that women eating too much food high in fat, such as butter, milk, meat, burgers, crisps, biscuits, and cakes, were more likely to get breast cancer than others whose fat intake was low.

THE FOOD INDUSTRY

The British are now eating a more highly processed diet than at any time in history. We consume a whole range of factory-produced food, which is often low in nutritional value and may well be harmful to health, because of additives like flavourings, colourings, preservatives, and various drugs. Revelations that large food-processing companies were 'bulking up' chickens destined for schools, hospitals, and restaurants with poultry skin, beef bits, and pig waste were of major concern in 2003. Highly processed junk food reinforces the trend towards a high-sugar, high-salt, and high-fat diet which is low in vitamins, minerals, protein, and fibre. Research in 2003 suggested that high doses of fat and sugar in fast and processed foods could be as addictive as nicotine and even hard drugs (like heroine and cocaine), causing hormonal changes creating a need for even more high-fat foods and generating obesity as a growing health problem. Why do people have unhealthy diets, and why are unhealthy foods allowed to be produced?

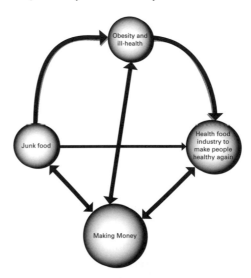

Figure 16.2 The food industry's triple whammy: making money and food production

ACTIVITY	Why do we eat unhealthy foods? Food production is often in the hands of multinational firms whose primary concern is with making money. The points below suggest some reasons why many of the foods sold for mass consumption are of poor quality.

- The need for food products to travel.
- The need for more imported food.
- The need for foods to have a relatively long supermarket shelf life.
- Marketing of a 'brand identity', with uniform colour, size, and quality of foodstuffs.
- The search for profit through marketing of factory-produced junk food.
- Keeping costs down, for both the producer and the consumer.

Study carefully the points above, and figure 16.2, and try to think of as many ways as you can that nutritionally poor food, profits, and poor health might be connected.

Photo: Ted Fussey

The activity on page 405 may have made you aware that many mass-produced foods are of poor quality.

The response to criticisms of the Western world's unhealthy diet is the 'health food' industry. Its products are more expensive, such as wholemeal bread and organic vegetables, and the food and drugs industry makes a lot of money through its marketing of 'healthy' foods, vitamins, and dietary supplements. It is estimated that around ten million people in the UK use dietary supplements, despite warnings from the Food Standards Agency that excess vitamins can themselves be harmful to health.

The slimming industry – to offset the effects of obesity-producing junk food – is very big business. Vegetarianism and fitness centres have become money spinners, and we can now buy every manner of food which is 'low-calorie', 'slimline', 'low-fat', 'high-fibre', 'sugar-free', and so on. Health itself has become a product for companies to sell in a big way, while continuing to produce those products which often contribute to the original ill-health.

INEQUALITIES IN HEALTH

The following section quotes statistics on health. However, like the crime statistics discussed in chapter 9, some of these should be treated with care.

Health statistics may be inaccurate because:

■ They depend on people persuading doctors they are ill, and are therefore simply a record of doctors' decision-making.

■ Doctors may diagnose illnesses or the causes of death incorrectly, reflecting the state of the doctor's knowledge – and therefore recorded illnesses and causes of death statistics may not be accurate. For example, there may have been many AIDS deaths recorded as pneumonia, etc., before doctors 'discovered' AIDS.

- Not all sick people go to the doctor, and not all people who persuade doctors they are ill are really sick.

- Private medicine operates to make a profit, and therefore is possibly more likely to diagnose symptoms as a disease.

Social class differences in health

Official statistics reveal massive class inequalities in health. Nearly every kind of illness and disease is linked to class. Poverty is the major driver of ill-health, and poorer people tend to get sick more often and to die younger than richer people. Those who die youngest are people who live on benefits or low wages, in poor-quality housing, and who eat cheap, unhealthy food.

A 1995 Department of Health report noted that if everyone were as healthy as the middle class, there would have been 1500 fewer deaths a year among children under age 1, and 17,000 fewer deaths among men aged 20–64.

In contemporary Britain:

- The death rate in class 5 (unskilled manual workers) is about twice that of class 1. A person born into social class 1 (professional) lives, on average, about seven years longer than someone in social class 5.

- About twice as many babies are still-born or die in the first week of life in unskilled families as in professional ones. In the first year of life, nearly twice as many children die among unskilled workers as in class 1. The risk of dying before the age of 5 is twice as great for a child born into social class 5 as for social class 1.

- Men and women in class 5 are twice as likely to die before reaching retirement age as people in class 1. About 90 per cent of the major causes of death are more common in social classes 4 and 5 than in other social classes.

- Lung cancer and stomach cancer occur twice as often among men in manual jobs as among men in professional jobs, and four times as many women die of cervical cancer in social class 5 as in social class 1.

- Working-class people, especially the unskilled, go to see doctors far more often and for a wider range of health problems than people in professional jobs.

- Semi- and unskilled workers are more likely to be absent from work through sickness than those in professional and managerial jobs. Long-standing illness is around twice as high among unskilled manual workers as for class 1 professionals.

■ All of the above are worse for the long-term unemployed and other groups in poverty.

These patterns of sickness and death provide strong evidence that it is society and the way it is organized that influences health, rather than simply our biological make-up.

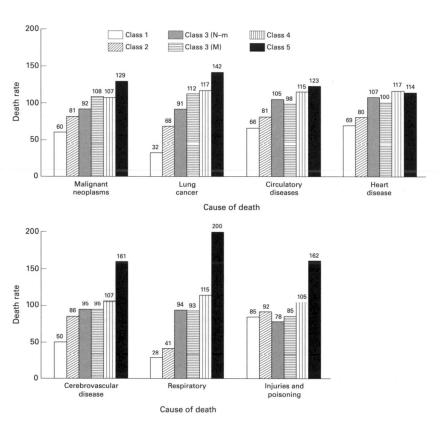

The average expected from the population as a whole is 100. Death rates are higher than expected above 100, and lower than expected below 100.

Figure 16.3 Mortality (1976–89) of men aged 15–64 at death: by cause of death and by their social class in 1971, United Kingdom

Source: Data adapted from *Population Trends*

The characteristics of people aged 16–64 who are more likely than most to consult their doctor

Those who:

- Live in urban areas.
- Are council property tenants or live in other rented accommodation.
- Live alone.
- Are in social classes 4 and 5.
- Are unemployed.

- Are smokers.
- Are widowed or divorced.
- Are adults with young children.
- Work in construction, service, and industrial occupations.
- Belong to a minority ethnic group.

Source: Adapted from *Morbidity Statistics from General Practice*, HMSO

ACTIVITY

Study figure 16.3:

1 Which disease shows the greatest difference in deaths between social class 5 and social class 1?

2 Which disease shows the smallest difference in deaths between social class 1 and social class 5?

3 Which social class shows the lowest deaths from lung cancer?

4 Identify two trends shown in figure 16.3.

5 Which social class for deaths from what disease is exactly in line with the number expected from the population as a whole?

6 Refer to the list of the characteristics of people aged 16–64 in the box opposite, and suggest reasons why each of the groups identified might be more likely to consult their GPs than other groups.

The inverse care law

Social class differences in health are made worse through inequalities in the NHS. The inverse care law suggests that healthcare resources tend to be distributed in inverse proportion to need. This means that those whose need is least get the most resources, while those in greatest need get the least. For example, poor working-class communities tend to have the most overcrowded facilities in the NHS as poorer people suffer more ill-health, and yet they don't get the extra money spent on them that they need. Poorer people whose need is greatest therefore get less time with their GPs, and hospital waiting lists are longer than in more prosperous areas.

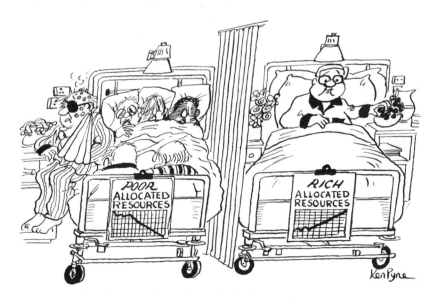

The inverse care law

ACTIVITY

1 How does the cartoon above illustrate the inverse care law?

2 Suggest reasons why people in more deprived areas are more likely to suffer from poorer health and get worse healthcare than those in richer areas.

Explanations for social class inequalities in health

There are two main types of explanation for social class inequalities in health.

Cultural explanations

Cultural explanations suggest that those suffering from poorer health have different attitudes, values, and lifestyles which mean they don't look after themselves properly. Such explanations suggest that the victims of ill-health have only themselves to blame. Examples of this might include smoking and drinking too much, using too much salt or sugar, eating junk food, or not bothering to take any exercise.

Material explanations

Material explanations suggest that those suffering poorer health lack enough money to eat a healthy diet, have poor housing, dangerous or unhealthy working conditions, live in an unhealthy local environment, and so on.

Figure 16.4 identifies a range of possible factors which might explain health differences.

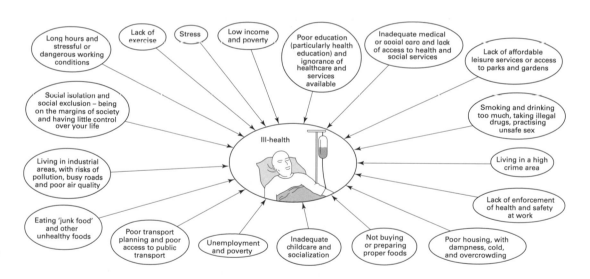

Figure 16.4 Cultural and material influences on health

Gender differences in health

As well as a pattern of social class differences in health, there is also a big difference between the health of men and women. At all ages, women's death rates are much lower than men's. Men's death rates are almost double those of women in every class and on average women live five years longer than men. Almost two-thirds of deaths before the age of 65 are male. After age 65, there are almost 40 per cent more women than men in

ACTIVITY

Figure 16.4 suggests a series of points which contribute to social class inequalities in health. Study figure 16.4 and do the following activities:

1 Divide the explanations into 'cultural' and 'material' ones.
2 Suggest ways each point might explain class inequalities in health.
3 Suggest other reasons of your own for social class differences in health.
4 Do you think cultural or material explanations (or a bit of both) are better in explaining health inequalities? Give reasons for your answer.
5 In view of the explanations for social class inequalities in health, suggest policies and measures government and other authorities should take to reduce these inequalities.
6 Go to <www.doh.gov.uk/cmo/progress/inequalities> and identify and briefly describe four measures that the government is taking to tackle inequalities in health.

the population. (Some reasons for this are discussed in chapter 15 on population.)

Are women healthier than men?

The answer is 'yes' if we use only the indicators of death rates and life expectancy. However, statistics show that men, who in general die younger, don't seem to experience as much ill-health as women, who live longer. Women are the major users of healthcare services and apparently get sick more often than men.

Compared to men, women:

▪ Go to the doctor about 50 per cent more often over the age of 16.

▪ Report more head and stomach aches, high blood pressure, and weight problems.

▪ Consume more prescription and non-prescription drugs.

- Are admitted to hospital more often and have more operations.

- Go to see doctors about conditions like insomnia, tension headache, and depression (which are often labelled as 'psychiatric problems') about twice as often.

- Receive far more prescriptions for tranquillizers, sleeping pills, and anti-depressants.

- Are off work with reported sickness more often and spend more days in bed.

Why do women appear to suffer more sickness?

- *Stress.* Many women suffer a double burden of being both low-paid workers and responsible for housework and childcare. In many cases this involves having to manage limited household budgets with pressure to make ends meet, and a long day with little time to relax.

- *Poverty.* In low-income households, it is usually women who go without to ensure other family members get enough to eat. Women are therefore more likely to suffer the effects of poverty more directly than men.

- *Domestic labour* (housework). Domestic labour is rarely fulfilling (for further discussion on this, see chapter 5 on gender). Depression may be linked to the unpaid, repetitive, unrewarding, low-status nature of housework, in a society where only paid employment carries any status. The high accident rates at home might be influenced by the isolated nature of housework.

- *Socialization.* Women are socialized to express their feelings and talk about their problems more than men. Since women are generally the ones who 'manage' family health matters, they are often more aware of health and healthcare matters. Women may therefore be more willing

than men to report physical and mental health problems. The higher rates of recorded illnesses among women could then be due not necessarily to greater health problems than men's, but to women's greater willingness to admit to problems and to take them to doctors. While women go to doctors for prescribed drugs like tranquillizers, men opt for non-prescribed drugs like alcohol. Men's higher death rates may simply be because they bottle everything up until it is too late.

▓ *Different diagnoses.* Due to gender roles, it may be that doctors are more likely to see symptoms reported by women as mainly mental, while men's are seen as physical. Women are therefore more likely to be diagnosed as depressed or suffering from anxiety than men. Until recently, women had a much higher chance than men of being institutionalized in mental hospitals.

ACTIVITY

1 Refer to the activity on p. 400 about the four stages, and suggest reasons why women might be more likely to end up as a health statistic than men.

2 Discuss the explanations suggested above for women apparently suffering more sickness than men. Do you think women really do suffer more ill-health, or do you think they are simply more open and honest about it than men?

Ethnic differences in health

Social class and gender are not the only important social inequalities in health. There are also some differences between ethnic groups. Compared to the white majority ethnic group:

▓ African-Caribbeans seem more biologically vulnerable to developing sickle cell anaemia (a blood disease), they are more likely to suffer from strokes, and they are more likely to be compulsorily admitted to hospitals for mental illnesses.

▓ Asians (Indians, Pakistanis, and Bangladeshis) suffer more heart disease and are more likely to die from it.

▓ Most minority ethnic groups have higher rates of stillbirths, infant mortality (deaths of children within the first year of life), and mortality in general.

▓ African-Caribbeans, Pakistanis, and Bangladeshis are between 30 and 50 per cent more likely to suffer ill-health.

Why do some minority ethnic groups suffer poorer health?

▓ *Racism and poverty.* Many of the health problems of some minority ethnic groups arise for the same reasons as social class inequalities, as they are more likely to be among the poorest groups in society. Racism in society means some minority ethnic groups are more likely to find themselves living in the worst housing, unemployed, or working for long hours in low-paid jobs in hazardous and unhealthy environments.

■ *Diet.* Higher levels of heart disease may arise from aspects of the high-fat Asian diet, which also generates higher levels of obesity – itself a cause of heart disease.

■ *Language and culture.* Asian women are less likely to visit ante- and post-natal clinics, which helps explain their higher levels of infant mortality. Asian women often prefer to see female doctors, and many find it difficult to discuss health issues with white male doctors, but the number of female GPs is lowest in those areas which have the highest concentrations of Asian households. Many older Asian women, and some older men, speak poor English, and this may create difficulties communicating with, and obtaining treatment from, doctors and other health professionals.

This chapter has shown that 'health', 'illness', 'disease', and inequalities in health are very much products of society rather than simply of biological factors. Social and economic life has major influences on the patterns of illness and death. So long as inequalities of wealth, income, education, occupation, and social privilege continue, so will inequalities in health.

CHAPTER SUMMARY

After studying this chapter, you should be able to:

■ Explain what is meant by 'health', 'illness', and 'disease'.

■ Identify and explain the difference between the medical and social models of health.

■ Suggest the reasons why some people may seek medical help while others may not.

■ Explain what is meant by the 'sick role', and identify the rights and obligations of it.

■ Identify and explain a range of social factors which influence health and disease.

■ Identify some problems with health statistics.

■ Explain social class, gender, and ethnic inequalities in health.

KEY TERMS

disease
health
illness
sick role

COURSEWORK SUGGESTIONS

1   Carry out a survey among men and women to find out when they were last
    ill enough to take time off work, school, or college, when they last visited
    the doctor, and how many times a year they visit the doctor. See if there are
    any differences between men and women. You could also do the same type
    of survey to identify any differences between social classes or ethnic
    groups.

2   Using secondary sources (see chapter 17), try to find out whether there are
    differences in the health of people in various areas of your city or county or
    in the country as a whole, for example between richer and poorer areas.
    Draw on the material in this chapter to try to explain your findings.

17 Doing Sociological Research

KEY ISSUES

- Key issues in social research.
- Quantitative and qualitative data.
- Primary and secondary sources.
- Social surveys.
- Observation.
- Doing your own research: coursework.

As has been seen throughout this book, sociology is concerned with a wide range of issues in social life, spanning the continuing existence of poverty, the influence of the mass media on our views about the world, the things that make work interesting or not, and how the very centre of our personalities is constructed through socialization into gender roles. The interests and concerns of sociologists are not that different from those of most people in society. However, what makes the views of sociologists different from those likely to be aired in a pub, in the canteen at work, or in other daily situations where views get exchanged is that sociologists try to provide evidence to back up what they say. This evidence is collected from a variety of sources and through the use of a number of research methods. In this section, we will examine the types of data (or information) sociologists collect, the range of sources used, and the methods sociologists use to collect their own information.

KEY ISSUES IN SOCIAL RESEARCH

There are three key issues that should always be considered when carrying out or assessing research. These are the issues of reliability, validity, and the ethics of research.

- Reliability is concerned with *replication*: whether another researcher using the same method for the same research on the same group would achieve the same results. For example, if different researchers used the same questionnaire on similar samples of the population, then the results should be more or less the same if the techniques are reliable.

- Validity is concerned with notions of truth: how far the findings of research actually provide a true picture of what is being studied. Data can be *reliable* without being valid. For example, official crime statistics may be reliable, in so far as researchers repeating the data collection would get the same results over and over again, but they are not valid if they don't give us the full picture on the extent of crime.

- The ethics of research are concerned with morality and standards of behaviour when sociologists carry out research. These important ethical issues are considered in the box at the top of the page opposite.

THE ETHICS OF RESEARCH

When doing research, sociologists should always consider the following points:

■ They should take into account the sensitivities of those helping with their research. For example, it would not be appropriate to ask about attitudes to abortion in a hospital maternity ward where women may be having babies or have suffered miscarriages.

■ Findings should be reported accurately and honestly.

■ The physical, social, and mental well-being of people who help in research should not be harmed by research – for example, by disclosing information given in confidence which might get the person into trouble, or cause them embarrassment.

■ The anonymity, privacy, and interests of those who participate in your research should be respected. Sociologists should not identify them by name, or enable them (or an institution) to be easily identified.

■ As far as possible, your research should be based on the freely given consent of those studied. Researchers should make clear what they're doing, why they're doing it, and what they will do with their findings.

When you are doing your own research for coursework, ask your teacher or lecturer for further advice on ethical issues.

QUANTITATIVE AND QUALITATIVE DATA

Quantitative data is anything that can be expressed in statistical or number form or can be 'measured' in some way, such as age, qualifications, or income. Such data is usually presented in the form of statistical tables, graphs, pie charts, and bar charts. There is more about interpreting statistical data in the appendix.

Qualitative data is concerned with descriptions of or people's feelings about some issue or event, and tries to get at the way they see things. Such data is normally in the form of the sociologist's describing and interpreting people's feelings and lifestyles, often using direct quotations from the people studied.

This data may be gathered from either primary sources or secondary sources.

| DEFINITION | Content analysis is a way of trying to analyse the content of documents and other qualitative material by quantifying it. This is done, for example. by sorting out categories, and then going through documents, books, magazines, television programmes, and so on systematically, recording the number of times items in each category appear. Examples might include feminist researchers analysing reading books for children seeking evidence of gender-role stereotyping, using categories such as male leader/female led, female works or plays indoors/male outdoors, and so on. |

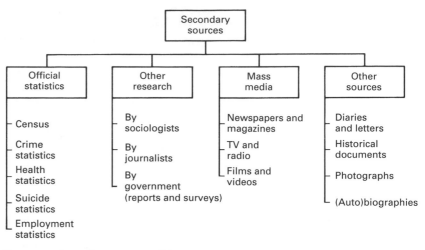

Figure 17.1 Secondary sources of data

PRIMARY AND SECONDARY SOURCES

Secondary sources of data are those which already exist. Secondary data has already been collected by others. Figure 17.1 shows a range of secondary sources which might be used by sociologists in carrying out research.

Because the existing data required for research may be unreliable or may simply not have been collected, sociologists often have to collect their own data from primary sources. Primary data is that which is collected by sociologists themselves – it only exists because the sociologist has collected it. Such information is usually obtained by carrying out a social survey or by participant observation (these will be discussed shortly).

The advantages of secondary sources

Secondary sources have the main advantage that the material is readily available and so is cheap and easy to use. There is no need to spend time and money collecting data, and some data, such as that provided by the census, would be impossible for an individual to collect. In some cases, secondary sources may be the only sources of information available in an area, such as in historical research, and sociologists may therefore have no alternative but to use them.

The problems of secondary sources

Secondary sources do present problems for use in sociological research. The information may be unrepresentative, and therefore may not apply to the whole population. For example, before the beginning of compulsory education in Britain in 1880, it was mainly only the well-off who could read and write, and so it was mainly they who left documents behind them.

The information may be inaccurate in some way and therefore *unreliable* or lacking in *validity*. It may be forged or biased, contain errors, or be exaggerated. Newspaper reports, for example, are notoriously unreliable as sources of evidence, as discussed in chapter 8.

Official statistics

Sociologists very often use official statistics, which are those produced by the government, in their research, such as those on crime, unemployment, and health. Such statistics must be treated very cautiously by sociologists. Chapter 9 showed the problems involved in using the official crime statistics as evidence of the real extent of crime, chapter 14 showed the limitations of unemployment statistics, and chapter 16 showed the limitations of health statistics. You should refer to these now. When sociologists use such secondary data, they must be very aware of their limitations, question their *validity* and *reliability*, and therefore approach them with care.

ACTIVITY

Read the following passage and then answer the questions:

Suicide is, by definition, the death of a person who intended to kill himself or herself. The problem for coroners is they can't ask dead people if they meant to kill themselves, so they can only guess at the truth by looking for 'clues' in the circumstances surrounding the death. Atkinson has suggested there are four main factors which coroners take into account when deciding whether a death is a suicide or not:

- Whether there was a suicide note.
- The way the person died, for example by hanging, drowning, or a drug overdose. Death in a road accident rarely results in a suicide verdict.
- The place the death occurred and the circumstances surrounding it; for example, a drug overdose in a remote wood would be more likely to be seen as a suicide than if it occurred at home in bed. A coroner might also consider circumstances such as whether the person had been drinking before taking the drugs, and whether the drugs had been hoarded or not.
- The life history and mental state of the dead person, such as her or his state of physical and mental health, and whether the victim was in debt, had just failed exams, lost her or his job, got divorced, or was depressed or not.

Coroners do not always agree on the way they interpret these clues. For example, Atkinson found one coroner believed a death by drowning was likely to be a suicide if the clothes were left neatly folded on the beach, but another coroner might attach little importance to this.

1 How is suicide defined in the passage?
2 Why do you think coroners attach such importance to suicide notes?
3 Suggest two reasons why the presence or absence of a suicide note might be an unreliable 'clue' to a dead person's intention to die.
4 Suggest ways relatives and friends might try to persuade a coroner that a death was not a suicide but an accident.
5 On the basis of the evidence in the passage, suggest reasons why (a) some deaths classified as suicides may have been accidental, and (b) some deaths classified as accidents may in fact have been suicides.
6 With reference to the evidence in the passage, suggest reasons why a sociologist should be very careful about using official statistics on suicide as a record of the real number of suicides in society.

SOCIAL SURVEYS

Surveys involve the sociologist in systematically gathering information about some group of people. This is done by questioning them using questionnaires and interviews.

The survey population

One of the first steps in any social survey is the selection of the group of people to be studied. This group is called the survey population. The choice of survey population will depend on the hypothesis which the sociologist is investigating. For example, a hypothesis like 'teachers treat males more favourably than females' might mean the survey population would include all pupils and teachers in a particular school.

DEFINITION	A hypothesis is an idea which the sociologist guesses might be true, but which has not yet been tested against the evidence.

If the survey population is small, such as a class of college students, it may be possible to question everyone in it. In some cases, because the organization doing the research has enough time and money, it may be possible to investigate everyone even in a very large survey population. For example, the government has the resources to survey the entire population of the United Kingdom in the census every ten years – at a cost of £250 million in 2001. Such costs are way beyond the reach of most sociologists and market research organizations, and because of cost and time, most surveys are limited to studying a *sample* of the survey population.

Sampling

A sample is simply a small group drawn from the survey population. It is a way of making general statements about the whole survey population based on the responses of only a small percentage of the total survey population.

If the results obtained from the sample are to be used to make valid (true) generalizations about the whole survey population, it is important that the sample is *representative*. Sociologists obtain representative samples by using various sampling methods.

DEFINITION	A representative sample is one that contains a good cross-section of the survey population, such as the right proportions of people of different ethnic origins, ages, social classes, and sexes. The information obtained from a representative sample should provide roughly the same results as if the whole survey population had been questioned.

Methods of obtaining a representative sample

1 Drawing up a sampling frame

A sampling frame is simply a list of names of all those included in the survey population from which the sample will eventually be selected; for example, the names of all schoolchildren in a school taken from registers, or doctors in a town. A commonly used sampling frame is the Electoral Register, which includes nearly all the names and addresses of adults over the age of 18 in Britain who are eligible to vote in elections. Doctors' lists of patients are also commonly used as sampling frames, as most people are registered with a doctor.

The choice and completeness of the sampling frame are very important if the results obtained are to be generalized to the whole survey population. For example, a telephone directory would be an unreliable sampling frame if we wanted to select a sample which was representative of the entire adult population, as it only contains those on the telephone and excludes those who may not be able to afford or want a telephone, who are ex-directory, or who are on cable, and therefore not included in the phone book.

2 Deciding on the sample size

The size of the sample will depend on the amount of time and money available. However, if the sample is too small the results obtained may not be representative of the whole survey population. The ideal size of a sample is that at which the results obtained won't be made much more accurate by increasing the size of the sample.

3 Deciding on a sampling method

A sampling method is the process by which the sociologist selects representative individuals from the sampling frame to question. There are a number of sampling methods used by sociologists to try to gain a representative sample.

Simple random sampling

Simple random sampling means that every individual in the survey population has an equal chance of being picked out for questioning. For example, all names are put in a hat and enough names picked out to make up the required sample size. This is most commonly done by numbering all the names in the sampling frame and then getting a computer to select enough numbers at random to make up the size of sample required.

The problem with this method is that, purely by chance, the random sample may not be representative of the survey population. For example, there may be too many people of one sex, of one age group, or who live in the same area.

Systematic sampling

Systematic sampling is a method where names are selected from the survey population at regular intervals until the size of sample is reached. For example, every tenth name in the sampling frame is selected.

Quota sampling

Quota sampling is a method where interviewers are told to go and select people who fit into certain categories according to their proportion in the survey population as a whole. For example, an interviewer may be asked to select and question thirty men and women over the age of 45. The choice of the actual individuals chosen is left to the honesty of the interviewer (unlike other sampling methods where actual named individuals are identified).

Stratified random sampling

Stratified random sampling is a way of attempting to avoid the possible errors caused by simple random sampling. In this case, the sampling frame is divided into strata (layers) or sub-groups relevant to the hypothesis being investigated, such as groups of a similar age, sex, ethnic group, or social class, and a random sample is then taken from each sub-group. For example, in a survey of doctors, we may know from earlier research that 8 per cent of all doctors are Asian, and so the sociologist must make sure 8 per cent of the sample are Asian. To do this, the sociologist will separate out the Asian doctors from the sampling frame of all doctors, and then take a random sample from this list of Asian doctors to make up the 8 per cent of the sample of all doctors. In this way, the final sample is more likely to be representative of all doctors in the survey population. Stratified random sampling has the advantage of being much more representative than simple random sampling, because all the characteristics of the survey population are more certain to be represented in the sample.

If one of the sampling methods shown in the box (below and opposite) is used, the information provided by the sample can be generalized with great accuracy to the whole survey population. For example, opinion polls on the voting intentions of electors often produce extremely accurate predictions of the outcome of general elections from questioning only about one thousand voters.

EXAMPLES OF SIMPLE RANDOM, SYSTEMATIC, AND STRATIFIED RANDOM SAMPLING

Survey population
    400 students in a school
    50 per cent are male and 50 per cent are female.
    This information would be known from earlier research,
        such as school records.
    In each group, 75 per cent are white and 25 per cent
        are black.

Sample size required
    10 per cent (40)

A simple random sample

To obtain a simple random sample:

1   Draw up a sampling frame: a list of the names of the 400 students in the survey population.

2   Pick out 40 names at random.

A systematic sample

To obtain a systematic sample:

Pick out every tenth name from the sampling frame until 40 names are collected.

The possible problem with these random and systematic samples is that, purely by chance, they might consist of too many males or females or too many black or white students. If this happened, the sample would be unrepresentative of the survey population, and therefore the survey results would give biased, inaccurate, and unrepresentative results. Stratifying the sample can avoid this problem.

A stratified random sample

To obtain a stratified random sample, complete the following stages:

1 Draw up a sampling frame (list of names) of the 400 students in the survey population.

2 Divide this sampling frame into the same proportions as the survey population. We know 50 per cent are male and 50 per cent are female, so in this case divide the sampling frame into two.

3 We know that 25 per cent of males and females are black, and 75 per cent are white, so divide *each of* these sampling frames into two.

4 Now take a 10 per cent random sample from each sampling frame. This produces a sample made up like the one here.

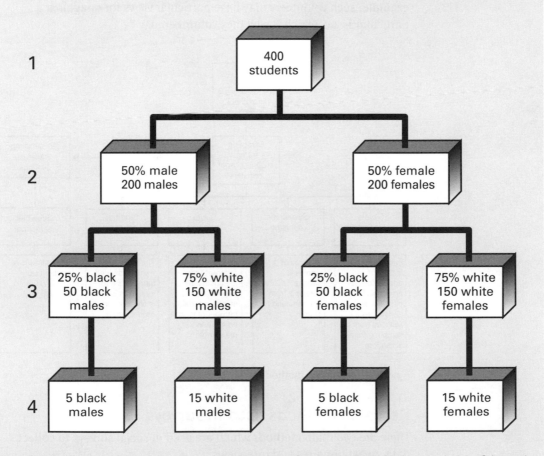

This stratified random sample should be representative of the sex and ethnic characteristics of the entire school population, as these features of the survey population are now certain to be included in the 10 per cent sample.

Snowball sampling

Snowball sampling is used when a sampling frame is difficult to obtain or doesn't exist, or when a sample is very difficult to obtain. The researcher may identify one or two people with the characteristics they're interested in, and ask them to introduce the researcher to other people willing to cooperate in the research, and then ask these people to identify others. In this way the sample gradually builds up, just like a snowball getting bigger as you roll it in the snow. For example, Laurie Taylor in In the Underworld used this technique to investigate the lifestyles of criminals. There was no readily available sampling frame of criminals. He happened to know a convicted criminal, who was willing to put him in touch with other criminals who were willing to cooperate in his research. These criminals in turn put him in touch with other criminals, and so he was able gradually to build up his sample of criminals.

Such samples may be useful, but they are not random or representative. They rely on volunteers recommending other volunteers to the researcher, and the sample is therefore self-selecting, and this may create bias. For example, such volunteers may have particular views for or against a particular issue, which is why they volunteered.

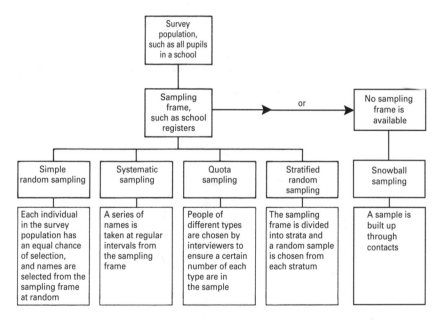

Figure 17.2 Sampling methods

Research methods used in surveys

There are two main methods which are used in social surveys to collect data: questionnaires and interviews.

Questionnaires

Most surveys involve the use of a questionnaire of some kind. A questionnaire is a printed list of questions to be filled in either personally

ACTIVITY

1 In each of the following cases, suggest a hypothesis you might wish to test, how you might obtain your sampling frame, and the sampling method you would choose to select your sample, giving reasons in each case.

■ The attitudes of family doctors (GPs) to changes in the NHS.

■ The reasons why shoplifters commit the crime.

■ The attitudes of football supporters to soccer hooliganism.

■ The reasons why few female school leavers in a town go on computer courses at a local college.

■ A survey of young mothers.

■ A survey of old age pensioners.

■ The opinions of adults in your neighbourhood about how they will vote in the next election.

■ The attitudes of gay men.

2 Ellolova College has 3000 full-time students and 6000 part-time students. Half of the full-time students and three-quarters of the part-time students are women. You want to do a survey among students at Ellolova College. You haven't the time or the money to question every student, so you need to take a 10 per cent sample. In order to make this as representative as possible, you have decided to use a stratified random sampling method.

(a) Explain the stages you would go through to select this 10 per cent sample.

(b) Give the actual numbers of the different groups in the survey population which will be included in your sample.

by the respondent (the person answering the questions) or by an interviewer. All respondents answer exactly the same questions.

There are two main types of questionnaire: the pre-coded questionnaire and the open-ended questionnaire.

The pre-coded questionnaire

The pre-coded questionnaire involves the individual being asked a number of pre-set questions with a limited number of multiple-choice answers. The person filling in the questionnaire will tick off the answer. A typical question might be 'Do you think wages should be paid for housework?' with available answers being 'Yes/No/Don't know'. The problem with this type of questionnaire is that it does not allow respondents to explain their views fully or to develop their answers. An example of a pre-coded questionnaire (to be carried out by an interviewer) is shown in figure 17.3.

The open-ended questionnaire

Like the pre-coded questionnaire, the open-ended questionnaire usually has a number of pre-set questions, but there is no pre-set choice of answers. This allows respondents to write their own answer or dictate it to an interviewer.

An example of an open-ended question is: 'What is your opinion of the present government?' Such questions give respondents scope to express their own views. Such a questionnaire may form the basis for an unstructured interview (see page 429).

In a survey, both pre-coded and open-ended questions may be combined in the same questionnaire.

Newspaper survey

Conduct the interview politely. Ask questions clearly. Do not give extra emphasis to any words. Use only the words that are underlined. Mark the answer given by putting a circle round the appropriate code number.

Good morning/afternoon/evening. I am conducting a survey on newspapers and I would be grateful if you would help me by answering some questions.

		Code	
A	Sex of respondent:		
	Male	1	
	Female	2	
B	Estimated age of respondent:		
	16 or under	1	
	17–21	2	
	22–40	3	
	41–60	4	
	61 or over	5	
C	Would you please tell me which of the following categories best describes your occupation: (show list)		
	Professional/senior manager	1	
	Manager in business	2	
	Administrator/clerical	3	
	Self-employed/business owner	4	
	Manual	5	
	Housewife	6	
	Student	7	
	Retired	8	
	Unemployed	9	
	Other	10	

Question			Code	Route
Q.1	Do you read a daily morning newspaper			
	every day		1	Q.2
	4–5 times a week		2	Q.2
	2–3 times a week		3	Q.2
	once a week		4	Q.2
	less than once a week		5	Q.2
	never?		6	Classify
Q.2	Do you usually read:			
	all the newspaper		1	Q.3
	most of it		2	Q.3
	part of it		3	Q.3
	or just glance through it?		4	Q.3
Q.3	Which newspaper or newspapers do you read?			
	Sun *Star* *Independent*		1 5 9	Q.4
	Mirror *Telegraph* *Financial Times*		2 6 10	Q.4
	Mail *Guardian* Others (please		3 7 11	Q.4
	Express *Times* write in)		4 8	Q.4
Q.4	Where do you usually get most of your news about what's going on in Britain today? Is it from:			
	Newspapers		1	Q.5
	Television		2	Q.5
	Radio		3	Q.5
	Other (specify)		4	Q.5
	Don't know?	5		Q.5
Q.5	Which of the following do you think gives the most truthful account of the news:			
	Newspapers		1	Q.6
	Television		2	Q.6
	Radio		3	Q.6
	Don't know?	4		Q.6

Figure 17.3 Example of a pre-coded questionnaire conducted by an interviewer

Note the instructions given to the interviewer at the top of the questionnaire. These seek to ensure objectivity and consistency between different interviewers.

DESIGNING A QUESTIONNAIRE

To design a successful questionnaire, you should follow these rules:

- It should be clearly laid out and well printed, and instructions for completing it should be easily understood by the respondent. The questionnaire should be easy to follow and complete.

- Questions should only be asked which the respondents are likely to be able to answer accurately. For example, people can only give opinions on things they know about and can remember accurately.

- The number of questions should be kept to the minimum required to produce the information. Respondents may be unwilling to spend a long time answering questions, or might stop answering the questions seriously.

- Questions should be simple and direct, and able to be answered briefly.

- Questions should be phrased in simple, everyday language so they are easily understood by the respondent. Technical words and 'jargon' should be avoided as the respondents may not understand the question. For example, a question about 'marital status' should be avoided – it is better to ask if someone is married, single, or divorced.

- Questions should be unambiguous, and their meaning quite clear. For example, a question like 'Do you watch television often?' is a bad question because people might interpret 'often' in different ways – it is better to specify actual time periods such as 1–2 hours a day, 3–4 hours a day, and so on.

- 'Leading' questions which encourage people to give particular answers should be avoided – otherwise the respondent might feel he or she is expected to give a particular answer. This might then produce invalid (or untruthful) answers.

- Pre-coded questionnaires should provide enough alternative answers to apply to all the respondents. There should be an opportunity for the respondents to give a 'Don't know' answer.

Questionnaires should be phrased in straightforward, everyday language

The postal questionnaire

A postal questionnaire is one which is sent to the respondents through the post with a pre-paid envelope for the reply. The respondents fill in the form themselves.

A key problem with postal questionnaires is that of non-response – often people don't bother to return them. The percentage returning them may sometimes be less than 20–30 per cent of the sample, and this may mean the results obtained may not be valid, but inaccurate, biased, and unrepresentative. For example, those not replying might have answered differently from those who did reply, and those replying may be more educated, be interested in the topic being investigated, or have some 'axe to grind'.

To try to overcome the problem of non-response, postal questionnaires often have covering letters from well-known individuals or organizations, or offer free gifts, and other rewards. A reply-paid envelope is essential if the questionnaire is not to be dropped into the nearest paper recycling bin.

ACTIVITY

1. The following questions, which are intended to be filled in by the respondent, all have *at least* one thing wrong with them. In each case, describe what is wrong with the question and rewrite the question in a more correct or more appropriate way:

   (a) Do you watch television: 1–2 hours a night?
                                    2–4 hours a night?
                                    4–6 hours a night?

   (b) Don't you agree sex before marriage   YES/NO
       is wrong?

   (c) Don't you think you should vote   YES/NO/DON'T KNOW
       Labour if there were a general election
       tomorrow?

   (d) Which recommendation of the
       Government Road Safety Committee
       regarding the change in the upper
       speed limit on class A roads and
       motorways do you support?

   (e) Are you happy with your washing   YES/NO/DON'T KNOW
       machine?

   (f) Do you have joint conjugal roles in   YES/NO/DON'T KNOW
       your household?

   (g) Which social class do you belong to?

   (h) Do you bonk with your partner a lot?   YES/NO

   (i) Are you a good driver?   YES/NO/DON'T KNOW

   (j) Do you read newspapers: A LOT?
                                   QUITE A LOT?
                                   OFTEN?
                                   SOMETIMES?
                                   A BIT?
                                   NOT MUCH?
                                   NEVER?

2. Do you think any of the questions above in their present form would be either unlikely to be answered or answered dishonestly? How would this affect the *validity* of the research? Give reasons for your answer.

THE STRENGTHS AND LIMITATIONS OF POSTAL QUESTIONNAIRES

Strengths

- Fairly cheap compared to paying interviewers.
- Large numbers of people over a wide geographical area can be questioned.
- Results are obtained quickly.
- People have more time to reply than when an interviewer is present, so more accurate answers may be obtained.
- Questions on personal, controversial, or embarrassing subjects are more likely to be answered than if they are asked by an interviewer.
- The problem of interviewer bias is avoided.
- Answers are easy to compare and put into statistical form (numbers and percentages) – for example, '87 per cent of women questioned said they had to do all the housework.'

Limitations

- Non-response, leading to unrepresentative, invalid, biased results.
- Extra questions cannot be asked or added, to get the respondents to expand or explain themselves more fully. The depth of information is therefore limited.
- With pre-coded questionnaires, the limited range of questions and answers may mean the researcher isn't getting at what the respondent really thinks, so results may not be valid.
- The wording may be confusing to the respondent, and the questions therefore misunderstood. There is no interviewer present to explain the question if necessary.

Interviews

Questionnaires are often conducted by an interviewer. There are two main types of interview: the structured or formal interview and the unstructured or informal interview.

The structured or formal interview

The structured interview is based on a pre-coded questionnaire. The interviewer asks the questions and does not probe beyond the basic answers received. It is a formal question-and-answer session.

The unstructured or informal interview

This type of interview is based on an open-ended questionnaire, or simply a list of topics the interviewer wishes to discuss. The interviewer will ask the respondent open-ended questions which may trigger off discussions or further questions. The interviewer will try to put the respondent at ease in a relaxed, informal situation and encourage him or her to express his or her feelings and opinions. This means the interviewer can obtain much greater depth of information than is possible in a structured interview or in a postal questionnaire. It is a bit like a TV chat show.

Interviewer bias

A major problem with interviews, particularly unstructured ones, is that of interviewer bias. Interviewer bias is the way in which the presence or behaviour of the interviewer may influence in some way the answers given by the respondent. There is always the possibility that the respondent

Interviewers may not always get the cooperation they hope for ...

... especially if they choose the wrong moment

THE STRENGTHS AND LIMITATIONS OF INTERVIEWS

Strengths

- They are the best way of getting questionnaires completed – the problem of non-response found with postal questionnaires is much rarer. Skilled interviewers can persuade people to answer questions.
- There is more flexibility than with postal questionnaires – questions may be explained and, except with pre-coded questionnaires, extra questions can be asked and more detail obtained.
- Unstructured interviews allow the respondent to be more open and honest, and therefore more valid information about the respondents' attitudes, values, and opinions can be obtained.
- Unstructured interviews enable the ideas of the sociologist to develop during the interview, and the interviewer can adjust questions and change direction as the interview is taking place if new ideas and insights emerge. By contrast, structured interviews have already decided the important questions.

Limitations

- Interviews are more time-consuming and costly than postal questionnaires – interviews are often slow and interviewers have to be paid. Many more people can be questioned with a postal questionnaire for the same cost.
- Because interviews tend to be slow and expensive, often only a small number can take place – this means the sample size is often small, and therefore risks being unrepresentative of the survey population.
- Interviews tend to be artificial situations, and there is no way of knowing whether what people say in an interview is what they really believe or how they behave in real life.
- The success of interviews depends heavily on the skill and personality of the interviewer, especially in unstructured interviews; for example, in getting people to answer questions that produce useful information and in keeping the conversation going.
- There is a risk of interviewer bias, leading to results that are neither reliable nor valid.

might adapt his or her answer according to the status, class, ethnicity, age, sex, speech, accent, tone of voice, style of dress, or behaviour of the interviewer. The interviewer may give the impression of wanting to hear a certain answer, and the respondent may try to impress the interviewer by giving answers she or he thinks the interviewer wants to hear and would approve of, rather than giving her or his real opinions.

Interviewer bias is a serious problem, as it could mean that respondents do not give answers which they really believe, and therefore the results of the survey may not be valid or reliable – that is, they may not give a true picture of what is being studied, and other interviewers may not get the same results. To overcome interviewer bias, interviewers are trained to avoid giving any impression of approval or disapproval based on their own opinions and feelings about the answers they receive. They should give the impression of polite indifference to the answers received.

ACTIVITY

Consider the following situations, and in each case:

1 Suggest possible ways in which interviewer bias might occur.

2 Suggest what might be done to help remove the bias.
- A white person being questioned by a black interviewer about his or her racial attitudes.
- An adult interviewing pupils in a school.
- A British person interviewing a French person about her or his attitudes towards the English.
- An adult interviewer asking teenagers about their attitudes to cannabis use or other drug abuse.
- A well-dressed, middle-class sociologist asking gypsies questions about their lifestyle.
- A middle-class interviewer asking lower-working-class people about their attitudes to social welfare payments.
- A female interviewer asking a married or cohabiting couple about how household tasks are divided between them.
- An interviewer asking questions on birth-control techniques.
- An older woman asking questions of a young mother about the way children should be brought up.
- An interviewer who is a committed Christian asking questions about religious belief.

The stages of a survey

Before carrying out a large-scale survey, it is important to carry out a pilot survey. This is a trial run of the final survey, using fewer people than the final sample. Its purpose is to iron out any problems which the researcher might have overlooked. For example, some questions may be unclear, some of the sample may have died or moved away, or there may be problems with non-response or non-cooperation by respondents.

After the pilot survey is completed, the results are reviewed, any necessary changes are made, and the main survey can then proceed. The stages of a survey are shown in figure 17.4 on page 432.

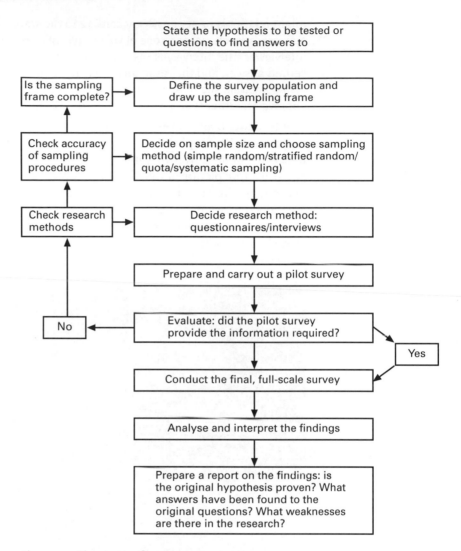

Figure 17.4 The stages of a survey

OBSERVATION

Apart from surveys, sociologists also collect data by observation. There are two main kinds of observation: non-participant observation (or direct observation) and participant observation.

Non-participant observation

The researcher observes a group or situation without taking part in any way. This has the advantage that the sociologist can study people in their 'natural setting' without their behaviour being influenced and changed by the presence of the researcher. For example, a researcher may observe people queuing in a supermarket to see how impatient they get. However, observation without involvement in the group means it is often not possible to understand what is really happening, or to find out more by asking questions. Therefore sociologists more often join in with a group to observe it. This is known as participant observation.

Participant observation

Participant observation is a very commonly used observation technique. In this method, the researcher actually joins in the group or community she or he is studying. The researcher tries to become an accepted part of the group and to learn about the group as a member of it. For example, the sociologist may spend time as a mental patient in a hospital, join a gang, live as a gypsy or as a 'down and out', spend time in prison, or teach in a school.

ACTIVITY

1 What does the cartoon above suggest might be some of the difficulties involved in a participant observation study of a gang?

2 Many participant observation studies have been concerned with the study of various forms of deviance, such as gay groups, street gangs, religious cults, or drug users. Suggest ways you might get in touch with and be accepted by such a group to study it, and outline any difficulties you might have with staying in the group.

In an actual piece of research, sociologists will probably use a variety of methods to collect the data they require. The methods chosen will be influenced by the questions or hypothesis being investigated, the information required (whether quantitative or qualitative), the scale of the research, and the time and money available to complete it. Figure 17.5 on page 435 illustrates the relationship between some of these factors.

THE STRENGTHS AND LIMITATIONS OF PARTICIPANT OBSERVATION

Strengths

- The sociologist gains first-hand knowledge of the group being studied. She or he sees the world through the eyes of members of the group. This provides much more detail and depth than other methods like questionnaires and interviews.

- Questionnaires and interviews tend to provide information only at one point in time. Participant observation takes place over a long period and can therefore give a much fuller and more valid account of a group's behaviour.

- With other methods, the sociologist has already decided on a hypothesis, which affects what questions are asked and therefore what is found out. With participant observation, interesting new ideas to explore may emerge during the research itself and the sociologist may discover things she or he would not even have thought of asking about, producing more valid results.

- Participant observation may be the only possible method of research. For example, a criminal gang is hardly likely to answer questionnaires or do interviews for fear of the consequences, and a group like gypsies may well see an interviewer as 'official' and prying, and may fear harassment by councils, police, and other official bodies. By adopting a *covert* role – keeping her or his identity secret – the researcher may be able to investigate such groups. Even if the group knows who the researcher is (this is known as an *overt* role), the researcher may, after a time, win the trust of the group.

- People can be studied in their normal social situation, rather than in the somewhat artificial context of an interview or questionnaire.

Limitations

- It is very time-consuming and expensive compared to other methods, as it involves the sociologist participating in a group for long periods.

- Because only a small group is studied, it is difficult to make generalizations.

- It depends a great deal on the personality of the investigator and his or her ability to fit in with the group.

- There is a danger of the researcher becoming so involved with the group and developing such loyalty to it that he or she may find it difficult to stand back and report his or her observations in a neutral way. The research would not then be valid.

- There is no real way of checking the findings of a participant observation study. There is no real evidence apart from the observations of the researcher, and what one researcher might regard as important may be missed or seen as unimportant by another.

- There may be a problem of gaining the group's confidence (getting into the group) and maintaining it (staying in), especially if criminal and other deviant activities are involved. What does the researcher do if a group involves itself in criminal activities like theft, drug-dealing, or acts of violence? Failure to take part may result in the group's loss of confidence and trust, and the effective end of the research.

- The presence of the researcher, if she or he is known to the group as a researcher (an overt role), may change the group's behaviour simply because they know they are being studied. This may produce invalid information.

- With a covert role, the researcher has to be very careful when asking questions, in case her or his real identity is revealed or people become suspicious. This may limit the information obtained. There are also serious ethical difficulties involved in a researcher concealing his or her real identity and purpose.

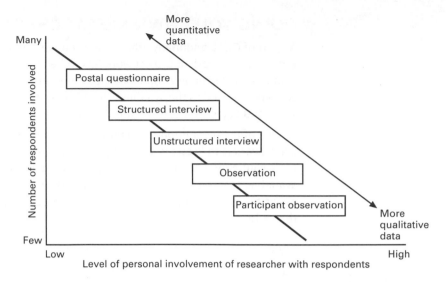

Figure 17.5 Methods of data collection

ACTIVITY

1 According to figure 17.5, which method of data collection involves the largest number of respondents?

2 Which method has the highest level of personal involvement of the researcher with the respondents?

3 Which method, apart from observational methods, provides the most qualitative data?

4 Briefly describe in your own words two advantages and two disadvantages of each of the methods of data collection identified in figure 17.5.

5 Refer to the strengths and limitations of participant observation opposite. Suggest two advantages and two disadvantages of adopting (a) an overt role (b) a covert role.

6 Imagine you have two months to carry out a small-scale research project on one of the following issues, using both primary and secondary sources:
■ The difficulties facing the elderly.
■ The opinions of adults in your neighbourhood about how they will vote in the next election.
■ How household tasks are divided between men and women in the home.
■ Gender stereotyping in a school or college.
■ The attitudes of people towards religion.
■ The lifestyle of teenagers.

Select one of the issues above, and:

(a) Suggest a hypothesis you might wish to test or questions you want to find answers to.
(b) Identify at least one secondary source of information you might use, and explain what information you would expect to obtain from it.
(c) Explain how you might select the group of people to be studied.
(d) Explain carefully what research method or methods you would use to collect your primary data.
(e) Identify three problems or difficulties you might face in carrying out your research, and in each case suggest how you might overcome them.

DOING YOUR OWN RESEARCH: COURSEWORK

As part of GCSE and many other introductory sociology courses, some form of coursework or project work has to be carried out. This coursework component is usually a small-scale piece of research into an area of sociology related to the syllabus. The AQA suggests a length of between 1,500 and 2,500 words, while the OCR suggests 2,000 words.

One of the most important factors in successfully completing coursework is to keep research small-scale and manageable, to choose a topic you're interested in, and to recognize the limited time and resources available. Marks are awarded for the quality of the research and not simply quantity – a short (but not too short), well-executed project is far better than a long rambling one.

SAFETY AND ETHICS IN RESEARCH

Before carrying out your coursework, you should refer to the ethical issues discussed at the beginning of this chapter. You should also consider issues of your own safety – do not put yourself at risk, and certainly do not do anything that might be harmful in any way to the people you are researching. If in doubt, ask your teacher or lecturer for further advice.

Planning a coursework project

In planning and carrying out a project, the sampling techniques and research methods discussed in this chapter should be applied. A successful project should follow the stages of research shown in figure 17.6.

You should also follow these guidelines:

- Set yourself only one or two aims – these should be simple, concise, and achievable given the time and money you have to do the research.

- If information is collected from a sample of people, you should explain how you selected your sample. Was it representative? (It usually won't matter if it is unrepresentative, so long as this limitation of the research is explained in your evaluation.)

- Try to use only one method and give convincing reasons for the method you choose, explain why it is particularly suited to the aims of your research and why it was more suitable than other methods you might have used to research your aim, and give a clear description of how the information was collected.

- Your report should include:
  - A title page, including the title of your project, your name, centre number and candidate number.
  - A table of contents. (The OCR 'Enquiry' additionally requires after the contents page a summary or abstract.)
  - Clearly marked and separated chapters.
  - Good layout.
  - Clear language.
  - The use of relevant diagrams and illustrations, with any pie charts,

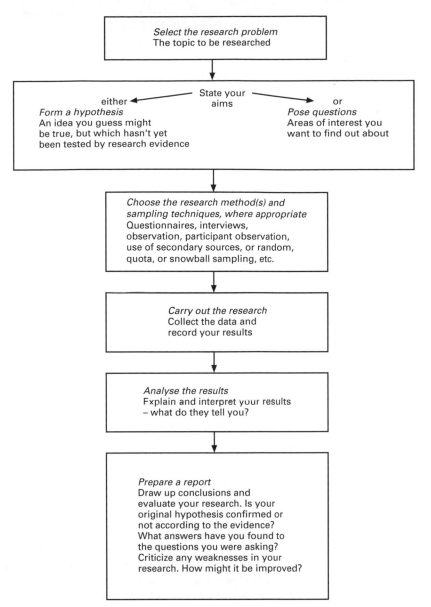

Figure 17.6 The stages of research

graphs, tables, photographs, or cassette or video tapes being clearly labelled and referred to in the text.
– A list of books and other sources, including websites, you used – this is known as a bibliography.

Below is a project checklist, based on the AQA and OCR Sociology GCSE specifications, for you to use. However, you should check the latest requirements with your teacher or lecturer.

Suggestions for possible projects are included at the end of each chapter in this book, except chapter 1 and this chapter, but you can usually choose any topic which interests you, so long as it is relevant in some way to the specification you are following.

YOUR PROJECT CHECKLIST

☐ Has your project got a title page, with a *project title, your name, centre number,* and *candidate number?*

☐ Have you included a table of contents, and, if you are studying the OCR course, a separate page with a summary or abstract?

☐ Does your project contain a clearly and fully explained *aim* (what you set out to do and why) or a *hypothesis* (a 'guess' about what you expect to find), with an explanation of what it is you expect to find? Is there some background explaining why you chose this particular aim or hypothesis, perhaps referring to other pieces of information or research in the area? What made you interested in this topic?

☐ Does your project use one or more sociological methods (for example, questionnaires, interviews, or observation/participant observation, and/or use of secondary sources)?

☐ Do you fully discuss *why* you chose the research method you did, explaining why this was the most suitable method for what you were investigating (your aim or hypothesis)? Do you explain the advantages/disadvantages of this method compared to using other methods for what you were investigating? Does your project contain a sample questionnaire, etc.?

☐ If you selected a sample of people to investigate, do you explain why you selected them, how you selected them (what sampling method you used), and why you chose this method as the most suitable?

☐ Are your research findings and the sources of information you used relevant to what you said you were going to investigate in your aim or hypothesis?

☐ Does your project deal fully with all the aims you set yourself? Do you describe and explain fully all the evidence you collected? Do you explain what your findings show – in confirming and/or disproving your aims/hypothesis?

☐ Does your project have an evaluation – clear conclusions drawn from your research, indicating what you have found out, whether your aims have been achieved (and if not, an explanation of why not) or whether your hypothesis has been proven (and if not, an explanation of why not)? What are the limitations and weaknesses of your research and the methods you used? How might it have been improved? What are its strengths? Does your project have any interesting insights?

Does your project contain:

☐ numbered pages?

☐ a table of contents (with page numbers)?

☐ clearly separated chapters (for example, Title, Contents, Introduction (with an aim or hypothesis, and some background to your research), Methodology, Content and Results (your findings and evidence), Analysis and Conclusions, Evaluation, Bibliography)?

☐ a clearly planned layout (does it follow a sensible order)?

☐ good grammar and spelling (if in doubt, use a dictionary!)?

☐ a bibliography – a list of the books, statistics, newspapers, websites etc., you used, with their authors, publishers, and dates?

If it is all complete – hand it in!

CHAPTER SUMMARY

After studying this chapter, you should be able to:

■ Explain the issues of reliability, validity, and ethics in social research.

■ Explain the difference between quantitative and qualitative data.

■ Explain, with examples, the difference between primary and secondary sources of data, and their advantages and disadvantages.

■ Explain the various methods sociologists use to obtain samples to study.

■ Outline the stages of a survey.

■ Describe and explain the use of questionnaires, interviews, and non-participant and participant observation in sociological research, and explain their various strengths and limitations.

■ Outline the stages a sociologist would go through in carrying out a piece of research.

■ Carry out a small-scale piece of research of your own, using the various sources, sampling techniques, and research methods covered in this chapter.

KEY TERMS

ethics
hypothesis
interviewer bias
pilot survey
primary data
qualitative data
quantitative data
reliability
representative sample
sample
sampling frame
secondary data
survey
survey population
validity

Appendix: Reading Statistical Data

The evidence that sociologists use in their research comes in a variety of forms, but often consists of statistical data presented in the form of tables, graphs, bar charts, pie charts, and various combinations of these. These often prove difficult for newcomers to sociology to understand. This appendix is designed to introduce you to the use and interpretation of these forms of data, and give you practice in doing so. This should make it easier to read the tables and figures appearing in this book, and construct your own should you wish. Answers to all activities in this chapter (except the graphs you are asked to draw) are at the end of the chapter.

STATISTICAL TABLES

When confronted with a statistical table, you should first read carefully the heading of the table – this will tell you what subject the statistics refer to. Tables generally show the relationship between two or more factors, and the key thing to note is what the statistics refer to – whether they are in actual numbers or percentages and what units the numbers are in. For example, the numbers might be in thousands or millions or they might be in the form of numbers per thousand of the population.

Table A1 is derived from a series of official government statistics on divorce. The data in this table will be used to show the variety of ways in which statistical evidence can be presented.

Table A1 shows the relationship between a number of factors (shown in the left-hand column) and how these have changed over time (the dates shown along the top row). Notice that:

- The table refers to the different countries making up the United Kingdom. There are references to England and Wales, Scotland, Northern Ireland, Great Britain, and the United Kingdom.

- There are three ways in which the figures are expressed:
  - 'Petitions filed', 'decrees nisi granted', 'decrees absolute granted', and 'estimated numbers of divorced people who had not remarried' are expressed in *thousands*.
  - 'Divorces where one or both partners had been previously divorced' are expressed in *percentages*.
  - 'Persons divorcing' are expressed as '*per thousand* married people' (this is known as the divorce rate).

Table A1 Divorce: 1961–2001

	1961	1971	1981	1991	2001
Petitions filed[a] (thousands)					
England and Wales	30	110	176	179	162
Decrees nisi[b] granted (thousands)					
England and Wales	27	89	147	161	147
Decrees absolute[c] granted (thousands)					
England and Wales	25	74	145	158	143
Granted to husband	11	30	42	44	44
Granted to wife	14	44	102	114	99
Scotland	2	5	10	12	11
Northern Ireland	–	–	1	2	2
United Kingdom	27	79	156	172	156
Persons divorcing per thousand married people					
England and Wales	2.1	6.0	11.9	13.5	13.0
Percentage of divorces where one or both partners had been previously divorced					
England and Wales	9.3	8.8	17.1	25.4	29.4
Estimated numbers of divorced people who had not remarried (thousands)					
Great Britain					
Men	101	200	653	n/a[d]	n/a
Women	184	317	890	n/a	n/a
Total	285	517	1543	n/a	n/a

[a] A petition is a request to a court to grant a divorce.
[b] A decree nisi is the stage before the divorce is finalized.
[c] A decree absolute is the final divorce, representing the legal termination of the marriage.
[d] Not available
Source: Data adapted from *Social Trends*; *Population Trends*; Marriage, Divorce and Adoption Statistics, Office for National Statistics

ACTIVITY

Study table A1 carefully and answer the following questions to check whether you are reading the table correctly:

1 How many decrees absolute were granted to husbands in England and Wales in 1991?

2 How many divorced women in Great Britain in 1971 were estimated not to have remarried?

3 How many decrees absolute were granted in Scotland in 2001?

4 By how many had the number of decrees absolute granted in the United Kingdom increased between 1961 and 2001?

5 How many decrees absolute were granted to wives in England and Wales in 2001?

6 How many persons were divorcing per thousand married people in England and Wales in 1981?

7 What percentage of divorces in England and Wales in 2001 involved at least one partner who had been previously divorced?

8 What was the total number of divorce petitions in England and Wales in 1991?

DESCRIBING A TREND

When interpreting statistical data, you will often be expected to describe a trend, or how the pattern shown changes over time. In describing a trend, you should normally say whether there is an upward or downward trend, state whether the figure has increased or decreased, and by how much, and give the starting figure and date and the finishing figure and date.

For example, with table A1 you might be asked: 'What trend is shown in the number of decrees absolute granted in the United Kingdom between 1961 and 2001?' Your answer might take the form: 'The number of decrees absolute has shown an upward trend, increasing by 129,000, from 27,000 in 1961 to 156,000 in 2001' (the figure of 129,000 being obtained by subtracting the figure of 27,000 in 1961 from 156,000 in 2001).

ACTIVITY

Using table A1, practise describing the following trends:

1 What trend is shown in the number of persons divorcing per thousand married people in England and Wales between 1961 and 2001?

2 What trend does the table show in the number of decrees nisi granted in England and Wales in the period covered by the table?

3 Comparing the number of decrees absolute granted to husbands and wives in England and Wales between 1961 and 2001, identify *three* trends that are shown.

GRAPHS

Statistics are commonly presented in the form of graphs. These show the relationship between two factors and how they change over time. These are shown on the vertical and horizontal axes, which are labelled to show what they represent. Trends can be spotted immediately by studying whether the line rises or falls between two dates. It is always important to note what the figures on the axes refer to – numbers, percentages, dates, and so on.

Figure A1, using the data given in table A1, illustrates how the number of decrees absolute granted in the United Kingdom has changed over

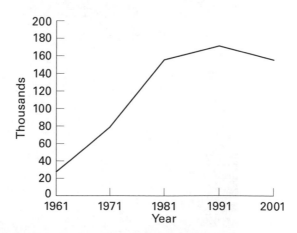

Figure A1 Decrees absolute granted: United Kingdom, 1961–2001

Using figure A1:

1 About how many decrees absolute were granted in 1971?
2 About how many decrees absolute were granted in 1991?
3 What trend is shown in the graph?
4 Using the data given in table A1, practise drawing your own graph to illustrate the changing number of persons divorcing per thousand married people in England and Wales between 1961 and 2001. Make sure you label the axes correctly and put a title on your graph.

time. Notice how the horizontal axis gives the date and the vertical axis gives the number of divorces (in thousands).

Graphs may have more than one curve on them to show more information, and this is useful for making comparisons. For example, figure A2 shows that both the number of petitions filed for divorce and the decrees absolute granted (in thousands) have increased over time, and it is easy to see at a glance that there are large differences between them.

What does figure A2 show about the number of divorce petitions compared to the number of decrees absolute granted over the period covered by the graph? How might you explain this difference?

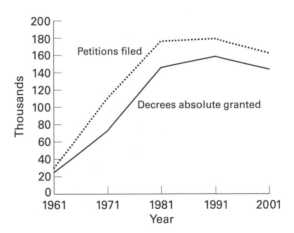

Figure A2 Divorces: England and Wales, 1961–2001

Cumulative graphs

Sometimes graphs may show how a total figure is made up by adding one set of figures to another. This is called a cumulative graph, as the figures 'build up' to the total. This is illustrated in figure A3 on page 444, using the data from table A1 on 'decrees absolute granted to husbands and wives in England and Wales'.

In figure A3:

- The top line shows the total number of decrees absolute granted.

- The bottom line shows the number of husbands granted a decree absolute.

- The space between the two lines represents the number of wives granted a decree absolute.

By subtracting the number of husbands (the bottom line) from the total (the top line), it is possible to calculate the number of wives granted a decree absolute. For example, in 1991, there was a total of about 158,000 decrees absolute (point A), with 44,000 granted to husbands (point B). The number of wives granted a divorce is therefore about 114,000 (A minus B).

It is immediately obvious from looking at the graph that:

- Far more wives are granted divorces than husbands, as the gap between the top line and the bottom line is much wider than the gap between the bottom line and the horizontal axis.

- The gap between the curves widens over time (although it decreases slightly after about 1991), showing that the number of wives granted a divorce has grown at a faster rate than that of husbands granted a divorce.

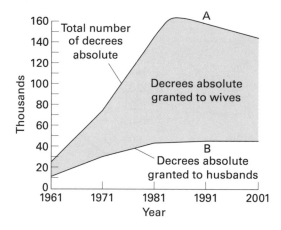

Figure A3 Decrees absolute granted to husbands and wives: England and Wales, 1961–2001

Referring to figure A3:

1 About how many wives were granted a decree absolute in 1961?

2 Identify three trends that are shown in the graph.

3 Using the data in table A1, draw a cumulative graph showing the estimated numbers of men and women in Great Britain who had been divorced but who had not remarried in the period 1961 to 1981. Don't forget to label your graph correctly and give it a title.

BAR CHARTS

Bar charts are another very commonly used way of presenting data and showing comparisons and trends in a visually striking way. Bar charts are constructed in much the same way as graphs, but columns are used instead of lines.

Figure A4 shows a bar chart comparing the estimated numbers of divorced people in Great Britain who had not remarried between 1961 and 1981.

ACTIVITY

Referring to figure A4, answer the following questions:

1 About how many divorced women were estimated not to have remarried in 1981?

2 About how many divorced men were estimated not to have remarried in 1971?

3 Identify two trends shown in the chart.

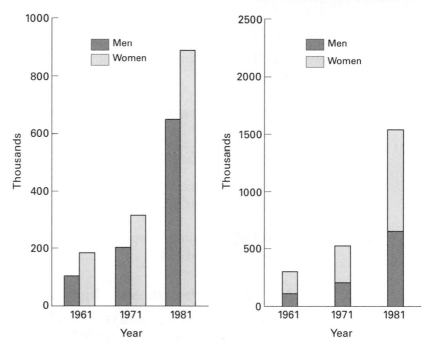

Figure A4 Estimated numbers of divorced people who had not remarried: Great Britain, 1961–81

Figure A5 Estimated numbers of divorced people who had not remarried: Great Britain, 1961–81

Cumulative bar charts

Bar charts may, like graphs, be cumulative and show how totals are made up. Compare figure A4 with figure A5, in which exactly the same information is presented in a different form (note, however, that the scales on the vertical axes differ between the two).

ACTIVITY

Using the data in table A1 (see page 441), construct a bar chart comparing the decrees absolute granted for divorce in England and Wales to husbands and wives for the years 1961, 1981, and 2001.

PIE CHARTS

Pie charts present data by dividing a circle into sectors, with the size of each sector being proportional to the size of the item it represents. Pie charts are very effective in showing statistics in an easily digestible and striking way. For example, using the data given in table A1, the number of decrees absolute granted to husbands and wives in England and Wales in 2001 might be presented as in figure A6.

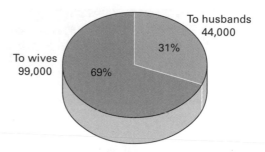

Figure A6 Divorces (decrees absolute) granted to husbands and wives: England and Wales, 2001

ACTIVITY

Draw a pie chart illustrating the way your 24-hour day is divided up between school/college work or paid employment, travelling to and from work, leisure activities, domestic jobs in the home, and sleeping and eating.

Throughout this book there are many examples of statistics presented in a variety of forms, often with activities to develop your understanding of them. You should not simply ignore them, but try to read and interpret them. They often contain important information which will help you to understand the text better.

Answers to questions in this chapter

p. 441   (1) 44,000. (2) 317,000. (3) 11,000. (4) 129,000. (5) 99,000. (6) 11.9. (7) 29.4 per cent. (8) 179,000.

p. 442   (1) Upward trend, increasing by 10.9, from 2.1 in 1961 to 13.0 in 2001. (2) Upward trend, increasing by 120,000 from 27 000 in 1961 to 147,000 in 2001. (3) All upward trends, although the wives' figure declined between 1991 and 2001, and the husbands' was the same in 1991 and 2001. Increasing by 33,000 for husbands, from 11,000 in 1961 to 44,000 in 2001; increasing by 85,000 for wives, from 14,000 in 1961 to 99,000 in 2001; and those granted to wives have increased more than those granted to husbands – by 85,000 compared to 33,000. The gap between them has therefore grown over time.

p. 443   (1) About 80,000. (2) About 170,000. (3) Upward trend, rising from about 28,000 in 1961 to a peak of about 170,000 in 1991, with a small decline after 1991.

p. 443   There are a lot more petitions than there are divorces granted.

This suggests that some people who apply for divorce then change their minds for some reason before it is too late.

p. 444   (1) About 20,000. (2) There are four trends you could mention: total divorces increasing; divorces granted to husbands increasing; divorces granted to wives increasing; and the divorces granted to wives increasing far more than those granted to men.

p. 445   (1) About 900,000. (2) About 200,000. (3) There are three possible trends: the number of divorced men who had not remarried has increased; the same for women; and the number of divorced women not remarrying has increased much more than the number of men.

Glossary

Words highlighted within entries refer to terms found elsewhere in the glossary.

Absolute poverty. Poverty defined as lacking the minimum requirements necessary to maintain human health. (See also relative poverty.)

Achieved status. Status which is achieved through an individual's own efforts. (See also ascribed status.)

Affluent worker. Well-paid manual worker.

Agenda-setting. The list of subjects which the mass media choose to report and bring to public attention.

Alienation. A lack of power and satisfaction at work.

Anomie. Confusion and uncertainty over social norms.

Anti-school sub-culture. A set of values, attitudes, and behaviour in opposition to the main aims of a school.

Arranged marriage. A marriage which is arranged by the parents of the marriage partners, with a view to background and status. More a union between two families than two people, and romantic love between the marriage partners is not necessarily present.

Ascribed status. Status which is given to an individual at birth and usually can't be changed. (See also achieved status.)

Authority. Power which is accepted as fair and just.

Automation. Production of goods by self-controlling machines with little human supervision.

Bias. A subject being presented in a one-sided way, favouring one point of view over others, or deliberately ignoring, distorting or misrepresenting issues.

Bigamy. Where monogamy is the only legal form of marriage, the offence of marrying a second partner while still married to the first.

Birth rate. The number of live births per 1000 of the population per year.

Blue-collar workers. Manual workers.

Bourgeoisie. Class of owners of the means of production.

Caste system. A stratification system (see social stratification) based on Hindu religious beliefs, where an individual's position is fixed at birth and cannot be changed.

Chivalry thesis. The suggestion that paternalism or sexism on the part of the police and courts means they regard female offenders as a less serious 'threat' than men, particularly for minor offences, and treat women more leniently than men.

Churches. Large, world-accommodating (see world-accommodating groups) religious organizations with a hierarchy of clergy and paid officials generally accepting the dominant norms and values of a society.

Citizenship. The legal, social, civil, and political rights and responsibilities of individuals (citizens) living in a democratic society.

Class consciousness. An awareness in members of a social class of their real interests.

Classic extended family. A family where several related nuclear families or family members live in the same house, street or area. It may be horizontally extended, where it contains aunts, uncles, cousins, etc., or vertically extended, where it contains more than two generations.

Closed society. A stratification system (see social stratification) where social mobility is not possible.

Coercion. Rule by violence or the threat of violence.

Communes. Self-contained and self-supporting communities, where all members of the community share property, childcare, household tasks, and living accommodation.

Communism. An equal society, without social classes or conflict, in which the means of production are the common property of all.

Compensatory education. Extra educational help for those coming from disadvantaged groups to help them overcome the disadvantages they face in the education system and the wider society.

Conflict theory. A sociological approach that emphasizes social differences and conflicts, with inequalities in wealth, power, and status all creating conflicts between individuals and social groups. (See also consensus theory.)

Conjugal roles. The roles played by a male and female partner in marriage or in a cohabiting couple.

Consensus theory. A sociological approach that emphasizes the shared norms and values that exist between people, and sees society made up of individuals and social institutions working together in harmony, without much conflict between people and groups. (see also conflict theory.)

Consumption property. Property for use by the owner which doesn't produce any income, such as owning your own car.

Core workers. The well-paid and qualified, skilled workers who make up the full-time, permanent employees in a workplace. (See also periphery workers.)

Corporate crime. Crimes committed by large companies which directly profit the company rather than individuals.

Craft production. The production of goods by hand tools.

Crime. Behaviour which is against the law – law-breaking.

Cults. World-affirming (see world-affirming groups) religious-like groups open to anyone who can afford to participate, offering individuals access to spiritual or supernatural powers to help them lead happier and more successful lives.

Culture. The language, beliefs, values and norms, customs, roles, knowledge and skills which combine to make up the 'way of life' of any society.

Culture of poverty. A set of beliefs and values thought to exist among the poor which prevents them escaping from poverty.

Customs. Norms which have existed for a long time.

Dealignment. In voting, no clear alignment (matching up) of particular social classes with one of the two main political parties. In particular, the working class (see social class) is no longer clearly aligned with the Labour Party, nor the middle class with the Conservative Party, and most voters no longer show loyalty to a party according to their social class.

Death rate. The number of deaths per 1000 of the population per year.

Democracy. A form of government where the people participate in political decision-making, usually by electing individuals to represent their views.

Demography. The study of population.

Denominations. World-accommodating (see world-accommodating groups) religious organizations, similar to churches but smaller, with a hierarchy of clergy and paid officials, generally accepting the dominant norms and values of a society, though with some criticisms of them.

Dependency culture. A set of values and beliefs, and a way of life, centred on dependence on others. Normally used in the context of those who depend on welfare state benefits.

Dependency ratio. The proportion of the population which is dependent (see dependent population) compared to those who are working.

Dependent age groups. The under 16s, who are at school, and the over 60s (women) and 65s (men), who are retired.

Dependent population. That section of the population which is not in work and is supported by others, such as those in full-time education, pensioners, and the unemployed.

Deskilling. The removal of skills from work by the application of new machinery which simplifies tasks.

De-urbanization. The movement of people away from towns and cities.

Deviance. Failure to conform to social norms.

Deviancy amplification. The process by which the mass media, through exaggeration and distortion, actually create more crime and deviance.

Deviant career. Where people who have been labelled as deviant (see deviance) find conventional opportunities blocked to them, and so are pushed into committing further deviant acts.

Deviant voter. Someone voting against the political party representing the interests of her or his social class.

Dictatorship. A form of totalitarianism where power is concentrated in the hands of one person.

Disease. A biological or mental condition that usually involves medically diagnosed symptoms.

Division of labour. The division of work into a large number of specialized tasks, each of which is carried out by one worker or group of workers.

Divorce rate. The number of divorces per 1000 married people per year.

Domestic labour. Unpaid housework, including cooking, cleaning, childcare, and looking after the sick and elderly.

Ecumenical movement. A movement which seeks to achieve greater unity between different Christian churches.

Education Action Zones. Areas which face a range of social problems, such as poverty and unemployment, in which schools are given extra money and teachers to help children overcome difficulties at school arising from their home and social class backgrounds, and improve educational achievements.

Educational Priority Areas. Areas which face a range of social problems, such as poverty and unemployment, in which schools are given extra money and teachers to help children overcome difficulties at school arising from their home and social class background and improve educational achievement.

Elaborated code. A form of language use involving careful explanation and detail. The language used by strangers and individuals in some formal context, like a job interview, writing a business letter, or a school lesson or textbook. (See also restricted code.)

Elite. A small group holding great power and influence in society.

Embourgeoisement. The idea that, with higher wages, the working class (see social class) are becoming part of the middle class. The opposite of proletarianization.

Emigration. The movement of people out of a country or area on a permanent basis.

Endogamy. Where marriage must be to a partner of the same kinship or social group.

Equality of educational opportunity. The principle that every child should have an equal chance of doing as well in education as his or her ability will allow.

Ethics. Ideas about what is morally right and wrong.

Ethnic group. A group of people who share a common culture.

Ethnicity. The shared culture of a social group which gives its members a common identity in some ways different from other groups.

Ethnocentrism. A view of the world in which other cultures are seen through the eyes of one's own culture, with a devaluing of the others. For example, school subjects may concentrate on white British society and culture rather than recognizing and taking into account the cultures of different ethnic communities (see ethnic group).

Evangelicalism. A form of Christianity involving a fundamentalist (see fundamentalism) belief in the Bible and a commitment to preaching the Christian gospel.

Extended family. A family grouping including all kin (see kinship). There are two main types of extended family: the classic extended family and the modified extended family.

False consciousness. A failure by members of a social class to recognize their real interests.

Feminist. Someone who believes that women are disadvantaged in society, and should have equal rights with men.

Feudalism. A closed (see closed society) system of stratification (see social stratification) based on land ownership and legal inequalities.

Floating voter. A voter with no fixed political opinion or committed support for any political party.

Folk devils. Individuals or groups posing an imagined or exaggerated threat to society.

Fordism. The mass production of standardized goods using assembly line technology, involving few skills and repetitive work by employees.

Fundamentalism. A return to the literal meaning of religious texts.

Gate-keeping. The media's refusal to cover some issues.

Gender. The culturally created differences between men and women which are learnt through socialization.

Gender identity. People seeing themselves, and others seeing them, in terms of their gender roles and biological sex.

Gender role. The pattern of behaviour which society expects from a man or woman.

General fertility rate. The number of live births per 1000 women of child-bearing age (15–44) per year.

Glass ceiling. An invisible barrier of discrimination which makes it difficult for women to reach the same top levels in their chosen careers as similarly qualified men.

Globalization. The growing interdependence of societies across the world, with the spread of the same culture and economic interests across the globe.

Health. Being able to function normally within a usual everyday routine.

Hidden curriculum. Attitudes and behaviour which are taught through the school's organization and teachers' attitudes but which are not part of the formal timetable.

Household. An individual living alone or a group living at the same address and sharing facilities.

Hypothesis. An idea which a researcher guesses might be true, but which has not yet been tested against the evidence.

Identity. How individuals see and define themselves and how other people see and define them.

Illness. The subjective feeling of being unwell or unhealthy.

Immigration. The movement of people into a country or area on a permanent basis.

Income. The flow of money which people obtain from work, from their investments, or from the state.

Infant mortality. The death of babies in the first year of life.

Infant mortality rate. The number of deaths of babies in the first year of life per 1000 live births per year.

Institutional racism. 'The collective failure of an organization to provide an appropriate and professional service to people because of their culture, colour or ethnic origin. It can be seen or detected in processes, attitudes and behaviour which amount to discrimination through unwitting prejudice, ignorance, thoughtless and racist stereotyping which disadvantages minority ethnic people' (Macpherson Report, 1999).

Integrated conjugal roles. Roles in marriage or in a cohabiting couple where male and female partners share domestic tasks, childcare, decision-making, and income earning.

Inter-generational social mobility. A way of measuring social mobility by comparing an adult's present occupation with that of the family she or he was born into (usually measured against the father's occupation). It therefore shows how much social class mobility there has been between two generations.

Interviewer bias. The answers given in an interview being influenced or distorted in some way by the presence or behaviour of the interviewer.

Intra-generational social mobility. A way of measuring social mobility by comparing a person's present occupation with her or his first occupation. It therefore shows how much mobility an individual has achieved within her or his lifetime.

Inverse care law. In relation to the welfare state, the suggestion that those whose need is least get the most resources, while those in the greatest need get the least resources.

Juvenile delinquency. Crime committed by those between the ages of 10 and 17, though the term 'delinquency' is often used to describe any anti-social behaviour by young people, even if it isn't criminal.

Kibbutz. A community established in Israel, with the emphasis on equality, collective ownership of property, and collective child rearing.

Kinship. Relations of blood, marriage, or adoption.

Labelling. Defining a person or group in a certain way – as a particular 'type' of person or group.

Laws. Official legal rules, formally enforced by the police, courts, and prison, involving legal punishment if they are broken.

Liberation theology. A Christian doctrine mixing Communism and Catholicism, and supporting the poor and oppressed in their fight for freedom.

Life chances. The chances of obtaining those things defined as desirable and of avoiding those things defined as undesirable in a society.

Life expectancy. An estimate of how long people can be expected to live from a certain age.

Marginalization. The process whereby some groups are pushed by poverty, ill-health, lack of education, racism, and so on to the margins of society and are unable to take part in the life enjoyed by the majority of citizens. (See also social exclusion.)

Market situation. The rewards that people are able to obtain when they sell their skills in the labour market, depending on the scarcity of the skills they have and the power they have to obtain high rewards.

Master status. The dominant status of an individual which overrides all other characteristics of that person, such as that of an 'ex-con'.

Matriarchy. Power and authority held by women.

Matrilineal descent. Property or title passing through the female side of the family.

Matrilocal residence. Where, on marriage, the husband is expected to live with or near his wife's family.

Means of production. The key resources necessary for producing society's goods, such as factories and land.

Mechanization. The process where production of goods by hand is replaced by machinery.

Meritocracy. A society where social positions are achieved by merit, such as educational qualifications, talent, and skill.

Migration. The movement of people from one country or area to another.

Minority ethnic group. A social group which shares a cultural identity (see culture) which is different from that of the majority population of a society.

Modified extended family. A family type where related nuclear families, although living apart geographically, nevertheless maintain regular contact and mutual support through visiting, the phone, letters, and e-mail.

Monogamy. A form of marriage in which a person can only be legally married to one partner at a time.

Moral panic. A wave of public concern about some exaggerated or imaginary threat to society, stirred up by exaggerated and sensationalized reporting in the mass media.

Neo-local residence. Where, on marriage, the couple are expected to live away from both sets of parents.

Net migration. The difference between the number of people entering a country (immigrants) and the number leaving (emigrants) in a given period.

New religious movements. New religious organizations which have emerged in the period since 1945, and particularly since the 1960s. These are mainly sects and cults, and many have little in common with established churches and denominations.

New social movement. A broad movement of people who are united around the desire to promote, or block, a broad set of social changes in society. Unlike political parties or pressure groups, they are often only informally organized through a network of small, independent, locally based groups.

News values. The values and assumptions held by journalists which guide them in choosing what to report and what to leave out, and how what they choose to report should be presented.

Norm-setting. The process whereby the mass media emphasize and reinforce conformity to social norms, and seek to isolate those who don't conform by making them the victims of unfavourable public opinion.

Norms. Social rules which define correct behaviour in a society or group.

Nuclear family. A family with two generations, of parents and children, living together in one household.

Objectivity. Approaching topics with an open mind, avoiding bias, and being prepared to submit research evidence to scrutiny by other researchers.

Open society. A stratification system (see social stratification) in which social mobility is possible.

Patriarchy. Power and authority held by men.

Patrilineal descent. Property or title passing through the male side of the family.

Patrilocal residence. Where, on marriage, the wife is expected to live with or near her husband's family.

Peer group. A group of people of similar age and status with whom a person mixes socially.

Perinatal death. Still-births and deaths within the first week of life.

Periphery workers. Workers who are part-time, or on temporary or short-term contracts, employed on a casual, temporary basis and therefore easily dispensable and replaceable. (See also core workers.)

Pilot survey. A small-scale practice survey carried out before the final survey to check for any possible problems.

Political party. A group of people organized with the aim of forming the government in a society.

Politics. The struggle to gain power and control in a society or group, by getting into a position to make decisions and implement policies.

Polyandry. A form of marriage in which a woman may have two or more husbands at the same time.

Polygamy. A form of marriage in which a member of one sex can be married to two or more members of the opposite sex at the same time.

Polygyny. A form of marriage in which a man may have two or more wives at the same time.

Population projections. Predictions of future changes in population size based on past and present population trends.

Positive discrimination. Giving disadvantaged groups more favourable treatment than others to make up for the disadvantages they face.

Post-Fordism. A system of industrial production involving computer-controlled, multi-purpose machinery, specialized products for consumer choice, and a multi-skilled, flexible workforce able to do a range of jobs.

Poverty line. The dividing point between those who are poor and those who are not. The official poverty line used in Britain today is 60 per cent of average income – the definition of poverty used by the European Union.

Power. The ability of people or groups to exert their will over others and get their own way.

Pressure groups. Organizations which try to put pressure on those with power in society to implement policies which they favour.

Primary data. Information which sociologists have collected themselves. (See also secondary data.)

Privatized nuclear family. A nuclear family unit which is separated and isolated from wider kin (see kinship) and the community, with members spending time together in home-centred activities.

Productive property. Property which provides an unearned income for its owner, such as factories, land, and stocks and shares.

Proletarianization. The process of decline in the pay and conditions of sections of the middle class (see social class), so they become more like the working class. The opposite of embourgeoisement.

Proletariat. The class (see social class) of workers, who have to work for wages as they do not own the means of production.

Proportional representation. A voting system where the number of representatives elected accurately reflects the proportion of the votes received.

Qualitative data. Information concerned with the meanings and interpretations people have about some issue or event.

Quangos. Quasi-autonomous non-government organizations. Bodies which are financed by public funds, whose leaders are appointed by the government, but are not elected by or accountable to the public.

Quantitative data. Information that can be expressed in statistical or number form.

Race. Humans classified into different groups according to physical characteristics, like skin colour.

Racial discrimination. When racial prejudice causes people to act unfairly against a racial group (see race).

Racial prejudice. A set of assumptions about a racial group (see race) which people are reluctant to change even when they receive information which undermines those assumptions.

Racism. Believing or acting as though an individual or group is superior or inferior on the grounds of their racial (see race) or ethnic (see ethnic group) origins.

Reconstituted family. A family where one or both partners have been previously married, and bring with them children of a previous marriage.

Relative deprivation. The sense of lacking things compared to the group with which people identify and compare themselves.

Relative poverty. Poverty defined in relation to a generally accepted standard of living in a specific society at a particular time. (See also absolute poverty.)

Reliability. Whether another researcher, if repeating research using the same method for the same research on the same group, would achieve the same results.

Representative sample. A small group selected from the survey population for study, usually by interviews or questionnaires, containing a good cross-section of the characteristics of the survey population as a whole, and producing similar results as if the whole survey population had been studied.

Restricted code. A form of language use which takes for granted shared understandings between people. Colloquial, everyday language used between friends, with limited explanation and use of vocabulary. (See also elaborated code.)

Role conflict. The conflict between the successful performances of two or more roles at the same time, such as worker and mother.

Role model. Patterns of behaviour which others copy and model their own behaviour on.

Roles. The patterns of behaviour which are expected from individuals in society.

Sample. A small group drawn from the survey population for questioning or interviewing.

Sampling frame. A list of names of all those in the survey population from which a representative sample is selected.

Sanction. A reward or punishment to encourage social conformity.

Scapegoats. Individuals or groups blamed for something which is not their fault.

Secondary data. Data which already exists and which the researcher hasn't collected herself or himself. (See also primary data.)

Sects. Small, tight-knit and often short-lived world-rejecting (see world-rejecting groups) religious groups, often under the control of a single charismatic leader.

Secularization. The process whereby religious thinking, practice, and institutions lose social significance.

Segregated conjugal roles. A clear division and separation between the roles of male and female partner in marriage or in a cohabiting couple.

Selective exposure. Individuals exposing themselves only to media output that fits in with their existing views and interests. (See also selective perception, selective retention.)

Selective perception. Individuals filtering and interpreting media output so they only see or hear that which fits in with their own views and interests. (See also selective exposure, selective retention.)

Selective retention. Individuals ignoring or forgetting media output that is not in line with their own views and interests. (See also selective exposure, selective perception.)

Self-fulfilling prophecy. People acting in response to a prediction of their behaviour, thereby making the prediction come true. Often applied to the effects of streaming and labelling in schools.

Serial monogamy. A form of marriage where a person keeps marrying and divorcing a series of different partners, but is only married to one person at a time.

Sex. The biological differences between men and women.

Sex ratio. The proportion of males to females in the population, expressed as the number of males per 1000 females.

Sexism. Prejudice or discrimination against people (especially women) because of their sex.

Sexual division of labour. The division of work into 'men's jobs' and 'women's jobs'.

Sick role. The pattern of behaviour which is expected from someone who is classified as ill.

Social class. An open (see open society) system of stratification (see social stratification) consisting of broad groups of people (classes) who share a similar economic situation, such as occupation, income, and ownership of wealth.

Social control. The process of persuading or forcing individuals to conform to values and norms.

Social exclusion. The situation where people are marginalized (see marginalization) or excluded from full participation in mainstream society. Those who lack the necessary resources are denied the opportunities most people take for granted.

Social institutions. The organized social arrangements which are found in all societies.

Social mobility. Movement of groups or individuals up or down the social hierarchy.

Social stratification. The division of society into a hierarchy of unequal social groups.

Social structure. The social institutions and social relationships that form the 'building blocks' of society.

Socialization. The process of learning the culture of any society.

Sociology. The systematic (or planned and organized) study of human groups and social life in modern societies.

Status. The amount of prestige or social importance a person has in the eyes of other members of a group or society. (See also ascribed status, achieved status.)

Status frustration. A sense of frustration arising in individuals or groups because they are denied status in society.

Status group. A group of people sharing a similar social standing and lifestyle.

Stereotype. A generalized, oversimplified view of the features of a social group, allowing for few individual differences between members of the group.

Sub-culture. A smaller culture held by a group of people within the main culture of a society, in some ways different from the main culture, but with many aspects in common.

Survey. A method of gathering information about some group of people by questioning them using questionnaires and interviews.

Survey population. The section of the population which is of interest in a survey.

Symmetrical family. A family where the roles of husband and wife have become more alike (symmetrical) and equal.

Tactical voting. In an election, where supporters of a political party which has no chance of winning vote for another party which is not their preferred choice, in the hope of defeating the predicted winning party.

Totalitarianism. A system of government where society is controlled by a small powerful group or an individual, and ordinary people lack any control over government decision-making.

Tripartite system. The system of secondary education established in 1944 in which pupils were selected for one of three types of secondary school according to their performance in the 11+ exam.

Underachievement. The failure of people to achieve as much as they are capable of.

Underclass. A social group who are right at the bottom of the social class hierarchy, who are in some ways cut off or excluded from the rest of society.

Urbanization. The movement of population from rural (country) areas to urban areas (towns and cities), which become the major centres of population in a society.

Validity. Whether the findings of research actually provide a true picture of what is being studied.

Value consensus. A general agreement around the main norms and values of society.

Value freedom. The idea that the beliefs and prejudices of the sociologist should not be allowed to influence the way research is carried out and evidence interpreted.

Values. General beliefs about what is right or wrong, and the important standards which are worth maintaining and achieving in any society.

Wealth. Property which can be sold and turned into cash for the benefit of the owner.

White-collar crime. Crime that is committed by people in the course of their middle-class jobs.

White-collar workers. Non-manual clerical workers, sales personnel, and other office workers whose work is non-professional and non-managerial.

Work. The production of goods or services that usually earns a wage or salary, though housework remains unpaid.

World-accommodating groups. Religious groups that generally accept the dominant norms and values of a society, and are more concerned with spiritual behaviour and everyday morality than 'other worldly' activities.

World-affirming groups. Religious groups that generally accept society as it is, and offer individuals the opportunity to be successful in society and in terms of existing values through providing access to spiritual or supernatural powers.

World-rejecting groups. Religious groups that are in opposition to the world, and reject many of the dominant norms and values of a society, and replace them with alternative beliefs and practices.

Index

Using the Index

If you are looking for general topics it is probably best to refer first to the contents pages at the beginning of this book. If you want to find a particular item of information, look it up in this index. If the item is not listed, then think of other headings it might be given under: the same information is often included several times under different headings. This index only includes the main references found in the book rather than every single occurrence of the theme and it is sensible to check the largest references first, such as pages 152–9 before 147, 148, and 177. The chances are that what you're looking for will be in the largest entry, and this will save you time wading through a lot of smaller references.

Page numbers in **bold** refer to items in the glossary.

absolute poverty 52–3, **448**
abstention (in elections) 142–3
achieved status 12, **448**
affluent workers 34–6, **448**
age distribution 372, 381–2, 383
ageing population 235, 381–5
agenda-setting 169, 175, 189, 195–6, **448**
alienation 350–3, **448**
anomie 216–17, **448**
anti-school sub-culture 294, **448**
arranged marriage 227, 229, **448**
ascribed status 12, **448**
assembly line production 344–6
asylum seekers 126, 128, 181, 389
authority 130, 227, **448**
automation 344, 348–9, **448**

bar charts 445
BBC 163
'beanpole' family 235–6
Beveridge Report (1942) 63
bias **448**
    in the mass media 171–9
    interviewer bias 144, 429–31, **453**
bigamy 229, **448**
birth rate 371, 373, 379–81, **448**
births outside marriage 232, 251
bourgeoisie 17–20, 49, **448**
British Crime Survey 123, 208–10
broken homes 243
burden of dependence 382, 384

caste system 13, 313, 314, **448**
casualization (of employment) 356–7

census 370, 420
'cereal packet' family 251–4
child abuse 257–8
children
    and poverty 57, 287
    and the family 241–2, 257–8, 380
    changing position of 241–2
    neglect, emotional, sexual and
        physical abuse 257–8
chivalry thesis 204, **448**
church 315–16, 317, 321, 326, 331–3,
    449; see also religion
citizenship 132–3, 279, **449**
class conflict 17–21
class consciousness 19, **449**
class see social class
class structure in Britain 27, 33–9
classic extended family 226–7, 233–5,
    449
clerical work 32, 37–9, 40
closed society 12, 13–14, **449**
coercion 130–1, **449**
cohabitation 250–1
communes 262, **449**
communism 19, 350, **449**
community 393–5
compensatory education 295–6, **449**
comprehensive schools 268–71
conflict theory 8–9, **449**
conjugal roles 236–9, **449**
consensual definition (of poverty) 54–5
consensus theory 8–9, **449**
Conservative Party 134, 138, 139–41
consumption property 47, **449**
content analysis 417

core workers 356–7, **449**
corporate crime 207–8, **449**
coursework 436–8
craft production 343–4, 350, **450**
crime 192–223, **450**
  and age 202–3, 206, 218–19
  British Crime Survey 123, 208–10
  and the chivalry thesis 204, **448**
  conflict approach 199–200
  consensus approach 199
  corporate crime 207–8, **449**
  and deviance 196–200
  explanations for 216–20
  and gender 203–5
  and inner cities 392
  and marginality 219
  and the mass media 182–4
  and minority ethnic groups 122–4
  pattern of 200–8
  policy solutions 221–2
  and relative deprivation 219
  and social class 205–8
  and social exclusion 219
  statistics 200–1, 208–16, 419
  and status frustration 202–3
  white-collar crime 207–8, **460**
crisis of masculinity 94
cult 315–17, **450**; see also religion
culture 5, **450**
  culture clash 290–1, 298
  dependency culture 69–70, 72, 75, **450**
  of poverty 74–5, **450**
  sub-culture 218–19, 294, 304, **459**
cycle of deprivation 75

dealignment (in voting) 142, **450**
death rate 371, 374–9, 407, **450**
defensive groups 148
deference voters 140
democracy 131–3, 147–58, 188–9, **450**
  and the mass media 188–9
demography 370, **450**; see also population
denomination 315–16, 317, **450**; see also religion
dependency culture see culture
dependency ratio 372, 382, **450**
dependent age groups 372, **450**
dependent population 372, **450**
deskilling 37, 344, 348, **450**
de-urbanization 389–90, **450**
deviance 8, 192–223, **450**

conflict approach 199–200
consensus approach 199
  and crime 196–200
  explanations for 216–20
  and the mass media 169–71, 179–80, 182–4, 195–6
  and the sick role 400–1
  and voting 139–42
deviancy amplification 182, **450**
deviant career 220, **451**
deviant voter 139–42, **451**
dictatorship 131, **451**
disease 375–6, 398–9, 403–5, **451**; see also health
division of labour 344, **459**
  in the home 95, 100–2, 236–41, 260–1
  sexual 95, 103–4, **459**
divorce 243–8, 263
  statistics on 244–5, 440–7
domestic labour 100–2, 236–40, **451**
domestic violence 213, 257–60

ecumenical movement 327, **451**
education 267–310
  anti-school sub-culture 294, **448**
  and citizenship 132, 279
  and the class structure 279–80, 285–96
  compensatory 295–6, **449**
  comprehensive schools 268–71
  conflict approach 279, 281
  consensus approach 279, 281
  culture clash 290–1, 298
  and the economy 272–3, 279–81, 283
  Education Action Zones 278, 296, **451**
  Educational Priority Areas 295–6, **451**
  equality of educational opportunity 271, 278, 285, 306, 309, **451**
  and ethnicity 120, 296–9
  and the family 232, 287, 288–9
  and gender 86–7, 299–305
  grammar schools 267–70
  and health 377–8
  and the hidden curriculum 86, 195, 279, 281–2
  independent schools 306–8
  inequality in 285–309
  and labelling 292–3, 294
  and language 289–90, 299
  national curriculum 87, 132, 274, 276, 279, 283, 305

education (*cont'd*)
  private education 306–8
  recent developments in 272–8
  role in society 278–83
  and the self-fulfilling prophecy 269,
    270, 292–3
  secondary modern schools 267
  selection in 268–70, 275, 277–8
  and social class 276, 277, 279–81,
    285–96, 306–9
  and social control 195, 281–2
  specialist schools 275, 277–8
  streaming in 195, 268, 270, 292–3,
    294
  tripartite system 267–8
  underachievement in 120, 285–305,
    460
  and work 271, 272–3, 279–81, 283,
    348
Education Action Zones 278, 296, **451**
Educational Priority Areas 295–6, **451**
elaborated code 289–90, **451**
elite 42, 44, 131, 157–8, 307–8, **451**
embourgeoisement 34–6, **451**
emigration 371, 385–9, **451**
employment *see* work
  social class differences in 32–3
endogamy 13, 14, **451**
Equal Pay Act (1970) 96, 108
equality of educational opportunity
    271, 278, 285, 306, 309, **451**; *see
    also* education
estates, feudal 13–14
ethics (in research) 416–17, 436, **452**
ethnic group 112–13, **452**; *see also*
    minority ethnic groups
ethnic minority groups *see* minority
    ethnic groups
ethnicity and race 112–28, 296–9,
    413–14, **452, 457**
  and identity 112–13
  see also minority ethnic groups
evangelicalism 333, **452**
extended family 226–8, 233–6, 394, **452**
  'beanpole' 235–6
  classic 226–7, 233–5, **449**
  modified 226–8, 234, **455**

false consciousness 18, **452**
family 225–65
  alternatives to 261–2
  'beanpole' 235–6
  'cereal packet' 251–4

changes in 231–51, 263–4
changing functions of 231–2
changing roles in 228, 236–42
and children 239–42, 257–8, 380
classic extended 226–7, 233–5, **449**
and cohabitation 250–1
conflict approach 225–6
consensus approach 225–6
'darker side' of 257–60
diversity 251–6
and divorce 243–8, 263
and education 232, 287, 288–9
and ethnicity 229, 235, 254–5
extended 226–8, 233–6, 394, **452**
feminist criticisms of 260–1
forms of 226–31
gay and lesbian 262
and gender socialization 83–6
and industrialization 232, 233–5
lone-parent 59, 227, 228, 248–50
modified extended 226–8, 234, **455**
nuclear 226, 227, 233–4, **455**
one-parent *see* lone-parent
and political socialization 135
privatized nuclear 233–4, **456**
reconstituted 227, 228, 251, 254, **457**
single-parent *see* lone-parent
size of 242–3, 379–81
and social control 193–4, 232
symmetrical 227, 228, 236–41, **460**
violence in 258–60
and women 100–2, 236–41, 258–60
femininity 78–82, 90, 92–3
feminism 260–1, **452**
feminization
  of clerical work 38
  of poverty 58
feudalism 13–14, **452**
flexible worker 347, 348, 356–7
floating voters 137, **452**; *see also* voting
folk devils 179–80, 182–4, **452**
food industry 405–7
Fordism 344–8, **452**
functionalism 8–9, 16
fundamentalism 315, 333, **452**

gate-keeping 169, 175, **452**
gender 78–111
  and crime 203–5
  and education 86–7, 299–305
  and the family 83–6, 100–2, 236–41
  and femininity 78–82, 90, 92–3
  and the glass ceiling 106, **452**

and health 376, 378–9, 410–13
and identity 80, 92–4
and life expectancy 376, 378–9,
and masculinity 78–82, 91, 92–4
and the mass media 88–92
and the peer group 87–8
and poverty 58, 412
roles 78–80, **452**
and sex 78–80
and social mobility 42
socialization 80–92,
and stereotyping 80–92, 204
see also women
general fertility rate 371, **452**
glass ceiling 106, **452**
globalization 150, **453**
grammar schools 267–70
graphs 442–4

health 375–7, 397–415, **453**
and education 377–8
and ethnicity 413–14
and the food industry 405–7
and gender 376, 378–9, 410–13
and illness 398–9, **453**
inequalities in 30–1, 62, 397, 407 14
and inverse care law 409, **454**
medical model 399–400
and medicine 375–6, 397–8, 402–3
and poverty 62, 407–8
and the sick role 400–1, **459**
and social class 30–1, 407–10
and social control 400–1
social influences on 375–8, 402–5, 410
social model 399–400
statistics 400, 407
and the welfare state 63, 377, 409
hidden curriculum 86, 195, 279, 281–2,
453
homelessness 60–2
household 252, **453**
housework *see* domestic labour
hypothesis 420, **453**

identity 5–6, **453**
and ethnicity 112–13
and gender 80, 92–4
and leisure 364
and work 338
illness 398–9, **453**; *see also* health
immigration 113, 371, 385–9, **453**
income 29–30, 47–51, 57–8, **453**; *see
also* wealth

independent schools 306–8
industrial sabotage 352
industrial society 343
industrialization 343–8, 354, 363
and the family 232, 233–5
infant mortality 30, 242, 371, 375–8,
380–1, **453**
inner cities 390–2
Institute of Practitioners in Advertising
(IPA) 22, 26
institutional racism 118–19, 123, 124,
125, 128, **453**
integrated conjugal roles 236–41, **453**;
see also domestic labour; family
interest groups *see* pressure groups
Internet 151, 153, 161, 188, 283, 347,
349
interviewer bias 144, 429–31, **453**
interviews 429–31
inverse care law 72, 409, **454**

job satisfaction 350–3
juvenile delinquency 196, 202–3,
217–19, **454**

kibbutz 262, **454**
kinship 225, 232, **454**; *see also* family;
marriage

labelling **454**
and crime and deviance 219–21
in education 292–3, 294, 298
and the mass media 179–80, 182–4
Labour Party 133–4, 139–42
language
and education 289–90, 299
and gender socialization 82
and the mass media 176–7
in questionnaires 427
leisure 336, 362–7
and identity 364
and work 337, 338, 362–3, 367
liberation theology 315, **454**
life chances 12, 15, 29, 337, **454**
life expectancy 30–1, 247, 371, 374–9,
379, 381, **454**
lobbying 153
lone-parent families 59, 227, 228,
248–50

Macpherson Report 123, 124, 128
marginalization (marginality) 54, 219,
319, **454**

market situation 21, **454**
marriage 13, 14, 15, 43
  decline of 250–1
  forms of 227, 229–30
  inequality in 100–2, 236–41, 260–1
  rape in 214, 260
  see also family
Marx, Karl 9, 17–20, 313–14, 350
masculinity 78–82, 91, 92–4, 219
mass media 161–91
  bias in 171–9
  content of 171–9
  and crime and deviance 169–71,
    179–80, 182–4
  and democracy 188–9
  and deviancy amplification 182–4
  effects of 92, 137–9, 185–8
  formal controls on 162–3
  and gender socialization 88–92
  and the law 162
  and minority ethnic groups 180–2
  and moral panics 179–80, 182–4
  and news values 173–4, **455**
  ownership of 163–5, 189
  and poverty 70–1
  selective exposure, perception and
    retention 186, **458**
  and social class 165–7
  and social control 168–71, 195–6
  and stereotyping 88–92, 179–81
  and violence 92, 187–8
  and voting 137–9
  and youth 179–80, 182–4
master status 219–20, **454**
matriarchy 227, 231, **454**
matrilineal descent 227, 230, **454**
matrilocal residence 227, 230, **454**
means of production 17–21, **454**
means-testing 69–70
mechanization 344, 389, **454**
media see mass media
medical model (of health) 399–400
medicine 375–6, 397–8, 399, 402–3
  and social control 400–1
meritocracy 15, 39, 271, 280–1, **454**
middle class 22, 24, 25, 26, 27
  and crime 205–8,
  and education 276, 277, 279–81,
    285–95, 306–8
  and health 30–1, 72, 407–10
  proletarianization of 37–9, 142
  and voting 139, 141–2
  and the welfare state 72, 409

migration 371, 385–9, **455**
minority ethnic groups 112–29, **455**
  and crime 122–4
  and education 119–22, 296–9
  and employment 115–16, 118–22
  and the family 229, 235, 254–5
  and health 413–14
  and housing 116–17, 118–22
  and identity 112–13
  and income 115
  and institutional racism 118–19, 123,
    124, 125, 128, **453**
  and policing and the law 122–4
  problems faced by 114–24, 127–8
  and racist attacks 123–4
  and social mobility 43
  and mass media stereotyping 180–1
  and voting 135–6
modified extended family 226–8, 234,
  455
monogamy 227, 229, **455**
moral panics 179–80, 182–4, **455**
mortality
  infant 30, 242, 371, 374–8, 380–1,
    453
  see also death rate

national curriculum 87, 132, 274, 276,
  279, 283, 305
National Statistics Socio-economic
  Classification (NS-SEC) 22, 24
natural science 3–4
negative sanctions 8, 192
net migration 371, 386–9, **455**
New Labour see Labour Party
'new man' 93–4, 236
new religious movements 316–20, **455**
new social movements 149–56, 158, **455**
new working class 34–6, 141
news values 173–4, **455**
newspapers 137–8, 164–8, 171–4, 176–8
norms 5, 7–8, 169–70, 192, 216–17, **455**
norm-setting 169–70, 175, 189, 195–6,
  455
nuclear family 226, 227, 233–4, **455**

objectivity 4, **455**
observation 432–4
occupation, defining class by 21–7
occupational scales 22–7
occupational structure 33–4, 353–6
Office for Standards in Education
  (Ofsted) 276

Office of Communications (Ofcom) 163
official statistics 419
    on crime 200–1, 208–16, 419
    on divorce 244–5, 440–7
    on health 400, 407
    on suicide 419
    on unemployment 339
old age *see* ageing population
old boys' network 156, 308
one-parent families *see* lone-parent
    families
open society 12, 15, 39, **455**
opinion polls 143–6

parliamentary democracy 131–2
participant observation 433–4
party images 136–7
party political broadcasts 137–8
patriarchy 98, 227, 231, **455**
patrilineal descent 227, 230, **455**
patrilocal residence 227, 230, **456**
peer group 87–8, 195, 202–3, 219, 294,
    304, **456**
periphery workers 356–7, **456**
pie charts 446
pilot survey 431, **456**
police 122–4, 192–3, 202, 203, 204,
    206, 210–14, 215, 221, 392
political parties 133–5, 136–7, 148,
    151–2, 158, **456**
politics 130–60, **456**
polyandry 227, 230, **456**
polygamy 227, 229–30, **456**
polygyny 227, 229–30, **456**
population 370–96
    ageing 235, 381–5
    key terms 371–2
    minority ethnic 113–14
    survey population 420, **460**
positive discrimination 295–6, **456**
positive sanctions 8, 192
postal questionnaires 428–9
post-Fordism 346–8, **456**
poverty 51–76
    absolute 52–3, **448**
    consensual definition 54–5
    culture of poverty 74–5, **450**
    cycle of deprivation 75
    definitions of 52–7
    and dependency culture 69–70, 72,
        75, **450**
    feminization of 58
    groups in 59, 60–1

and health 62, 407–8
and marginalization 54, 219, **454**
poverty line 57, 59–63, **456**
relative 52, 54, **457**
at school 62
and social class 59
and social exclusion 52, 54, 55, **459**
subsistence 52–3
and the underclass 24, 27, 34, 72–3,
    460
and the welfare state 63–8, 69–73
at work 61
why it continues 68–76
power 18, 130, 199–200, **456**; *see also*
    politics
pressure groups 65, 147–9, 151–6, **456**
    different from political parties 148
primary data 418, **456**
private education 306–8
privatized nuclear family 233–4, **456**
productive property 47, **457**
proletarianization 37–9, 142, **457**
proletariat 17–20, **457**
promotional groups 148–9
proportional representation 157, **457**
protective groups 148–9
protest movements 147–56, 158
public opinion 168–70, 189; *see also*
    opinion polls
public schools 44, 306–8

qualitative data 417, **457**
quangos 156, **457**
quantitative data 417, **457**
questionnaires 424–9
quota sampling 422

race and ethnicity 112–28, 296–9,
    413–14, **452**, **457**; *see also* minority
    ethnic groups
racial discrimination 118–19, **457**
racial prejudice 118–19, 121, **457**
racism 44, 118–19, 122–4, 126–8, 181,
    298, 341, 392, **457**
    causes of 126
    institutional racism 118–19, 123, 124,
        125, 128, **453**
    racist attacks 123–4
random sampling 421, 422, 423
rape 213, 214,
    in marriage 214, 215, 260
reconstituted family 227, 228, 251, 254,
    457

relative deprivation 219, 319, **457**
relative poverty 52, 54, **457**
reliability (in research) 416, 419, **457**
religion 311–35
    and politics 136, 315
    and secularization 247, 250, 321–34,
        379, **458**
    and social change 315
    and social control 196, 313–14
    church, denomination, sect and cult
        315–17, **449, 450, 458**
    conflict view of 313–14
    consensus view of 312–13
    defining 311–12
    new religious movements 316–20, **455**
religious organizations 315–16, 317
representative sample 144, 420–3, **457**
research methods 416–35
restricted code 289–90, **458**
riots 390–1
role 6, **458**
    conjugal role 236–9, **449**
    gender role 78–80, **452**
    role conflict 6–7, **458**
    role model 86, **458**
    sick role 400–1, **459**
ruling class 18
rural life 393–5

sample (representative) 420–3, **458**
sampling frame 421–2, 423, **458**
sampling methods 420–4
sanctions 8, 192, **458**
scapegoating 126, 179–80, 182–4, 343,
    392, **458**
schools
    comprehensive 268–71
    grammar 267–70
    independent 306–8
    public 44, 306–8
    secondary modern 267
    specialist 275, 277–8
    see also education
science (and sociology) 3–5
secondary data 417–19, **458**
secondary modern schools 267
sect 315–17, **458**; see also religion
secularization 247, 250, 321–34, 379,
    458
segregated conjugal roles 236–41, **458**;
    see also domestic labour; family
selection (in education) 268–70, 275,
    277–8

selective exposure, perception and
    retention 186, **458**
self-fulfilling prophecy 269, 270,
    292–3, **458**
self-report studies 209, 210, 211
serial monogamy 227, 229, **458**
Sex Discrimination Act 96
sex/gender differences 78–80, **452, 459**;
    see also gender; women
sexism 98, 106, **459**
sexual division of labour 95, 103–4, **459**
sick role 400–1, **459**
single-parent family see lone-parent
    families
snowball sampling 424
social class 14–27, 28–45, **459**
    conflict views of 17–21
    consensus view of 16–17
    and crime 205–8
    defined by occupation 21–7
    and education 279–81, 285–96,
        306–9
    functionalist view 16–17
    and health 30–1, 407–10
    inequalities 29–33, 40–1, 72,
        285–95, 407–10
    Marxist theory of 17–20
    and the mass media 165–7
    in modern Britain 28–45
    and poverty 59
    and social mobility 39–45
    and voting 139–42
    Weber's theory of 21
    see also middle class; upper class;
        working class
social control 8, 192–6, **459**
    agencies of 192–6
    and education 195, 281–2
    and the family 193–4, 232
    and the mass media 168–71, 195–6
    and medicine 400–1
    and the peer group 195
    and religion 196, 313–14
    and the sick role 400–1
social exclusion 52, 54, 55, 73, 219, **459**
social institution 1, 9, **459**
social mobility 12, 13, 14, 15, 39–45,
    459
    inter-generational 40–1, **453**
    intra-generational 40, 41, **453**
social model (of health) 399–400
social research 2, 4, 416–35
social stratification 11–16, **459**; see also

ethnicity and race; gender;
   income; poverty; social class;
   underclass; wealth
social structure 1, 34, **459**
social surveys 420–32
socialist revolution 19
socialization 3, 5–6, 232, 279, **459**
   and gender 80–92
   and voting 135
sociological research 2, 4–5, 416–35
sociology 1–5, **459**
specialist schools 275, 277–8
spin doctors 138, 179
Standard Occupational Classification
   (SOC2000) 22, 25
statistical tables 440–1
statistics *see* official statistics;
   quantitative data
status 12, 16, 336, **459**
   achieved 12, **448**
   ascribed 12, **448**
status frustration 202–3, 217–19, 319,
   459
status group 12, 21, **459**
stereotyping 80–92, 122, 123, 179–82,
   203, 204, 206, **459**
stratification *see* social stratification
stratified random sampling 422–3
streaming (in schools) 195, 268, 270,
   292–3, 294
structured interviews 429–31
sub-culture 217–19, 294, 304, **460**
subsistence poverty 52–3
suffragette movement 95, 97–8
suicide 94, 419
survey population 420, **460**
surveys 420–32, **460**
symmetrical family 227, 228, 236–41,
   460
systematic sampling 421, 423

tabloid press 165–6
tactical voting 149, **460**
taxation 50–1
teachers
   and gender socialization 86
   and racism 298
   and the self-fulfilling prophecy
      292–3
   and streaming and labelling 292–3
   see also education
technology 343–9, 353, 364, 376–7
   and clerical work 37, 39, 348

effects on society 348–9
   in the home 100
   and job satisfaction 350–1
   and schools 272, 279, 283, 349
Tory Party *see* Conservative Party
totalitarianism 131, **460**
trade unions 359–62
traditional working class 34–6, 141,
   234–5, 255, 361, 395
trends, describing 442
tripartite system 267–8, **460**

underachievement (in education) 120,
   285–305, **460**
   and ethnicity 120, 296–9
   and gender 299–305
   and social class 285–96
underclass 24, 27, 34, 72–3, **460**
unemployment 338–43
   causes of 339–40
   consequences of 341–3
   and crime 202, 205–6
   groups at risk 341
   and inner cities 391
   and minority ethnic groups 115–16,
      118–22
   and poverty 59, 61
   statistics on 339
unstructured interview 429–31
upper class 15, 17, 26, 27, 41, 48–50,
   157–8, 307–8
urban dispersal 389–90
urban life 393–5
urbanization 389, 394, **460**

validity (in research) 416, 418, 419, **460**
value consensus 9, 225–6, 312, **460**
value freedom 4, **460**
values 7–8, 192, **460**
   and crime and deviance 206, 217–19
   news values 173–4, **455**
   value consensus 9, 225–6, 312, **460**
   value freedom 4, **460**
victim surveys 209, 210
violence
   against women 258–60
   and gender 92, 258–60
   and the mass media 92, 187–8
   in the family 258–60
   see also domestic violence
vocational education 271, 272–3, 341,
   348
volatility (in voting) 142

voluntary organizations 65, 66
voting 95, 97–8, 135–46, 156–7
    deference voters 140
    deviant voters 139–42, **451**
    factors influencing 135–42
    floating voters 137, **452**
    pragmatic voters 141
    tactical voting 146, **460**

wealth 29–30, 47–51, **460**; see also
        income
Weber 9, 21
welfare state 63–8, 69–73, 232, 239,
        377
white-collar crime 207–8, **460**
white-collar workers 22, 37–9, 359, **460**
women 95–109
    changing role of 95–100, 245, 250,
        357–8, 380
    and crime 203–5, 258–60
    discrimination against 96, 98, 106
    and domestic labour 100–2, 236–41
    and education 86–7, 299–305
    and the family 100–2, 236–41,
        258–60
    and the glass ceiling 106, **452**
    and health 376, 378–9, 410–13
    and housework see domestic labour
    inequality of 42, 58, 100–9, 236–41,
        260–1
    and leisure 366
    life expectancy of 376, 378–9
    in paid employment 38, 102–9,
        357–8
    and poverty 58
    and social mobility 42
    and socialization 80–92, 95, 378,
        412–13
    women's 'triple shift' 238, 260
    women's movement 98
    see also gender

work 336–62, **461**
    and alienation 350–3, **448**
    attitudes to 337–8
    casualization of 356–7
    changing nature of 347–8, 353–8
    class inequalities at 32–3
    and deskilling 37, 344–8, **450**
    and education 271, 272–3, 279–81,
        283, 348
    and flexibility 347, 348, 356–7
    Fordism and post-Fordism 344–8,
        452, 456
    and identity 338
    importance of 336–7
    and leisure 337, 338, 362–3, 367
    poverty at 61
    preparation for 271, 272–3, 279–81,
        283, 348
    and technology 37, 39, 343–9, 350–3
    and women 38, 95, 100–9, 236–41,
        260–1, 357–8
working class 22, 24, 25, 26, 27
    and crime 205–6, 216–19
    and education 279–80, 285–96
    embourgeoisement of 34–6, **451**
    and health 30–1, 407–10
    new 34–6, 141
    and poverty 59
    traditional 34–6, 141, 255, 361, 395
    and voting 139–41
world-accommodating groups 316,
        461
world-affirming groups 316, **461**
world-rejecting groups 315, **461**
world wars 98–9

youth
    and crime 202–3, 206, 217–19
    and leisure 365
    stereotyping and scapegoating of
        179–80, 182–4